Hinduism in the Modern World

D0218411

Hinduism in the Modern World presents a new and unprecedented attempt to survey the nature, range, and significance of modern and contemporary Hinduism in South Asia and the global diaspora. Organized to reflect the direction of recent scholarly research, this volume breaks with earlier texts on this subject by seeking to overcome a misleading dichotomy between an elite, intellectualist "modern" Hinduism and the rest of what has so often been misleadingly termed "traditional" or "popular" Hinduism. Without neglecting the significance of modern reformist visions of Hinduism, this book reconceptualizes the meaning of "modern Hinduism" both by expanding its content and by situating its expression within a larger framework of history, ethnography, and contemporary critical theory. This volume equips undergraduate readers with the tools necessary to appreciate the richness and diversity of Hinduism as it has developed during the past two centuries.

Brian A. Hatcher is Packard Chair of Theology at Tufts University, where he is also Professor and Chair of the Department of Religion. He is the author of several monographs on Hindu reform movements in colonial Bengal, the dynamics of modern Hindu eclecticism, and the life and activities of the social reformer, Ishvarchandra Vidyasagar. In his other published work he has explored the transformation of Sanskrit learning in colonial Bengal, highlighted the world of vernacular intellectual life, and worked to understand contemporary Hinduism against the backdrop of colonial history and postcolonial theory.

Religions in the Modern World

Available:

Hinduism in the Modern World

Edited by Brian A. Hatcher

Routledge
Taylor & Francis Group

NEW YORK AND LONDON

First published 2016
by Routledge
711 Third Avenue, New York, NY 10017

and by Routledge
2 Park Square, Milton Park, Abingdon, Oxon, OX14 4RN

Routledge is an imprint of the Taylor & Francis Group, an informa business

Library of Congress Cataloging-in-Publication Data

A catalog record for this book has been requested

ISBN: 978-0-415-83603-6 (hbk)
ISBN: 978-0-415-83604-3 (pbk)
ISBN: 978-0-203-36203-7 (ebk)

Typeset in Goudy
by Apex CoVantage, LLC

Printed and bound in the United States of America by
Edwards Brothers Malloy on sustainably sourced paper

Graham Stuart Hatcher
1923–2014
Per ardua ad astra

Contents

Maps and Images

Maps

Images

Acknowledgments

A book like this is a collective endeavor and I would like to say a special word of thanks to the many contributors whose chapters really make it what it is. Their enthusiasm for the project and commitment to meeting deadlines are appreciated in equal measure, as is their willingness to share their work in a concise and engaging fashion. To those who offered images for inclusion, I remain especially grateful. I also thank the various editors who were engaged at various stages in the commissioning, planning, and completion of the book, especially Lesley Riddle, Steve Wiggins, Eve Mayer, and Laura Briskman. Finally, I want to acknowledge the hard work and critical input of Hayden Lizotte, who read and responded to early drafts of the work and who offered sound suggestions for improving the overall appeal of the book. If it proves to be even half as stimulating to discuss as we discovered, then I will consider it a success.

Notes on Contributors

Donald R. Davis, Jr. is Associate Professor of Sanskrit and Indian Religions at the University of Texas at Austin. He is the author of *The Boundaries of Hindu Law: Tradition, Custom, and Politics in Medieval Kerala* (2004) and *The Spirit of Hindu Law* (2010).

Timothy S. Dobe is Associate Professor of Religious Studies, Grinnell College. His research focuses on Hinduism, Indian Christianity and the shared idioms of South Asian religions. His recent publications include "Vernacular Vedanta: Autohagiographical Fragments of Rama Tirtha's Diglossic Indo-Persian Mysticism" (2014) and *Hindu Christian Faqir: Modern Monks, Global Christianity and Indian Sainthood* (2015).

Jason D. Fuller is Associate Professor of Religious Studies, Chair of Religious Studies, and Director of the Asian Studies Program at DePauw University in Greencastle, IN. He specializes in the study of modern Hinduism and Bengali social history. His publications include "Re-Branding Gaudiya Vaishnavism," *Journal of Vaishnava Studies* (2014) and "The Accidental Pilgrim: Vaishnava Tirthas and the Experience of the Sacred," in H. Rodrigues ed. *Studying Hinduism in Practice* (2011). He is currently working on a book entitled, *Selling Krishna: Bhaktivinoda Thakura and the Branding of Gaudiya Vaishnavism in 19th Century Bengal*.

Brian A. Hatcher is Professor and Packard Chair of Theology at Tufts University. His research addresses the transformation of social, religious, and intellectual practices in colonial Bengal and the modern expression of Hindu traditions. His publications include *Eclecticism and Modern Hindu Discourse* (1999), *Bourgeois Hinduism, or the Faith of the Modern Vedantists* (2008), and, most recently, *Vidyasagar: The Life and After-life of an Eminent Indian* (2014).

Pralay Kanungo is Professor/ICCR Chair at Leiden University and a Fellow at IIAS. Earlier he taught at Jawaharlal Nehru University and was a Fellow at NMML, New Delhi. He is the author of *RSS's Tryst with Politics* (2002) and his coedited volumes include *The Cultural Entrenchment of Hindutva* (2011) and *Public Hinduisms* (2012).

Eliza Kent is Professor of Religion at Skidmore College. A scholar of religion in South Asia, she is the author of *Converting Women: Gender and Protestant Christianity in Colonial South India* (Oxford University Press, 2004) and *Sacred Groves, Local Gods: Religion and Environmentalism in South India* (Oxford University Press, 2013).

Meena Khandelwal is Associate Professor of Anthropology and Gender, Women's and Sexuality Studies at the University of Iowa. Her work on Hindu renunciation includes *Women in Ochre Robes* (2004) and *Women's Renunciation in South Asia*, coedited with S. Hausner and A. Gold (2006).

Hanna H. Kim is Associate Professor of Anthropology at Adelphi University in New York. Her research interests include the anthropology of religion, religious subjectivities, and transnational religious movements. Recent publications include "Swaminarayana: Bhakti Yoga and the Aksharbrahman Guru" in *Gurus of Modern Yoga* (2013) and "The BAPS Swaminarayan Temple Organisation and its Publics" in *Public Hinduisms* (2012).

Prema Kurien is Professor of Sociology at the Maxwell School of Syracuse University, where she is also the Founding Director of Asian/Asian American Studies. Her recent research focuses on race and ethnic group relations, as well as the role of religion in shaping group formation and mobilization among contemporary ethnic groups.

Timothy Lubin is Professor of Religion, and Adjunct Professor of Law, at Washington and Lee University. He publishes on Indic legal institutions recorded in inscriptions and in scholastic texts in Sanskrit. He coedited *Hinduism and Law: An Introduction* (Cambridge, 2010), and is at work on a study of Brahmanical authority.

Karline McLain is Associate Professor in the Religious Studies Department at Bucknell University. She is the author of *India's Immortal Comic Books: Gods, Kings, and Other Heroes* (Indiana University Press, 2009) and is currently working on a book about Shirdi Sai Baba.

Brian K. Pennington is Professor of Religious Studies and Director of the Center for the Study of Religion, Culture, and Society at Elon University. He is author of *Was Hinduism Invented?: Britons, Indians, and the Colonial Construction of Religion* (2005). He is currently working on a book on entrepreneurial religion in the North Indian pilgrimage city of Uttarkashi.

Leela Prasad is Associate Professor of Religious Studies at Duke University. She studies ethics through narrative, media, performance, and art. Her first book was *Poetics of Conduct: Narrative and Moral Being in a South Indian Town* (2006). She is currently writing on enchantment and historical imagination in colonial India, and directing an ethnographic film *Moved by Gandhi*.

Anantanand Rambachan is Professor of Religion at Saint Olaf College. Among his books are *The Advaita Worldview* (2012) and, most recently, *A Hindu Theology of Liberation: Not-Two Is Not One* (2015).

Amiya P. Sen is currently Heinrich Zimmer Chair at the South Asia Institute, Heidelberg. A historian by profession, his academic interests lie in the fields of intellectual and cultural histories of colonial India. He has published extensively, the latest being *Religion and Rabindranath Tagore: Select Discourses, Addresses and Letters in Translation* (2014).

Usha Shukla is professor of Languages, Linguistics & Academic Literacy at the University of KwaZulu-Natal, South Africa. Her work examines the role of Ramayana traditions in diaspora contexts. She is the author of *Ramcharitmanas in the Diaspora: Trinidad, Mauritius and South Africa* (2011).

Frederick M. Smith is Professor of Sanskrit and Indian Religions at the University of Iowa. His research interests include Vedic sacrificial ritual, deity and spirit possession, the Mahabharata, and the devotional thought of Vallabhacharya. His recent books include *The Self Possessed: Deity and Spirit Possession in South Asian Literature and Civilization* (2006) and a coedited volume with Dagmar Wujastyk, *Modern and Global Ayurveda: Pluralism and Paradigms* (2008).

Ruth Vanita is Professor of Liberal Studies at the University of Montana. Formerly, she taught at Delhi University and was founding coeditor of *Manushi*, India's first nationwide feminist magazine. She coedited the pioneering *Same-Sex Love in India* (2000; updated 2008) and her latest book is *Gender, Sex and the City: Urdu Rekhti Poetry in India, 1780–1870* (2012).

Rupa Viswanath is Professor of Indian Religions and Director of the Center for Modern Indian Studies at the University of Göttingen, Germany. Her research addresses caste subordination, national minorities and techniques of minoritization, theories of representative democracy, and comparative secularisms. Her most recent book is *The Pariah Problem: Caste, Religion and the Social in Modern India* (Columbia University Press, 2014).

Maya Warrier is Reader in the Department of Theology, Religion and Philosophy at the University of Winchester, UK. Her research explores Hindu traditions in modern transnational contexts. She is coeditor of *Public Hinduisms* (Sage, 2012). Recent publications include works on Hinduism in Britain, the 'hugging guru' Mata Amritanandamayi, and modern transnational Anglophone Ayurveda.

Lola Williamson is Associate Professor of Religious Studies at Millsaps College in Jackson, Mississippi. She is the author of *Transcendent in America: Hindu-Inspired Meditation Movements as New Religion* (2010) and coeditor of *Homegrown Gurus: From Hinduism in America to American Hinduism* (2013).

Introduction

Brian A. Hatcher

Readers of *Hinduism in the Modern World* are presented with an exciting challenge. On the one hand, the book offers an opportunity to think about what it means to be Hindu or, for those with some prior familiarity, to add greater complexity to what they already know about Hinduism. On the other hand, the book aims to promote reflection on the more specific question of what it means to be Hindu in the modern world. In both respects, the goal of the book is to highlight and to complicate the relationship between categories like 'Hinduism' and 'modernity.' As this Introduction will suggest, the goal of this book is not to categorically define Hinduism but, through its various chapters, to offer a series of occasions for asking where and how we might look for Hinduism in the world around us. As will become clear, there is no one version of 'modern Hinduism,' no single place, person, movement, or text to which we can point that would fully and finally reveal what it means to be Hindu today. Recognizing this, the goal here is to explore the ways in which the complex experience of modernity can be put in relation to the equally complex experience of being Hindu. The approach is necessarily selective; the volume is oriented around the exploration of important themes in modern Hinduism. This means that readers will not find here a chronological overview of the tradition. That said, an attempt has been made to balance an awareness of historical change with the attempt to explore selected modern and contemporary expressions of Hinduism.

Plan of the Book

Part I contains three chapters that are intended to provide differing but complementary perspectives on modern Hinduism as observed in three geographical contexts: south India, north India, and the diaspora. These chapters raise three broad issues. First, they invite readers to reflect on commonalities and differences in Hindu life and practice as observed in differing locales and cultural contexts. Here, readers will encounter a range of religious narratives and divine actors, types of landscape and sacred geography, forms of religious architecture, modes of ritual and spiritual practice, and varieties of theological reflection.

Second, these chapters encourage readers to consider in what respects the concept of modernity can be invoked to make sense of modern Hinduism in various local, regional, and global contexts. Is modernity best approached in terms of the advent of something radically new or does it reflect the on-going articulation of lived traditions in a changing world? How do the people, places, and traditions discussed in these chapters represent specific ways in which Hindus have responded to the opportunities or challenges associated with the modern world? Third, and finally, these three chapters call attention to the interpretive stance taken by their respective authors. How do they choose to make sense of Hinduism? Where do they start? What do they choose to emphasize? Here, it is worth recalling that we are often confronted with the choice between looking 'inside' a tradition in order to appreciate what and how it is meaningful for its adherents and standing 'outside' in order to apply tools borrowed from disciplines like sociology or economics to give an account of why that tradition looks the way it does today. Each approach is important for helping us understand the meaning and the function of religion in human life and society. In these first three chapters, readers are invited to consider the way particular authors in this volume deal with this choice.

By pairing a review of south and north Indian Hinduism with an exploration of its transnational expression, this volume begins by emphasizing that any attempt to understand Hinduism in the modern world must include a global perspective. Hindus today make up significant portions of the population in numerous countries around the globe, from Bali in the South Pacific to South Africa, the United Kingdom, and the United States. The example of Bali, to which Hindus began migrating in the first millennium of the Common Era, also reminds us that global Hinduism is not even solely a modern phenomenon. Hindu traders, travelers, saints, and pilgrims have been an important force in shaping religious, aesthetic, political, and moral life across South and Southeast Asia for the past two thousand years or more. When thinking about the premodern diffusion of Hinduism, we need to be careful not to associate the tradition too closely with 'India'. After all, the modern nation-state of India comprises only one portion of the larger South Asian subcontinent throughout whose history Hinduism has played an important role (see Map 0.1). It is important to bear in mind that Hinduism has been on the move within and beyond South Asia for millennia. Processes of movement and migration are therefore not in themselves something new, even if these processes were radically altered and accelerated during the modern era through the combined forces of European imperial expansion, systems of colonial indenture, and global economic migration.

Needless to say, Hinduism in the modern world cannot be understood without attending to the enormous and complex set of developments we associate with European imperialism and colonialism. The chapters in Part II have been chosen to introduce readers to a set of critical problems that emerge during the colonial era, roughly from the mid-eighteenth to the mid-twentieth century. These chapters address a set of intellectual, theological, and legal developments

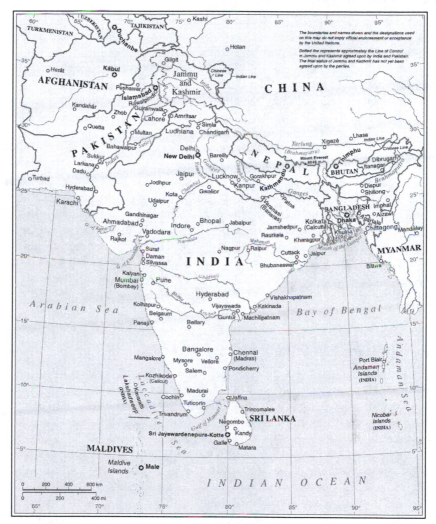

Map 0.1 South Asia

that have each contributed to the emergence of modern Hinduism. Whether we consider the ramifications of material and technological innovations like the printing press, social changes associated with urbanization and mass education, innovations in colonial law and bureaucracy, or the attempts of various Hindu actors to negotiate the challenges of life under imperial rule, it becomes clear the degree to which the very concept of 'Hinduism' itself emerges during colonial era.

This issue, to which we will return below, cannot really be addressed without some understanding of the spread of Hindu beliefs, practices, and institutions around the globe during this same period, a set of concerns addressed in

Part III. Here, some of the colonial-era movements first encountered in Part II (such as the Arya Samaj) will reappear, allowing readers to reflect on the historical connectivity and dynamic interrelationships among Hindu modes of life around the globe over the past 200 years. By exploring the themes of transnational movement and global interconnectivity, readers are able to trace what we might call (following Leela Prasad) 'networks of meaning' in modern Hindu life. The chapters in Part IV are then dedicated to examining a range of selected issues in a thematic fashion, themes such as the role of cosmopolitan religious teachers, the global flow of practices like yoga, the contemporary meaning of renunciation, and the vital role played by visual media in the transmission of Hindu meaning. It should become clear that the modern history of Hinduism reflects a series of on-going and vigorous debates not only among Hindus, but also between Hindus and others who may have challenged, appropriated, or otherwise engaged with Hindu values, practices, and modes of social organization. Tackling such debates is essential for a responsible understanding of contemporary Hinduism. In this spirit, Part V includes chapters dedicated to addressing a number of critical social and political issues, including debates over sexuality, gender, untouchability, the Indian nation, and the environment.

Complicating 'Hinduism'

One of the things we can take away from the study of Hinduism in the modern world is an awareness of just how much the processes that we associate with imperialism, colonialism, Indian nationalism, and diasporic migration can be said to have contributed to the emergence of the tradition we now recognize as 'Hinduism.' While scholars have today become comfortable discussing the modern invention or construction of Hinduism, this is understandably a concept that may either confuse or anger some Hindus. There are two dimensions to this problem, one historical and the other hermeneutical.

The historical problem involves asking whether we can in fact tell the story of Hinduism as the continuous transmission of a set of truths and practices. It is certainly the case that many Hindus understand their tradition to be essentially timeless, an eternal set of truths (*sanatana dharma*), and not really even a 'religion' at all if by that term we mean a dogma and institution traceable to a single founder. Such a view clearly depends on defining religion in terms of a stereotype of the great Semitic monotheisms like Judaism, Christianity, and Islam and then defining Hinduism as something completely different. But the very context in which such a comparison tends to be drawn and the polemical contexts in which it might become a useful strategy already puts us in mind of some the profound concerns that have shaped Hinduism in the modern era, not least the pressure to define a unique Indian identity in the face of western cultural imperialism. We may choose to be skeptical of such a definition, but we must also recognize that many Hindus do trace the roots of their tradition at least as far back as the ancient Vedic era and would be inclined to view the tradition as one of the world's longest-lived religions. And isn't it the case that we routinely speak of scriptures like the Vedas and Upanishads (ca. 1200–200 BCE) as 'Hindu' texts? If these and later texts like the Bhagavad-gita (ca. 100 CE) are Hindu texts, then what could it mean to say Hinduism is a modern concept? Perhaps, on one level, we simply need to acknowledge the force of such an argument; what is wrong with asserting the great historical longevity of Hindu teachings and practice, especially when one considers the incredible longevity of Vedic ritual as illustrated in the chapter by Frederick Smith?

On another level, this formulation raises the question of hermeneutics. After all, in order to speak of these texts and practices as 'Hindu' it seems we must have in mind an idea of what constitute the essential characteristics of the tradition such that we may say one text is Hindu and another is not (such as the *Buddhacharita*, for instance?). In other words, we set off to learn about Hinduism and begin looking for evidence—like ancient scriptures—that can help us understand the tradition. And yet, how do we know which scriptures to read unless we already have some idea of what Hinduism is? And so we enter what is known as the hermeneutic circle. We have a prior conception of Hinduism that allows us to go off and find the Hinduism we expect to find. One thing readers will discover in this volume is that many of the essential things said to constitute Hinduism are in some respect the legacy or residue of colonial-era categories and classifications, whether these be traced to European scholarship, Christian missionaries, Hindu reformers, or Indian nationalists. Each of these groups had particular interests (legal, bureaucratic, theological, and cultural) for finding a way to speak of the Hindu world. Whether we think of the East India Company committing to administer 'Hindu' law among Hindus, a missionary denunciation of Hindu superstition, or the Indian Supreme Court defining what it means to be 'Hindu,' we encounter important factors shaping the emergence of 'Hinduism' as a recognizable category. This is not to say that there were not long-standing Hindu legal traditions or that the missionaries weren't responding to actually existing practices and customs they could correlate to textual traditions and patterns of received learning. But it is to suggest that, prior to the colonial era, there had not emerged a single, overarching, and widely shared understanding of what it meant to be 'Hindu'— that term at one time indicating nothing more than that one was a resident of the lands east of the Indus (or Sindhu) River. If we say 'Hinduism' is a modern construction, the goal is not to take away from the dignity or historical depths of the tradition, but to point to the way our categories (just like our academic disciplines) are of relatively recent origin.

Put differently, the point of such reflections is not to question the legitimacy or meaning of Hinduism but to remind us of the need to become aware of how we think about all forms of religion, past and present. There is clearly a tendency in both popular thought and scholarly discourse to think of religions as neatly bounded entities. We routinely speak of religions like Hinduism as if we are certain about what distinguishes them from other religions like Buddhism, Christianity, or Islam. We tend to presume that religions are defined by essential and exclusive attributes and we only really contemplate the question of 'fuzzy' boundaries when we choose to call into question what we take to be unorthodox or inadmissible mixing (typically referred to as 'syncretism'). Clearly, such a concern with mixing only makes sense if religions are assumed to be clearly bounded entities. While religious teachers and defenders of orthodoxy may have an interest in defending such concrete boundaries, the student of religion does well to contemplate the degree to which the history of religion is far more complicated. Ironically, some Hindus prefer to refer to Hinduism as a 'way of life' precisely because they don't like to think of Hinduism as such a tightly bound entity. They wish to preserve room in their understanding for those Hindus who may revere Jesus as a great *yogi*, who may attend Christian festivals or seek the spiritual guidance of a Sikh or Muslim holy figure.

In the case of religion in South Asia, we have to recognize that convenient categories like Hinduism, Buddhism, and Jainism often work to impose a measure of discontinuity on what was in fact a world of overlapping and continually shifting religious experience. Recent scholarship has demonstrated, for instance, that *yoga* was never originally the property of one religious system; if anything, yogic theory and practice could themselves be thought of as a set of crucial strands within ancient South Asian religious life; the techniques and metaphysical assumptions of yoga were thus often shared by a range of like-minded teachers and practitioners across what we take to be religious 'boundaries.' The same may be said for a range of widely shared practices related to renunciation and austerity. These have been a characteristic marker of South Asian religion at least since the earliest Greek travelers reported finding 'naked philosophers' in the forests of India around the third c. BCE. And while we often associate the arrival of Islam in South Asia after the eighth c. CE with a clear distinction between monotheistic iconoclasm and indigenous polytheism and image worship, the historical record speaks again and again of rich interchanges—not just those initiated by philosophically inquisitive rulers like Emperor Akbar (sixteenth c.), but those that take place in a myriad everyday experiences in India and abroad.

Far from being monolithic entities, therefore, religious traditions might better be understood as a conglomeration or loose confederation of what we variously (and sometimes misleadingly) call sects, movements, denominations, or schools. Sometimes such religious communities are identifiable at the level of theology or doctrine so that one may distinguish between followers of non-dualist (*advaita*) or dualist (*dvaita*) Vedanta; sometimes they are identifiable by the particular reverence their members show for a particular deity, as when we distinguish among devotees of Shiva, Vishnu, or the Goddess (or Shaivas, Vaishnavas, and Shaktas, respectively); and sometimes one notices differences based on allegiance to spiritual lineages, so that among Vaishnavas one can point to those who revere the teacher Ramananda or to those who revere the teacher Chaitanya (among many others). And it is worth noting that, in some cases, one may be able to distinguish a particular Hindu movement on each of these grounds. Here, one thinks of the Swaminarayan tradition, where we can speak of those who follow a particular teacher (Saha-janand Swami), who, though himself nominally a devotee of Vishnu, is today worshipped as the incarnation of supreme reality (*purushottama*), a theological claim that is predicated on a distinctive set of theological and scriptural interpretations.

As these general reflections suggest, the apparently self-evident nature of the tradition can easily be complicated in any number of ways: Is God one or many, masculine, feminine, or both? What are the central sources of religious knowledge: scripture, reason, or meditative experience? Does worship require intense self-deprivation, careful ritual practice, or emotional surrender? Is there room for blood sacrifice or are cultic practices strictly vegetarian? Does a particular group conform to or challenge the norms of social order we associate with patriarchy, caste exclusion, and untouchability? The alternatives embedded in each of these questions should encourage readers to balance their desire to identify a single Hindu tradition with a willingness to consider the tradition in all its complexity. Each of the chapters in this volume is intended to support this kind of inquiry and the suggested readings and bibliographies will provide many avenues for further reading and discovery.

Colonialism and Modernity

When we say that an understanding of modern Hinduism requires reflection on the history and legacy of imperialism and colonialism, what is it we hope to emphasize? Clearly, no history of modern Hinduism can be written that does not address the series of developments associated with the European 'discovery' of India as a land of wealth and spices, the arrival in South Asia of Portuguese, French, Dutch, and British trading companies, the eventual rise to power of the East India Company and the British 'Raj,' and the modes of anticolonial resistance that gave shape to the present-day nation-states of South Asia. To study this history is to confront fundamental transformations in the religious, social, moral, and political world of South Asia—and, to be fair, of Europe and America as well. While it would be inaccurate and unhelpful to say that modern Hinduism is entirely a product of colonial rule, there is no denying that Hindu life and society were profound transformed during the colonial era. One need only think of such obvious colonial interventions as the printing press, the telegraph, the law court, the railway, and steamship to get a sense for how comprehensive change was during this period.

Beyond such material and technological interventions, it is widely acknowledged that one of the central goals of British colonial ideology was to regulate and control the economic, social, political, and religious world of South Asia. British rule was predicated on the amassing of information, the codification and classification of all manner of natural and social phenomena, and the attempt to expand the potential for economic profit through the imposition of bureaucratic and governmental order. In this respect, the sheer complexity of South Asian religious life was a source of near-constant fascination and frustration for British administrators and scholars (often the two roles were synonymous). While the fabled India of mystic insight and marvelous wealth remained beguiling to many Europeans right through the colonial period, missionaries, utilitarian policy makers, and die-hard imperialists found little to admire in a land associated with wandering holy men, multi-armed deities, and alien social customs. Whether framed as demonic, superstitious, immoral, or child-like, the figure of the Hindu was often viewed as in need of conversion, education, or moral improvement. Even if we set aside the least charitable of missionary characterizations of Hinduism as superstitious polytheism and immoral ritualism, it remains the case that colonial-era observers often could do little more than plug Hindu history and experience into their own familiar categories. By and large, these reflected a post-Protestant Reformation and Enlightenment view of the world structured around key concepts like 'scripture,' 'reform,' 'faith,' and 'reason.'

Linking our understanding of Hinduism in this way to the legacy of European colonialism and European self-understanding is one of the best ways to begin wrestling with the question of Hinduism and modernity. The title of this volume, *Hinduism in the Modern World*, is meant to suggest an important point in this connection. This is not a book about 'modern Hinduism,' if by that phrase one means only those forms of Hinduism that show signs of emerging from a direct engagement with the modern west. Many forms of Hinduism in the modern world betray such direct and sometimes intentional engagement, but many do not. By choosing not to restrict our gaze to only those forms that could be said to have attempted to be 'modern,' we hope to show that the expression and meaning of Hinduism today is far richer and more varied than a survey of so-called modern movements might suggest. Why does this matter?

The quest to define and ultimately ratify a distinctively 'modern' form of Hinduism represents a long-established mode of thinking about religion in modern South Asia, stretching back at least as far as John Nicol Farquhar's book, *Modern Religious Movements in India* (1915). That book took it as self-evident that the most consequential and therefore most interesting developments taking place in twentieth-century India were those in which the so-called traditional South Asian religions underwent profound transformations after encountering the salutary effects of western culture and Christianity during the age of British colonialism. This is one way to highlight the moral framework of European Christian exceptionalism within which Farquhar operated. For him, as for numerous other early twentieth-century scholars, the advent of a truly 'modern' Hinduism depended upon the arrival of the earliest Protestant missionaries in Bengal, who began critically scrutinizing religions like Hinduism while working to 'improve' (which is to say Christianize) the religious landscape of India.

Farquhar is representative of one dominant mode of thinking about 'modern Hinduism' in the past century that stressed the importance of those thinkers and movements that were presumed to bear the clear 'impress' of western, Christian values. We see such a trend even in a recent text like Arvind Sharma's anthology, *Modern Hindu Thought*, which opens with the revealing statement: 'A fundamental religious and cultural corollary of British Rule over India . . . was the cultural encounter between the two countries and the religious encounter between Christianity and Hinduism' (2002: 2). The goal of Sharma's book is to gather together texts written by a range of elite, male Hindu thinkers who are taken to represent something like the 'essence' of modern Hinduism. Prominent are figures who loomed large already for Farquhar a century earlier, men like Rammohan Roy (see Image 0.1). Sharma, like Farquhar, sees in Rammohan Roy's promotion of a monotheistic, ethical, and nonidolatrous Hinduism a debt to Christian missionary teachings, which we are told prompted Roy to repudiate the purportedly polytheistic, superstitious, and idolatrous practices of 'traditional' Hinduism. This way of viewing modern Hinduism operates as a kind of 'domino theory' in which Roy's Brahmo Samaj is pictured as providing the motive force for the subsequent 'reformation' of Hinduism along 'modern' lines. Both Farquhar and Sharma are most interested in those Hindus who sought in one way or another to purify Hinduism's tainted record of so-called nonmodern practices, from female infanticide and widow immolation to image worship and the reverence of holy men and priests. In this respect, 'modern Hinduism' was synonymous with 'reformed' Hinduism.

What an awareness of colonialism allows us to see, however, is that behind the idea of religious reform stands a series of European debates over the meaning and place of religion in society. British attitudes toward Hinduism were in fact heavily colored by Protestant animosity toward any forms of religion that reminded them of the purported errors of Catholicism, not least iconography, ritualism, and the excessive authority granted to priests (known in the colonial idiom as 'priestcraft'). So pervasive was the trope of 'reform' that it was even employed within groups that Farquhar might have seen as more 'traditional' than the Brahmo Samaj. Here one thinks of Swami Dayananda and the Arya Samaj. In the chapters that follow, readers will learn that it was Dayananda who sought to reform Hinduism by reasserting a proper orientation to ancient Vedic scripture. Hence, even this 'defense' of traditional Hinduism (as Farquhar understood it) suggests a fundamental modality of reform. It is no surprise that Dayananada figures as one of the essential figures in Sharma's collection. His is a 'modern Hinduism.'

There is no way to think about Hinduism in the modern world without wrestling with the work of major reformers like Rammohun Roy and Swami Dayananda. And yet, *Hinduism in the Modern World* is not a book about 'modern Hinduism' in this sense; we are not solely concerned with the Hinduism one encounters in works by authors like Farquhar or Sharma. In the present context, readers will be asked to think of Rammohun and Dayananda only as two examples of a far wider spectrum of Hindu experience in the modern era. While there is room for disagreement over what constitutes modernity, for the purposes of this volume, it is important to stipulate that 'modernity' does not stand for a kind of superior religious or moral vision that is taken to represent the 'reform' or 'improvement' of a so-called traditional religion. To be sure, the Hinduism that readers will encounter in this volume has been touched by the work of modern reform; in many and various ways, modern

Figure 0.1 Rammohun Roy

Hindus have clearly embraced, wrestled with, or rejected the idea of reform, whether imposed by a colonial other or generated by coreligionists. Indeed, the development of modern Hinduism has entailed a range of explicit and sometimes unregistered engagements with the values and projects associated with reform. But to put the matter simply, while it is necessary to reflect upon reform as a modality of modern Hinduism, it is not sufficient for understanding the full range of Hinduism in the modern world.

In order to dissociate a conception of the 'modern' from normative assumptions about what a modern religion *should* look like, it may help to think of modernity as a particular era, most simply defined as 'the time we are living in.' If this seems too minimal, we might go further and say that, for many, the onset of the modern era is associated with such historical events as the French Revolution, the emergence of industrialism in the west, or rise of the great European colonial systems under the Portuguese, Dutch, French, English, and Belgians. For the purposes of this volume, this sort of periodization is both adequate and useful, as long as we avoid the temptation to think that such temporal markers correspond to a set of ideal moral or civilizational values that we associate with the idea of western, Christian supremacy.

One might ask, if the concept of the 'modern' poses such problems, why not simply speak of 'contemporary Hinduism'? This question may seem especially pertinent insofar as much of this book will focus on figures, movements, or events associated with the present day. However, no matter how much we wish to move away from the kind of Eurocentric, teleological histories that tell the story of modern Hinduism as the 'progress' of an inferior religion toward greater perfection, we cannot escape the fact that recent and contemporary Hinduism can only be understood when placed in the context of a range of developments we associate with the modern era, including colonialism, nationalism, anticolonial resistance movements, transnational migration, the global networking of diaspora communities, and the impact of new technologies—from steamships and telegraphs to television and the internet. To be Hindu in this 'modern world' is to live through, negotiate, contest, appropriate, and reconfigure all the many challenges, opportunities, crises, tools, and situations that go along with 'modernity.' The authors of the chapters herein do not presume there is (or has been) a right way to go about such negotiation; they endorse no particular expression of modernity as most valid. Instead, they aim to be attentive to the complex dynamics associated with modernity, dynamics that make the history and expression of Hinduism over the past two centuries so complex and exciting.

References

Farquhar, J. N. (1915). *Modern Religious Movements in India*. Reprint ed. Delhi: Munshiram Manoharlal.

Sharma, Arvind (2002). *Modern Hindu Thought: The Essential Texts*. New Delhi: Oxford University Press.

Part I
Hinduism Today
Three Perspectives

1 Hinduism in South India

Leela Prasad

As new technologies and new diasporas emerge across the world, as tourism and the marketplace offer new religious mobilities and goods, and as modern governance exerts its claim on ancient political structure, Hinduism in modern South India invents and adapts itself. One illustration is a weekly Telugu-language television program called *Dharma Sandehalu* (*Doubts about Dharma*) that is viewed both through a live broadcast and through YouTube recordings by more than five million viewers across Asia, the Middle East, and North America. The program features an expert on South Indian Hindu traditions who resolves callers' dilemmas of practicing Hinduism amidst the exigencies and diversity of modern life. In another example, temples in the Hindu diaspora commonly adjust their ritual calendars to accommodate the work routines of host countries and extend maps of traditional Hindu sacred landscapes to include their new local geographies. The Sri Venkateshvara temple in suburban Pittsburgh, the oldest temple in North America, uses its hilly geographic setting to authenticate its belonging to the network of temples in the tradition of the famous hill temple of Sri Venkateshvara in Tirupati in South India. Almost every temple today has a cyber-presence: an elaborate website and Facebook pages that detail its origin stories and devotional experiences, web links to related temples, audiovisual streaming media of the worship rituals, and, often, facilities for 'e-worship' through which devotees can request and pay for particular rituals. Cell phone apps bring ritual procedures to handheld devices such as goddess worship in a South Indian format to an iPhone app. These new applications and mediations reflect the changing contours of sacred space and time and religious experience.

Modern adaptations, nevertheless, are embedded in histories and traditions that make regional forms of Hinduism distinctive. Modern South Indian Hinduism is best understood, not as one undifferentiated religion, but as a confluence of histories of rulership and patronage, lineages of spiritual authority, languages and styles of worship, and geographic and economic orders that are specific to South India. And modern South Indian Hinduism must also be understood as a negotiated identity within new contexts of race and culture. It is therefore important to take a longer view of South India than is provided by post-Independent India whose modernity downplays the enormously complex changes and exchanges that took place across Tamil, Kannada, Telugu, and Malayalam regions for many centuries, especially between the fifth and the seventeenth centuries. These regions not only had a variety of religious orientations that predate narrower definitions of 'Hindu' produced and contested during the period of British rule and beyond, but they also spawned a deeper cultural cross-fertilization between Hindu, Islamic, Jain, and Buddhist imaginations. For example, the city of Madurai (in modern-day Tamil Nadu) portrayed in the great Tamil epic *Cilapattikaram* (*The Tale of an Anklet*), ascribed to Ilango Atikal (about fifth century CE), depicts the strong currents (and uneasy undercurrents) between Jainism, Hinduism, Buddhism, and the so-called tribal religions that prevailed in this prosperous city of early South India. Between the fifteenth and the seventeenth centuries CE, engaging with an Islamic cultural and political climate, Hindu temple architecture borrowed distinct Islamic features such as arches, framed doorways, and stylized flower motifs. In the same way, the soaring roofs of a South Indian temple in a North American or European city are made possible only after the local Hindu community has negotiated its place through both tense and productive exchanges with other religious orders and with local laws of construction.

Thus, one way to discern the flows of the past in the modern and the interflows between different facets of the modern itself is to imagine a network—a necessarily fuzzy network—that gets created through reflections and reminiscences, people and precepts, and materials and methods. The portraits of South Indian Hinduism in this chapter illustrate different kinds of ancient and modern networks that are at play at consecrated sites, in worship rituals, in sacred embodiment, and, most of all, in devotees' perceptions and experiences.

Networks of Narratives

Avani, a small, rocky, and temple-dotted village in Kolar district, about sixty miles from the silicon city of Bangalore in Karnataka, South India, is an excellent example of how South Indian landscapes fashion their identity around epic narrative. Avani inhabits the ancient pan-Asian epics of the Ramayana and the Mahabharata in a way that ensures its own place in the perpetuity of these epic traditions and simultaneously locates itself in a network of places and temples across South India that are connected to each other through these epics. Photographs of Avani along with narrative sketches on Internet sites indeed register Avani primarily as an epic landscape that is a necessary part of tours through Karnataka.

According to contemporary oral traditions of Avani, Rama, the central hero of the Ramayana, and his wife, Sita, stayed at Avani—a motif of association that recurs in many towns and temples. The landscape remembers sage Valmiki, the author of the Sanskrit Ramayana and also one of its visionary characters, through the Valmiki Parvata (Valmiki Hill) with its cave residence. But unique to Avani is the familial claim that it makes on Sita through one of the few Sita temples in India. In fact, the very name Avani, which means 'earth' in Sanskrit, foregrounds the story of how King Janaka found the baby Sita in a furrow while he was plowing his fields and adopted her as his daughter. (Sita is also called Avanisuta, child of the earth.) Just as Mithila in North India displays its affectionate custody over Sita who was born and grew up there, it is to Avani, the story goes, that the pregnant Sita retreated, heartbroken at Rama's unjust—even if heart-torn—rejection of her. And it is here that she raised her twin sons in the sanctuary of Valmiki's hermitage and the surrounding forest. Landmarks in Avani's rocky terrain record these stories: Valmiki's cave contains an antechamber where Sita is believed to have birthed her boys; Tottalagundu (cradle-rock) is the boulder upon which Sita nurtured them; Kudregundu (horse-rock) is where the teenaged twins precociously tethered Rama's roaming sacrificial horse, challenging his kingship. The local community's folklore attributes the reddish hue of the rocks to the tears of blood that Sita shed as she watched her husband and young sons wage their battle with each other below on the plains (Vijailakshmi 2014).

But Avani's temples are also part of a South Indian network of rulerships and patronages, and they reflect the shifting religious preferences of many centuries of rulers. Although generally believed to have been built by rulers of the Nolamba-Pallava dynasty between the eighth and eleventh centuries CE, these temples successively saw new construction and renovation under later rulers such as the Chola kings. Avani's rulers were either Shaivas or Vaishnavas (worshippers of Shiva or Vishnu, the two prominent Hindu gods), but they built temples that accommodated the more diverse religious constituencies of their kingdoms. Hence, many of Avani's temples, although built by Vaishnava rulers, enshrine lingas which are iconic representations of the god Shiva, such as the Ramalingeshvara temple.

Avani also enshrines a story from the other inexhaustible epic, the Mahabharata. This story links both epics (the Ramayana and the Mahabharata) through the memory of one of the Mahabharata's characters, the ageless bear-king Jambavan, who was Rama's devotee from an earlier epoch. In the story, Krishna goes in search of a precious jewel called Shyamantaka whose loss is erroneously attributed to him, and finds that Jambavan has it. A struggle ensues. After twenty-one days of wrestling, Jambavan suddenly recognizes that Krishna is none other than his beloved Rama, reincarnated. Overcome with devotion, he immediately surrenders the jewel to Krishna. A temple on Avani's Valmiki Hill celebrates this story, with local lore also claiming that Jambavan's daughter (Jambavati) was given in marriage to Krishna here. These and other stories and their variants are part of Avani's mythic memory and they continue to be expressed there in daily worship, votive rituals, and healing practices. What is also important to note is that in an implicit network, Avani's Jambavan temple coexists with another rare

Jambavan temple roughly 250 miles northeast of Avani, in Nellore (Andhra Pradesh). Called the Krishnaswami temple, it too celebrates the same origin story from the Mahabharata as the Avani temple. In this way, epic narrative yields many opportunities for claims and identities that do not—at least commonly—challenge one another but become part of the fuzzy network of shrines in South India discussed earlier.

Hindu Architecture of South India: Networks of Sacrality and Secularity

A temple is called *kovil* in Tamil, *devasthana* in Kannada, *gudi* in Telugu, and *ambalam* in Malayalam. Regional variations notwithstanding, the ambience of a contemporary South Indian temple in India is routinely busy: outside is a marketplace with stores selling prayer books, devotional music, icons, trinkets, and framed or glossy pictures of deities associated with the temple; vendors are selling flowers and fruits that are usable in worship or small compact baskets with ritual paraphernalia. The streets of more touristy temples, additionally lined with small restaurants, see large numbers of buses and cars that take pilgrims and tourists on regional circuits of sacred and heritage sites. The interior of a temple displays a different kind of busy-ness with worshippers waiting in lines to see the deities, offer pujas (worship), and be blessed by the priest. Although physical access to the innermost space of the shrine is limited to temple priests, these days, one is likely to find closed circuit television screens and loudspeakers in larger temples that provide the worshippers who are standing in line a mediated experience of the inner shrine. This reciprocal flow between 'sacred space' and 'secular space' (i.e. worldly, mundane) has modern makings, but as the history of South India shows, temples through the centuries have supported networks of interdependence between the commercial enterprise of local communities and the religious duties of temple administrations.

The modern form of the South Indian temple, traditionally classified as 'Dravida,' has evolved over nearly seven hundred years, with each ruling dynasty or patron often modifying existing structures. In early Hindu political theology (that put secular political order in conversation with divine order), deities and rulers shared a sovereign status: the deity was a supreme and timeless sovereign, and the ruler was temporal potentate. Through a system of endowments, the ruler would ensure continuity of worship for the deity. In return, the temple accorded special privileges at the temple to the ruler. This shared sovereignty over territory is marked by a tall flagpole (*dhvajastambham*) in the courtyard of South Indian temples, usually positioned in front of the main door. While modern temples will have structures such as the *dhvajastambham*, it is a symbol that today, in the absence of a king, can serve to evoke the sole sovereignty of the deity or, in the diaspora, convey the arrival and belonging of a religious community.

A South Indian temple has two defining axes: one is horizontal (east-west) and the other is vertical. These axes symbolize and materialize the relationship between the human and the divine, the mundane and the extraordinary. The horizontal axis along which a worshipper walks to reach the inner shrine draws out the earthly location of the divine. The vertical axis, expressed through tall gateways and roofs, connects the earthly to the cosmic. The most sacred intersection of the two axes is the inner sanctum itself. These understandings are calculated through a precise mathematics elaborated in various architectural and iconographic texts. Two keystone texts on the principles of Hindu architecture and material culture, the *Manasara* ('essence of measurement') and the *Mayamata*, are from South India (Howes 2003).

It is important to remember that subjective preferences ultimately determine the diverse ways in which worshippers engage with temple spaces. Typically, however, a worshipper enters a South Indian temple through an ornate, tall gateway (*gopura*). She moves toward the east-facing deity, passing through one or more pillared halls (*mantapas*) and reaches the main structure called the *vimana* that is comprised of the inner sanctum called *garbha griha* (womb-house) and an elaborate pyramidal-dome directly above the sanctum. The garbha griha is smallish and cave-like, usually lit only by the lamps that surround the deity (*murti*). The deity's resplendent adornment reflecting in the lamplight creates an aura of auspiciousness and regality. The *vimana* is a precise mathematical configuration of a square plan on which the inner sanctum is built, while the pyramidal dome itself is a tiered projection of that plan. The vertical alignment suggests that the universe of secular forms and fantastical phenomena depicted in the pyramidal dome is ultimately born from the 'womb' that holds the deity. At the summit of the pyramidal dome-roof is a special kind of vase or pot (or a line of pots) called *kalasha*. While kalasha has many meanings, in essence, it symbolically contains the seed and the water of life. A circular pathway around the sanctum allows the worshipper to circumambulate the deity and thus express an intimate bond with an embodied, organic, and sovereign life-source.

The earliest phase (seventh to ninth CE) of South Indian temple architecture is associated with Pallava rulers who built rock-cut temples such as the chariot shrines (*rathas*) and the 'Shore temple' in Mahabalipuram in Tamil Nadu. The rathas depict scenes from the Puranas and the Mahabharata such as the descent of the heavenly river Ganga, or the warrior Arjuna's penance. Later temples added elements that define the South Indian temple today such as pillared halls, passageways for circumambulation, and walled courtyards. The tenth to eleventh centuries marked another culturally effervescent era when massive structures reflected the power and wealth of kings. A vibrant center to this day for the worship of Shiva, the granite Brihadeeshwara temple at Thanjavur, built by the Chola kings in 1,000 CE, has a tower that is nearly 200 feet high with just the top of the pyramidal structure weighing nearly eighty tons. The twenty-five-foot tall Shivalinga is the largest in

India. Nandi, Shiva's bull—each deity has a distinctive animal as vehicle—is a twenty-foot long monolithic statue. During festive processions today, large bronze statues, the famous Chola bronzes, go out draped in silk, flowers, and jewels on chariots into streets of the town, reminding us of the public role of deities.

If grandeur through scale and embellishment came to signify Hindu architecture by the twelfth century, it was taken to even further heights by the Vijayanagara and Nayaka rulers between the fourteenth and eighteenth centuries. The South Indian temple as a 'gigantic urban ensemble' came to index the widening importance of the temple in urban life (Michell 1995: 149). While the garbha griha continued to be the focal spiritual point of the temple, expanding enclosures, walls and soaring gateways, and halls for cultural performances, discourses, and civic meetings transformed the temple into a temple complex that accommodated worldly exchange. Still in active worship today, the Virupaksha-Pampa (Shiva-Parvati) temple in Hampi, the former capital of the Vijayanagara Empire, is a classic example of accrued architectural form. While the sanctuary in this temple existed even in the ninth and tenth centuries, it was the many generations of Vijayanagara rulers from the fourteenth century who made the temple—with gateways, water tanks, colonnaded streets leading into the surrounding bazaar, and public celebrations such as the grand Navaratri festival—virtually iconic of 'empire.' The display of regality is an integral part of a tradition in Shringeri, Karnataka, which dates to the fourteenth century when the then guru of Shringeri's monastic center (*matha*) strategically advised the two brothers, Hakka and Bukka, who soon established the Vijayanagara Empire. Tradition narrates that in gratitude, the brothers offered the guru the kingdom itself but, as a renunciant (*sannyasi*), he declined. He agreed instead to hold a symbolic royal court (*durbar*) for the ten days of Navaratri, the nine-night festival of the goddess in the Sharada temple there. Thus each night, even today, the matha's guru, wearing royal insignia, presides over music and dance performances in a durbar setting in the main temple. Hundreds of people gather for his durbar in the large hall of the temple, which is illuminated by fluorescent lights and traditional long brass wick lamps.

South Indian temples continue to embody the idea of interwoven worlds. While the deity has primordial importance, the temple's immersion in the everyday and its aesthetic construction of the sacred creates intricate networks between the worldly (commercial, political, or literary) and the cosmic. The bustling Meenakshi temple complex (see Image 1.1) at Madurai (Tamil Nadu) has two main linked shrines: one to Meenakshi (Parvati) and the other to her husband Sundareshvara (Shiva). The fourteen acres of the temple complex also house the main administrative offices, religious schools, sheds for the temple's animals, the Golden Lotus ritual bathing tank, the thousand-pillared hall, and the marriage hall where Meenakshi and Sundareshvara's marriage is celebrated annually. The temple re-creates Tamil literary pasts through shrines dedicated to scholars of the ancient literary academy called Sangam (Baker Reynolds 1987).

Figure 1.1 Meenakshi temple complex

Networks of Deities and Devotion

As discussed earlier, gods and goddesses are known in South India through multiple forms and by the particular devotions these evoke in their worshippers. The powers and personalities of deities are vividly charted by oral traditions, iconographic schemes, material practices, and worship texts while the lives of exemplary devotees are highlighted through hagiographic memory. Contemporary circuits of pilgrimage link sacred places in such a way that pilgrims are offered an immersion in a deity's manifestations; the goddess network in the Malnad mountains of Karnataka is an example. Two points need to be borne in mind as we discuss modern South Indian Hinduism: first, while there are significant interflows between pan-Indian Hindu conceptions of deities and worship and South Indian ones, regionalization offers us a glimpse into aesthetics and practices that remain unique to South Indian Hinduism. Second, deity networks are no longer limited to locations in South India. The god Murugan (also called Kartikeya, Subramanya, Kumara, or Skanda), son of Shiva and Parvati (their other son is the immensely popular elephant-headed Ganesha) for example, is worshipped in countless ancient and new shrines across Tamil Nadu. While he is associated with the bustling town of Palani, Murugan temples are today inseparable from the Tamil diaspora in Southeast Asia and North America.

The Goddess

South Indian Hinduism conceptualizes the goddess as an omniscient, independent feminine force (Devi) who is at once maternal and martial—as a *shakti* that empowers her male consort—and as a distinctive region-specific form. Thus Parvati, Shiva's wife, is known as Meenakshi (one with fish-shaped eyes) in the 'Madurai Meenakshi Temple' where she is represented both as an independent four-armed goddess and also as the wife of Sundareshvara (Shiva). In Kanchipuram, Parvati is Kamakshi (one with 'eyes of desire'), the goddess who passionately courts Shiva until he is persuaded to marry her. The image of Kamakshi in the 'Kanchi Kamakshi Amman Temple' displays symbols associated with Kama (the god of love) such as a bow of sugarcane and arrows of flowers. She also carries in her other arms a whip and a goad that suggest her resemblance to Kali, who is Parvati in her darker energy.

Lakshmi (also called *Sri*, or 'auspicious'), the goddess of wealth and good fortune and wife of Vishnu, adorns every South Indian Hindu home or business shrine. Popular art depicts her as a bejeweled, four-armed goddess, seated or standing in a red lotus, flanked by white elephants (symbols of royalty and fertility). Two hands hold lotuses that symbolize her spiritual autonomy, fertility, and her purity. Another hand, held in the boon-endowing gesture (*varada hasta*), showers gold coins. The fourth either holds a kalasha or is in the fear-dispelling gesture (*abhaya hasta*). Lakshmi's identity becomes localized in Tirupati (Andhra Pradesh), the site of the famous Sri Venkateshvara temple, through a legend: Lakshmi, angered by Vishnu's submissiveness toward a sage who has insulted him, stomps down to earth. Searching for her, Vishnu forgets himself and falls in love with Padmavati, a local princess—whose very name evokes the lotus (*padma*) of Lakshmi. On the eve of the marriage, the gods frantically substitute Padmavati with Lakshmi, and Lakshmi and Padmavati become synonymous with each other. Venkateswara is hence always depicted with 'two' goddesses on his chest: Padmavati and Lakshmi, also known as Bhudevi (goddess of the earth), and Sridevi (goddess of wealth). Padmavati has her own temple at the foothills of Tirupati and pilgrims customarily visit both shrines.

The worship of Parvati and Lakshmi demonstrates the cultural emphasis on fertility, marriage and domestic prosperity, and the belief that these can be enabled through women's worship traditions. Pujas to these goddesses involve the recitation of texts (such as the Lalita Sahasranamam, or the Thousand Names of Lalita) that extol the Devi in all her forms and Puranic stories that mark the conclusion of these pujas emphasize the rewards of female piety. In Karnataka, for instance, women and girls perform a ritual fast (*vrata*) on Bhimana amavasya (the new moon day between June and July) by fashioning small images of Parvati and Shiva out of mud and decorating them with vermillion and ash. Following the popularization through audiocassettes and prayer books of a Sanskrit prayer composed in the 1970s in Chennai, Lakshmi is also worshipped as Ashtha Lakshmi (The Eight Lakshmis), a group manifestation of eight forms such as Dhanalakshmi (goddess of wealth), Dhanyalakshmi (goddess of grains), Veeralakshmi (goddess of courage), and Santanalakshmi (goddess of progeny). Exclusive Ashtha Lakshmi temples in Chennai, Hyderabad, Houston, and North Hollywood indicate the aspirations of a globalizing middle-class and its imagination of prosperity as multifaceted.

Also unique to South India is the popular goddess Sharada who is a form of Saraswati, the patron of learning and the arts. In iconography, Sharada is depicted as seated, and in her four arms she holds a rosary, a parrot (evocative of speech), a palm-leaf book and a pot of divine nectar. Residents of Shringeri, where there is a 1,200-year-old temple dedicated to her, ascribe the nearly 100% literacy rates of the region to the presence and blessings of Sharada, but her worship indicates the high value placed on education in general in South Indian society. During the ten days of Navaratri, she takes on the larger persona of the goddess assuming a different form each day. Nearly twenty thousand people, from diverse communities and places, participate in Shringeri's Navaratri events each year, and partake in the free meals provided by the temple. From the 1990s, when improved transportation made travel through the winding mountain ghats easier and connected temple towns to Shringeri, the temple has expanded its facilities, replaced the boat ferry with a bridge over the river Tunga, and built large dining halls and lodges. Temple towns like Shringeri face a paradox with modernization. Modernization has boosted local economies and diversified the occupations of local residents who, alongside traditional agriculture, now run businesses like Internet cafes and cellphone stores. Yet, at the same time, the high tourist volume presents a challenge to local cultural rhythms and social life.

In another worship tradition, women devotees mostly from nonbrahmanical communities in South India pray to a distinctive network of goddesses who belong to the pantheon of *gramadevatas* (village deities), guardian deities often conceptualized as Seven Sisters. In the Telugu-speaking Telangana region, one of these goddesses is Pochamma, the eldest of the Seven Sisters. Pochamma bears tremendous heat that has the potential to break out in the form of measles or mumps or cause other calamities. For this reason, at the end of summer (July-August) her searing heat and heightened hunger are lowered by elaborate cooling and feeding rituals. Women carry on their heads a small, covered brass or terracotta container (*bonam*) that is decorated with symbolic eyes of the goddess, turmeric (*pasupu*, in Telugu) and vermillion (*kumkum*). These auspicious pots, covered by a wick-lamp, and containing rice, jaggery, neem leaves, yoghurt, and palm wine (*kallu*) are offered at Pochamma temples where a goat or a chicken is also sacrificed. Thus cooled and fed, Pochamma becomes a protectress and wish-granting goddess. The annual festival (*jatara*) of Pochamma ends in a procession to her temple whose external iconography includes the figure of Potu Raju, the only brother and youngest sibling of the Seven Sisters. In the procession, Potu Raju is represented by a bare-bodied man, painted in ritual colors, who dances vigorously, occasionally lashing himself in ecstasy with twisted coir or leather ropes. Potu Raju embodies Pochamma's shakti; his performance indicates his transformation from a man to an energized goddess. The Gangamma tradition that flourishes in Tirupati (*Andhra*), the site of the Sri Venkatesvara and Padmavati temples discussed earlier, is similarly about 'transformation'—becoming intensively female—that is mediated through material and ritual processes and renewed through narrative and enactment (Flueckiger 2013). In more empowering ways than pujas performed to Lakshmi or Parvati, worship in the Seven Sisters tradition is feminine endorsing, female protecting, and female energizing, thus creating a discourse and a space to confront gender inequities prevalent in modern society.

The Gods: Vishnu and Shiva in South India

The resurgence in the worship of Shiva and Vishnu that transformed South India between the seventh and the thirteenth centuries created vivid networks of sacred places, guru-lineages, texts, and ritual traditions that gave rise to South Indian devotional (*bhakti*) traditions with their own vernacular resonance. The shaping impact of this period is seen in many performance arts such as the sophisticated musical tradition known as 'Carnatic music,' whose founding composer, Purandara Dasa (1484–1564) was an ardent devotee of Vitthala (Krishna) while his contemporary, Annamaiyya (1408–1503), was a poet-devotee of Sri Venkateshvara. The motifs of modern Hinduism in South India are elaborated in the Carnatic musical compositions of South Indian singer-saints and have seen tremendous popularization through modern hagiographical movies, numerous international societies for the promotion of music and dance, and exclusive television channels owned by religious groups. For example, the Trust of the Sri Venkateswara Temple in Tirupati owns a twenty-four-hour cable and satellite TV channel that relays devotional music concerts, documentaries, and live broadcasts of pujas being performed in the temple.

Vishnu

Between the sixth and tenth centuries CE, twelve poet-saints (the Alvars, the immersed ones) are believed to have visited various Vishnu shrines in South India mapping a 'Divya desham' (sacred country). They expressed their visionary experiences in poems, which, like the Vedas, came to be regarded as divine revelation by a new community of Vishnu adherents called Srivaishnavas that consolidated in the eleventh century CE. The tradition's first teacher Nathamuni (tenth century CE) incorporated Alvar songs into daily liturgy, and, since then, they have been sung regularly in Srivaishnava homes and temples (Narayanan 1987). The lyrical poems composed by Andal, the only woman-saint among the twelve Alvars, are especially sung all over South India in December and January. Alvar poetry specially praises Ranganatha, the reclining form of Vishnu, in the temple at Srirangam, Tamil Nadu. This temple is the largest in India: its 150 acres enclose towering structures and seven walled rectangles at the center of which is the main shrine to Ranganatha, a large, dark stone image of Vishnu reclining on his giant serpent, Ananta. The image faces south and not east as is conventional. It is this Vishnu as Ranganatha on whom the young Andal, living in the compound of a temple in Srivilliputtur 140 miles south of Srirangam, sets her heart and Ranganatha himself (appearing in a dream to her father) asks to marry her in Srirangam's temple. Considered the ideal devotee by the Srivaishnava community, by the twelfth century, Andal had become identified as Bhu Devi, the earthly form of Lakshmi, Vishnu's consort (Venkatesan 2013).

Shiva

In the eleventh century, the Chola court poet Nampi recovered at the Chidambaram temple compositions of three poet-saints, Sambandar, Appar, and Sundarar, who wrote poems to Shiva prolifically between the sixth and eighth centuries CE. These (and preceding) saints are celebrated as the sixty-three Nayanars ('leaders') of Tamil Shaivism. The collected poems of the three saints are called the *Tevaram*, a foundational scripture for Tamil Shaivas. The poems, inspired by the experiences of the saints as they visited 274 Shiva shrines across South India, illuminate an extensive Shaiva landscape that becomes exalted in worship. This place-centered yet omnipresent Shiva is described in the following poem by Appar:

> In Nallur he danced for a long time,
> in Palaiyaru, mounted his white bull.
> He wandered begging in many towns,
> sojourned in Cerrur for the whole world to see,
> then hid in the shrine at Talaiyalankatu.
>
> He dwelt with delight in Peruvelur's temple,
> halted in Patticcuram for the night,
> entered Manarkal,
> revealed himself in Cattankuti's shrine,
> and swiftly reached Tiruvarur,
> where he stayed.
> (Viswanathan Peterson 1991: 151)

One of the most praised Shiva temples in these hymns is the temple at Chidambaram where Shiva is represented as Nataraja, the king of dance, and as Akasha, space. Notwithstanding secularization, Tevaram hymns continue to be a strong marker of Tamil Shaiva identity and are sung in temples and homes—a fact that played into widespread public protest when, in 2009, the Tamil Nadu state government took over the management of the Chidambaram temple from traditional caretaker priests. This followed a caste-based controversy over who could sing Tevaram hymns inside the sanctum sanctorum: the otuvars (professional Tevaram singers who have for generations sung the songs but just outside the sanctum) or the brahman priests who conduct the worship in the inner sanctum.

If grandeur is the aesthetic appreciated by the Tamil Shaivas, its opposite is spelled out by followers of another crucial South Indian Shaiva movement called the Virashaiva ('heroic' Shaivism) founded by the poet Basava after a violent revolt against King Bijjala in north Karnataka in the twelfth century. The philosophy of the Virashaivas, who are also known as Lingayats, is expressed in *vachanas* ('utterances'), poems in Kannada composed by

Basava and other Virashaiva saints around the twelfth century. An illustrative vachana by Basava says:

> The rich make houses for Shiva.
> What can I make?
> I am but poor.
>
> My legs are themselves the pillars,
> My body is itself the temple,
> My head the gold kalasha
>
> Listen, you god of Kudalasangama![1]
> The fixed (*sthavara*) has loss,
> the itinerant (*jangama*) has no loss.
>   (Basava; translation mine)

This vachana rejects the formalism and fixity (*sthavara*) of temple structure and instead offers as the dwelling of Shiva the moving devotee's (*jangama*) body. As a mark of this embodied philosophy, lingayats today carry a personal linga. At the core of the vachanas is a trenchant critique of ritual-and-palace-based Shiva worship and a reformulation of 'community.' Indeed, the Virashaiva movement brought a new modernity to bhakti-based worship. The Sri Siddhaganga matha near Bangalore continues to revitalize the central Virashavia tenet 'kayakave kailasa' (work is worship) through a network of modern educational and philanthropic institutions. The vachanas themselves which were previously only sung within Lingayat communities, today appeal, because of their modernity, to a newer generation of South Indian classical vocalists who include them in their repertoires.

Born out of the union of Shiva and Vishnu is a uniquely South Indian god, the celibate ascetic, Ayyappan, famous for vanquishing the ravaging demon Mahishi. The annual pilgrimage to Ayyappan's temple on the mountain Sabarimalai, Kerala, is the largest in South India, drawing tens of millions of men from all over South India between mid-November and mid-January. Men dress in a black dhoti and an upper garment, wear no footwear, and observe a forty-one-day period of fasting, prayer, and abstinence. Until recently, the temple, in the remote Nilimala forests of Kerala, was difficult to reach. In recent years, a special train network across South India takes pilgrims to nearest points of the forest trek. The Kerala state government and private companies have created illuminated pathways that pilgrims now use to reach the temple, stopping traditionally at the mosque of a Muslim saint, Vavar, who is known to have provided assistance to Ayyappan in his battle against the demons. While men from all castes, even religions, participate in the tradition, women roughly between ten and fifty years of age are prohibited, in the belief that it preserves the celibate energy associated with the tradition. This prohibition of women is being challenged in recent times in Indian courts, with a few women breaking the tradition by entering the main temple.

Networks of Philosophy

Three widely influential foundational schools of philosophy took root in South India between the eighth and the thirteenth centuries CE. The founders and philosophers associated with these schools wrote extensive commentaries on a resonant body of literature called Vedanta, which may be understood to mean 'conclusion to the Vedas' or 'the purpose of the Vedas.' The earliest of these schools was Advaita (absolute non-dualism) founded by Shankara (eighth century CE), who established a monastic center (*matha*) at Shringeri for its study and propagation. Shankara argued that there is one single reality, a One-ness without any attributes, and that the world of form and experience is an illusion (*maya*), a distraction, caused by ignorance (*avidya*). Liberation from the endless cycle of life and death comes when the individual realizes One-ness (and thereby becomes it). The worship of deities, according to Shankara, is valuable to cultivating devotion, but it is to be superseded by the higher intellectual pursuit and ethical practice of Oneness. Smartha Brahmins of South India follow the tradition of worship of five deities (Surya, Devi, Shiva, Vishnu, and Ganesha) established by Shankara. Interpreting Vedantic texts differently, Ramanuja (1017–1137 CE) established the school of philosophy called Vishistadvaita (qualified non-dualism) which gave the Srivaishnava tradition its philosophical foundation. Ramanuja, founding the Srivaishnava matha at Melkote in Karnataka, argued that while there is a single ultimate reality (Vishnu), the differentiated (*vishista*) world consisting of acts, forms, devotees, and so on is also real and the path to that ultimate single reality is through devotion and surrender (*prapatti*) to Vishnu. A third school of philosophy was formulated in the thirteenth century by Madhava who proposed that there are graded differences (*bheda*) between things, but all things are permanently subordinated to the supreme reality, understood as Vishnu. Vishnu pervades everything, all things depend entirely on him, and liberation consists in the self's joyful and steady awareness of this always-distinct and supreme inner divinity. The matha founded by Madhava at Udupi in southwestern Karnataka propagates Madhava's teaching and guides dvaita practice. These various mathas today have vibrant networks that include international locations that also run philanthropic and outreach programs. Modern politicians often visit the prominent mathas and seek the blessings of their spiritual leaders, recalling the historical connection between rulers and renunciant gurus. Another modern facet of this nexus can been seen in the public sphere of national media, where some spiritual leaders comment on national political events that involve religion or even take a lead in organizing social movements.

Conclusion: Who Owns the Vaults of Vishnu?

The case of the Ananta Padmanabha Swami temple in Tiruvananthapuram (formerly Travancore) in Kerala sums up what we have discussed in this chapter: the networked roles of memory and materiality in creating the experience of Hinduism in South India. The Ananta Padmanabha temple tells the story of a deity's autonomy caught between the hereditary patronage of a royal family and the claims of modern legalistic public. Till Indian Independence in 1947, the temple was strongly connected to Travancore, one of the larger kingdoms of South India. After consolidating Travancore in 1750, King Marthanda Varman I, dedicated the kingdom and its vast wealth to the deity, Padmanabha, the form of Vishnu in the temple at Thiruvananthapur. In the paradigm of shared sovereignty between deity and ruler discussed earlier, Varman ruled symbolically as the deity's vassal. Travancore became one of the richest and most progressive kingdoms in India. In 1936, for instance, the last Maharaja of Travancore, Chitira Tirunal Balarama Varma, issued the historic Temple Entry Proclamation that permitted Dalits (so-called Untouchable castes) to enter and worship at all temples in Travancore. The modernity of the temple, one could easily argue, was demonstrated by this radical proclamation that was approved by Mahatma Gandhi.

The colonial English government's Religious Endowments Act of the 1860s and its later amendments by state governments in independent India replaced the ancient tradition of shared sovereignty with a new system of governance. Instead of titular royal families, now boards and committees appointed by a government administered the temple. However, the close association of the erstwhile royal family with the Padmanabha temple was not erased from public memory. Its members continued to be de facto custodians of the temple. In 2007, a public interest litigation was filed challenging the family's custodianship of the temple and alleging misappropriation of temple funds. The community in Thiruvananthapur itself was split over this matter, but a large number of citizens showed allegiance to the royal family. At stake in the debate, ongoing in 2014, are six secret vaults in hitherto unknown recesses of the temple. The courts ordered two vaults to be opened and its contents audited. The royal family, with public support, claimed that the vaults belonged to no one but the deity Padmanabha and violation would cause serious misfortune in the city. Despite this, in the only vault that was ultimately opened (the royal family was prohibited from access to the temple), riches worth billions of dollars have been discovered: gold bricks and ropes, precious gems including large diamonds, silver furniture, rare artifacts, foreign coins, and exquisite ornaments, among other items. A furious debate continues in the Supreme Court of India about whether other vaults should be opened. According to belief, some vaults are protected by mystic powers that should not be disturbed. Yet, what is not so mystical is that the temple today is 'protected' by lawsuits, gun-carrying commandos, hidden cameras, and other surveillance mechanisms. One could end this chapter by reflecting on the question: What happens to deities and devotees when a great tradition modernizes (see Singer 1972)?

Summary

Modern South Indian Hinduism is best envisioned not as one undifferentiated religion, but as a multiplicity of traditions that emerge from the interaction between an early South Indian past of royal patronage and artistic form and a modern present that is rapidly changing, marked by new technologies, diasporas, and governance. These interactions across time and space that make South Indian Hinduism both distinctive and modern can be understood through the idea of networks—fuzzy networks—that connect people, precepts, memories, and materials. Some of the networks illustrated in this chapter are networks of narratives that connect different places across South India and her diaspora, networks of sacrality that link regional and cosmic orders, and networks of deities and schools of philosophy that highlight patterns of worship and sacred embodiment. These networks demonstrate how "modernity" has always been negotiated over the last two millennia by traditions of South Indian Hinduism, which have redefined continuity and invention in the light of experience, power, and resources.

Questions for Discussion

- How do religious and other cultural networks in South India function? How do these alter and expand over time, and how are they affected by modernity in particular? Do we need flexible understandings of modernity?
- What role do history and artifacts play in South Indian religious identity today? Where and how does the past meet the present?
- How do broader social issues like gender norms and political structures influence South Indian religious practice?
- How are material elements and spatial organization within temples and other sacred spaces related to concepts of the deities and their divine power?
- What is the relationship between fixity of place and devotional itinerancy in the spatial context of South Indian religious traditions?

Note

1   Kudalasangama is a place in Bagalkot district of north Karnataka where the two rivers Malaprabha and Krishna meet.

Suggested Readings

Flueckiger, Joyce F. (2013). *When the Goddess Becomes Female: Guises of a South Indian Goddess*. Bloomington: Indiana University Press.

Fuller, Christopher J. (2003). *The Renewal of the Priesthood: Modernity and Traditionalism in a South Indian Temple*. Princeton: Princeton University Press.

Michell, George (1995). *The New Cambridge History of India: Architecture and Art of Southern India*. Cambridge: Cambridge University Press.

Narayanan, Vasudha (1987). *The Way and the Goal: Expressions of Devotion in the Early Sri Vaisnava Tradition*. Washington, D.C.: Institute for Vaishnava Studies.

Prasad, Leela (2007). *Poetics of Conduct: Oral Narrative and Moral Being in a South Indian Town*. Columbia: Columbia University Press.

Waghorne, Joanne P. (2004). *Diaspora of the Gods: Modern Hindu Temple in an Urban Middle-Class World*. New York: Oxford University Press.

Viswanathan Peterson, Indira (1991). *Poems to Siva: the Hymns of the Tamil Saints*. Delhi: Motilal Banarsidass.

Bibliography

Clothey, Fred W. (1978). *The Many Faces of Murukan: The History and Meaning of a South Indian God*. The Hague, The Netherlands: Mouton.

Cohen, Andrew L. (1992). 'The King and the Goddess: The Nolamba Period Laksmanesvara Temple at Avani.' *Artibus Asiae* 52, No. 1/2: 7–24.

Flueckiger, Joyce F. (2013). *When the Goddess Becomes Female: Guises of a South Indian Goddess*. Bloomington: Indiana University Press.

Fritz, John M. and George Michell (1992). *Vijayanagara Research Project Monograph Series*. New Delhi: Manohar.

Fuller, C. J. (1980). 'The Divine Couple's Relationship in a South Indian Temple: Mīnākṣī and Sundareśvara.' *History of Religions* 19, No. 4: 321–348.

Hardy, Adam (1995). *Indian Temple Architecture: Form and Transformation, the Karnāta Drāvida Tradition, 7th to 13th Centuries*. New Delhi: Indira Gandhi National Centre for the Arts & Abhinav Publications.

Howes, Jennifer (2003). *The Courts of Pre-Colonial India: Material Culture and Kingship*. London: RoutledgeCurzon.

Michell, George (1995). *The New Cambridge History of India: Architecture and Art of Southern India*. Cambridge: Cambridge University Press.

Narasimhachar, R., ed. (1976). *Archaeological Survey of Mysore. Annual Reports: 1910–1911*. Volume III. Dharwar: Karnatak University.

Narayanan, Vasudha (1987). *The Way and the Goal: Expressions of Devotion in the Early Sri Vaisnava Tradition*. Washington, D.C.: Institute for Vaishnava Studies.

Prasad, Leela (2007). *Poetics of Conduct: Oral Narrative and Moral Being in a South Indian Town*. Columbia: Columbia University Press.

Reynolds, Holly Baker (1987). 'Madurai: Koyil Nakar.' In *The City as a Sacred Center: Essays on Six Asian Contexts* (pp. 12–44). Eds. Bardwell Smith and Holly Baker Reynolds. Leiden: E.J Brill.

Rodrigues, Hillary (2006). *Introducing Hinduism*. New York: Routledge.

Singer, Milton (1972). *When a Great Tradition Modernizes: An Anthropological Approach to Indian Civilization*. New York: Praeger.

Sekar, Radhika (1992). *The Sabarimalai Pilgrimage and Ayyappan Cultus*. Delhi: Motilal Banarsidass.

Vijailakshmi, Usha R. (2014). 'Uttarkhand in Avani: Sita's Life in Exile and the Chola's Religious Policy in the aftermath of the Govindaraja Controversy (1186–1279).' Proceedings of the Conference on 'The Ramayana in Literature, Society and the Arts.' Chennai: C.P.R. Publications. Pp. 425–435.

Viswanathan Peterson, Indira (1991). *Poems to Siva: the Hymns of the Tamil Saints*. Delhi: Motilal Banarsidass.

Venkatesan, Archana (2013). 'Ecstatic Seeing: Adorning and Enjoying the Body of the Goddess.' In *Contemporary Hinduism* (pp. 217–231). Ed. Pratap Kumar. Durham, U.K: Acumen.

Waghorne, Joanne P. (2004). *Diaspora of the Gods: Modern Hindu Temples in an Urban Middle-Class World*. New York: Oxford University Press.

2 Hinduism in North India

Brian K. Pennington

In 2001, I was traveling with friends attempting to complete a Hindu pilgrimage called the Char Dham Yatra in the Indian Himalayas. This route stops at four sacred sites (*dhams* or 'abodes' of the deity) near the glacial source of a sacred river. As we were traveling by car from Yamunotri, where the Yamuna River begins, to Gangotri, where the Ganges River emerges from a glacier, our driver urged us to stop at a roadside cave in which a village had recently established a shrine to the Hindu god Shiva. We hiked a short distance up the mountainside where we encountered a villager seated in front of the narrow cave opening. We learned he served as priest at the shrine. After we had squeezed in, we were shown rock formations that our local guide explained were naturally formed images of the gods and goddesses of the Hindu pantheon. Later, when we interviewed the village head, he explained that he had recently discovered the cave while searching for an underground water source for the village. The god Shiva had spoken to him in a dream and led him to this spot. He discussed his plans to organize the village in order to make news of the cave visible to the auto and bus traffic passing along the road during the pilgrimage season. He also had plans to build a proper temple that would attract pilgrims and their offerings. Over the years since then, there has been occasional controversy in the village over which castes can rightfully conduct rituals and guide visitors inside the sacred enclosure. However, during this same period, the site has grown and expanded as busloads of pilgrims from all over India have stopped to marvel at the cave shrine, captivated not only by the remarkable natural forms of the gods but also by the vivid storytelling of the village guides. Today, on the basis of successful marketing to tour organizers and drivers, this temple—known as Prakateshwar Panchanan Mahadev—has become one of the most popular stopping points on the Char Dham Yatra, and the story of its miraculous discovery is told and retold to throngs of visitors whose donations have helped build a bustling pilgrimage center. However, two successive years of dramatic monsoon flooding in the region, attributed by some to the effects of climate change at high altitudes, led to steep declines in pilgrimage during 2012 and 2013. Today, those whose livelihoods depend on the success and possible expansion of the pilgrimage economy face great uncertainty about the future. What will become of religious tourism in a region threatened by increased climactic disruption?

I open with this vignette because it highlights a particular set of dynamics that characterize North Indian Hinduism in the early twenty-first century: religious entrepreneurship, rapid economic expansion, the commodification and politicization of sacred space and pilgrimage, and the challenges of ecological deterioration. As we proceed, we shall also see that North Indian Hinduism demonstrates the ways in which religion can become a resource for various kinds of activism as well as a potent source of regional and national contestation. The transformations we see Hinduism undergoing in the North represent a distinctly modern, or even postmodern, environment. While the categories of 'modern' and 'postmodern' are endlessly debated, for the purposes of this chapter, I use 'modern' to signal a religious environment in North India that contrasts with premodern settings in at least four different ways: first, religious authority is diffuse and contested; second, religious identities are politicized; third, accelerating globalization introduces outside influences into India while India itself becomes the source of many globalizing trends; fourth, opportunities for invention and innovation flourish in a milieu characterized by a wide array of religious options.

Is There a North Indian Hinduism?

For centuries, people have observed that North India and South India are two distinct places in many important respects. There are good reasons for believing so. The most fundamental difference between these two regions of the South Asian subcontinent is linguistic: whereas the languages commonly spoken in the four states considered South India belong to the Dravidian family of languages, those of the North generally are Indo-European languages, a completely separate and unrelated family that also includes Latin, Greek, most of the languages of modern Europe and North America, as well as Sanskrit, the ancient religious language of India. Because language, especially one's mother tongue, is such a powerful influence on one's sense of personal identity in India today, the North/South linguistic divide remains one that Indians themselves have strongly felt.

Correlated with differences in language, however, is a whole set of social and cultural differences. When I posted a question to an email listserv asking others scholars of Hinduism to name the ways in which they thought North and South India differed, a variety of specific practices and traits were noted: the traditional calendars of North and South use different starting and ending days for their months; the grain staple of the north is wheat, while in the south it's rice; wedding practices and family structures vary; the caste system is quite different; names for shared gods are not the same, and each region has its own unique deities; food, temple architecture, and music each have characteristic North and South Indian styles. History gives us another set of compelling reasons for drawing a line between North and South: whereas areas of North India have been ruled by various Muslim dynasties with connections to Persia and modern Afghanistan and Pakistan, the South largely avoided conquest by these northern powers and has seen Hindu monarchies who proudly claim to have resisted the imposition of ruling authority from outside the region. Finally, today we see important demographic differences: markers for human development such as health, literacy, the status of women, are all better in the South (see, e.g., Drèze and Sen 2013: 72–80, 168–171, and 233–239).

Do these divergences point to wider, more pervasive, or more meaningful differences in styles of religiosity? Does it make sense to speak of a North Indian Hinduism? Even though India has become more and more homogenized since it achieved political independence in 1947, I would argue that there are good reasons for talking about Hinduism in India today in terms of its northern and southern varieties. Emerging out of the Enlightenment in Europe and then spread around the globe by colonialism, modernity refers to the growing power of science and reason over tradition and the valorization of the individual, free self. These forces made possible many common global realities today that have dramatically affected religion: democracy, capitalism, consumer economies, technology, and the media. In the rest of this chapter, I will focus on three features of the religious culture of contemporary North India that embody these modern transformations in Hinduism: first, specific practices that express an attachment to the religious landscape; second, modes of Hindu activism on behalf of the environment or the nation; and third, an entrepreneurial spirit that is now generating exciting if sometimes problematic developments in Hindu religious life. In this chapter, I will emphasize what an intelligent and educated observer might notice about how Hinduism is evolving in North India today. Readers are encouraged to note how closely connected these different facets of North Indian Hinduism are to one another. Indeed, I would like to suggest that, taken together, they help us to understand North India today as a distinctive religious region. Readers will also notice how many of the ideas and themes that other chapters of this textbook develop are interwoven here in particularly interesting ways.

The Sacred Landscape of the North

Although its distinct topographies include broad plains that can resemble a checkerboard of neatly bordered agricultural fields, desert, highlands, and the awe-inspiring peaks of the Himalayas, North India can be said to form a distinct geocultural region that is typically thought to be physically separated from the South by a rising plateau known as the Deccan. North Indian Hindus have shared a common reverence for the remarkable features of this landscape and participated in pilgrimages to various sacred sites since at least the time of the composition of the Hindu epic the *Mahabharata* nearly 2,000 years ago (Bhardwaj 1973: 31–34). Three kinds of pilgrimage destinations are most significant: mountains, rivers, and holy cities. Although each pilgrimage destination has its own distinct character and expresses unique ideas about how and why journeying to that spot is important, they may all be thought of using the Hindu concept of *tirtha*, that is a 'crossing point' (literally a 'ford' in a river) at which humans make contact with the gods and goddesses of Hinduism and gain access to powerful sources of energy (Bhardwaj and Lochtefeld 2004).

The Ganga, or Ganges River (the latter being the name adopted by the British during the colonial period), is one of the defining features of the North Indian landscape. This broad and powerful stream of water is part of a larger river system that covers much of North India, originating at many points in glaciers and springs in the Himalayas, tumbling down through the mountains, and then flowing across the plains, eventually emptying into the Bay of Bengal. These waters are critical to agriculture and therefore to life itself in North India. Today, through complex irrigation networks, they water the fields of countless farmers growing the wheat, rice, lentils, and vegetables that form the major portion of the diet of North India. At the same time, the Ganga is regarded as supremely sacred by all Hindus. Many believe that its waters wash away all the accumulated sins from the souls of those who bathe in it (see Image 2.1). Among the Hindus of North India, the Ganga is an ever-present focal point, shaping their religious lives and imaginations. By contrast, Hindus living in the South or in the diaspora have a less immediate connection to the river, which nonetheless structures their religious ideas and imagination. Indeed, Hindus believe the sanctity of the Ganga can be accessed locally in other bodies of flowing water, whether it be the Kaveri River in South India or the Allegheny River in Pennsylvania.

The Ganga itself is regarded as the earthly form of a goddess who descended from the heavens when the ancient King Bhagirathi begged her to come to earth so that the ashes of his ancestors could be cleansed by her waters and they could proceed on their journey to the afterlife (Eck 1996: 145). All along her length are holy cities, each with its own distinct character, myths, and religious institutions such as temples and meditation retreat centers called *ashrams*. But central to religious life in each of these sacred sites is the act of bathing in the Ganga.

Every city and town along the Ganga will include spots set aside for bathing; these typically feature a series of stone or concreate steps down to the river (called *ghats*). In addition, one will often also find temples dedicated to the goddess Ganga herself as well as to the other major deities. Nearby these temples and ghats, lines of people can almost always be found heading to and from the river. On the ghats, they will submerge themselves for bathing or simply frolic in the waters, almost always in gender-segregated groups. Men will typically strip down to their underwear and enthusiastically jump in the water, whereas women often bathe more discreetly, keeping their clothes on and then changing into dry ones while shielded from view by other women. Bathing like this takes place as an individual activity and often simply as part of the fun of living in one of these pilgrimage cities. However, many people

Figure 2.1 Bathers in the Ganga

also bathe before undertaking worship of their gods or in connection with a religious vow. Such vows typically involve asking a god or goddess for help in getting pregnant, overcoming an illness, or securing a good job. The river is also a focal point for great seasonal and calendrical festivals that sometimes draw millions of bathers to the most sacred sites, like Hardiwar and Allahabad. Finally, as we shall see, the river plays a role in the final rites of Hinduism associated with death, cremation, and the afterlife.

Put simply, the Ganga exerts a kind of magnetic pull over Hindus, drawing daily worshippers and pilgrims from far and wide. In this way, it has helped to shape the life of North Indian Hinduism. In what follows, I will briefly profile four of the most popular sacred cities along the Ganga to give a sense of the religious culture that stretches along this critical artery of North Indian Hinduism.

We begin with Gangotri, a small city high in the Himalayas at an altitude of around 10,000 feet. Today, pilgrims arrive in Gangotri by private cars or bus, traveling along a bumpy and vertiginous road that traces a winding path along sheer cliffs. They come to bathe and to visit the Gangotri Temple, which marks the spot where Hindu myth says King Bhagirathi stood on one leg and prayed for 5,500 years for the river goddess to descend and bless the earth. Here, the great god Shiva graciously allowed Ganga to strike his head so that he could absorb the tremendous force of her fall and protect the earth from destruction (a day's hike further into the mountains of Gangotri brings the pilgrim to Gaumukh, the spot where the river first emerges from a glacier). Gangotri is one of the four pilgrimage destinations in the upper Himalayas that together form the Char Dham Yatra, or the Pilgrimage (*yatra*) to the Four (*char*) Sacred Abodes (*dham*) of the divine.

While bathing in the icy waters at Gangotri is thought to be especially meritorious, the journey is not only about religion. Himalayan pilgrimage in the modern era is in fact a kind of devotional tourism whose attractions include meaningful spiritual experience but also the sense of adventure, the chance to glimpse firsthand the breathtaking scenery, and the opportunity to be entertained by stories about the mythical Bhagiratha and his ancestors, all of which point to the gracious descent of Ganga, who now offers herself to all who come to her. Towering, snow-capped mountains hem in the rushing river whose roar as it crashes down the huge rocks of the riverbed often drowns out all other sounds. The air is thin, and pilgrims from the plains often struggle to catch their breath, exhilarated by the combination of majestic scenery and powerful religious devotion, not to mention by the experience of being in such a lofty and remote location.

About 155 miles downstream from Gangotri are the sister cities of Haridwar and Rishikesh. Each is the home for important religious institutions with far-reaching influence (McKean 1996: 43–70). Rishikesh, some fifteen miles from Haridwar, is a frequent destination for pilgrims, but today it is primarily associated with the many meditation complexes along the river where Indians and foreigners often spend extended periods of time, just as the Beatles famously did in 1968. Haridwar is the traditional gateway to the Himalayas and it features a temple marking the point where the Ganga leaves the Himalayas and enters the North Indian plains. Hindu nationalist organizations such as Vishva Hindu Parishad (VHP) are powerfully present in Haridwar, and many national politicians travel here for major speeches and for opportunities to have their picture taken with important gurus. Some pilgrims come to Haridwar to begin the Char Dham Yatra, while others arrive every year to perform life cycle rites, to consult with the many human and divine powers who live here, or to collect Ganga water to take home for ritual purposes (Lochtefeld 2010: 171–202). Among the more recent innovations in the religious life of Haridwar are temples and ashrams along the riverbank that seek to promote a vision of India as a fundamentally Hindu nation. Like the perennial presence of politicians in the city, these temples remind us how closely religion and politics can be integrated.

Further downstream in the state of Uttar Pradesh, two large cities are particularly noteworthy for their roles in consolidating North Indian Hinduism: Allahabad and Varanasi. Allahabad is thought to represent the confluence (*sangam*) of the Ganga River with the Yamuna, the second major river of North India that flows through Delhi and is considered the mythological sister of Ganga (in myth, a third stream, the Sarasvati, is also thought to merge here). Allahabad, known in Sanskrit as Prayag (an ancient term for a place of sacrifice), is home to what is said to be the largest gathering of human beings on earth for any single purpose, the giant bathing festival called the Maha Kumbha Mela (Maclean 2008). Taking place once every twelve years over a period of several weeks, the Maha Kumbha Mela is led by bands of naked *sadhus*, or ascetic holy men, who belong to specific religious orders and who typically live in isolated forests in the Himalayas (Lochtefeld 2008). In 2013, an estimated sixty to one hundred million Hindus came to bathe at astrologically auspicious times; the city filled with festival goers and large camps were set up on the wide river banks by influential *sadhus* and *sadhvis* (holy women) and their many disciples.

Probably the most celebrated and ancient city in all of Hinduism is Varanasi (or Benares), believed to be as old as time itself, the oldest portions of which offer a confusing maze of narrow, twisted lanes that all seem to lead inevitably to the city's crowning feature, the many banks of steep *ghats* that line the length of the river's western edge (Eck 1982: 211–251). Each of these ghats has its own mythology, purpose, and history. The famous Manikarnika Ghat is the busiest of the burning ghats in Varanasi, where many Hindus come to live out their final days and where funeral cremations are held continuously through the day and night. Manikarnika Ghat is the final destination of the many funeral processions that can be seen every day as families carry their loved ones to this sacred spot to be cremated and have their ashes placed in the Ganga River so that their souls may be released (Parry 1994: 33–72).

Activist Hinduism

A second distinctive feature of modern North Indian Hinduism is a public spirituality that promotes a set of social and political causes on the basis of certain Hindu ideals. The modern era witnessed a gradual extension of civic participation to all members of society, beyond elite or dominant groups like Brahmins, landlords, or kings. In the process, modernity witnessed the formation of innumerable voluntary associations and societies for promoting a wide range of social and political ends. Beginning in the nineteenth century with religious associations like the Brahmo Samaj and Arya Samaj (discussed in later chapters), by the twentieth century, this trend would lead to the formation of diverse groups promoting the interests not only of religion, but of caste identity, political protest and environmental activism.

In this section, I will examine associations organized around three activist agendas: environmental, anticorruption, and Hindu nationalist. The movements I discuss should help illustrate what it means to be both modern and Hindu. As we shall see, such groups can be liberal and broadly inclusive in character, or they can be intolerant and divisive. Two features make them distinctly northern in style and scope. First, these movements are often headquartered in one of the sacred cities discussed above, thereby aligning themselves with the status and prestige of such North Indian sites. Second, except where such movements are focused on specific regional concerns (such as in the Punjab), the preferred language of communication is a kind of standard spoken Hindi intelligible across North India. Thus, even though the magnetic pull of North India's rivers and sacred sites makes it a diverse ethnic, linguistic, and multicultural milieu, the specific political aspiration of activist Hinduism tends to mobilize through the lingua franca of North India.

Environment

Given that the landscape of India is so supremely sacred in Hindu religious thought and practice, it is sometimes surprising to visitors that her mountains are deforested and her rivers tremendously polluted, not to mention often dammed to produce hydroelectric power for the rapidly expanding economy in India. In response to the degradation of India's environment, however, individuals and organizations inspired by their religious devotion to the land have spearheaded environmental movements that have grabbed the world's attention. Among the most famous of these may be the Chipko Andolan, or tree-hugging movement, which started in the mid-1970s in the Indian Himalayas as villagers, particularly women, began surrounding or grasping trees (hence the term, *chipko*, 'embrace' or 'hug') to save them from lumbermen awarded harvesting contracts by the government. Although their initial motivations were largely economic and ecological rather than religious, Chipko activists employed the principles of nonviolent resistance developed by Mahatma Gandhi. Gandhi's methods, based on his interpretation of Hindu teachings, have proven influential for other environmental movements, which explicitly call upon Hindu beliefs about the divine presence in the landscape as a means of generating popular support. This has been particularly true among individuals and organizations whose emotional bonds with the Ganga have moved them to clean up polluted sections of the river and to oppose dam construction (Drew 2013). Even though religious belief in the divine character of mountains and rivers can lead people to deny scientific findings about climate change and pollution (Alley 1998; Drew 2012), it has also occasionally spurred them to heroic action.

A major environmental activist in North India is Sunderlal Bahguna, who explains his regular hunger fasts to halt dams and other forms of environmental degradation in the simplest of terms: 'I love rivers because they are God; they are our Mother' (Haberman 2006: 71). The Sankat Mochan Foundation in Benares was founded in 1982 by the high priest of an important Hanuman temple who also happened to be a civil engineer. He was committed to a single goal: 'seeing the spiritual purity of Ganga reflected in the river's physical purity' (Sankat Mochan Foundation 2013). Today, the Ganga Ahvaan led by Hemant Diyani is an organization that believes protection of the Ganga is critical to the preservation of Hindu culture and has successfully helped convince the Indian Supreme Court to halt dam construction in the most ecologically sensitive areas of the Ganga in the Himalayas.

Anticorruption

In the summer of 2011, it seemed as if the same global energies that generated the Arab Spring uprisings in the Muslim world and the Occupy Wall Street movements in the United States had found expression in India in the form of anticorruption protests. Indians came out into the streets by the millions to demand an end to government inefficiency and the widespread extortion of bribes by public servants. These demonstrations were especially acute in the North, spear-headed by two men allied with one another but with very different religious sensibilities. The two sets of protests illustrate the regular resurgence of Gandhian activism that we see in North India; one shows how these ideas can downplay the religious roots of that kind of political engagement in order to reach a broad audience, while the other shows how activists often underscore Hindu themes as a means for energizing popular support.

Anna Hazare has worked as a social activist in India since the 1960s (see Image 2.2). He achieved regional and occasional national notice through the 1980s for his work in reforming and rebuilding his ancestral village community based on principles espoused by Mahatma Gandhi. Emphasizing such personal and social virtues as self-reliance, community service, rural development, and self-discipline, Hazare began his work by rebuilding the village's Hindu temple as a center for community life and organizing. For over two decades, he led the village to attack such social ills as alcoholism, untouchability, and poverty through community action (Sengupta 2012). When Hazare turned his attention to corruption, he brought with him his reputation as a committed Gandhian as well as his skills at effective, populist political action. In 2011, he launched a series of hunger strikes (another Gandhian tactic) demanding the adoption of a strong anticorruption bill that drew thousands of supporters to rallies and virtually nonstop media coverage. The images of an aged, weakening activist dressed in simple white cotton not only evoked the spiritual and social principles that animated Gandhi's campaigns for moral reform and Indian self-governance, but also inspired a mass movement captured best by his followers' widespread adoption of the slogan, 'I am Anna' and their donning of his signature white Gandhian cap (Visvanathan 2012).

An occasional partner in Hazare's protests, Baba Ramdev is a national celebrity headquartered in the city of Haridwar who first achieved fame in 2003 for his daily television programs teaching yoga and promoting a diet based on the traditional medical system of Hinduism known as Ayurveda. When I was doing research in the North Indian state of Uttarakhand in 2006–2007, my sixty-year-old host, like millions of other Hindus in North India at the time, rose every morning to practice the meditations and postures taught by Baba Ramdev. When I would travel to Haridwar for research, he would send me with a lengthy shopping list of dietary supplements and herbal remedies to bring back from the medical dispensary at his ashram. My host, whom I simply called 'Tauji' ('Uncle'), oriented many elements of his daily life according to the inspiration he received every morning via the cheerful and charismatic

Figure 2.2 Anna Hazare

young TV star. Baba Ramdev often seemed to avoid any explicit discussion of Hindu ideas, and he was even the first non-Muslim religious leader to lecture to the faculty at a famous Muslim university. There is little mistaking, however, the overtly Hindu character of his teaching and celebrity (Chakraborty 2007). In a saffron robe, he is dressed as a traditional Hindu ascetic; the yoga he promotes so energetically is based on centuries-old Hindu philosophy and meditation practice; his wealthy institution is styled as an ashram, and in the fashion of the Hindu nationalists I will discuss below, his rhetoric trumpets 'our Vedic culture' as India's ancient, distinctive, and unifying heritage.

In the beginning of the second decade of the 2000s, Baba Ramdev began experimenting with a political career. As Hazare's protests gained steam, Ramdev launched his own agitation singling out 'black money,' the term for funds obtained through illegal means in India but hidden in foreign banks, as his target. Like Hazare, Baba Ramdev framed his protests as a *satyagraha*, Gandhi's term for nonviolent confrontation with injustice that means 'clinging to the truth.' He also employed the strategy of the public hunger strike, another element of political action inherited from Gandhi. While Hazare's protests reflected the secular commitments of Gandhi, Ramdev's employed a Hindu idiom. His major June 4, 2011 rally in New Delhi against black money drew around 65,000 supporters. While Ramdev was surrounded on the dais by leaders of other religious groups in India, his celebrity as a yoga teacher and his dress clearly appealed to a Hindu audience. Since those protests were broken up by police the day after they started, Ramdev has associated himself more and more with right-wing Hindu political groups and leaders. During the 2014 national elections, he endorsed Narendra Modi, previously a major voice among Hindu nationalists in the Bharatiya Janata Party (BJP), who eventually won the election and is currently the prime minister of India.

Hindu Nationalism

The politicization of Hinduism, especially in the divisive brand of Hindu nationalism known as *Hindutva*, is addressed elsewhere in this volume, but it bears noting when thinking about North Indian modes of religious activism. In essence, Hindutva is a political philosophy committed to preserving and strengthening Hindu identity as the essence of Indian society and the defining feature of the Indian nation. Hindutva ideas and programs are propagated through a variety of organizations, such as grassroots paramilitary and social service organizations, political parties, and youth camps. These groups tend to be stronger and more numerous in the North than in the South. The influence of such organizations as the Rashtriya Swayamsevak Sangh (RSS) and the Vishva Hindu Parishad (VHP) is not hard to detect in temples throughout North India; the party most closely associated with Hindu nationalism, the currently ruling Bharatiya Janata Party (BJP), has had much greater electoral success in the North over time, where it might be said that religion plays a larger role in peoples' voting patterns than the South, where caste and language have typically been more powerful rallying points. In the north, Hindu nationalist ideologies have flourished among segments of India's new middle class (discussed below) by promoting a politics of exclusion that singles out Muslims and Christians, who are viewed as 'antinational' insofar as they represent communities with origins outside the nation (Fernandez 2006: 168–172; see also Lutgendorf 2007: 360–376).[1]

Entrepreneurial Religion

Capitalism and consumerism are two ways that modernity expresses itself economically. A logical development of the Enlightenment ideal of free and rational selves pursuing their desires in a world of other similar individuals, these forces have deeply affected North Indian Hinduism. Beginning in 1991, India embraced free-market capitalism and undertook dramatic economic reforms, moving from a state-controlled economy to a market-based one. The rapid development that quickly followed has seen India become one of the world's fastest growing economies; the past two decades have witnessed the corresponding growth and increased influence of India's middle class (Jaffrelot and van der Veer 2008: 18). The effects of these economic changes for religious life in India have been similarly dramatic (Hawley 2001). With larger disposable incomes, India's middle class has engaged in forms of consumption that are often marked by signs of its religious devotion; in fact, middle-class habits and new patterns of behavior are rapidly transforming the face of North Indian Hinduism (Sharma forthcoming). Throughout the developing world, the growth in private car ownership and improvements in basic infrastructure like roads and public transportation have made India's sacred sites far more accessible, while the availability of cable and satellite television has made TV a prime medium for religious experience and expression. Simultaneously, countless new religious movements, groups, leaders, and sites have come on the scene, adding to the vibrancy and complexity of North Indian Hinduism today (Stausberg 2011: 219–225).

These new expressions of religiosity rely on the energies of two principal groups of actors: consumers and entrepreneurs. The mutually reinforcing behaviors of these two groups have created a lively, colorful, and 'spirited' atmosphere of religious pursuits that reflects an exuberant, grass-roots capitalism. At the risk of sounding reductionist, we can say that the desires of religious consumers to augment their faith with the acquisition of religious goods, to travel to famous temples and sacred rivers and mountains, and to experience firsthand the teachings of important religious leaders are met by the inventive and strategic methods of entrepreneurial individuals and organizations eager to establish or expand the reach of their 'products.' The result is a competitive religious marketplace in which entrepreneurial gurus and temples seek to attract the attention of an ever-growing audience of Hindus eager to expend capital on religious undertakings.

As I attempted to illustrate in the opening section of this chapter, such entrepreneurial and consumerist modes of devotion have recently been the subject of my research in the small but historic city of Uttarkashi, in the state of Uttarkhand. Situated on the ancient pilgrimage routes of the Indian Himalayas, the once isolated region around Uttarkashi has been transformed over the last decade by some of the same economic forces mentioned above. Whereas, in prior eras, few Hindus had the opportunity to visit the sacred peaks and rivers extolled in Hindu myth and legend, today, the pilgrimage industry in this region is rapidly expanding. Clearly one reason for this growth has to do with such factors as increased private ownership of automobiles and the proliferation of easy package tours to the holy places of the Himalayas. At the same time, India's expanding demands for electrical power have led to improved and expanded networks of roads to facilitate access to remote areas for the construction of dams and power plants. The expansion of roadways, along with a booming tourism market, has sparked, in turn, massive in-migration of young men from hitherto remote mountain villages. Such economic migrants come to cities like Uttarkashi in search of work in the many hotels and restaurants that have sprouted along the main highways (Young and Jeffrey 2012). Finally, there is the fact that Uttarkashi serves as one of the district headquarters within the relatively new state of Uttarkhand. Uttarkhand itself was created in 2000 as the result of agitation by regional activists who sought to achieve political and economic autonomy for their region; activists argued not only that their culture was distinct from that of the plains (which now lie in the state of Uttar Pradesh), but that the natural resources of their region were being exploited by outside interests. For all these reasons—economic, political, religious—Uttarkashi represents a kind of laboratory for observing and documenting the kinds of developments taking place across large portions of North India. However, because of its location in the Himalayas and its booming tourism and pilgrimage trade, it also throws into relief some of the more dramatic consequences of recent development. Thus in the catastrophic floods of 2012 and 2013, nearly ten thousand people were killed and the local tourist economy suffered a tremendous blow. Such a crisis raises a question about the dangers inherent in recent religious entrepreneurship, dangers exacerbated by climate change and rapid population growth. The future course of North India's exuberant religious economy will surely become clearer as time goes on.

We began the chapter with a visit to the cave temple at Prakateshwar Panchanan Mahadev, which provides an excellent example of a successful new religious venture. It may be appropriate now to examine the failure of a similar attempt to build a lucrative religious establishment by capitalizing on the rise of Hindu pilgrimage through Uttarkashi. Such a case study can show us just how important it is when launching a new spiritual venture to achieve a kind of compatibility between entrepreneur and consumer. Sometime around 2004, a guru began constructing a new religious retreat center outside Uttarkashi. He called himself Pilot Baba since he had once flown combat missions for the Indian Air Force (*Baba* is the term for 'father' that is often applied to Indian holy men). Pilot Baba, who already boasted an international following, told of a miraculous intercession that set him on a spiritual quest: once, while flying a mission over India's border with Pakistan, he lost control of his plane and faced certain death. At that very moment, a sage appeared in his cockpit and safely landed his aircraft. This sage, known as Hari Baba, claimed to have performed severe penances in the icy Himalayan peaks for years, through which he acquired immense spiritual powers. After his miraculous escape, Pilot Baba resigned from the Air Force and followed the sage into the distant Himalayas where he spent years learning Hari Baba's secrets. Only then did Pilot Baba begin the public phase of his career as an international guru. This brings us to the developments concerning his new religious establishment. Pilot Baba created a complex along the Ganga above Uttarkashi, which he began to advertise as the 'Fifth Dham,' thereby suggesting that pilgrims intent on visiting the traditional four *dhams* would somehow fail to acquire spiritual merit if they did not also stop to offer prayers at his ashram. This outraged local residents and led to public protests; many people expressed their opposition to this apparent attempt to commercialize on the sacred environs of Uttarkashi. Despite Pilot Baba's large international following, his complex was bulldozed under court order in late 2011 and Pilot Baba fled to the North Indian plains. Was his a religious failure or an economic one? Were his opponents outraged for spiritual reasons or material ones? The answer is tricky. On one level, we might say that Pilot Baba failed to properly insert his new religious project into the sacred world of Uttarkashi religion; we might say he misread the desires of his prospective religious consumers. But on another level, it seems clear that Pilot Baba also ran afoul of the already entrenched interests of other religious sites and organizations. The experience of Pilot Baba thus provides an excellent example of the difficult transitions that accompany the transformation of modern Hinduism in North India.

Producing Hinduism in North India

Taken together, devotional practices related to sacred geography, activist forms of spirituality, and entrepreneurial religion show us not simply how Hinduism is distinctive in North India, but how new forms are being actively produced by religious authorities and devotees alike. Traditional ideas and rituals continue to function as powerful symbols of the religious heritage of India and they remain immensely influential in the lives of individuals and the nation. Like all elements of the past, however, they are subject to constant reinterpretation, reimagining, and sometimes active contestation. North Indian Hinduism helps us see how tradition serves as a valuable resource for living in a rapidly changing present as economies, societies, and political systems evolve.

While I began by emphasizing the distinctive character of North India, it remains true that we could see developments similar to those discussed in this chapter if we turned our gaze on other regions of the subcontinent. All across India, there are regional movements and popular leaders that are reinvigorating local languages, reinterpreting ancient traditions, and generating new pride in the deities and rituals of any number of religious, ethnic, and linguistic groups. In fact, if we were to include emerging practices in Islam and Christianity in our study of North Indian religion, we would see the roles played by the media, travel, and mass communication in fostering new possibilities for the expression of religious devotion just as they do among Hindus. North Indian Hinduism is, however, one of the most visible of the emerging religious phenomena in South Asia today. Animated by the energy and devotion of millions of Hindus watching their country rapidly develop, and sometimes fragmented by the conflict that development sparks, North Indian Hinduism represents the unfolding future of one of the world's most ancient religious traditions.

Summary

Because of its particular history and its shared, related languages, North India presents a distinctive version of Hinduism whose contours continue to evolve under conditions of rapid development and globalization. An examination of three features of the religious culture of contemporary North India—practices that express an attachment to its landscape, modes of Hindu activism on behalf of the environment or the nation, and religious entrepreneurialism that is now generating exciting if sometimes problematic developments in Hindu religious life—show us how the transformations we see Hinduism undergoing in North India represent a distinctly modern, or even postmodern, environment. Shaped by the commodification of religion and the politicization of religious identity, these emerging realities reveal not simply how Hinduism is distinctive in North India, but how new forms are being actively produced by religious authorities and devotees alike.

Discussion Questions

- How does the author distinguish the religious environment of modern North India from what might have been the case in premodern India?
- Discuss the various ways that North India can be considered a distinctive cultural and religious region.
- Explain how the geography of India is especially meaningful to North Indian Hindus. What are the practices and beliefs by which attachment to the land is expressed?
- Discuss how the legacy of Gandhi may be invoked to achieve different kinds of social and political objectives.
- Are entrepreneurial ventures authentic expressions of the Hindu tradition? Why or why not?

Note

1   It bears noting, nonetheless, that voting patterns in the 2014 general election showed some support for the BJP among Muslims. This should caution against falling into overly simple understandings of political behavior, which reflects not merely religious identity, but concerns of caste, class, community, and other local factors.

Suggested Readings

Eck, Diana (2012). *India: A Sacred Geography*. New York: Three Rivers.
Feldhaus, Anne (1995). *Water and Womanhood: Religious Meanings of Rivers in Maharashtra*. New York: Oxford University Press.

Gold, Ann Grodzins (1990). *Fruitful Journeys: The Ways of Rajasthani Pilgrims*. Berkeley: University of California Press.
Haberman, David L. (2013). *People Trees: Worship of Trees in Northern India*. New York: Oxford University Press.

Bibliography

Alley, Kelly D. (1998). 'Idioms of Degeneracy: Assessing Ganga's Purity and Pollution.' In *Purifying the Earthly Body of God: Religion and Ecology in Hindu India* (pp. 297–330). Ed. Lance E. Nelson. Albany: SUNY Press.
Bhardwaj, Surinder Mohan (1973). *Hindu Places of Pilgrimage: A Study in Cultural Geography*. Berkeley: University of California Press.
Bhardwaj, Surinder M. and James G. Lochtefeld (2004). 'Tirtha.' In *The Hindu World* (pp. 478–501). Eds. Sushil Mittal and Gene Thursby. London: Routledge.
Chakraborty, Chandrima (2007). 'The Hindu Ascetic as Fitness Instructor: Reviving Faith in Yoga.' *International Journal of the History of Sport* 24, No. 9: 1172–1186.
Drew, Georgina (2012). 'A Retreating Goddess? Conflicting Perceptions of Ecological Change near the Gangotri-Gaumukh Glacier.' *Journal for the Study of Religion, Nature and Culture* 6, No. 3: 344–362.
——— (2013). 'Why Wouldn't We Cry? Love and Loss along a River in Decline.' *Emotion, Space and Society* 6: 25–32.
Drèze, Jean and Amartya Sen (2013). *An Uncertain Glory: India and Its Contradictions*. Princeton: Princeton University Press.
Eck, Diana (1982). *Benaras: City of Light*. New York: Alfred Knopf.
——— (1996). 'Ganga: The Goddess Ganges in Hindu Sacred Geography.' In *Devi: Goddesses of India* (pp. 137–153). Eds. John Stratton Hawley and Donna Marie Wulff. Berkeley: University of California Press.
Fernandez, Leela (2006). *India's New Middle Class: Democratic Politics in an Era of Economic Reform*. Minneapolis: University of Minnesota Press.
Haberman, David L. (2006). *River of Love in an Age of Pollution: The Yamuna River of North India*. Berkeley: University of California Press.
Hawley, John Stratton (2001). 'Modern India and the Question of Middle-Class Religion.' *International Journal of Hindu Studies* 5, No. 3: 217–225.
Jaffrelot, Christophe and Peter van der Veer, eds. (2008). *Patterns of Middle Class Consumption in India and China*. New Delhi: Sage.
Lochtefeld, James G. (2008). 'Getting in Line: The Kumbha Mela Festival Processions.' In *South Asian Religions on the Move: Religious Processions in South Asia and in the Diaspora* (pp. 29–44). Ed. Knut A. Jacobsen. London: Routledge.
——— (2010). *God's Gateway: Identity and Meaning in a Hindu Pilgrimage Place*. New York: Oxford University Press.
Lutgendorf, Philip (2007). *Hanuman's Tale: The Messages of a Divine Monkey*. New York: Oxford University Press.
Maclean, Kama (2008). *Pilgrimage and Power: The Kumbh Mela in Allahabad, 1765–1954*. New York: Oxford University Press.
McKean, Lise (1996). *Divine Enterprise: Gurus and the Hindu Nationalist Movement*. Chicago: University of Chicago Press.
Parry, Jonathan P. (1994) *Death in Benares*. Cambridge: Cambridge University Press.
Sankat Mochan Foundation (June 2013). 'Welcome.' Retrieved June 17, 2013. http://www.sankatmochanfoundationonline.org/index.html.

Sengupta, Mitu (2012). 'Anna Hazare and the Idea of Gandhi.' *Journal of Asian Studies* 71, No. 3: 593–601.

Smith, David (2003). *Hinduism and Modernity*. Oxford: Blackwell.

Sharma, Sheetal (forthcoming). 'Consuming Krisna: Women, Class, and Ritual Economies in Pushtimarg Vaisnavism.' In *Ritual Innovation in South Asian Religion*. Eds. Brian K. Pennington and Amy Allocco. Albany: SUNY Press.

Stausberg, Michael (2011). *Religion and Tourism: Crossroads, Destinations, and Encounters*. London: Routledge.

Visvanathan, Shiv (2012). 'Anna Hazare and the Battle against Corruption.' *Cultural Critique* 81: 103–111.

Young, Stephen and Craig Jeffrey (2012). 'Making Ends Meet: Youth Enterprise at the Rural-Urban Intersections.' *Economic and Political Weekly* 47, No. 30: 45–51.

3 Transnational Movements

Hanna H. Kim

In a modest room at the Swaminarayan temple guesthouse, there were suitcases everywhere, on the floor, in between and around the two single beds, and in the adjacent outside bathroom area with its built-in clothes lines. These suitcases belonged to members of an extended family whose stop in Ahmedabad, Gujarat was the last one following their pilgrimage to BAPS Swaminarayan temples in New Delhi and Gujarat. In the closet along one wall of the room, there were even more suitcases amongst the clothes waiting to be packed. Also in one corner of the closet, piled on top of a suitcase lying flat, was an oddly charming heap of stainless steel pressure cookers. As it turned out, these were not new purchases, destined for stovetops far away from India. Rather, these used cookers had made the journey in suitcases from Australia, Britain, and Zanzibar, and were soon to be brought to the pressure cooker manufacturer's shop in Ahmedabad. Here the old cookers could be exchanged for a discount on a brand new model with its yet unstretched rubber gasket and shiny pressure regulator.

The journey of these cookers traveling via airplane to Gujarat and their replacements making a reverse trip back to their owners' home countries offers an accessible image for the ease of global travel and the circulation of goods across national boundaries. Behind the scenes, as it were, of these traveling pots is a much more complex story of Swaminarayan devotees and their relationship to a transnational Hindu movement known formally as Bochasanwasi Shri Akshar Purushottam Swaminarayan Sanstha (BAPS). BAPS has, in just over a century, evolved from a regional devotional community into a globalizing religious movement with a highly organized institutional infrastructure to connect its members to the center of its administrative and religious leadership in Gujarat. The Swaminarayan devotees who were transporting the pressure cookers embody a story of devotional motivations and individual desires that contribute to the shape of transnational Hinduism today. Who are these Gujarati Hindu travelers and devotees from multiple nations; what connects them to India despite lives mostly lived elsewhere; and, what is the relationship between these devotees and Swaminarayan teachings and devotional practices?

This chapter is an introduction to modern Hindu transnational religious movements, with a particular focus on the BAPS Swaminarayan Sanstha as a case study. If we understand transnationalism 'as the processes by which immigrants forge and sustain multi-stranded social relations that link together their societies of origin and settlement,' then many Hindu communities can be considered to be transnational movements by virtue of the organized networks that connect them to the geographic locus, institutional center, and historical sources of their tradition (Basch, Glick Schiller, and Blanc 1994: 7). Additionally, the concept of transnationalism calls attention to the construction of relational ties between 'people, goods, information, and other resources across national boundaries'; in the context of global mobility, it thus raises questions about how these flows and relations are generated and sustained over space and time (Wuthnow and Offutt 2008: 211). A transnational religious movement, such as the BAPS Swaminarayan Sanstha, is made up of followers who live in multiple countries and continents, including India.[1]

For their daily devotional practices and individual efforts to achieve a certain ideal of living as a Swaminarayan devotee, BAPS followers are not dependent on knowing about or even visiting India. This raises an important question: How is the leadership of BAPS able to ensure that its devotional teachings and practices can be circulated and realized throughout communities spread across the globe? Put differently, how is it possible that followers of a movement like BAPS—which possesses a strong historical, institutional, and ideological base in India—are able to pursue meaningful religious lives in places where Hindus are often a minority community? Needless to say, these are questions that could be asked of all transnational religious movements.

As noted in the Introduction, Hindus began traveling and settling outside the South Asia subcontinent long before the emergence of the modern nation-state; thus one might say Hinduism was 'trans-local' long before it was 'transnational.' While this observation is historically accurate, thanks to more rapid, fluid, and cost-effective modes of capital transfer, travel, and media communication, today's transnational movements have developed more innovative ways to support and sustain their constituencies across territorial distances. Many contemporary Hindu transnational movements may be broadly described as devotional, or *bhakti*, movements; often they look for leadership to a single figure, typically regarded as *guru*, or religious teacher. The guru is the leader of the devotional community, or *satsang* and devotees are known as *satsangis*. The *satsangis'* various acts of devotion to the guru constitute the core relationship in many Hindu transnational movements. Many, but not all, gurus travel extensively, visiting the transnational communities of their followers. Some gurus are comfortable with English and others speak only their mother tongue and regional languages. Most of these transnational movements embrace print media and new technologies for the dissemination of their movement's teachings. Increasingly, many transnational movements are active in humanitarian causes, including the creation of educational, medical, and social service institutions that serve a wider community both locally and internationally.

Some, though not all, transnational movements have inserted themselves into religious, nationalist, or political movements originating in India (Nanda 2009; Rajagopal 2000). It could also be argued that all transnational movements, when settling beyond India, have had to engage with the governmental, political, and religious discourses of their new homelands (Eisenlohr 2012; Zavos 2013). Thus, even though some movements profess an apolitical stance, transnational movements are *de facto* situated within discursive fields with which they must necessarily engage, not least in their new host countries. This means that transnational movements are not immune to the categories, assumptions, and misconceptions operating in the context of their new homes. Often, the encounter between transnational movements and dominant discourses about concepts such as religion or religious pluralism will be a key factor in shaping how a movement reconstitutes itself in a new territory (Kim 2009). And these encounters between religious communities and new kinds of 'public' do not merely affect the life of transnational communities outside of India; ideas emanating from a community in one national context can travel to another and then reverberate across a range of transnational networks. In this way, even those movements that arose in very particular contexts generate ideas and practices that may in turn become universalized, exported, and subsequently reinstitutionalized in complex new ways (Srinivas 2010).

Transnational movements arising out of India have become visible owing to what are often savvy programs for public relations, to their skillful use of media technologies, and their ability to develop strategies for engaging with religious publics who are no longer residents of one region of India but members of communities now spread across many nations. This sophistication in reaching out to various audiences is not, however, achieved at the expense of the consolidation and effective transmission of their own devotional teachings and practices. In this respect, transnational movements provide an interesting area of modern Hinduism for us to closely examine how religious teachings become portable in different cultural and national contexts. It is well worth asking the question: What accounts for the appeal of these guru-led movements? Do our answers to this question tell us something about the expression of religious identity in the modern era? And can we at the same time come to understand something about religion in general as the human effort to live and find meaning in the world?

This chapter provides a sketch of one important transnational movement, the BAPS Swaminarayan community, drawing upon a range of ethnographic data. The chapter has two goals. First, to consider how BAPS maximizes the channels of global movement, most notably in technologies, travel, and communications, in its efforts to disseminate knowledge about Swaminarayan ways of being; second, to demonstrate how BAPS fosters the kinds of relationships and networks that—from the Swaminarayan perspective—are necessary for attaining the devotional goals and purposes of being a Swaminarayan Hindu.

The picture of transnational Hinduism that emerges from this exercise is one that stresses both the desire of Swaminarayan devotees to attain a particular kind of devotional knowledge and the challenge faced by the movement in translating this particular desire into a more universal language framed in terms of the modern concept of 'religion.' The chapter will conclude by reflecting on how the success of such a transnational movement is tied to the needs of devotees and the almost perennial human search to find satisfaction in one's life. In this search, devotees often turn to the teachings of a specific guru and find in the guru's teachings the inspiration to lead an ethical life. Despite the unpredictability of life in a global world order predicated on neoliberalism and pervasive strands of secularism and skepticism about religion, such devotees are able to experience what Jane Bennett (2001) artfully terms, 'the enchantment of modern life.'

Flows, from Local to Transnational

'We are nomads,' said the 'Uncle' in the Swaminarayan guesthouse room as he saw me staring at the pressure cookers in the open closet. He added: 'We live in four places and we keep things in all four places.' The cookers belonged to his wife and her three sisters, all of whom had come from different Commonwealth countries and converged together in July 2014 in India. The main reason for the reunion was to visit BAPS Swaminarayan temples, beginning with the new and immensely popular New Delhi Swaminarayan Akshardham temple complex, followed by a pilgrimage to the five historic temples constructed under the guru, Shastriji Maharaj, the founder of the BAPS.

For followers of BAPS, Shastriji Maharaj (1865–1951) holds the double distinction of establishing the Bochasanwasi Shri Akshar Purushottam Swaminarayan Sanstha and of being the third guru in the nonhereditary BAPS guru lineage. When he inaugurated the first BAPS temple (*mandir*) in 1907 in the central Gujarati village of Bochasan, the structure was incomplete due to a shortage of funds. Nevertheless, Shastriji Maharaj ritually installed two icons (*murtis*) of Akshar and Purushottam, respectively. For devotees, these represent the images of the ideal *sadhu* or guru (in whom God is fully present) and God himself. This moment marks the formal beginning of BAPS and, correspondingly, it signals the distinction between the 'breakaway' BAPS *satsang*, or community, and the 'original' Swaminarayan community, which dates back to 1801, having been established by Sahajanand Swami (1781–1830) in the region of Gujarat in western India.

It is important to note these dates and names because they help us situate the Swaminarayan Hindu tradition historically within colonial India. Sahajanand Swami, originally from north India, came to Gujarat as a wandering holy man. In Gujarat, he began teaching his new doctrine and took up projects of social reform. He was recognized early on by the British colonial administration as both a religious leader and notable social reformer. For BAPS devotees, or *satsangis*, Sahajanand Swami is the physical manifestation of God, also known as Bhagwan Swaminarayan, who had temporarily come to Gujarat and whose presence on earth remains in the physical and always male form of the living guru. As a result, BAPS has a lineage of gurus (*guru parampara*) dating to Sahajanand Swami's time and it is the present guru in whom the power and divinity of God resides. This relationship between guru and Bhagwan is personified in the two icons of Akshar and Purushottam installed in the central shrine of all BAPS temples. Shastriji Maharaj, as the founder of BAPS, is revered by BAPS devotees as the third guru in the lineage of Akshar gurus; his tenure as guru was followed by Yogiji Maharaj (1892–1971), while the present BAPS guru is Pramukh Swami Maharaj (b. 1921).

An empirical mapping and enumeration of the growth of BAPS, beginning from 1907, would show that this community began as a small, financially pressed, and localized Gujarat-based group. Shastriji Maharaj, as BAPS history recounts, expended tremendous energy to ensure the survival of the new devotional community he founded. Under the guidance of the next guru, Yogiji Maharaj, there was a direct effort to reach those Gujaratis who by this time—owing to colonial labor migration—were living in East Africa. Through his visits to East Africa, Yogiji Maharaj nurtured a growing community of East African devotees. He was particularly noted for encouraging youth participation, and among his BAPS legacies are age-grade temple groups, regularized weekly meetings for *satsangis* at BAPS temples and centers, and the institutionalization of examinations for the testing of *satsang* knowledge. Yogiji Maharaj also built up the BAPS institution of *sadhus*, or male monks, who, in the service they gave to the Sanstha, were to play an enormous role in its growth. The various activities of BAPS, along with the guru's teachings and travels were recorded and distributed in publications printed by the Swaminarayan Aksharpith press, which also published the central BAPS devotional texts, histories, and hagiographies. All of these items traveled to wherever *satsangis* lived; they brought not just news of guru's latest activities, but a tangible feel and aroma of India, from the texture of the paper to its particular smell.

Circulations

During the late 1960s and into the '70s there was a large-scale, second migration of Indians from East Africa to Britain and other Commonwealth countries. The BAPS leadership, including guru and *sadhus*, undertook the requisite travel to support the development of communities in these new contexts. This pattern of guru traveling outside of India would be significantly increased under the leadership of Pramukh Swami Maharaj, who succeeded Yogiji Maharaj in 1971. Indeed, it might be said that under the leadership of Pramukh Swami, BAPS has fully emerged as a transnational movement. He was the first BAPS guru to travel to the United States where people of Indian origin had begun to immigrate after 1965 thanks to changes in official immigration policy. Pramukh Swami is credited by devotees for having nurtured the thriving American *satsang* from a small handful of *satsangis* into a North American community with temples and centers in many states.

Today, BAPS boasts one million devotees. They are nearly all Gujarati and the majority live in India, but significant communities exist in North America, Europe, parts of Africa, the Middle East, and Southeast Asia. With this global expansion, BAPS is ever more dependent on a rationalized organizational structure in order to reach its worldwide members and sustain its devotional tradition. The order of *sadhus*, as of October 2014, numbers 970 men and Pramukh Swami, at nearly 94 years of age, remains at the apex of BAPS administration—even if there are senior *sadhus* initiated under Yogiji Maharaj who oversee the management of *satsangis*, temples, and the larger BAPS temple complexes known as Akshardham.

For BAPS devotees, Pramukh Swami is the physical form in which Bhagwan Swaminarayan is fully present. As a celibate without any possessions or attachments to worldly things, the guru is the visible locus for Swaminarayan devotional practice. Devotees see no contradiction that their guru, who has no interest in matters of money and handles no money himself, has consistently endorsed the incorporation of the latest technologies in the dissemination of BAPS teachings, including the use of social media, the internet, and technologies for multimedia and filmmaking. As devotees point out, Pramukh Swami's willingness to support forms of social media and modern entertainment (such as the IMAX theaters found in some Akshardham complexes) is specifically tied to his devotional objective to ensure the widest possible reach for the transmission of BAPS bhakti. Alongside his approval of technologies to sustain his global following, Pramukh Swami has focused on temple construction as a central means to inspire devotees, current and potential, in their commitment to Swaminarayan teachings. These temples, ranging from repurposed buildings to edifices of entirely carved stone to the striking Akshardham temple complexes, are obvious signs of a devotional community with the resources to acquire land and build. These temples also provide something like a material testament to BAPS's skills at negotiating its new publics and the complex bureaucracy—legal, political, regional, and national—that temple construction entails (Kim 2009).

At the one hundred year anniversary celebration of BAPS held in Ahmedabad in 2007, Pramukh Swami was awarded a Guinness World Record for inaugurating the largest number of Hindu temples by a single individual. This award was presented along with the Guinness World Record for constructing the 'world's largest comprehensive Hindu temple,' in reference to the New Delhi Swaminarayan Akshardham temple complex (see Image 3.1). Images of the guru, with his simple ochre cloth wrapping and matching head covering, holding one side of the framed Guinness certificate, were broadcast around the world via satellite television. Not more than a day later, those who had missed the satellite feed could relive the movement through the internet, via the BAPS website. Throughout the transnational Swaminarayan community, the circulation of the images of Pramukh Swami during anniversary celebration days was meticulously recorded and shared via various technologies. Despite the tens of thousands *satsangis*, the elaborate stage settings, and the use of technology to broadcast the nightly events across a massive outdoor field,

Pramukh Swami appeared to have a singular focus: To convey the importance of knowing that through offering devotion to guru and God, devotees come to understand the relationship of their eternal self to God, Bhagwan Swaminarayan. Only then are they able to realize the possibility of serving God eternally.

The message of Pramukh Swami—conveyed with his unadorned style of self-presentation, even amid the most grandiose of settings—has inspired *satsangis* to dedicate innumerable hours of service, or *seva*, for the growth and support of BAPS activities. The offering of volunteered service is a significant means by which *satsangis* seek to cultivate a deeper understanding of their relationship to guru and to Bhagwan Swaminarayan. This service is not performed to allay a devotee's sense of debt to Pramukh Swami, but to support the devotee's desire to understand the self as separate from the biological and somatic being. Acquiring this knowledge of an eternal self, distinct from the sensory being that eventually disintegrates, is hard work. According to BAPS teachings, it is the guru who is the perfect devotee and the one who gives the guidance and inspiration for offering continuous service to God. The Swaminarayan guru is thus the model for an ontological ideal, a state of being whose devotional postures and gestures are those that devotees strive to emulate. To achieve the knowledge that one's atma is separate makes possible the attainment of a state of being, *atmarup*, without which devotees cannot offer continuous devotion to God (Kim 2013).

In this trajectory from desire to ontological goal, there is a direct connection between the Swaminarayan understanding of eternal self and its relationship to

Figure 3.1 Akshardham complex, New Delhi

guru and God. When the massive Akshardham temple complexes were inaugurated by Pramukh Swami, his message was typically simple and direct; he encouraged devotees to offer devotion and service to God and to inspire others to do the same. The construction of the Akshardham complex, though impressive by any number of measures, is, according to Pramukh Swami, part of a singular objective to foster the conditions for offering devotion to God by whose side devotees hope to gain a permanent position in eternity. Thus, we can see that there are highly specific ontological goals for the Swaminarayan devotee. However, for those who are not necessarily focused on these same goals, there is nevertheless the physical reality of the Swaminarayan temple. These temples, with their lush carvings and inspiring towers, exert a larger-than-life kind of magnetism over visitors and devotees alike. The moment of encounter that occurs between either a committed seeker or a casual visitor might well be understood as a crucial point of departure for interest in BAPS.

From the *satsangis'* perspective, the hundreds of Swaminarayan temples and centers for *satsang* throughout the world are predicated on a specific Swaminarayan devotional teaching that guru is 'the bridge that connects man with the Divine' (Brahmaviharidas 2004). For devotees, there is a wish to serve the 'Divine,' that is, Bhagwan Swaminarayan. Yet, this can only occur by learning from and emulating the guru and by trying to reshape the subjective being into a physical being who, like the guru, can become fully immersed in the joyful service of God. This relational connection between *satsangis*, guru, and God is the central engine of Swaminarayan transnational growth, of its temple building projects, its publications, and humanitarian services. As a technology of the self—a means by which to shape one's being into a desired conception of the self—the act of performing *seva* to guru is what underwrites the expansion of BAPS bhakti throughout the world.

Necessary Relationships

Darshan, for many Hindus, is the very individual devotional act of seeing and, in return, being seen by a divine entity who is accessible in some iconic form (*murti*). The murti may be made of paper, stone, or metal and be physically located somewhere such as at home, or in a temple, or even mediated by the internet. In fact, according to devotees, the BAPS website provides a highly appreciated means for 'doing darshan' in any number of settings—wherever an internet connection is available. The action of 'doing darshan of guru and Bhagwan Swaminarayan' sustains a cognitive and emotional relationship between devotees and their guru and God without which the *satsangis* cannot attain the devotional knowledge they desire. Thus, *satsangis*, no matter where they live, seek ways to maximize their darshan. The actual portability of BAPS bhakti is, one might argue, made possible by the ritual practice of darshan that does not require the devotee to be in the actual physical presence of guru. Rather, darshan supports a conscious orientation of *satsangis* toward looking, remembering, and thinking about guru and God while gazing directly into the eyes of these murtis.

For the North American BAPS *satsang*, the weeks from 6–19 August 2014 represented an unprecedented fortnight of 'unbelievable *darshan*.' During this fortnight, Pramukh Swami traveled to Robbinsville, New Jersey, where he was scheduled to inaugurate an elaborately carved stone temple in an as-yet-unfinished Akshardham temple complex. Known as Mandir Mahotsav or 'temple festival' 2014, this event would celebrate the opening of the first carved-stone temple in the northeastern United States. Robbinsville additionally marked the location of the first fledgling BAPS community in the United States (Williams 2001). Pramukh Swami had performed the inauguration of carved-stone temples in Atlanta, Chicago, Houston, Los Angeles, and Toronto, but Robbinsville would be an historic occasion as it was some forty-five years after the beginning of the American *satsang* in 1970 in New York. Far off in Ahmedabad, I met *satsangis* who asked me whether I would be going to Robbinsville to see Pramukh Swami. Besides marveling at how a small town in New Jersey of 11,000 residents was now known to so many *satsangis* in Gujarat, I also wondered if these same devotees might not themselves travel to the United States for this occasion. But as my circle of interlocutors went on to tell me, by living in India, 'we have much more opportunities to do darshan of Swamishri' (i.e. Pramukh Swami).[2] As one *satsangi* confided, 'let the Americans have a peaceful darshan without all of us coming from India!'[3]

On Wednesday, 5 August 2014, many hours before nightfall, *satsangis* who had just arrived in the United States from various locations around the world began preparing for the arrival of their guru. As the website, www.baps.org, reported, Pramukh Swami was en route from Gandhinagar in Gujarat. He would fly into Newark, New Jersey via a private aircraft that included onboard medical facilities to address his current treatment needs. As for those unable to be present in Robbinsville, the BAPS media and internet teams ensured that a steady stream of photographs and videos were placed on the BAPS website. Devotees could even sign up for text messages from the username 'MM14' (Mandir Mahotsav 2014); in tones of great excitement, these messages kept devotees updated regarding Pramukh Swami's current location, his destination, the timing of his itinerary, as well as suggestions on where devotees should situate themselves in order to best see their guru.

According to BAPS, some ten thousand people had lined the pathways and open spaces of the Robbinsville temple site by the time Pramukh Swami arrived at 12:52 am on 6 August 2014. The video coverage on the BAPS website, expertly edited, produced, and uploaded, showed devotees with the palms of their hands held together and poised near their hearts, and their bodies craned in the direction of Pramukh Swami's arrival. He appeared in a white multipurpose vehicle, altered to accommodate his wheelchair. The faces of the *satsangis*, all turned toward Pramukh Swami, glow with happiness. The official BAPS video and photographic coverage of this moment are riveting; they capture the intensity of the relationship that *satsangis* feel with their guru. For many of the young children, this was their first actual encounter with Pramukh Swami. For older devotees who had not traveled to India since their guru's restricted his movements, this darshan was memorable for the sheer fact of its having happened at all. These days, at nearly ninety-four years of age, Pramukh Swami is largely confined to a wheelchair; he no longer speaks easily nor eats much. And, yet, as *satsangis* told me, such was their guru's desire to serve devotees that he readily ignored the discomforts of his body to share with them his divine blessings.

Throughout the two weeks of his stay, *satsangis* were keenly aware that their guru was present on the temple grounds. As a number of young Swaminarayan *satsangis* shared with me, the 'atmosphere was indescribable.' Referring to their guru in the reverential manner of address, 'Swamishri,' these young *satsangis* expressed their enormous happiness knowing that 'Swamishri has come for us,' and 'the darshan Swamishri gave us was just amazing.'[4] More than one person observed with awe that, despite being 'much older and unwell,' Pramukh Swami had made the 'selfless' decision to journey from Gujarat to New Jersey to share his grace. 'Doesn't he look so well?' one young woman asked me. And, an older man commented with hopefulness, 'Bapa [guru] looks so well here [in New Jersey] that maybe he will stay past the 19th [of August].'[5]

On the evening of 10 August 2014, the day that the Robbinsville Swaminarayan temple was inaugurated, sixteen sets of brides and grooms were married in a large outdoor tent that had earlier been used for viewing the inauguration rituals on large screens. As the wedding couples, elaborately dressed and surrounded by family and friends, paraded to their allotted areas in the designated tent, a male *satsangi* volunteer carrying a camera called out: 'Isn't it wonderful that during a time when many want to make the day all about themselves . . . it isn't about them but about receiving Swamishri's blessing?'[6] The shimmer of the gold and silver threads in the wedding finery and the sparkle of the brides' jewelry in the still-bright evening sun, along with the palpable air of family members' excitement and anticipation were perhaps surpassed by the even greater realization that Pramukh Swami was close by. Following the marriage rituals, the new husbands and wives would have the privilege of darshan of their guru. And their new lives, like the awakening of the murtis in the new temple just a few hours earlier, would begin in the same auspicious way, within the divine presence of guru and God.

Portable Sociality

The presence of Gujaratis in different parts of the world is attributable to well-known patterns of postcolonial migration, the labor needs of established nations, and shifts in late twentieth century immigration laws in places like the United States. These political and economic shifts cannot of course explain why some Gujaratis have chosen to become devotees of BAPS. It is common among immigrant-oriented religious communities for new migrants to seek out the possibility of shared language, foods, customs, as well as the opportunity to discuss and learn from fellow immigrants, but this too cannot account for the particular nature of *satsangis* involvement in BAPS. We have to think of these BAPS devotees as more than just immigrants who seek out Swaminarayan temples in hopes of finding a network for job hunting, a symbol of middle-class success, or tips on preparing Gujarati food in the diaspora. For devotees from all caste and class backgrounds, there is something more onto-logical, more connected to a conception of how to be in the world, that plays a motivating role in their commitment to 'being Swaminarayan.' Devotees yearn for a personal relationship with their guru, and *satsang* activities, rituals, and *seva* are connected to strengthening this desire. So too does the construc-tion of temples and activity spaces, the circulation of guru and *sadhus*, and the vast publishing capacities of BAPS support the individual's cultivation of devotion to guru and Bhagwan Swaminarayan. In other words, being in BAPS provides a structure for those who are trying to experience their lives, actions, and consequences of actions according to a different ontological scheme. In the process, of course, *satsangi* devotion also works to reshape not just personal, religious lives but notions of cosmopolitanism (Van der Veer 2004), global citizenship (Zavos 2013), and religious subjectivity.

The success of BAPS as a transnational movement is clearly attributable to numerous factors. We may think of some of these as being external to the movement's teachings and some as directly tied to it. Devotional ideals are not immune from global channels of migration, individual desires for economic stability, and the controls established by governments and states for the regu-lation of religious institutions. And yet to reduce Swaminarayan devotion or religious ontology to these material and ideological realities would be to say very little about why young men and women, raised in Gujarat or India, are attracted to the Swaminarayan Sanstha; it would not be sufficient to explain why they will go on to contribute to the transmission of BAPS teachings on to future generations. One American male *satsangi*, brought up near Chicago in the United States, said that his reason for choosing to become a Swamina-rayan *sadhu* was motivated by the happiness he felt when he was 'doing things like bhakti and *seva*.'[7] This young man received admission into a competitive six-year medical program, but left after receiving an undergraduate degree in chemistry. 'Personally, my only goal as a *sadhu* is to live my life in such a way that it pleases Bapa [Pramukh Swami] and I can earn his blessings,' the *sadhu* shared. This *sadhu* is among numerous young men of Gujarati heritage who were raised in places like the United States, Canada, and the United Kingdom and who have made a decision to dedicate their lives to serving guru, God, and BAPS. As another *sadhu* who grew up in the Washington, D.C. area said:

> I was motivated by my guru, Pramukh Swami Maharaj. I mean that Swami never asked me to become a sadhu. He never mentioned it, or hinted it to me. But, I mean he is such a good person, so humble, so kind, so gentle. And, I have always trusted him. . . . Seeing Swami motivated me to become a sadhu.[8]

One can trace the desires of these young men to become *sadhus* to a number of motivating factors, including the migration history of their family, their identities as religious and ethnic minorities in the United States, changes in the political economy of postcolonial India, the legal and political language of religious pluralism, and more readily accessible modes of travel and communication. Even these factors, however, do not satisfactorily explain the relationships of trust, affection, and devotion that *sadhus* or lay followers have with their guru. For this, we must attend to the dimension of religious subjectivity, the experiencing of life through the lens of 'being Swaminarayan.' This is something that appears to be at least somewhat independent of other variables like economic status, nationality, or patterns of migration. Despite its obvious connections with Gujarat, the BAPS Swaminarayan Sanstha is an example of a Hindu transnational movement that can 'go global' precisely because it is possible for present and future devotees to sustain meaningful relationships with their guru and leaders of the movement wherever they may reside.

For *sadhus* and lay followers who are refining their relationship to the guru and who intentionally seek ways to increase their knowledge about BAPS bhakti, theirs is an ethical posture that is explicitly connected to the question of 'how do I live my life to help others so that I may gain knowledge about my own self, or atma?' This deeply personal quest to 'know one's atma' becomes an individual ethical project that ideally turns *satsangis* toward serving their guru; this in turn motivates service to others. The success of BAPS's growth can be connected to the ethical project of devotees who, in pursing their personal devotional goals, are reshaping themselves to be good neighbors and cosmopolitan citizens. This formula—where individual energies are directed toward a personal goal that in turn requires thinking beyond the self—is one that can be identified in other Hindu transnational movements, in which personal devotion supports an outward emphasis on social or humanitarian service (Van der Veer 2004).

It is interesting to consider that many of the more well-known transnational movements such as the International Society for Krishna Consciousness (ISKCON), Mata Amritanandamayi Mission, Satya Sai Organization, and the Swadhyay Parivar all emphasize social service and volunteer work (*seva*), as the central means to achieving desired changes in the self and society. This dual focus on service as helping others and service as refining one's ontological self may in fact be one aspect of modern Hindu movements that is distinctly portable. Tulasi Srinivas argues that the globalization potential of a particular religious movement is enhanced if there are 'cultural forms' in one location that can undergo 'cultural translation' into another location (Srinivas 2013: 238). This process does not occur automatically but passes through four phases. First, Srinivas suggests, a cultural form is intentionally selected for its potential translation and then 'disembedded'; second, the dislodged cultural form is then 'codified' by a guru or religious leadership in an effort to translate it into more universalist terms; third, outfitted to travel, the codified form seeks an anchor site in some new location; and, fourth, once such a site is located, the cultural form can undergo 're-embedding and contextualization' in the new location (Srinivas 2013: 238–243).

Srinivas's typology for cultural translation suggests that the success of a transnational movement may in some measure rest on the very practical consideration of just what ideas and practices can attain portability, since not all such forms may prove 'translatable' within different cultural contexts. Srinivas's focus on the Sathya Sai movement provides ample evidence that this transnational movement, reputedly one of the largest arising from India, owes its success to the flexibility it provides for the interpretation of its devotional ideals. This flexibility of meaning allows for what Srinivas terms a 'strategic ambiguity' where devotees have the agency to be active interpreters of their devotional practice (2013: 244). That the logics of devotees' praxis in one area may not match with the logics of devotees in another area is not itself troublesome to the overall devotional focus on attaining a Sai Baba understanding of the moral and virtuous devotional self.

The interpretive flexibility available in the Sathya Sai Baba movement is not obviously present in the Swaminarayan community. Such flexibility may in fact be less necessary within BAPS since *satsangis* share a distinctly Gujarati heritage compared to the extensive diasporic membership of the Sathya Sai movement. Nevertheless, BAPS, like other transnational movements, does face the challenge of engaging with publics outside of India that are not necessarily familiar with Hindu traditions. In these interactions—which range from bureaucratic negotiations around the acquisition of land for temple building and legal requirements for recognition as a 'religious' organization to the sheer building of trust among new communities—the leadership and members of BAPS have acquired significant knowledge about how to represent the movement. From the perspective of BAPS leaders, this active engagement with new publics who are unfamiliar with Swaminarayan Hinduism is a necessary feature of *satsangi* life wherever the community finds itself; it is a requirement to be met if devotion to guru and Bhagwan Swaminarayan are to continue in new contexts. As such, BAPS continues to seek out appealing and creative ways to present its vision of Hinduism and India, whether through cultural festivals, volunteer service, or large-scale public facilities like the Akshardham complexes, which are now so closely associated with the movement.

Conclusion

Hindu transnational movements, by virtue of their migration from the global south to metropolitan centers in Europe and North America serve to challenge the idea that prestige, value, and desirable goods move only from the north to the south. Indeed, global movements such as BAPS compel a reexamination of the migratory networks of modern religions and their efflorescence outside of their homeland in a colonial and postcolonial context; in addition, such movements should lead us to consider how best to make sense of modern religious subjectivity without either clouding it in the abstractions of theology or reducing it to the play of material and economic forces. Tracing the histories and strategies of such movements as they endeavor to inhabit, adjust to, and interact in new cultural and political spaces provides important opportunities to explore why and how modern devotees sustain their values and ideals across not just vast distances, but also across different discursive arenas, including political, legal, and sociological ones.

Do transnational movements contribute to religious pluralism or do they promote religious factionalism and the persistence of religion in an otherwise secular world? Does a religious community that evolves into a transnational community do so by accommodating a particular set of assumptions about what in fact constitutes a religion? When a regional religious movement becomes transnational, does it qualify to be labeled as a 'world religion'? The case of the BAPS, Swaminarayan Sanstha suggests that focusing on the relationships and forms of sociality or engagement that devotees have with their fellow *satsangis* and those outside of their tradition can lead to a more fine-tuned appreciation of why people join transnational movements and what they gain from this membership. Such a focus can also point to areas of stress and strain that inevitably appear when religious movements brush up against certain hegemonic projects, whether these are regional, national, or global. Once again, the Swaminarayan Sanstha has provided ample occasion for such reflection, since its regional roots in Gujarat are tied closely to the caste dynamics of western India while its success in contemporary India has (in the minds of some critics) been gained by forging comfortable alliances with the kinds of Hindu majoritarian projects we associate with Hindutva. Beyond India, one might well ask how the highly visible and clearly well-funded BAPS movement works to foster a particular vision of what it means to be Hindu.

Satsangis are aware of such critical questions and often take them very much to heart. Near the end of a long conversation in the Swaminarayan temple in Ahmedabad, a *satsangi* shared his bewilderment that BAPS's global presence and successful program of temple building might be interpreted as a sign of BAPS's intention to claim Hinduism as its own. Gaining control of his emotions, the *satsangi* said,

> Our only purpose is to work constructively in society, to live a better life, to use our energy in constructive, creative directions. . . . I am so happy, so happy but I also want to serve others so that they can lead a better life. It is one thing to write books, another thing to come up with concrete solutions to inspire people to lead a better life. You can bloody write hundreds of books, but how do you inspire people to live?[9]

Clearly, this *satsangi*'s response is framed by the Swaminarayan vision of how to live a moral and religiously meaningful life; his commitment to living well individually is clearly joined with a desire to live well with others. As we have seen, this dual conception of service may be a central factor in the success of the BAPS movement. Like other transnational movements, it thrives in part because of its specific teachings about finding personal religious fulfillment wherever the devotee may live. It remains a compelling question to ask why some are attracted to such a teaching while others are not. At the very least, the global vitality of modern Hindu movements suggests that they are social formations that can, at least for some, arrest the spread of the hypertrophic modern 'individual' in favor of an alternate religious subjectivity predicated on the sharing of spiritual wonderment as a higher personal and devotional priority.

Summary

Modern Hindu movements are not necessarily dependent on proximity to an Indian place of origin or a founder's institutional locus in order to thrive. Transnational Hindu communities, in particular, are composed of members who are settled inside and outside of India and whose growth across national boundaries is mediated by communication technologies as well as the ease of global travel and different channels of migration. This chapter considers some of the factors that support a portable Hinduism. How does a Hindu movement 'go global' and how are religious teachings and practices circulated and supported among the transnational membership? And, in what ways does the minority status of Hindus and their religious traditions in places of settlement outside of India influence the ways in which transnational movements interact with their publics? To sketch some answers to this question, this chapter looks at one example of a transnational movement, the BAPS Swaminarayan community.

Discussion Questions

1. What makes transnationalism today different from the movements of peoples and ideas in the past?
2. What are some characteristics of a transnational religious movement or community?
3. Based on the ethnographic material in this chapter, describe some challenges that transnational Hindu movements can encounter that may not arise in the Indian context. What are some reasons for these challenges?
4. Consider your concept of a world religion. How does the globalization of Hinduism through transnational movements disrupt or support the concept of world religions?

Notes

1   BAPS followers are especially oriented towards India and the western Indian state of Gujarat, since the latter is the historical center of their devotional tradition. In this sense, BAPS is itself a kind of diaspora; its members, while living in a transnational context, retain an attachment to Gujarat, the place of origin for the Swaminarayan Sanstha. In fact, most members of BAPS are Gujaratis. By contrast, one might note that there are other large Hindu transnational movements such as those centered on figures such as Mata Amritanandamayi Math or Sathya Sai Baba whose followers are both Indian and non-Indian.

2   Conversation in Ahmedabad, Gujarat, 30 July 2013.
3   Conversation in Ahmedabad, Gujarat, 13 July 2014.
4   Conversations in Robbinsville, New Jersey, 9–10 August 2014.
5   Conversations in Robbinsville, New Jersey, 9–10 August 2014.
6   Conversation in Robbinsville, New Jersey, 10 August 2014.
7   Conversation recorded, via a male intermediary, in Sarangpur, Gujarat, 21 July 2013.
8   Conversation recorded, via a male intermediary, in Sarangpur, Gujarat, 22 July 2013.
9   Conversation in Ahmedabad, Gujarat, 22 July 2014.

Suggested Readings

Jacobsen, Knut A. and P. Pratap Kumar, eds. (2004). *South Asians in the Diaspora*. Leiden: The Netherlands: Brill.

Transnational religious movements are often connected to specific diaspora communities. This edited volume offers chapters on Hindu and other South Asian communities, including Buddhist, Jain, Christian, Muslim, Parsi, and Sikh diasporas, some of whom are part of transnational religious movements seeking ways to sustain their traditions and practices.

Richardson, E. Allen (2014). *Seeing Krishna in America: the Hindu Bhakti Tradition of Vallabhacharya in India and its Movement to the West*. Jefferson: McFarland & Company, Inc.

The Pushtimarg followers in the Vallabha tradition are the focus of this highly accessible account that weaves history with an ethnography of Pushtimarg devotees in the United States. As its devotees strive to sustain their traditions in the United States, the author argues that Pushtimarg, in its American form, is evolving into an American religion.

Williamson, Lola (2010). *Transcendent in America: Hindu-Inspired Meditation Movements as New Religion*. New York: New University Press.

This engaging ethnography looks at the genealogical influence of Hindu gurus, concepts, and teachings on American meditation movements with a mostly non-Indian following. The author teases out the Christian and Hindu-inspired inflections in three meditation communities and shares insights into American practitioners' motivations for participation in these movements.

Zavos, John, P. Kanungo, D. Reddy, M. Warrier, and R. Williams, eds. (2012). *Public Hinduisms*. New Delhi: Sage Publications India.

Transnational Hinduism is constituted of leaders, devotees, and organizations aiming to adapt practices and teachings in the context of familiar and unfamiliar geographies, publics, and political contexts. This edited volume focuses on the myriad ways in which Hindu groups represent and become representations of a public Hinduism both within and beyond India.

Bibliography

Basch, Linda, Nina Glick Schiller, and Cristina Szanton Blanc (1994). *Nations Unbound: Transnational Projects, Postcolonial Predicaments and Deterritorialized Nation-States*. New York: Routledge.

Bennett, Jane (2001). *The Enchantment of Modern Life: Attachment, Crossings, and Ethics*. Princeton: Princeton University Press.

Copeman, Jacob and Aya Ikegame (2012). 'Guru Logics.' *Journal of Ethnographic Theory* 2, No. 1: 289–336.

Eisenlohr, Patrick (2012). 'Cosmopolitanism, Globalization, and Islamic Piety Movements in Mauritius.' *City & Society* 24, No. 1: 7–28.

Kim, Hanna H. (2009). 'Public Engagement and Personal Desires: BAPS Swaminarayan Temples and their Contribution to the Discourses on Religion.' *International Journal of Hindu Studies* 13, No. 3: 357–390.

——— (2013). 'Swāminārāyaṇa Bhakti Yoga and the Akṣarabrahman Guru.' In *Gurus of Modern Yoga* (pp. 237–260). Eds. Ellen Goldberg and Mark Singleton. Delhi: Oxford University Press.

Nanda, Meera (2009). *The God Market: How Globalisation is Making India More Hindu.* Delhi: Random House.

Rajagopal, Arvind (2000). 'Hindu Nationalism in the U.S.: Changing Political Configurations of Political Practice.' *Ethnic and Racial Studies* 23, No. 3: 467–496.

Brahmaviharidas, Sadhu (2004). 'Pramukh Swami Maharaj the Inspirer and Instiller of Philosophy in Life.' http://www.baps.org/Article/2011/Pramukh-Swami-Maharaj-The-Inspirer-And-Instiller-Of-Philosophy-Life-2181.aspx.

Srinivas, Tulasi (2010). *Winged Faith: Rethinking Globalization and Religious Pluralism through the Sathya Sai Movement.* New York: Columbia University Press.

——— (2013). 'Towards Cultural Translation: Rethinking the Dynamics of Religious Pluralism and Globalisation through the Sathya Sai Movement.' In *Religions in Movement: The Local and the Global in Contemporary Faith Traditions* (pp. 230–245). Eds. Robert W. Hefner, John Hutchinson, Sara Mels, and Christiane Timmerman. New York: Routledge.

Van der Veer, Peter (2004). 'Transnational Religion; Hindu and Muslim Movements.' *Journal for the Study of Religious Ideologies* 7 (Spring): 4–18.

Warrier, Maya (2005). *Hindu Selves in a Modern World: Guru Faith in the Mata Amritanandamayi Mission.* New York: RoutledgeCurzon.

Williams, Raymond B. (2001). *An Introduction to Swaminarayan Hinduism.* Cambridge: Cambridge University Press.

Wuthnow, Robert and Stephen Offutt (2008). 'Transnational Religious Connections.' *Sociology of Religion* 69, No. 2 (Summer): 209–232.

Zavos, John (2013). 'Transnational Religious Organisation and Flexible Citizenship in Britain and India.' In *Citizenship as Cultural Flow, Transcultural Research—Heidelberg Studies on Asia and Europe in a Global Context* (pp. 167–186). Ed. Subatra K. Mitra. Heidelberg: Springer-Verlag.

Part II
The Colonial Backdrop

4 Debates within Colonial Hinduism

Amiya P. Sen

In his unfinished autobiography, Debendranath Tagore (1817–1905), the leader of the reformist body called the Brahmo Samaj (founded 1828), recalls that in the early 1850s, some of his close religious associates and friends tried to determine the nature of god by a show of hands. If, for instance, someone proposed that god represented Bliss and Beatitude, this was then put to vote among the members gathered. The pious and essentially conservative man that he was, Debendranath found this quite blasphemous. Earlier too, he had regretfully noted that while he was interested in investigating the relationship between god and man, his associates seemed more keen on examining the ways in which man related to the physical world. On each of these occasions, he singled out in particular one associate by the name of Akshay Kumar Dutta (1820–1886). Dutta was an ardent deist and a scholar of natural theology. It was in fact Dutta who convinced Debendranath to take up the question of whether or not the Vedas could be treated as the final scriptural authority for Hinduism. As a result, by 1848–1849, the Brahmo Samaj under Debendranath's leadership took the radical step of renouncing faith in the Vedas as an infallible work of nonhuman (*apaurusheya*) revelation.

Such developments are symptomatic of the intellectual and moral concerns that may be found among the new Hindu intelligentsia in British India, most palpably in the three Presidency towns of Calcutta, Bombay, and Madras. These concerns included extended debates on conceptions of the divine, on the valid sources of religious knowledge and on man's manifold duties in the world. In this chapter, we shall focus on the city of Calcutta, then the administrative capital of British India, because in many ways it represented the nucleus of intellectual and cultural changes. As the first province to be brought under British colonial rule, Bengal exhibits the early impulses of progressive thinking as well as those of innate conservatism. The former impulses were derived from the intellectual and moral impact that contemporary European thought had made on the Hindu mind while the latter reflected an anxiety to defend indigenous culture against 'alien' influences. Arguably, Hindu Bengalis were perhaps the first social group in India to develop a new self-reflexivity and to critically negotiate the colonial encounter.

Religious Debates: Modern and Premodern

Internal differences and debates have long been a part of the religious life of the Hindus and, in general, tend to reflect the vibrancy of Indian intellectual life. Allowing for some exceptions, this was more visible in upper caste, literate society and remained almost exclusively confined to men. Elite Hinduism of this sort was often characterized by contestations around matters of faith or doctrine. In early medieval India, there had been sharp, theological exchanges between Vaishnavas and Shaktas on god or the nature of the world. At times, these even turned violent. The regularity with which such disagreements and debates surfaced is somewhat remarkable considering that the religion of the Hindus was not a homogenized or unified body of beliefs and practices. Hinduism had no organized church or a central authority that could effectively speak on behalf of all Hindus. This made it difficult to identify the Hindu 'dissenter' or 'heretic.' As such, theological differences were often a matter of sectarian self-righteousness.

Modern Hindu intellectuals moved away from this pattern by attempting to more rigidly determine the religious belief of the Hindus. It could be argued that religious and philosophical debates grew sharper in modern India precisely because an influential class of Hindus increasingly came to believe that 'Hinduism' was a name that could justly be given to a readily identifiable religion common to all Hindus. To a great extent, this reflected the growing perception that, whereas the Christians and Muslims claimed to be unified communities and could boast of following a single scripture, the Hindus had hitherto not been known to do so. Attempts to formulate a common religion for all Hindus and to identify a common scripture were soon to emerge as major objectives for modern Hindu leaders.

Debates within modern Hinduism can be separated from those occurring in the premodern era in one other respect. Before the establishment of British rule in India, religious discussions or debates (*shastrarth*) were often patronized by Hindu ruling chiefs who considered this to be a part of their royal duties or function. In colonial India, however, the state consciously withdrew itself from such debates. These were largely left to religious communities to sort out. The result was that modern religious debates often took place in the public domain. This was greatly facilitated by the rapid success of print culture. Understandably, such developments augured well for those patrons and publicists who were keen to establish a common religious identity for all Hindus. It was now possible not only to plead for a common scripture for all Hindus, but to actually make religious texts more freely available, at least to educated, urban Hindus.

Between 1815 and 1820, as part of a project to demonstrate that Hinduism was a monotheistic and nonidolatrous religion, the reformer Rammohun Roy (1774–1833, see Image 4.1) published the *Brahma Sutras* of Badarayana and select *Upanishads* in Bengali and English translations. This was in some ways a revolutionary act for it made public for the first time texts that were known only to a certain class of Hindus. What is more, contrary to all conventions,

Figure 4.1 Home of Rammohun Roy

Rammohan also declared that these highly esoteric texts could be made available to women and low castes (*shudras*), two social groups that had hitherto been denied this right. Such pronouncements signaled the possibilities of a religious democracy in a society that was highly differentiated and stratified in terms of social and ritual rights. Rammohun's Hindu opponents had little objection to his plea that Hinduism was at heart monotheistic. Ideas like this had been acknowledged earlier in the tradition. What his opponents found highly objectionable was Rammohun's willingness to open up 'sacred' knowledge to those who did not traditionally qualify for it. Nonetheless, once the idea of a common scripture for the Hindus was linked to the availability of these chosen texts in the public domain, it became possible to more clearly define who a Hindu was or what it meant to be a Hindu.

The Valid Sources of Knowledge

The need to identify a common scripture for the Hindus led Rammohun Roy to lay renewed emphasis on Vedic authority. This was tactically the easiest to perform since the Vedas had been traditionally accepted as canon. As *shruti* (literally, that which was only heard), they were taken to be superior to all other classes of religious literature. Interestingly enough, among the six schools of Hindu philosophy, there were some which tacitly contested the idea of god but not the authority of *shruti*. However, Rammohun's agenda led him to confront certain other problems. Under the influence of Islamic theology, with which he had been familiar in early life, Rammohun had become a staunch monotheist. The problem before him was that both Vedic and post-Vedic religion featured the worship of multiple deities. The religion of the medieval Puranas appeared to be even worse since it also sanctioned the practice of image worship (*murti-puja*). Such considerations led Rammohun to focus on the body of texts called the Upanishads. These texts were highly speculative in nature and spoke of a transcendental Absolute (*brahman*) that had no conceivable form or quality (that is, it was *nirakara* and *nirguna*). As such, this Absolute was very different from a god to whom one might emotionally relate.

The debate over valid scriptures could not be sorted out with any ease. Among Rammohun's followers were rationalists and sceptics who, under the spell of European deism, distrusted any notion of scripture as the revealed word of god. They were of the opinion that nature itself offered a better clue to god's presence and to Divine laws. To put this differently, they believed that the work of a creator-god as witnessed in the world in fact represented god's revelation. In the 1840s, the Brahmo Samaj was deeply divided on this question. Akshay Kumar Dutta, mentioned above, alleged that Vedic texts spoke with mutually conflicting voices. At Dutta's instigation Debendranath made enquiries and learned that the Upanishads appeared to speak of both a personal god and an impersonal Absolute; in the Upanishads, god was depicted as both pervading the world and as eternally separate from it.

Rammohun himself appears to have been well aware of these internal inconsistencies but, nonetheless, glossed over them. For the rationalists, something internally inconsistent could not be spoken of as the work of god, but Rammohun rejected their argument. In his *A Defence of Hindu Theism*, he argued instead that 'the explanation of the Veda and of its commentators must either be admitted as sufficiently reconciling the contradictions or must not be admitted.' He then added, 'in the latter case, the Veda must necessarily be supposed to be inconsistent with itself and therefore altogether unintelligible, which is directly contrary to the faith of Hindus of all description' (Roy 1946: 89). Rammohan thus affirmed the inherent intelligibility of the Vedas.

Debandranath found the critique of the rationalists to be more persuasive than the commitment of Rammohun to the Veda. As a result, Debendranath rejected the Vedas and Upanishads as authoritative sourcebooks. In the place of *shruti*, Debendranath introduced a new synthetic scripture, the *Brahmdharmagrantha* (1848–1850), based on his own selective reading of ancient texts like the Upanishads and the Laws of Manu. In place of the unquestioned faith in Vedic scripture found among orthodox Hindus, the *Brahmodharmagrantha* upheld the twin ideals of ethical purity and intuitive experience. Predictably, not everyone was happy with this experiment and this even included those who generally favored reform. Some latter-day Brahmos actually accused Debendranath of unduly giving up the Vedas as authority (*pramana*), of selectively using the texts he preferred, and of text torturing (Tattwabhushan n.d: 105–106; Pal 1972: 18, 194).

Disagreement on the issue of Vedic authority could even cause a change of heart in some. For instance, by the latter half of the nineteenth century, movements like the Arya Samaj, founded in north India by Swami Dayanand Saraswati (1824–1883), had begun to emphasize the need to reorient Hindus to the revealed literature of the Vedas. Dayananda's efforts in this regard—often likened to Martin Luther's cry of *sola scriptura* ('scripture alone')—were aimed at demonstrating that true Hinduism was not based in teachings about the illusoriness (*maya*) of the world (a teaching that Christian polemicists often used to question the truth of Hinduism) but on the scientific truths of ancient Vedic wisdom. At a time when Indians were beginning to recognize the need to articulate more 'nationalist' understandings of their religion in order to confront the fact of European racism and claims of Christian supremacy, this revival of the dignity of Vedic religion had tremendous appeal. We can sense the way this appeal took hold among some intellectuals if we consider the well-known Bengali novelist and intellectual, Bankim Chandra Chattopadhyay (1838–1894). Early in his career, Bankim had looked with skepticism on such calls for a revival of Vedic religion. However, as he wrestled with the question of articulating a meaningful Indian identity, he eventually came to support the idea—as evidenced by a series of lectures on Vedic literature he delivered to students of Calcutta University (Chattopadhyay 1969: 235, 149–169).

In trying to determine the 'true' or 'authentic' sources of their religion, both more traditional Hindus and more modernizing Brahmos were led into some confusion. In this they appear to have been driven by two competing desires. On one level, they were anxious to press the traditional claim that the religion of the Hindus was by nature timeless and immutable (*sanatan*). On another, they were too deeply influenced by contemporary European ideas not to take a historical-anthropological view of religion. But even here, they were pulled in two directions. While Utilitarianism and the ideas of Herbert Spencer and the European Positivists led them to take history as a linear movement in time that ushered in human progress, they also tended to believe that religion and culture had degenerated over time. This, incidentally, was consistent with both the kinds of Protestant theology with which they were familiar and the Hindu *yuga* theory which spoke of the degeneration of *dharma* over time. Once again, we get a sense for such confusion in the following passage from Bankim:

> Let us revere the past, but we must, in justice to our new life, adopt some new methods of interpretation and adapt the older, eternal, and undying truths to the necessities of that life. (Chattopadhyay 1969: 236)

Here, Bankim's use of the word 'adapt' is perfectly understandable given his belief that a religious tradition had to be interpreted afresh with the passage of time. And yet he seems to contradict himself with the suggestion that 'eternal and undying truths' could somehow be adapted to suit changing needs. In this, we sense the inherent conflict between the views of those who measured religion in social-utilitarian terms and those who did not.

New Conceptions of God and Religion

On the question of adapting religion to meet the needs of the day, we see a range of shifting opinions across the nineteenth century. Rammohun had himself adopted a utilitarian view of religion when he argued that Hindu religion could be useful only if it secured 'political advantage and social comfort' (Roy 1973: 462). However, this viewpoint was promptly rejected by his spiritual successor, Debendranath Tagore, who announced that '[w]e are not among those who seek both God and this world,' he argued; 'the world is acceptable to us only after we have made an acquaintance with God' (Tagore 1965: 172). When it came to advantage and comfort, the later Brahmo theologian Keshab Chandra Sen (1838–1884) sounded an even more skeptical note when he observed that '[t]he politics of the age is Benthamism, its ethics utilitarianism, its religion rationalism, its philosophy positivism. All seems dull, mechanical, unspiritual and lifeless' (Sen 1954: 37).

Bankim Chandra Chattopadhyay, who otherwise admired the Utilitarian thinker J. S. Mill and who had for a time taken to the Positivism of Auguste Comte, subsequently gave up both of these European systems for the sake of what he took as a rational view of Hindu theism. A few years after him, Swami Vivekananda (1863–1902) also radically departed from the notion of utility by arguing that this could never provide a stable or enduring basis for morality. Such a basis, he claimed, could only be found in the monistic metaphysics of Advaita Vedanta. Given the unity of all life, a man would be truly inspired to help others when he realized that in so doing, he also helped himself (Vivekananda 1973: vol. 3, 129; vol. 1, 75). Indeed, the Swami's criticism of the tendency found among European critics and some western-educated Hindus to understand religion as an appendage to society was even sharper:

> We are asked, 'what good is your religion to your society?' Society is made the test of Truth. Now this is very illogical. Society is only a stage in the growth which we are passing (through). . . . Society is good at a certain stage but it cannot be an ideal, it is in constant flux. (Vivekananda 1973: vol. 6, 144)

Among Hindus, such new conceptions of religion were clearly related to critical reflections on the nature of god. In the 1820s, Rammohun instigated a fierce debate over a range of questions that were traditionally linked to orthodox Hindu faith. For one, he unambiguously rejected the elaborate mythology of Puranic religious culture and, following from that, the popular worship of deities like Krishna, Shiva, or Durga. This, in turn, led him into a protracted controversy on the question of whether or not image worship was a valid means to advance one's religious life. In retrospect, Rammohun appears to have been more impressed with those religious traditions of medieval north India that stressed a formless (*nirguna*) god and were also socially radical in looking past the ordinary distinctions of caste and gender. This did not, however, make Rammohun an atheist or agnostic; he firmly rejected a purely secular culture.

When someone reported to him the case of an educated young man who had turned atheist, Rammohun is said to have quipped that he would next turn into a beast! To make sense of Rammohun's theological position it helps to imagine it as a combination of the monistic or non-dual (*advaita*) vision of the philosopher Shankara (c. ninth century CE) and the piety of a modern theist. Thus, although Rammohun was known to revere the transcendental Absolute (*brahman*) of the Upanishads, he also addressed this Absolute as 'Father,' an epithet that may betray a his debt to both Anglican Protestantism and the Vedic canon.

Roughly a half century after Rammohun's death in Bristol, England in 1833, a buoyant Hindu revivalism began to question the tendency among elite reformers to disavow the myths and practices associated with what we might call customary Hinduism. While both Rammohan and Dayananda sought to circumvent what they viewed as the 'excesses' of medieval Hinduism—with its many gods, elaborate temple worship and elaborate ritual ceremonies—a new generation of intellectuals began to emphasize the truths that could be found in the literature of post-Vedic India like the Puranas and the epic story of the Mahabharata. This tendency is most noticeable in the works of Bankim Chandra whose religion may in fact be described as neo-Puranic. Bankim's favorite god was not the formless Absolute of the Brahmos but the epic charioteer and incarnate deity Krishna, albeit suitably refurbished and given a moralizing makeover in light of modern-day concerns. In advancing his preference for the epic Krishna in his work, the *Krishnacharitra* (*The Life of Krishna*, 1886), Bankim clearly dissociated himself from worship of the pastoral Krishna who was thought to sport with the cowherd maidens (*gopis*) in Vrindavan. This latter Krishna, though widely worshipped in popular culture had proven greatly suspect in the eyes of Christian evangelists and western-educated Hindus alike due to his amorous exploits and trickster persona. In Bankim's work, Krishna emerges as a figure who combines reason, efficiency, and sagacity. Importantly, though, Bankim did cling to the concept of Krishna as an incarnation (*avatar*) of god. His embrace of this traditional Hindu conception of divinity was influential in fostering a revival of traditional Vaishnavism in Bengal, which may also be seen in the decision by some later Brahmos like Bijoy Krishna Goswami (1841–1899) to spread their message using popular modes of Vaishnava devotionalism.

Developments like these were characteristic of the late nineteenth century when Bengal witnessed something like a conservative backlash associated with the birth of nationalist sentiment, the rise of Hindu missionary organizations, and a more dogged defense of image worship. In the 1880s, fierce controversy broke out between the Hindu missionary Pandit Shashadhar Tarkachudamani (1851–1928) and the Brahmo theologian, Nagendranath Chattopadhyay (1843–1913), on whether or not god could be worshipped as an image. The Sasadhar-Nagendranath controversy proved to be as intense as it was inconclusive. In other cases, potentially disruptive tensions were smoothed over by recourse to the logic of theological inclusivism. A case in point may be found in the parables and preaching of the Hindu mystic, Ramakrishna Paramahamsa

(1836–1886), who came to be widely revered even by the likes of rationalistic and iconoclastic Brahmos.

Ramakrishna served as a priest in a temple and was an ecstatic devotee of the goddess Kali. Nonetheless, this did not keep him from praising Brahmoism, praising its worship of god as the formless Absolute. As Ramakrishna maintained, different forms of religious experience were only natural in view of the varying mental capacities and psychological dispositions in men and women. Religions were like pathways (*path*), and each corresponded to a different doctrine (*mat*). This led him to make the proclamation *yato mat tato path*—'there are as many pathways as there are doctrines.' All paths were valid in the eyes of god (for some parables, see Sen 2010). This teaching seems to have helped defuse some of the intense debates between advocates of image worship and their opponents. It also proved to be a guiding teaching for Ramakrishna's chief disciple, Swami Vivekananda, who went on to preach the universalistic possibilities in Hinduism.

Moral and Philosophical Debates

Throughout the nineteenth century in Bengal, we notice a range of new moral and philosophical concerns coming to the fore. Among the more pressing questions turned on the relationship between god and the world. Even though he had drawn inspiration from the non-dualist philosopher, Shankaracharya, Rammohun refused to treat the world as an 'illusion' or even as a mere 'appearance.' Followers of the non-dualist (*advaita*) school of Shankara typically held that the world was only relatively real in relation to the Absolute (*brahman*). This followed from the presupposition that there could be but a single Reality and that as such all worldly phenomena could be neither substantive nor permanent. As we have seen, Rammohun preferred to understand the Absolute in the terms of a personal god who created and sustained the world and who set worthy moral guidelines for men and women to follow. That Rammohun's religious outlook was not merely an 'otherworldly' spirituality is made clear from claims he made about the worshipper obtaining his 'desired' objects and from his conviction that anyone who sought worldly honor and advantage was bound to revere god (Roy 1946: 8). In this respect, Rammohun's position is akin to that of the ancient Vedic sage (*rishi*) who, like Yajnavalkya in the Brihadaranyaka Upanishad, could unabashedly covet gifts of a son or cattle. In advancing his viewpoint, Rammohun brought a new realism to the religion of his day; he granted greater importance to the world and acknowledged the positive role of human mediation.

In other words, for Rammohun, the world could be continuously improved. More importantly, though, activity in the world had to be guided by new social concerns. Rammohun believed that extending love and courtesy to other human beings made a devotee dearer to god. This view was strongly echoed by Debendranath Tagore (Roy 1973: 342; Basu 1957: 33–34). At the same time, as we have seen, Debendranath rejected the overly rationalistic natural theology of Akshay K. Dutta who worked to separate knowledge of the natural world from the human knower. By contrast, Debendranath emphasized the importance of intuitive spiritual experiences; he also pointed worshippers to a Higher Power who benignly and purposefully worked to ensure that nature served the interests of humanity. Such ideas, it may be noted, coincided with the simultaneous decline of deism in Europe and the emergence of more vibrant forms of modern theism.

The religious views of Rammohun and Debendranath were not seriously contested until the 1880s when they came under scrutiny by a new generation of Hindu intellectuals. This new generation was just as pious, cosmopolitan, and humane as Rammohun and Debendranath, but they began to question the powers or transformative agency of human beings. As an example, we may consider the viewpoints of key figures like Bankim Chandra Chattopadhyay and Ramakrishna. Both men were Brahmins, but their world views differed in significant ways. For instance, regarding the role of the Hindu *guru* or spiritual teacher, Bankim was a cynic; he ridiculed the guru as a self-seeking individual who lived off the blind reverence of followers. To an extent, Ramakrishna seems to have shared Bankim's skepticism and was apparently reluctant himself to assume the mantle of the guru. That said, his religious world was solidly founded upon the role of personal spiritual instruction derived from close contact with spiritual teachers. This is how he acquired the spiritual disciplines (*sadhana*) he mastered in his lifetime; and this is how he passed on his wisdom to a generation of young spiritual seekers.

Bankim and Ramakrishna also differed on how humans should best relate to god and the world. Bankim Chandra was by no means an agnostic, but he took the position that it was far more important for man to begin with an intellectual understanding of the world and only subsequently proceed toward the heights of God-realization. This put Bankim squarely on the side of ethical activism. In his mind, a pressing love (*priti*) for humanity constituted a valid and effective means to serve god. In this respect, he remained close to the moral and theological position advanced by the Brahmos. By contrast, Ramakrishna was a man with little or no formal learning and saw no benefit for religion by beginning with worldly knowledge. Rather, he held that it was our acquaintance with god the creator that helped us better understand his creation, the world (Sen 2010: 39–41). Once while visiting a mango orchard, he remarked that there was little point in counting the number of mango trees when one could simply savor the juicy mangos! We come to appreciate that, for Ramakrishna, religion begins with an ardent pining (*vyakulata*) for god.

In a similar fashion, Ramakrishna also rejected the possibility that direct experience of god could follow from forms of intellectual reflection or the dry study of scripture. He shared none of Bankim's historical or anthropological interest in religion. For Ramakrishna, religion was god's gift to man; it was not something humanly created. This ultimately led him to distrust forms of altruism and charity. While he was not averse to the idea of social service (*seva*), he doubted if humans were truly capable of the kind of selflessness required to help others. And more importantly, he believed that in the end, all transformative power belonged to god. As Ramakrishna saw it, all forms of charitable work were simply a distraction from the highest objective, which ought to be God-realization (Sen 2010: 198). It is somewhat ironic, therefore, that Ramakrishna's chief monastic disciple, Swami Vivekananda, should make social service the founding principle of the Ramakrishna Mission, the organization founded in 1897 in memory of his guru. Somewhat surprisingly, given his reverence for Ramakrishna, Vivekananda may have been the first modern Hindu intellectual to suggest that the path of selfless action (*karma yoga*) need not be founded on any conception of god or religion. In Vivekananda, we see one gesture toward a resolution of the debate between two kinds of morality, the theistic and the humanistic.

Caste and Social Change

Reflections on the cultural history of nineteenth-century India suggest that developments in Bengal represented a distinctly religious approach to questions of social change. The noted Maharashtrian reformer, Mahadev Govind Ranade (1842–1901), in fact once complained that Bengal had gone too far in privileging religious reform over the social (Ranade 1992: 159). There is some truth to this allegation. While Rammohun attained worldwide fame for his crusade against the inhuman practice of widow immolation (*sati*), the most innovative dimensions of his life and work concerned religion. After Rammohun, many would hold that social reform was meaningless without first attempting a reformation of religious beliefs and practices. Such was the view of the Brahmo leader Keshab Chandra Sen, who held that caste discrimination could only be addressed through a radical reorientation of Hindu religious life (Sen 1940: 146). We have seen that for someone like Ramakrishna, such social concerns were almost meaningless (Sen 2010: 195).

One way to account for the difference in emphasis between reformers in Maharashtra and south India and those in Bengal is by pointing to the relatively weaker history of caste-based tensions in the latter region. This had the important effect, in Bengal, of allowing the substance and pace of reform initiatives—whether in the fields of religion or society—to be determined by Brahmins and other high castes. It is surely no coincidence that the men to take the most radical or innovative postures regarding Hindu reform in Bengal were all Brahmins: Rammohun, Debendranath, and Bankim Chandra. By contrast, in places like Maharashtra and areas that constitute present day Tamil Nadu, upper-caste reformers were compelled to respond to significant challenges from low-caste leaders and constituencies. Bengal could thus boast no low-caste reformist figures on a par with Jyotirao Phule (1827–1890) and Bhimrao Ambedkar (1891–1956) in Maharashtra or E. V. Ramasamy Naicker Periyar (1879–1973) in the south.

Here it might be instructive to compare the attitudes of Vivekananda, Ranade, and Periyar, each of whom had distinct understandings of 'reform.' Vivekananda tended to be dissatisfied with contemporary reform movements (as embodied in the widow marriage and age of consent controversies) for two reasons. First, he disliked the idea of social or religious changes being introduced through government legislation; this was tantamount to delegating social change to the will of a foreign government and alien ruling class. In this objection, we sense the increasing nationalist sentiments of Vivekananda's day. Second, Vivekananda lamented the fact that reform work as conducted by Indian reformers or reforming institutions, could boast no real connection to the people and as such could not address 'grass roots' problems like poverty or the lack of education (Vivekananda 1973: vol. 3, 194–196, 213–220). Unlike Vivekananda, Maharashtrian reformers like Ranade sought the active intervention of the state to help bring about meaningful change in the religious and social life of the Hindus. Though himself a Brahmin, Ranade was the moving spirit behind the reformist Indian Social Conference. He expected the state to speak up for those, like women and low-caste groups, who could not speak for themselves (Kolasker 1902: 92–102). In the south, Periyar adopted a more radical posture, beginning with a rejection of the very paradigm of 'reform.' He suspected reform of being little more than a manipulative strategy adopted by upper castes to control change in a manner that preserved their own class interests. He preferred revolution to reform (Periyar 1965: 1–19).

By the close of the nineteenth century, the nature and range of debates within Hinduism underwent a significant transformation in the context of increased nationalist sentiment. As intellectuals became increasingly preoccupied with the new language of political rights, they began to demand increased representation in local governing bodies and legislative councils. In the major cities and towns of British India, Brahmo leaders took to politics alongside the more aggressive defenders of Hinduism. The Indian National Congress, a political party founded in 1885 and dominated from the outset by Hindus, nonetheless believed that intensive engagement with social and religious issues only worked to divide the nation, whereas political work held the promise of unification. Deep, underlying differences within Indian society were at least temporarily glossed over in favor of forms of consensus that in the end did not prove to be enduring. Thus, while the twentieth century was increasingly shaped by the demands for Indian independence, the challenge of religious change did not disappear, but manifested itself in new modes of intra-Hindu squabbling and interreligious discord.

Summary

The nineteenth century in Bengal was a productive period in the revision and contestation of Hindu belief and practice. Many of the leaders of reform were high-caste Hindu elites. Beginning with Rammohun Roy's promotion of the Upanishads (Vedanta) as the source of a monotheistic religion, the question of scriptural authority became a prominent topic for debate. Rammohan's successors in the Brahmo Samaj carried forward his emphasis on Vedantic monotheism while also going on to question Vedic authority, the role of reason, and the demands for social change. The last quarter of the century witnessed the appearance of more revisionist forms of Hindu thought, which returned to some of the texts and issues initially rejected by Rammohun, such as the significance of Puranic mythology and the status of the popular deity Krishna. Looking beyond Bengal, we note that the question of how to prioritize religious versus social reform found somewhat different resolution among thinkers like M. G. Ranade (in Maharashtra) and Periyar (in Tamil Nadu).

Discussion Questions

- What was distinctively 'modern' about the sorts of intellectual and theological debates that took place in nineteenth-century Bengal?
- What sources of authority did modern Hindu reformers turn to in their attempt to advance new understandings of their tradition?
- How would you distinguish between the religious and moral worldviews of figures like Rammohan, Bankim Chandra, and Ramakrishna?
- Can you identify the differing perspectives modern Hindu reformers had regarding such issues as the goal of reform, the value of the guru, the nature of religious experience and the significance of caste?

Further Reading

Baird, R. D., ed. (1989). *Religion in Modern India*. 2nd ed. Columbia: South Asia Books.
An accessible collection of essays surveying religious movements and figures in India in the past century, including Muslim and Hindu figures.
Hatcher, B. A. (2008). *Bourgeois Hinduism, Or the Faith of the Modern Vedantists: Rare Discourses from Early Colonial Bengal*. New York: Oxford University Press.
Provides a translation and detailed analysis of a published set of discourses delivered by middle-class Hindu reformers of the Tattvabodhini Sabha, an organization led by Debendranath Tagore.
Kopf, D. (1979). *The Brahmo Samaj and the Shaping of the Modern Indian Mind*. Princeton: Princeton University Press.
A detailed, expansive history of Brahmoism and its impact on the Bengali and Indian consciousness.
Pennington, B. K. (2001). 'Contesting Colonial Dharma. A Chronicle of Emergent Hinduism: 1830–31.' *Journal of the American Academy of Religion*, 69, No. 3: 577–603.
Examines a Bengali newspaper from 1830–1831 to explore how native Indians engaged in the production of a coherent Hindu identity.
Sen, A. P., ed. (2003). *Social and Religious Reform. The Hindus of British India. Debates in Indian History and Society*. Delhi: Oxford University Press.
A critical examination of common debates during the colonial period including a reader bringing the voices of the debaters to the fore.

Bibliography

Basu, R. (1957). *Brahmodharmer Lakshan O Vrittanta* (*The Principles and History of Brahmism*). Calcutta: Sadharan Brahmo Samaj.

Chattopadhyay, B.C. (1969). *Bankim Rachanavali* (*The Collected Works of Bankim Chandra Chattopadhyay*) Vol. III. Ed. J.C. Bagal. Calcutta: Sahitya Samsad.

Kolasker, M.B. (1902). *Religious and Social Reform. A Collection of Essays and Speeches by Mahadev Govind Ranade*. Bombay: Gopal Narayan & Co.

Pal, B.C. (1972). *Navajuger Bangla* (*Renascent Bengal*). 3rd ed. Calcutta: Bipin Chandra Pal Institute.

Periyar, E.V.R. (1965). 'Social Reformation or Social Revolution?' Translated from *Arivin Ellai* by A. M Daharmalingam. Madras: Viduthalai Publications.

Ranade, M.G. (1992). *Miscellaneous Writings of the Late Hon'ble Mr. Justice, M.G. Ranade*. New Delhi: Sahitya Akademi.

Roy, R. (1946). *The English Works of Rammohun Roy*. Eds. K. Nag and D. Burman. Calcutta: Sadharan Brahmo Samaj.

——— (1973). *Rammohun Granthavali* (Collected Works of Rammohun Roy). Ed. Ajit Kumar Ghosh. Calcutta: Haraf Prakashani.

Sen, A.P. (1993). *Hindu Revivalism in Bengal. 1872–1905. Some Essays in Interpretation*. New Delhi: Oxford University Press.

——— (2010). *The Preachings and Parables of Ramakrishna Paramahamsa*. New Delhi: Penguin Viking.

Sen, K.C. (1940). *Life and Works of Brahmananda Keshub*. Ed. Prem Sundar Basu. Calcutta: Nababidhan Publication Committee.

——— (1954) *Lectures in India*. Calcutta: Nababidhan Publication Committee.

Tagore, D. (1965). *Brahmodharmer Vyakhyan* (An Exposition of Brahmoism). Calcutta: Sadharan Brahmo Samaj.

——— (1982). *Maharshi Debendranath Thakurer Atmajivani*. Ed. A. Mitra and A. Mitra. Calcutta: Chariot International Edition.

Tattwabhushan, S. (n.d.). *Autobiography. With Details of Philosophical Study and Spiritual Endeavour*. Calcutta: Sadharan Brahmo Samaj.

Vivekananda, S. (1973). *The Complete Works of Swami Vivekananda*. 8 vols. Calcutta: Advaita Ashrama.

5 Colonial Devotional Paths

Jason D. Fuller

Introduction

It is hard for a sophisticated person to believe in God these days. An intellectually honest devotee of any personified deity in the twenty-first century must admit this. The environment for believers of all stripes has become increasingly hostile in recent years. In North America, for example, educated people often find themselves ashamed of admitting adherence to anachronistic devotional practices like petitionary prayer, ritualistic observance, belief in miracles, or the public affirmation that one is a follower of a particular deity. 'Merry Christmas' and 'Happy Hanukkah' have been bowdlerized and transformed into 'Happy Holidays' in the American town square. Campus 'ministers' and spiritual life 'directors' on most secular college campuses no longer worry themselves overmuch with the metaphysical idiosyncrasies of their own traditions, but instead function as spiritual cruise directors—tour guides to religious destinations to which they owe little allegiance. Indeed, the situation of partisan *theistic* belief in North America is such that one is tempted to postulate that if one were to corner an ordained minister from a mainline Protestant church today, one would have a fifty-fifty chance of finding a shame-faced agnostic hiding beneath the robes of tradition and rote piety.

The hobbling *theistic embarrassment* that so many feel today regarding serious discussions about the existence of God, the efficacy of prayer, and the nature of the afterlife are symptomatic of the hyper-rationalistic moods and demythologizing habits of thought characteristic of modernity as such. The troubled relationship between *theism* (i.e. belief in a personal deity who is actively engaged in the world) and *modernity* is not unique to twenty-first-century America. In fact, it has its roots in seventeenth- and eighteenth-century European conversations about the intellectual merits of atheism and Deism as replacements for the (supposedly) outmoded superstitions and theistic excesses of the Middle Ages. Important Enlightenment thinkers such as Spinoza (1632–1677), Voltaire (1694–1778), Hume (1711–1776), Diderot (1713–1784), and Kant (1724–1804) argued that reason should be privileged above revelation and faith in all discussions of religious matters. Whether they were skeptical atheists or loosely aligned Deists, the major thinkers of the European Enlightenment were unified in their belief that they had inaugurated in the history of human affairs a new 'Age of Reason' that would supplant the fideism of the Middle Ages. Inasmuch as traditional theistic understandings of Christianity (particularly Roman Catholicism) ran afoul of modernist common sense (what Enlightenment thinkers rather self-flatteringly called 'reason'), they were to be rejected and replaced by more 'enlightened' metaphysical notions.

Of course, Christians in Europe and North America were not the only religious practitioners to be put to the yolk of an Enlightenment-driven modernity forced upon them by elite intellectuals who felt that they had outgrown traditional religious belief and practice. Hindus in India too had to come to grips with the secularizing challenges posed by what David Smith has aptly called the 'Juggernaut of modernity' (Smith 2003: 21–26). The hyper-trophic rationalism and reformist zeal that characterized the Enlightenment in eighteenth-century Europe came to India in the nineteenth century as part of a colonial modernizing mission. As British missionaries and colonizers began to exert increasing influence on Indian society from Lord Clive's military victory over the ruling Mughal *nawab* at the Bengali battle of Plassey in 1757 straight through until the mid-twentieth century, they brought with them the Enlightenment prejudices of their small island culture. If the traditional monotheistic beliefs, attitudes, and practices of the Abrahamic traditions were seen as intellectually troubling, the 'pagan' religious proclivities of Indian 'Hindoos' were regarded by English modernizers as positively horrifying in their medieval turbidity.

The Colonial Bengali Intelligentsia and the Development of Hindu Modernity

Though the process commenced haltingly and superficially in the eighteenth century, the most meaningful and impactful efforts to modernize Hinduism began in the nineteenth century. The city of Calcutta in particular, the so-called second city of empire, formed the crucible within which Hindu modernity was forged. Modern Hinduism was, in fact, shaped on the anvil of an Enlightenment mindset brought to India by a colonizing power. The provincial region of Bengal served as the 'British Bridgehead' during an advance of colonial influence on the subcontinent (Marshall 2006). Confronted by British critiques of popular Hindu piety, Indian intellectuals in the nineteenth century turned their considerable mental gifts toward the reformation and revival of Hinduism within the restrictive limitations of a rationalist modernity that always and everywhere poses a mortal threat to popular faith and practice.

In nineteenth-century India, the peculiarly modern moods and motivations associated with hypertrophic rationalism and a belief in progress swept over the educated Hindu population like a tidal wave. The ideological and technological cargo of modernity came to the subcontinent in the eighteenth and nineteenth centuries on the very same ships that carried British merchants, missionaries, soldiers, and politicians. Along with the colonizers came new technologies and novel ideas about the nature of the world and how one should conduct oneself within it. The British began to exert an increasing and outsized influence on Indian culture throughout the nineteenth century (the period of high modernism in India) by opening schools, founding voluntary associations, creating international markets and houses of finance, introducing the printing press and modern conceptions of clock-time and workplace efficiency. As Indian intellectuals worked to align traditional Hindu institutions, ideas, and practices with a British understanding of 'modernity,' many found themselves forced to criticize their own religion(s) in ways that blurred the distinction between 'westernization' and 'modernization.'

By the middle of the nineteenth century, a class of Indian intellectuals, businessmen, journalists, teachers, lawyers, merchants, and politicians emerged in India to bridge the cultural divide between colonizers and colonized. As a mediating middle-class sandwiched between the British ruling class and the subcontinental masses, this group of elite culture producers found itself at the vanguard of a modernizing process that would accomplish in 100 years what it had taken Europeans 300 years to achieve—namely the complete transformation of political, economic, sociocultural, and religious life in their country.

The members of the new class of mediating culture producers who emerged in the mid-nineteenth century were known as the *bhadraloka* (*bhadra*: sophisticated; *loka*: people), and they became the people upon whom the hopes and dreams of Hindu renewal, reform, and revival would rest. The *bhadraloka* intellectuals of nineteenth century Bengal were acutely aware of the challenges posed to Hindu belief and practice by modern ideas about rationality and faith. They had the good sense (from an Enlightenment perspective anyway) to feel embarrassed about aspects of their own religious traditions that could not be easily squared with modern/colonial ideas regarding reason, progress, gender relations, caste equality, social welfare, democracy, and literacy. Social and religious problems that particularly occupied the attention of *bhadraloka* intellectuals included the traditional Hindu institutions of *sati*, childhood marriage, bans on widow remarriage, and the orality of Hindu culture versus the Biblicism of European Christian culture.

The *bhadraloka* intellectuals of the nineteenth century were, for the most part, fluent in English and conversant with the threads of Enlightenment discourse that their compatriot modernizers in Europe and America were also utilizing in their own revisions of religion within a nineteenth-century context. In point of fact, many of the challenges facing Hindu reformers in the colonial period were challenges that all traditions faced when confronting the finicky rationalism and moral prudery of modernity's greatest nineteenth-century advocates like G.W.F. Hegel (1770–1831), Karl Marx (1818–1883), Friedrich Nietzsche (1844–1900), and Sigmund Freud (1856–1939). Christianity in Europe had to deal with challenges similar to those given voice in Indian Hindu circles in the eighteenth and nineteenth centuries. Yet the Indian case was different precisely because modern ideas, institutions, and technologies were mediated and enforced upon the indigenous population by a foreign power. When considering the transformations of Hinduism into a modern religion—a process that was completed primarily in the mid to late nineteenth century—it is impossible to separate the challenges posed by the concept of modernity per se from the challenges posed by the British as westernizers. Nationalism, print culture, colonial reason, and British constructions of masculinity and femininity all became issues of concern for *bhadraloka* modernizers intent on transforming Hinduism in the nineteenth century.

Bengali *bhadraloka* intellectuals tackled the challenges of westernization and modernization head on, and they did so with an unflinching pragmatism and intellectual courage that makes an advocate of religious innovation swell with admiration. Names like Ram Mohan Roy (1772–1833), Debendranath Tagore (1817–1905), Dayananda Saraswati (1824–1883), Keshub Chandra Sen (1838–1884), Bhaktivinoda Thakura (1838–1914), Bijoy Krishna Goswami (1841–1899), Swami Vivekananda (1863–1902), Rabindranath Tagore (1861–1914), and Aurobindo Ghose (1872–1950) all loom large in the Indian imagination to the present day; for they were the intellectuals who invented what we now call 'modern Hinduism.' These great thinkers found themselves, to a greater or lesser degree, embarrassed by the popular piety of many ordinary Hindus and felt that changes had to be made in order to make Hinduism a religion befitting the title of 'modern.'

Early Movements of Modernist Reform—1820s–1860s

In the end, each reformer was forced to make his own peace with modernity and westernization on very important socioreligious issues. In every case, however, the momentum of 'tradition' pushed one way while the magnetic force of modernity pulled another. The most popular responses to the modern, westernizing spell that had been cast upon the Bengali intelligentsia in the early to mid-nineteenth century (roughly 1820s–1860s) were to either reject religion entirely or to embrace some form of universalizing Deism. Notable among the atheist group was the firebrand reformer Henry Louis Vivian Derozio (1809–1831) who advocated for a radical rejection of traditional Hinduism from his teaching post at the Hindu College of Calcutta. His acolytes were called Derozians and formed a cultural movement known as 'Young Bengal' primarily due to the age and iconoclastic ideals of its proponents. Derozio and his students held a view of Hindu society as corrupt, oppressive, and idolatrous at its core—in a word, antimodern. They pushed for a complete rejection of Hinduism and a break from the cultural past that produced its primary institutions.

The Deists of the Brahmo Samaj (Society of God) on the other hand, following the teachings of their spiritual leader, Ram Mohan Roy and his successor, Debendranath Tagore, found much to admire in Hindu thought. They promoted a sometimes monistic and sometimes monotheistic religion grounded in the Upanishads and modern Deistic ideas about the power of reason to unlock the revelatory mysteries of nature. They embraced the idea of a nameless God who did not intervene miraculously in the affairs of human beings. The Brahmos rejected idolatry, caste, the traditional Hindu belief in divine *avatars* (incarnations of deity), and the supreme authority of any given scripture. Though they differed in their interpretations regarding the useful-ness of religion qua religion, together, the atheists and the Brahmos shared an antipathy towards those aspects of Hinduism that they considered to be traditional, irrational, or embarrassingly premodern.

From the early nineteenth century until roughly the 1870s and 1880s, the primary conversation about modernization in India took place among unapol-ogetic proponents of religious reform. The terms of the conversation were laid out for the British-educated literati by the Derozians and Brahmos. God and religion were to be done away with or, if retained, forced to pass litmus tests regarding the reasonableness and social equity of any claims made by or about them. Hindu modernizers from roughly the 1820s through the 1860s, like their European and North American counterparts, searched for ways to make Hin-duism acceptable to British Enlightenment standards. The most common way of achieving this aim was to move away from dualistic and *theistic* (personal-ist) understandings of God with their attendant (and thoroughly 'irrational') devotional rituals, institutions, leaders, behaviors, and beliefs.

Something began to change, however, after the failed political and military rebellion of 1857 when the British crown took official possession of India as a legal subsidiary to be ruled from the royal ministries of Whitehall in cen-tral London. In the decade after the so-called Sepoy Mutiny, many *bhadraloka* intellectuals began to feel a growing sense of despair about the prospects of achieving social and political parity with their British overlords. At the same time, the disciplinary pressures and petite bourgeois demands of daily life in the urban metropolis of Calcutta began to weigh heavily upon the minds of the educated middle classes. Indian civil servants, small shop owners, teachers, lawyers, and mercantile agents were forced to serve under British managers and patrons. They had to follow British customs of dress and comportment, speak in English, read English newspapers and observe the disciplines of western 'clock-time.' In order to survive under colonial rule, middle-class Indians living in Calcutta were forced to embrace the consumerist and materialist underpin-nings of an urban culture of modernism that the demythologizing Enlighten-ment had brought to London, New York, Paris, Vienna, Cape Town, and Hong Kong as well as Calcutta. If the first half of the nineteenth century gave rise to a zeal and enthusiasm among the educated Indian population for all things modern and western (the term 'Renaissance' was often used to describe the period), the second half of that momentous century witnessed a disenchant-ment with the promises of the Enlightenment among many *bhadraloka* intel-lectuals. After a flurry of modernizing efforts attempting to purge traditional Hindu devotionalism of its embarrassing anachronistic elements in the first half of the nineteenth century, a new form of colonial devotional piety began to emerge in 1870s and 1880s India. This new form of colonial devotionalism or *bhakti* took note of modernizing pressures while explicitly rejecting or creatively inverting and coopting most of them. The change in attitude toward many traditional Hindu beliefs and practices such as image worship, reverence of *gurus*, and the mythological stories associated with Hindu deities marked a turning point in the development of modern Hinduism—one that witnessed the revalorization of Hindu theism in a way that would forever transform what it meant for an educated person to be both modern and Hindu.

Colonial India and Modernity's Challenge to Hindu Theistic Piety

Bhakti movements in India date back at least to the early centuries before the turn of the Common Era. Vaishnava, Shaiva, and Shakta traditions achieved particular cultural salience in the medieval and premodern periods as Hindus developed sophisticated theistic philosophical, ritualistic, and mythological traditions to support the worship of various deities. The *puranas* (sacred mythology) of the first millennium CE and the vernacular devotional literature of the early second millennium CE developed in response to the growing desire of Hindus to worship a personal God who was knowable and cared about the everyday lives and fates of individual devotees. There had always been non-dualistic understandings of Godhead that developed in parallel with the *bhakti* traditions, but the dominant mode of Hindu belief and practice for the two millennia before the coming of the modern era focused upon a complex gestalt of daily ritual adoration of a personal deity, fealty to a *guru* or priest, prayer, dietary laws, customary caste observance, and participation in traditional lifecycle rites. Hindu families of various theistic stripes would typically have small shrines in their homes or at least have access to local temples and sacred spaces where one could commune with a personal deity through the process of *seeing* the divine through the ritual act of taking *darsan* (visual prayer) of a physical *murti* (sacred image) considered to be charged with divine energy if not embodying the physical incarnation of God Him/Herself.

It was this traditional theistic practice of *murti puja* (worship of an 'idol' or physical image) that especially troubled the reformers of the nineteenth century. The 'father of Modern India' himself, Ram Mohan Roy (1772–1833), wrote: 'I have never ceased to contemplate with the strongest feelings of regret, the obstinate adherence of my countrymen to their fatal system of idolatry, inducing, for the sake of propitiating their supposed Deities, the violation of every humane and social feeling.'(Sharma 2002: 40) Roy, the first of a coterie of modernizers to take Hinduism explicitly and intentionally in the direction of Deism and a Unitarian-inspired Vedantism, expressed most coherently the embarrassment that he felt regarding traditional Hindu devotional piety:

> . . . We [Roy and his acolytes] reject Idolatry in every form and under whatsoever veil of sophistry it may be practiced, either in adoration of an artificial, a natural, or an imaginary object. The divine homage which we offer, consists solely in the practice of *daya* or benevolence towards each

other, and not in a fanciful faith or in certain motions of the feet, legs, arms, head, tongue or other bodily organs, in pulpit or before a temple. (Sharma 2002: 54–55)

Roy's views were typical of the educated *bhadraloka* reformers of the early to mid-nineteenth century. The modernizers of the Brahmo Samaj and other groups who favored non-dualistic or Deistic understandings of God held a very dim view of traditional Hindu *bhakti*. It is therefore all the more remarkable that by the 1870s and 1880s, large numbers of *bhadraloka* revivalists and disgruntled middle-class colonial functionaries began to embrace traditional forms of *bhakti* faith and practice.

Why the renewed interest in *bhakti* during the latter three decades of the nineteenth century? The answer most probably lies distally in the anomie associated with modern life for the *bhadraloka* mentioned above. The cold and hypertrophic rationalism of a pampered French *Philosophe* might prove satisfactory to single-minded scholars and professional curmudgeons, but it rarely helps ordinary human beings to make sense of life in times of acute existential need. As the pseudonymous writer A. Hindustani described the situation of colonial office workers in 1874:

> What with files of dockets to write, statements to give and accounts to examine, what with the impatience and excitability of his superiors manifesting themselves in those somethings called 'blowings up,' is it any wonder that the Babu [*bhadraloka* intellectual] is tired of his existence, and curses the day of his birth? (A. Hindustani 1875: 326)

The social and psychological pressures that educated Indians suffered under the colonial dispensation called for religious valves of release. The theistic *bhakti* revivalists of the 1870s and 80s provided these valves by developing new ways of talking about *bhakti* that appealed to a generation weaned on the mother's milk of Enlightenment 'reason.'

Proximally, the allure of *bhakti* most likely arose from the disrupted social and political modernizing projects embraced by the *bhadraloka* before the brutal quashing of the rebellion of 1857. After a decade of sorting out the social and political consequences of Crown rule in India—a decade that saw the development of the Imperial Civil Service (1858) and the implementation of the Indian Penal Code (1862)—the emerging middle class in postrebellion India turned away from the old enthusiasm for British modernizing efforts and entered an introspective phase. With little control over the political destiny of India, the *bhadraloka* reformers began to turn their energies and attention inward toward areas of social life where they could have some measure of influence free of British interference. To put it simply, the Enlightenment bloom was off the colonial rose after 1857 and middle-class modernizers needed to rethink the degree to which religious modernization had to be accomplished according to a European model.

The revivalists who turned their attentions toward traditional modes of Hindu piety in the 1870s and 1880s argued forcefully in favor of an independent trajectory of modernity for Hindu India that did not necessarily follow the European path toward secularization. Hinduism was seen by many who turned to theistic *bhakti* as the birthright of a nation that had been colonized and stripped of her traditional religious piety. In the 1870s and 1880s, we see the rise of increasingly nationalistic understandings of Indian identity rooted in the sphere of religious affiliation. Although theists were not the only religious modernizers to deploy nationalistic rhetoric in their reclamation of Hindu traditions after the rebellion of 1857, they were very adept at drawing distinctions between modernization and westernization as social forces at work on the Indian subcontinent.

Preoccupations with ridding Hinduism of 'superstition' and 'irrationality' through the denigration of the mythological traditions associated with various deities, the elimination of 'idolatry' and the suppression of faith or nonratiocinative ways of *knowing* were perceived by *bhakti* revivalists as colonial attacks on Hindu/Indian culture rather than as natural byproducts of modernization per se. The fact that Enlightenment ideals regarding the 'Age of Reason' had come to India through the auspices of colonial rulers and British-educated reformers gave the *bhakti* revivalists of the late nineteenth century pause; for how does one draw a clear distinction between the idiosyncrasies of eighteenth-century European rationalism and the more sweeping historical concept of modernity as such? Were the scientific, economic, political, social, philosophical, and theological ideas brought to India in the first half of the nineteenth century 'modern' ideas? Western ideas? Both? Neither? These are the sorts of questions that discontented *bhadraloka* revivalists began to ask themselves as they took a second look at the traditional *bhakti* movements that were by and large neglected by early reformers.

Vaishnava Bhakti and Revivalism—1870s–1880s

Although the rustic *Shakta* devotionalism of the very popular Hindu saint, Sri Ramakrishna Paramahansa (1836–1886), attracted many during the period, the major recipient of the *bhadraloka* revaluation of *bhakti* in Calcutta during the 1870s and 1880s was the tradition of Bengali Vaishnavism. Breakaway groups of middle-class revivalists turned away from the cold colonial rationalism of the Enlightenment toward more mystical and homespun religious frameworks in the 1870s and 1880s and they turned primarily to the religion of Krishna *bhakti*.

Leaders like Keshub Chandra Sen (1838–1884), Bijoy Krishna Goswami (1841–1899), and Bankim Chandra Chattopadhyay (1838–1894) emerged to direct the energies of modernity's discontented Hindus interested in *theistic* Vaishnavism. But the most significant and renowned *bhadraloka* proponent of Bengali Vaishnava revivalism was the fierce advocate of *bhakti* devotionalism, Bhaktivinoda Thakura (1838–1914). In late nineteenth century, Bengal

Bhaktivinoda Thakura utilized emerging technologies and 'western'-inspired institutions in order to recover and reappropriate a Vaishnava heritage that provided an alternative to, and in some cases rendered obsolete, both the Christianity of the British missionaries as well as the secularist modernizing agenda of the colonial bureaucratic establishment. Bengali Vaishnavism (theistic devotion to Krishna) during the eighteenth and nineteenth centuries had developed an unfortunate but widespread image as a degenerate and disreputable form of religion. Colonial missionaries and *bhadraloka* reformers saw in it the paradigmatic expression of Hindu licentiousness and degradation. Local Brahmans and those of privileged social status considered it to be an aberrant and 'unorthodox' form of traditional caste-Hinduism. So too, Vaishnavism found itself under attack from the harbingers of post-Enlightenment rationalism (indigenous and exogenous) who chose to deem all but the most ratiocinative forms of religion to be anachronistic and regressive.

Again, Ram Mohan Roy's critique of Krishna *bhakti* proves illustrative of reformer and modernist opinion regarding Vaishnavism in the first half of the nineteenth century:

> I begin with Krishna as the most adored of the incarnations [*avatars*], the number of whose devotees is exceedingly great. His worship is made to consist in the institution of his image or picture, accompanied by one or more females, and in the contemplation of his history and behavior, such as his perpetration of murder upon a female of the name of Putana; his compelling a great number of married and unmarried women to stand before him denuded; his debauching them and several others, to the mortal affliction of their husbands and relations; his annoying them, by violating the laws of cleanliness and other facts of the same nature. (Sharma 2002: 48)

If Bengali intellectuals in the nineteenth century faced the same general concerns that most religious practitioners in the modern era worry about—the legitimacy of an anthropomorphic understanding of deity; the purported existence of nonmaterial beings like devils, demons, and angels; reports of miracles and miraculous stories; and the efficacy of ritual—Hindu revivalists like Bhaktivinoda Thakura added to the general list of modern religious 'concerns' more specific issues peculiar to Vaishnavism such as the idolatry of image worship (*murti puja*), the licentious nature of mythological portrayals of Krishna, suspicion of the motives of Vaishnava *gurus* and *goswamis* (holy men), fears of corruption and racketeering at sacred Hindu pilgrimage sites, suspicion of ecstatic/nonrational religion and faith more generally, and a discomfort with the lack of scriptural traditions within Hinduism.

In order to confront the negative opinions of his modernizing compatriots, Bhaktivinoda Thakura established a printing press in 1878 in order to disseminate his message of Vaishnava revivalism. His strategy was not simply about printing books but using those books, with a mix of tracts and a monthly Vaishnava journal, in order to construct a community of like-minded and like-acting religious *bhadraloka* devotees who, through their printed texts, could participate in a revitalized Vaishnava world that had been denied them by the harbingers of Hindu modernity in the first century of British-Indian colonial interaction. Through the medium of print, individuals in remote locations could, for the first time in India, read identical texts thus allowing for a standardization of doctrine previously unattainable in Bengali Vaishnavism. One of Bhaktivinoda's first publications was a commentary upon the *Chaitanya Charitamrta* (considered by Bengali Vaishnavas to be the single most comprehensive and concise repository of Bengali Vaishnava doctrine) wherein he laid out the manner in which the text was to be interpreted. This was followed by the publication of innumerable documents expounding Bhaktivinoda's own brand of Vaishnava philosophy and practice. The act of publishing his works accomplished (at least) three things: 1) it resystematized Bengali Vaishnava doctrine and the bases of ritual; 2) it established a new form of centralized authority; and 3) it afforded a large number of people access to the very same systematized and centralized Vaishnavism that was now rooted in the urban center of Calcutta. In short, Bhaktivinoda engaged himself in a familiar modernist project—that of imagining a pure, ancient, and authoritative religious tradition that both provides meaning, context, and orientation for middle-class individuals while at the same time mirroring the sociocultural interests of their particular class position. But unlike the reformers before him, Bhaktivinoda embraced image worship, the importance of traditional Hindu *gurus*, and the authority of the supposedly 'scandalous' *Puranic* myths that so vexed Ram Mohan Roy and his acolytes.

Before the advent of the printing press in Bengal, Vaishnava thought and practice were decentralized and, for many, inaccessible. But through the printed medium, Bhaktivinoda was able to take advantage of the age-old Vaishnava emphasis on literacy by exploiting the ability of texts to structure consciousness in a dispersed population. The printing press extended an old practice of Vaishnava scholarship and commentary, but it magnified its import many times and became one of the new bases for sanctioning authority. In this way, the lay community (i.e. literate members of the Bengali *bhadraloka*) could participate in a larger community of devotees through print even though not physically present.

In a beautiful religious tract, based upon a speech that he gave in 1869, Bhaktivinoda addressed the rationalist reformers' criticisms of the *Puranic* literature associated with Krishna. He argued that most *bhadraloka* critics of Krishna had not actually read the *Bhagavata Purana*—a central Bengali Vaishnava text outlining the life-story of Krishna along with the major theological tenets of the tradition.

> The *Bhagavat* has suffered alike from shallow critics both Indian and outlandish. That book has been accursed and denounced by a great number of our young countrymen who have scarcely read its contents and

pondered over the philosophy on which it is founded. It is owing mostly to their imbibing an unfounded prejudice against it when they were in school. The *Bhagavat*, as a matter of course, has been held in derision by those teachers, who are generally of an inferior mind and intellect. (Bhaktivinoda Thakura 1998: 8)

Acknowledging the challenges against Krishna *bhakti* leveled by India's most famous modernizer, Ram Mohan Roy, Bhaktivinoda fired back:

Raja Ram Mohan Roy, the founder of the sect of Brahmoism, did not think it worth his while to study [the *Bhagavata Purana*]. . . . He crossed the gate of the Vedanta . . . and chalked his way out to the Unitarian form of the Christian faith, converted into an Indian appearance. (Bhaktivinoda Thakura 1998: 7)

In his many written works, Bhaktivinoda Thakura defended traditional religious practices like *murti puja*. Rather than rejecting mythological texts replete with miracle stories and fantastic tales associated with the physical manifestation of Krishna on the earthly plane in Vrindavana, Bhaktivinoda embraced the extraordinary and the magical. He argued that there are certain truths—Eternal Truths—that can only be glimpsed through the lenses of faith and devotion. He acknowledged the power of rationality to solve practical problems on the material plane, but he argued that religion should not be boxed within the limits of reason alone. If one could not understand how Krishna could have condescended to take birth in the realm of human beings and to have behaved in unpredictable ways, then one was simply applying the wrong criteria to the question of incarnation and manifestation. Similarly, the modernist's difficulty with accepting the possibility of divine manifestation in physical objects and images (*murtis*) was due to a lack of imagination and faithful intuition. Idolatry ceased to be an issue for Bhaktivinoda and his followers because they accepted the mystery at the heart of *murti puja* and argued that it made logical sense to accept the premise that, if Krishna exists as an all-loving God who wants to enter into relationship with His devotees, then if makes perfect sense that He would provide a means through which devotees could engage him physically in the material realm. If one considered the problem of so-called idolatry through the eyes of faith, then one could understand the internal logic of a ritual procedure that appeared pointless to nonbelievers. Faith (*shraddha*) was the key, according to Bhaktivinoda, to unlocking the door of religious experience—an experience that was desperately needed by a generation of rationalists who had mistaken the prejudices of Enlightenment atheists and Deists for truth itself. Bhaktivinoda argued that there are modes of reasoning available to the religious devotee not bound by hypertrophic rationality per se but perfectly consonant with its demands when premised upon different (i.e. nonmaterialist) foundations.

Conclusion

Bhaktivinoda's revivalist arguments with the reformers and modernizers who preceded him are telling to the historian of religions because they reveal a great deal about the contested nature of appropriate religious expression in the modern age. Bhaktivinoda was able to draw many followers to his quasi-fideistic way of thinking precisely because of the tensions and contradictions inherent in modern society itself. He was able to use logic and reason against proponents of logic and reason. He was adept at appropriating modern technologies and institutions like the printing press and voluntary societies in order to propagate ideas and practices that many *bhadraloka* intellectuals considered to be antimodern or traditionalist. By doing so, Bhaktivinoda marked out a path of theistic religious modernization that represented an independent trajectory of modernity that challenged the models presented by Enlightenment thinkers from Europe and early nineteenth-century Bengal alike. As one of several important revivalists from the 1870s and 1880s, Bhaktivinoda Thakura stands out as an exemplar of the types of arguments and strategies deployed by *bhadraloka* thinkers as they reclaimed traditional Hindu theistic devotionalism (i.e. *bhakti*), making it a legitimate path of religious aspiration in the colonial period.

Summary

The *theistic embarrassment* that many educated Americans and Europeans feel today regarding religious beliefs and practices deemed to be un-Enlightened or anachronistic is not new. Hindu modernizers in nineteenth-century India faced many of the same challenges and asked the same questions about the legitimacy of theistic devotion that we do today. And like Americans and Europeans today, the culture of educated Hindu India divided sharply along fault lines dividing religious 'progressives' from 'conservatives.' Many of the most significant Hindu reformers in the first half of the nineteenth century responded progressively to colonial modernizing pressures dictated by a foreign power by updating Hinduism along lines that blurred the distinction between westernization and modernization. Progress, westernization, and modernization were understood to be synonymous. Relegating God to a Deistic clock-maker or an impersonal cosmic force that lies at the ground of all Being had the advantage of obviating the sorts of challenges leveled at Hindu piety by critics from Roy to Derozio to Macaulay. But when the social and political circumstances became less favorable to *bhadraloka* hopes and aspirations following the rebellion of 1857, the hyperrationalist agendas of the early modernizers proved not entirely satisfactory to many disaffected Hindus looking for meaning and purpose in life. The anomie that gripped *bhadraloka* intellectual circles in the 1870s and 1880s demanded a new (old?) type of religion that nourished the soul as well as the mind. There was a feeling among many that something had been lost through the reformers' indiscriminate intermingling of Enlightenment ideas and progressive modes of Hindu religious expression. The Hindu revivalism of the 1870s and 1880s emphasized conservatism over progress and the nationalization of Hinduism over the westernization of Hinduism. Accommodations had to be made in order for *bhakti* movements in a modern context to thrive, but for revivalists like Bhaktivinoda Thakura and his Vaishnava coreligionists, modernization could be mapped out along a different trajectory than that laid out for Hinduism by Christian missionaries, Enlightenment rationalists, and reform-minded pandits who saw little place for traditional theistic piety in a 'modern' India. The revalorization, acceptance, and propagation of traditional devotional paths in the latter three decades of the nineteenth century proved influential and critical to the formation of Hindu nationalist identities, the reevaluation of the relationship between European Enlightenment ideals and Indian religious practice as well as the reconsideration of the relative values and porous boundaries between faith and reason within the context of an independent trajectory of Hindu modernity. By the end of the nineteenth, century the debate over what it means to be modern and religious had been engaged in full by India's cultural elites and that battle continues today. Given our own situation in modern-day North America and Europe, we have much to learn from the example of colonial India.

Discussion Questions

- What was at stake in colonial Hindu debates over the worship of images or 'idols'? Why is idolatry so troubling to 'reason' and the modern mind?
- How can the rise of *bhakti* revivalism be seen as a reaction to other sorts of reform-oriented changes taking place within colonial Hinduism?
- What are the similarities and differences between reformist and revivalist approaches to the modernization of Hinduism?
- Does it make sense to speak of *bhakti* movements as providing an 'escape valve' for the Bengali intelligentsia facing the challenges of an oppressive colonial regime and limited avenues to economic well-being?
- In what ways might modern *bhakti* movements contribute to Hindu nationalism (or a separatist communalism) either intentionally or unintentionally?

Suggested Readings

Fuller, Jason (2003). 'Re-membering the Tradition: Bhaktivinoda Thakura's "Sajjanatosani" and the Creation of a Middle-Class Vaisnava Sampradaya in Nineteenth-Century Bengal.' In *Hinduism in Public and Private: Reform, Hindutva, Gender, Sampradaya* (pp. 173–210). Ed. Antony Copley. New Delhi: Oxford University Press.
A good place to find more detailed information about Bhaktivinoda Thakura and the modernization of Bengali Vaishnavism in late nineteenth-century India.

Hatcher, Brian A. (2008). *Bourgeois Hinduism, Or the Faith of the Modern Vedantists: Rare Discourses from Early Colonial Bengal.* New York: Oxford University Press.
The first work on modern Hindu developments in the nineteenth century to take the issue of class seriously in our understanding of *bhadraloka* religious innovations.
Sarkar, Sumit (1998). *Writing Social History.* New Delhi: Oxford University Press.
Important collection of essays by a leading historian of colonial Calcutta; see especially the essay, 'Kaliyuga, Chakri and Bhakti: Ramakrishna and His Times' (pp. 282–357).
Sharma, Arvind (2002). *Modern Hindu Thought: The Essential Texts.* New Delhi: Oxford University Press.
An excellent collection of primary sources related to reform and revival movements from Ram Mohan Roy to Jiddu Krishnamurti.
Smith, David (2003). *Hinduism and Modernity.* Oxford: Blackwell Publishing.
Provides theoretical context for thinking about *modernity* as an intellectual construct applicable to the Indian case

Bibliography

Appadurai, Arjun (1996). *Modernity at Large: Cultural Dimensions of Globalization.* Minneapolis: University of Minnesota Press.

Basu, Shamita (2002). *Religious Revivalism as Nationalist Discourse: Swami Vivekananda and New Hinduism in Nineteenth-Century Bengal.* New Delhi: Oxford University Press.

Bayly, Susan (1999) [2001]. *Caste, Society and Politics in India from the Eighteenth Century to the Modern Age.* Cambridge: Cambridge University Press.

Beckerlegge, Gwilym (2000). *The Ramakrishna Mission: The Making of a Modern Hindu Movement.* New Delhi: Oxford University Press.

Berger, Peter L. (1967). *The Sacred Canopy: Elements of a Sociological Theory of Religion.* New York: Anchor Books.

Bhattacharya, Tithi (2005). *Sentinels of Culture: Class, Education, and the Colonial Intellectual in Bengal.* New Delhi: Oxford University Press.

Broomfield, John H. (1968). *Elite Conflict in a Plural Society: Twentieth-Century Bengal.* Berkeley: University of California Press.

Chatterjee, Partha (1993). *The Nation and Its Fragments.* Princeton: Princeton University Press.

Dalmia, Vasudha (1999). *The Nationalization of Hindu Traditions: Bharatendu Harishchandra and Nineteenth-Century Banaras.* New Delhi: Oxford University Press.

Dirks, Nicholas (2001). *Castes of Mind: Colonialism and the Making of Modern India.* Princeton: Princeton University Press.

Farquhar, J.N. (1967) [1914]. *Modern Religious Movements in India.* Reprint ed. Delhi: Munshiram Manoharlal.

Fuller, Jason (2003). 'Re-membering the Tradition: Bhaktivinoda Thakura's "Sajjanatosani" and the Creation of a Middle-Class Vaisnava Sampradaya in Nineteenth-Century Bengal.' In *Hinduism in Public and Private: Reform, Hindutva, Gender, Sampradaya* (173–210). Ed. Antony Copley. New Delhi: Oxford University Press.

——— (2005). 'Reading, Writing, and Reclaiming: Bhaktivinoda Thakura and the Modernization of Gaudiya Vaishnavism.' *Journal of Vaishnava Studies* 13, No. 2: 75–94.

———— (2009). 'Modern Hinduism and the Middle Class: Beyond "Reform" and "Revival" in the Historiography of Colonial India.' *Journal of Hindu Studies* 2, No. 2 (November): 160–178.

Guha, Ramachandra (1995). 'Subaltern and Bhadralok Studies.' *Economic and Political Weekly* 30, No. 33: 2056–2058.

Gupta, Shiv Kumar (1991). *Arya Samaj and the Raj (1875–1920)*. New Delhi: Gitanjali Publishing House.

Halbfass, Wilhelm (1988). *India and Europe: An Essay in Understanding*. Albany: State University of New York Press.

Hatcher, Brian A. (1999). *Eclecticism and Modern Hindu Discourse*. New York: Oxford University Press.

———— (2006). 'Remembering Rammohan: An Essay on the (Re)emergence of Modern Hinduism.' *History of Religions* 46, No. 1: 50–80.

———— (2007). 'Bourgeois Vedanta: The Colonial Roots of Middle-Class Hinduism.' *Journal of the American Academy of Religion* 75, No. 2: 298–323.

———— (2008). *Bourgeois Hinduism, Or the Faith of the Modern Vedantists: Rare Discourses from Early Colonial Bengal*. New York: Oxford University Press.

Hawley, John Stratton (2001). 'Modern India and the Question of Middle-Class Religion.' *International Journal of Hindu Studies* 5, No. 3: 217–225.

Hay, Stephen, ed. (1988). *Sources of Indian Tradition Volume II*. New York: Columbia University Press.

Heimsath, Charles (1964). *Indian Nationalism and Hindu Social Reform*. Princeton: Princeton University Press.

Hindustani, A. (1875). 'The Great Want of the Babu Community.' *The Bengal Magazine* 3: 326–332.

Jones, Kenneth (1976). *Arya Dharm: Hindu Consciousness in Nineteenth-Century Punjab*. Berkeley: University of California Press.

———— (1990). *The New Cambridge History of India Volume III, No. 1: Socio-Religious Reform Movements in British India*. Cambridge: Cambridge University Press.

Jordens, J.T.F. (1997) [1978]. *Dayananda Sarasvati: His Life and Ideas*. New York: Oxford University Press.

Joshi, Sanjay (2001). *Fractured Modernity: Making of a Middle Class in Colonial North India*. New Delhi: Oxford University Press.

Kopf, David (1969). *British Orientalism and the Bengal Renaissance: The Dynamics of Indian Modernization 1773–1835*. Berkeley and Los Angeles: University of California Press.

———— (1979). *The Brahmo Samaj and the Shaping of the Modern Indian Mind*. Princeton: Princeton University Press.

Llewellyn, J.E. (1993). *Arya Samaj as a Fundamentalist Movement: A Study in Comparative Fundamentalism*. New Delhi: Manohar Publishers and Distributors.

Ludden, David, ed. (1996). *Contesting the Nation: Religion, Community and the Politics of Democracy in India*. Philadelphia: University of Pennsylvania Press.

Majumdar, B.B. (1967) [1996]. *History of Indian Social and Political Ideas: From Rammohun to Dayananda*. Calcutta: Firma KLM.

Marshall, P.J. (2006). *Bengal: The British Bridgehead: Eastern India (1740–1828)*. Cambridge: Cambridge University Press.

McGuire, John (1983). *The Making of a Colonial Mind: A Quantitative Study of the Bhadralok in Calcutta, 1857–1885*. Canberra: Australian National University.

Misra, B.B. (1961). *The Indian Middle Classes: Their Growth in Modern Times*. London: Oxford University Press.

Ray, Rajat Kanta, ed. (1995). *Mind, Body and Society: Life and Mentality in Colonial Bengal*. Calcutta: Oxford University Press.

Raychaudhuri, Tapan (1999). *Perceptions, Emotions, Sensibilities: Essays on India's Colonial and Post-colonial Experiences*. New Delhi: Oxford University Press.

Sarkar, Sumit (1983). *Modern India 1885–1947*. Delhi: Macmillan.

——— (1998). *Writing Social History*. New Delhi: Oxford University Press.

——— (2002). *Beyond Nationalist Frames: Postmodernism, Hindu Fundamentalism, History*. Bloomington: Indiana University Press.

Schiffrin, Andre, ed. (1997). *The Cold War and the University: Toward an Intellectual History*. New York: The Free Press.

Sen, Amiya P. (1993). *Hindu Revivalism in Bengal 1872–1905: Some Essays in Interpretation*. New Delhi: Oxford University Press.

———, ed. (2005). *Social and Religious Reform: The Hindus of British India*. New Delhi: Oxford University Press.

Sharma, Arvind (2002). *Modern Hindu Thought: The Essential Texts*. New Delhi: Oxford University Press.

Smith, David (2003). *Hinduism and Modernity*. Oxford: Blackwell Publishing.

Thakura, Bhaktivinoda (1998) [1869]. *The Bhagavata: It's Philosophy, Ethics and Theology*. Kovvur, Andhra Pradesh: Sri Ramananda Gaudiya Math.

Waghorne, Joanne (2005). *The Diaspora of the Gods: Modern Hindu Temples in an Urban Middle-Class World*. New York: Oxford University Press.

6 Hinduism and Colonial Law

Donald R. Davis, Jr. and Timothy Lubin

Imagine a US government suddenly swept away by a commitment to animal rights that sought to ban the consumption of turkey at Thanksgiving or prohibit the proverbial Christmas goose. To those who relish meat on religious holidays, such a law would threaten a tradition that many closely connect with their religious lives. The motivation behind the law might be noble, even ethically justified, but the sense of intrusion into a sacred habit would remain all the same. We can imagine that some people would just ignore the law and find ways to carry on eating meat; others would no doubt follow the new law, placing adherence to the law or commitment to the nation or their respect for the government above religious commitments. We can imagine meat eaters coming up with vigorous and creative ways to defend the centrality of the practice, perhaps including recourse to scriptural authority or theological arguments in support of the ritual meal. Even those who chose to abstain would almost certainly feel compelled to find ways to argue that meat eating had never been essential to American Thanksgiving celebrations. In either case, we can imagine the eventual emergence of a very different version of the Thanksgiving holiday.

Even though the particular scenario imagined above is thoroughly grounded in American experience, it serves to illustrate in very general terms the sort of predicaments created for Hindus by virtue of colonial legislative and judicial actions. Thanks to the intrusion of colonial administrative bureaucracy and legal processes, Hindus found themselves compelled to wrestle with a variety of issues that struck at the heart of their religious and cultural identity and served to reshape many practices central to Hindu life. In some cases, as with the fictional example of meat eating at Thanksgiving, arguments arose regarding the classification and enumeration of what constituted the essential characteristics of Hinduism. As colonial legislators, lawyers, judges, and Hindu reformers wrestled with such questions, the impression arose that Hinduism itself stood in need of definition and more clearly demarcated boundaries. What should count and what was essential in Hinduism were questions that colonial law forced upon the minds of both Indians and colonizers. Moreover, this history raises broader questions about the proper role of government in relation to religion and religious institutions. When is it desirable or necessary for a government to intervene in religious matters? Can religion ever be a purely private matter? The intrusion of colonial power into Hindu social life was profound, often explicit, and regularly challenged in ways that help us see the complexities of answering such questions. Two important social locations of Hindu religious life are the household and the temple. By tracing legal actions related to these two areas, we can acquire an overall sense of the changes wrought on modern Hinduism.

The major transformation of Hinduism under colonial law was this: a wide variety of Hindu practices and institutions were regulated for the first time by the general laws of a state. Aided by Indian social reform movements, colonial law helped to create a homogenous, unitary conception of Hinduism within which internal differences were hard to recognize. Initially, the British legal policy in India was intended to be as unobtrusive as possible, a policy in effect of 'noninterference.' This principle, established in Warren Hastings's *Judicial Plan* of 1772, was invoked to justify the publication of the 1776 *Code of Gentoo Laws*.[1] Aiming to promote 'every Circumstance that may conciliate the Affections of the Natives, or ensure Stability to the Acquisition,' the translator of the *Code* proposes that 'Nothing can so favourably conduce to these two points as a well-timed Toleration in Matters of Religion, and an Adoption of such original Institutes of the Country, as do not immediately clash with the Laws or Interests of the Conquerors' (Halhed 1776: ix). In spite of this policy, during two centuries under British authority, religious practices were subjected to governmental control in a way that they had never been before. Many of these practices had long been the subject of debate and dispute within Hindu communities, but the use of state law to settle those disputes was in most cases new.

Hindu religious law, known as Dharmashastra in Sanskrit, had existed for more than two thousand years when the British established a formal colonial presence in India. Like Jewish law, Canon law, and Islamic law, these treatises (Shastra) on religious and legal duty (*dharma*) represented a scholastic law transmitted by the elite class of Brahmins. This means that a scholarly class separate from the state was responsible for the preservation and elaboration of laws pertaining to daily life, crime, ritual practice, inheritance, corporations, rites of passage, penances, and a myriad other topics that collapse the firm boundaries we sometimes make between religion and law. Brahmin scholars of Dharmashastra had to navigate between the recognized authority of the scholastic textual tradition and the acceptance of customary law (*achara*) as practiced among diverse communities (in fact, awareness of this distinction exists even in the scholastic texts). The existence of a great many Hindu groups alongside the Brahmins meant that in its textual form, Hindu law never encompassed or governed anything close to the whole of the Hindu community, even if it provided a symbolic point of reference for many Hindus (who might like to seal an argument by claiming: 'It's in the shastra!'). Being primarily concerned with the elite classes of Brahmins and royalty, texts on Hindu law found their greatest direct purchase within those same communities; even so, the texts did, in variable ways, also influence the legal and religious thought and practice of other groups lower in the social hierarchy. In daily practice, however, law and religion tended to be organized through local councils and corporate groups (such as guilds, caste groups, temples, military organizations, etc.) with the scholastic texts serving only as a background of legal and religious consciousness. Understanding this, it is possible to appreciate what it meant when the early colonial administrators chose to identify the texts of Dharmashastra as the center of Hinduism. In effect, they created a new and distinct personal law that came to be called 'Hindu law' and which was to be administered in state courts.

It goes without saying that states and governments had existed in India long before the British colonial period (1757–1947). These states and governments were also involved in various ways with religious and legal institutions and practices. Major temples were built, maintained, and staffed with patronage from the king or other individuals at court, with the expectation that support would be sustained (or that at least the endowments would be recognized) by later rulers. Sanskrit texts and public inscriptions provide evidence that kings were expected to judge disputes, including those involving religiously defined statuses and rights, and even to ensure that penances prescribed by religious authorities were actually performed. When the East India Company first came to power, they assumed a similar set of roles, taking over the management of temples and pilgrimage places, adjudicating temple-related disputes, and overseeing caste matters—just as earlier rulers had done (Appadurai 1981).

One important difference would become manifest during the colonial period. While precolonial political entities engaged, patronized, and contended with religious institutions and practices, they almost never made laws specifically to regulate them. Initially, the British adopted the same policy, in keeping with an official policy not to interfere with the religious practices of Indians. They sought to distance themselves from what they took to be religious matters, for instance declining to interfere in caste council rulings 'unless some civil and proprietary right was alleged to have been violated' (Derrett 1968: 291). Here, in effect, castes were treated as analogous to private clubs in England; they were organizations over which courts had no jurisdiction so long as fundamental rights are not violated. Over time, however, the policy of nonintervention was put to the test, especially as evangelical Christian voices in Britain questioned the propriety of their government giving tacit support to what were thought to be heathen superstitions. By the first quarter of the nineteenth century, the policy of noninterference began to be violated in a piecemeal fashion, as colonial administrators sought to regulate aspects of Hindu religion that were deemed harmful to society and the body politic, or to suppress customs that offended British views of equity and natural law. Many educated Hindus who began to internalize Western attitudes toward religion also tended to share these British attitudes and became themselves active supporters of religious reform. In could be said that modern Hinduism emerged through the force of governmental legal power and educated Hindu opinion operating in tandem to 'reform' Hindu institutions and practices. This is, in fact, the focus of several excellent studies of what scholars now refer to as the 'colonial construction of Hinduism' (see Viswanathan 2003; King 1999). Since the complex processes involved in this construction are addressed across many of the chapters in this volume, the particular focus of this chapter will be on the role of colonial law in directly and indirectly transforming Hinduism through acts of legislation and adjudication.

Hindu Households and Women

Many colonial interventions bearing on religion concerned social practices that in precolonial India would have been seen as matters of custom with support among various communities. To British observers, however, especially those back in London, many of these customs came to be stigmatized as violations of basic decency or of natural law. This rendered them fit in the British mind to be regulated in the interests of sound governance. Several of these customs, such as 'suttee' (or widow immolation) were treated as 'crimes peculiar to India,' and, these in particular, the colonial state sought to suppress (Stokes 1887: vol. 1, 7). Many also had to do with the status and treatment of women. In fact, scholars have recently argued that the distinctive character of what came to be called 'Anglo-Hindu law' was defined and justified under the rubric of 'protecting women' (Mani 1998; Williams 2006; Sturman 2010). The gendering of reform under conditions of colonial patriarchy thus needs to be acknowledged, since, as Gayatri Spivak has boldly argued, many legal attempts to transform Hinduism reflected the attempt by 'white men to save brown women from brown men' (1988: 296).

The first religious rite to be banned by the British was 'suttee,' a relatively uncommon practice in which a widow was immolated on the funeral pyre of her husband. On the basis of certain contentious passages in some medieval Hindu legal texts (Brick 2010), defenders of the practice argued that it represented a voluntary act of moral heroism on the part of the widow. In fact, it was through this act that the wife proved herself 'a holy woman' (*satī*, whence the English term 'suttee'). Real-life *satī*s were commemorated in legend and received worship at memorial sites that still dot the countryside. Historical evidence also suggests that women used *satī* (or the threat of it) for political manipulation and for the expression of their cultural role as 'husband-protector' (Moran 2014). The British, like most Indians, found the practice repugnant and suspected (not without reason) that, in practice, such immolations were often acts of despair, social pressure, or coercion rather than of piety. Suttee was thus readily classed with human sacrifice as a monstrous form of barbarism. Following a campaign by the reform-minded Bengali Brahmin Rammohun Roy (whose own sister had 'become a *satī*'), the Governor-General, Lord Bentinck succeeded in having suttee criminalized in Bengal under Regulation VII of 1829. Suttee was thus the first successful justification for colonial legal intervention in Hindu religious practice. Today, some view the ban in terms of an attempt by the British to bolster their power by promoting a noble cause, remarking that apart from this legal intervention, the colonial government showed little concern for actual widows (Mani 1989).

Widows once again served as a focus for legal control in the debate over widow remarriage. In 1855, Ishvarchandra Vidyasagar, another Bengali reformer, marshaled scores of traditional Sanskrit texts to argue for a law permitting widows to remarry, a practice contrary to many regional customs in India. The public influence of his writing enabled the colonial administration under Lord Dalhousie to legalize widow remarriage with Act XV of 1856, despite the vocal objections of Hindu traditionalists. Vidyasagar's work reflected both the traditional domain of innovative Sanskrit commentary and the emerging colonial view that Hindu scripture, rather than custom, should guide the framing of laws (Hatcher 2012: 44–47). As such, it further cemented the growing colonial legal habit of defining Hindu law and, by extension, Hinduism solely through textual sources. Moreover, Vidyasagar's style of argumentation depended on what might be called 'caste-based law' in that he excluded from consideration the numerous non-Brahmin communities among whom widow remarriage was in fact already accepted. By advocating a policy solely directed toward the officially sanctioned rules of Bengali Brahmins, Vidyasagar effectively subsumed all Hindus (and Hinduism) under the authority of the Brahmin. One result of this was that the customary legal practices of Hindus increasingly came to be seen as in fact legally different from colonial Hindu law (Derrett 1963a: 12–13). This led to the ironic situation in which Hindus found themselves compelled to prove the legitimacy of a custom before British judges by attacking the validity of the very Anglo-Hindu law that was recognized by the colonial government. Put simply, the validity of Hindu customs had to be proven by demonstrating they were not Hindu law! We can begin to see that what counted as Hinduism under colonial law began to have very little to do with what actual Hindus actually did. Colonial knowledge of Hindu law, grounded in reliance on textual 'codes' thus carried more weight than what Hindus themselves expressed in the British courts.

The remarriage of widows was only one of several major changes to the legal parameters of Hindu marriage toward the end of the nineteenth century. The Special Marriage Act (Act III of 1872) opened the path for secular marriages of a form where both bride and groom had disavowed any religious affiliation. However, it also banned polygamy and marriage of girls under fourteen, while further guaranteeing rights to widow remarriage and intercaste marriage. The Brahmo Samaj, a reform movement intending to purge the idolatrous rituals from the spiritual devotion of Hinduism, had pushed for passage of this legislation. For many, however, Act III represented a rupturing of the intimate connection between ritual and marriage in Hindu communities; as a result, the legitimacy of these marriages was questioned in social circles, despite colonial efforts to treat marriage as a civil and contractual matter (Majumdar 2009: 167ff.).

That said, customary differences continued to be recognized in marriage legislation by the British; courts would often inquire into such practices so that the particular rituals surrounding marriage continued to find a place within legislative acts. However, this should not be seen as evidence that the British worked to preserve the diverse customary practices associated with Hindu marriage. Even if diverse marriage rituals continued to be performed according to local, customary laws, the legal recognition granted to Brahminical, or high-caste, ritual forms nonetheless worked to standardize Hindu marriage rites such that 'practices that had historically been the exclusive privilege of the high castes were in the colonial courts interpreted as normative and extended to lower castes as well' (Sturman 2010: 95). In some cases, as in the Indian Penal Code of 1861, the law went so far as to criminalize certain lower-caste practices of divorce and remarriage. In the major codification of the Hindu Marriage Act (1955), references to specific interpretations of kin relationships, conditions for divorce, and the specific rite of *saptapadi* ('seven-steps') should be seen not as the culmination of British effort to secularize marriage, but rather as proof of the colonial attempt to limit Hindu marriage procedures and practices to one legally preferable form (Sreenivas 2004: 940; Sturman 2010: 101).

The fact that courts have required such ritual acts as the seven steps, ritual fire offering (*vivahahoma*), and the formal gift of the bride (*kanyadana*) as elements 'essential for solemnizing a Hindu marriage' (Agnes 2001: 87) only further bolsters the claim that colonial law worked to promote one specific form of Hinduism. The symbolism of that legally preferable form has had far-reaching consequences in television and film portrayals of marriage. In spite of the continued existence of many diverse rituals across India and abroad, the trend has undeniably been toward a standardization of Hindu marriage practices in a form that closely resembles those 'essential elements' identified in either current or historical statutes of Indian law.

Related to marriage laws, and often included within them, were acts regarding the legal age of consent for both marriage and sex. The controversial Age of Consent Act of 1891 raised the age of consent for sexual intercourse from ten to twelve for girls (whether married or unmarried). Many Hindu leaders and journals viewed this bill as the first major intrusion of the colonial government into the religious affairs of the Hindus. In this respect, these outcries point to the emergence during the late nineteenth century of concerted nationalist resistance to colonialism in the name of Hinduism (Sarkar 1993). Hindu leaders beginning with Lokamanya Tilak and ending with Sir Romesh Chunder Mitter, a member of the Legislative Council, argued on the one hand that the Age of Consent Act undercut traditional Hindu law; on the other hand, they argued that if positive social change was a desired end, it could not be achieved through the passage of laws (Heimsath 1962). Subtle arguments about the distinction between marriage and consummation were made to acknowledge the immorality of sex with prepubescent girls, especially in the practice of child marriage. The Sharda Act of 1930 reaffirmed the minimum ages of fourteen and eighteen for bride and groom respectively, while the now-amended Hindu Marriage Act of 1955 has raised these to eighteen and twenty-one. Even so, these limits have remained so controversial that they have rarely been enforced, even down to the present day (Derrett 1963a).

Finally, whether directly or indirectly, many of the practices relating to women and marriage involved questions of family property. Among many examples, one of most direct changes with respect to the practice of Hindu inheritance came in the Religious Disabilities Removal Act of 1850 (Cassels 2010: 256–272). The stated purpose of the act was to protect the inherited shares of any member of the family, even those who had renounced their religion or fallen from caste. In other words, the Act sought to ensure that religious preference would not be used to determine an individual's rights to a share in family property. The law was passed in the face of vigorous protest that it contravened existing Hindu personal law; it was subsequently upheld judicially in 1851. In this case, as in so many colonial cases, the judge invoked the principle of 'justice, equity, and good conscience' as justification for interfering in the existing norms of Hindu society (Derrett 1963b). This principle was the legal mechanism by which most innovations and changes to the law governing Hindus were introduced or upheld.

Hindu Temple Practices and Institutions

Beyond the household (and especially the place of women within it), the other major Hindu institution that drew the attention and reforming energies of the colonial authorities was the temple. A particular target of British scorn was the temple dancer, a special case of a wider tradition of dancer–concubines who performed in royal courts. Temple dancers were women dedicated in childhood to be a 'servant of God' (*devadasi*) in a temple; their service took the form of dancing before the divine image as part of the regular offering cycle. The rite of dedication was modeled on the wedding ceremony, and insofar as such women were considered to be married to the deity, they would not take a human husband. They were allowed, however, to form nonmarital relationships with priests or other men. It was this last circumstance that led the British to condemn the practice as a form of prostitution. In spite of this harsh view, no direct effort was made to legislate against it, even in the Indian Penal Code. As a result, it was left to the colonial courts to establish the criminality of what was referred to as 'temple harlotry,' this concept being from a contemporary perspective 'a pure judicial invention' (Parker 1998: 562).

Cases involving temple dancers often centered on questions of family status and inheritance disputes. Dancers in a particular temple tended to organize themselves like a Hindu joint family, and colonial observers increasingly treated the temple dancers as a sort of caste, even if it represented a peculiar kind of caste since these women controlled their property and their daughters were allowed to inherit (Parker 1998: 571). Relatedly, it was not uncommon for temple dancers to adopt daughters, even if this practice was routinely rejected by court-appointed pandits, who argued on textual grounds that the Dharmashastras did not recognize the adoption of girls.[2]

The issue of 'adoption' of daughters raised other questions: were they adopted, kidnapped, or had they been sold? Did it matter, legally, if they were forced into the sex trade? Although it might be assumed that the British authorities would frown upon slavery and prostitution, as we have seen, after 1772, they committed themselves to applying 'native laws' as far as the maintenance of public order would permit. Moreover, until 1833, the three administrative divisions of British India (the Bengal, Madras, and Bombay presidencies) were fully independent legislatively. At first, 'Mahomedan' (or Muslim) criminal law was the general norm (except in places like Bombay, where a separate Hindu criminal code was applied to Hindus). Up to this point, prostitution among minors was not recognized as a crime; the rights of the guardian alone were protected. However, in the wake of an important case (*Govt. v. Golab Peshagur*, 6 R.N.A. 4, 1841), the sale of a child into prostitution was eventually criminalized in Bengal in 1853. In addition, slavery was officially abolished in India by Act V of 1843. Soon thereafter, the notorious 'Monghyr case' (*Govt. v. Mussamut Amirun*, R.N.A. 343, 1858), dealing with the life-long 'leasing' of two infants to a prostitute, generated sufficient outrage that the prostitution of minors was specifically outlawed with the passage of the Indian Penal Code of 1860, which was applied throughout British India.

British courts reached diametrically opposed conclusions in relation to *devadasis*. On the one side, in the *Mathura Naikin* decision of 1880, they judged that the temple dancer offered 'the injurious example of a flagrant and prosperous immorality' that was deemed inimical 'to what mankind, in general, have learned to recognize as the highest conception of social progress and happiness' (*Mathura Naikin v. Esu Naikin*, 4 Bom. 545, 1880, at 549). On the other hand, the *Mathura Naikin* decision was challenged by those who argued against judicial activism; critics warned against judges who presumed to discern the 'nobler' sentiments of a judicially constructed generic 'Hindu' community. Critics also recognized the adoption of dancers as a heuristically valid 'caste custom' in the eyes of most Hindus in Madras (*Venku v. Mahalinga*, 11 Mad. 393, 1889). An important irony emerges from such debates: a law that on its face intended to protect the interests of a vulnerable section of the populace was applied in such a way that it served to limit their rights. As a result, temple dancers had to resort to significant legal contortions in order to be recognized under the law as a legitimate 'caste' or as a kind of 'temple officiant' rather than as a 'mere veil' for trade in prostitution.

British legal interference in Hindu temple and festival practices, however, extended well beyond the status of temple dancers. An early problem facing the British was the traditional pilgrim tax levied by political rulers to facilitate festivals and holy days at major temples in places like Puri and Tirupati (Cassels 2010: 319–337). For some forty years, colonial officers were charged with collecting taxes from visiting pilgrims; in exchange, they were called upon to arrange the labor—in some cases of up to 30,000 individuals—required to prepare both the central ritual processional and the necessary accommodations for hundreds of thousands of pilgrims. By 1840, this close involvement of the colonial government in the functioning of Hindu temples was brought to an end through the combined religious pressure of Christian evangelicals and the force of rumored corruption.

Meanwhile, there were other Hindu religious practices that the British sought to suppress outright, either through legislation or in the courts. Among the most controversial were those rituals dubbed 'hook-swinging,' which were common both in south India and Bengal. In general, hook-swinging represented a rather more spectacular form of what might be called 'votive piercing.' In this non-Brahmanical observance, devotees were pierced in the back and limbs by large hooks and suspended or swung before crowds, in fulfillment of a vow to a particular deity (Shiva, Murugan, or a village goddess), as part of a pilgrimage, or for the health or prosperity of one's village (Oddie 1995: 28–48, 61). Efforts by missionaries and reform-minded Hindus to discourage the practice met with great opposition, since the performances had broad-based financial and social support from the public, from temple officiants, and (in Bengal especially) some urban elites. At first, legal interventions were only piecemeal, with the government issuing orders relating to specific regional festivals that they justified on the grounds of safety and public welfare (despite the fact that no specific injuries were ever documented). Eventually, despite Queen Victoria's Proclamation of 1858 that promised freedom of religion in India, hook-swinging was banned in Bengal in 1865 and in Madras in 1894.

Nor was interference in religious practice limited to the suppression of ostensibly injurious or immoral activities. From early in the nineteenth century, the colonial state claimed the right and responsibility to oversee religious institutions themselves. Three regulations passed in 1810 (Reg. XIX of Bengal), 1817 (Reg. VII of Madras), and 1827 (Reg. XVII of Bombay) officially recognized the duty of the three respective presidencies to undertake the financial administration of Hindu temples, mosques, and other public institutions (Baltutis 2005: 456; see also Presler 1987). Moreover, forty-two laws passed in 1820, known as 'Bruce's Code,' regulated the wealthy Tirupati temple complex in south India (Kumari 1998). These laws are important for marking early colonial intervention in Hindu religious endowments. However, just as Christian groups in England had protested against British management of pilgrimages and festivals, they also agitated against any official role in the maintenance of 'idolatrous' religious institutions. As a result, efforts were made to cede supervision of religious endowments to governmentally recognized groups. The matter took on a new complexion after the so-called Indian Mutiny of 1857 and the subsequent official incorporation of the East India Company's territories within the British Empire. What followed was a shift in the official treatment of religion. For instance, the Religious Endowments Act (Act XX of 1863) sought to scale back government involvement in temple administration by creating boards of trustees staffed by Indians and devolving such functions to them (Ganapathy Iyer 1905). In practice, the law was unpopular and proved to be unwieldy (Frykenberg 2000). In an attempt to rectify the situation, the Religious Societies' Act (Act I of 1880) was introduced with the goal of simplifying the creation, operation, and dissolution of temple boards; a secondary purpose was to further distance the government from direct responsibility in such matters. By 1925, many states in colonial India had adopted proactive legislation intended to curb temple mismanagement and the misappropriation of funds, including provisions for the creation of boards of trustees who would assume oversight of temples.

It is worth noting in this context that the involvement of precolonial Indian states in the affairs of temples was both long-standing and well-attested (Kane 1930–1962: vol. 2, 912–914; Derrett 1968: 489, 508). As the primary patrons of temples, Hindu kings held a vested interest in the proper maintenance and operation of the temples they endowed. Viewing colonial interventions in temples as a case of continuity, Derrett has argued that the colonial legislation pertaining to Hindu religious endowments had 'little if any' effect on religion and that the regulations could 'hardly affect the notion of religion held by the mass of the people' (1968: 508–509). Somewhat ironically, however, Derrett identifies one major change to Hinduism under colonial law, namely that even if state involvement with temples was nothing new, the role of the colonial state in determining what counted as Hinduism was something new: 'the State has selected for the citizen an approved path from amongst several formerly possible paths, and has made it worth his while to keep to that path' (1968: 510). In fact, this comment may be taken to apply as much to the regulation of religious endowments as to the development of Hindu personal law or the reform of social practices. While Derrett is right to suggest that individual Hindus and temples experienced little disruption to their worship practices, the state's control of temple administration and finances gathered all public Hindu temples under one umbrella, thereby furthering the notion that Hinduism was one single thing. For the state to select one particular way to regulate temples and enforce that regulation across India weakened or denied all other existing ways of managing temples and conducting worship. As a result, what were once considered temples to singular deities like Venkateshvara or Guruvayurappan became for legal purposes simply 'Hindu' temples. This homogenization of difference is a big part of the colonial transformation of Hinduism that can be directly traced to developments in the area of law and official policy.

Hindu Law and the Personal Law System

Undergirding the social reformation of Hindu households and temples through colonial law was the development of Hindu personal law as a distinct body of law separate from that of Muslim personal law. The idea that religious communities should have separate personal laws applicable to matters such as marriage, adoption, and inheritance and that these laws should be administered by the official courts was one way the British sought to manage the complex religious landscape of India. There were other models they might have adopted, such as the *millet* system of the Ottomans, in which religious communities (Muslims, Jews, and Christians) were allowed to administer their own laws. The British decision to create a separate Hindu personal law would prove to be just as consequential as the other reforms and innovations they introduced. In order to determine the character of 'Hindu law,' the British privileged textual sources in Sanskrit along with the opinions of a narrow range of elites, such as Brahmin pandits. In point of fact, while pandits were employed in colonial courts until 1864, as early as 1828, the procedural law enacted in colonial courts had ceased to rely on such 'native law officers' in favor of looking to a body of substantive 'Hindu law.' In the process, case law amassed in India and even case law from Britain began to supersede the opinions of Indian legal experts. This selective and textually oriented approach to resolving highly charged questions of inheritance and family property had the effect of channeling the varied norms and practices of existing Hindu communities into a singular law recognized by the courts. Even though differences in custom were in theory admitted, getting a custom recognized by the court was rendered difficult due to the stringent judicial litmus tests put in place by the British.[3] We see that even a well-intentioned attempt by the British to administer 'native law' served to elevate singular forms of Hindu law to the exclusion of a myriad other legal norms (Lariviere 1989). Debates over the continued use of Hindu law in contemporary India persist, though, today, we notice that the politics have shifted in surprising ways. If the colonial era found traditional Hindu pandits opposed to the codification of Hindu personal law, in postindependence India, we find certain Hindu nationalist parties arguing for the creation of a Uniform Civil Code (Narula 2010). In the latter case, Hindu nationalist groups, aggrieved by what they take to be excessive concessions granted to Muslim personal law (a claim pressed forcefully in connection with the Shah Bano case during the 1980s), have taken to arguing that the only solution is a single code binding on all citizens (see Kishwar 1986).

A fundamental question that emerges when considering the issue of Hindu personal law is who counts as a Hindu? Even if one is able to find an uncontentious way to answer that question, a further thorny question arises: what should be the legal status of someone who converts either to or from Hinduism? The issue is unavoidable, since India's colonial personal law system requires litigants in the area of family law to be identified before the court in order for the appropriate personal law to be applied. Determining which law applies to litigants who happen to have converted to a new religion became a point of frequent contention, generating thousands of cases during the colonial period. Whether articulated directly or not, there is a presumption that the judge in any such case will have some idea of how to identify 'Hinduism.' As soon as the judge renders a decision about the *legal* identity of a person, this immediately entails a decision about that person's *religious* identity; this becomes of necessity a decision about the boundaries of the religion itself. Typically, the view of Hinduism presumed in such cases favors a Hinduism that avows one God (even if with many aspects), the philosophy of Vedānta, the devaluation of caste and image worship, and the centrality of belief in *karma* and *moksha*. If this has become one dominant way of understanding modern Hinduism among middle- and upper-class Hindus (both in India and in the diaspora), then we are now able to see the role played by colonial legislation and official court decisions in fostering this unitary view of Hinduism.

Conclusion

From the perspective of current legal and social sensibilities, the regulation of Hindu institutions and practices by the British colonial state poses an important dilemma. On the one hand, it is easy to feel sympathy with colonial efforts to ban exploitative practices like child marriage, widow ostracism, and caste discrimination. On the other hand, we are far less comfortable with the idea of interfering with socially harmless religious practices like pilgrimages, festival processions, or image worship. And yet all of these were targets of colonial legal regulation in connection with the concept of 'Hindu' practices. The question is where do we draw the line? What criteria can governments legitimately use to intervene in the sphere of religion? All modern states intervene and regulate religious institutions and practices to some extent. In fact, it can be argued that colonial-era legal reforms actually became the basis for the 'ameliorative' posture of secularism enshrined in the constitution of independent India (Jacobsohn 2005). Regardless of how we view this matter, we can at least appreciate the historical legacy of colonial legal interventions in the area of religion.

The colonial regulation of religion clearly helped foster the legal view that *all* religion is a private matter, something to be based primarily on scriptural foundations and delimited by in terms of clearly defined beliefs. Readers will see in this a decidedly modern, Protestant Christian view of religion. This serves to demonstrate that the growth of large, bureaucratic, modern states—whether in the colony or the metropole—have entailed the emergence of a particular (and particularly European) concept of religion. The case of Hinduism is particularly acute, since, as we have seen, colonial law helped ushered into existence a unified conception of Hinduism that has spread far beyond the court and legislature. As other chapters in this volume attest, there were many factors contributing to this process of unification, but clearly colonial legal regulation was prominent among them. Beyond this, it is important to note how colonial law contributed to the privatization of religion in general, since the historically successful attempt in Europe and the United States to relegate religion to the private sphere (hence removing it from politics and government) has been challenged in other regions of the world. Today, the privatization of religion is contested not just in South Asia, but elsewhere in the world by so-called conservative or fundamentalist religious movements. An important source of this as-yet-unresolved tension in modern political life was the application of colonial law to the regulation of Hindu religion.

Summary

Legal administration in British India consisted of a long-term effort to bring the law-making and law-applying institutions of Hindu societies (and of other communities) under the power and authority of the colonial state. This chapter examines transformations of religious practice in Hindu households and temples, as well as the formation of Hindu personal law. The colonial intention not to interfere in indigenous religious life nonetheless required knowledge of the legal limits of Hindu religious practice and of Hindu identity. The colonial desire to standardize Hindu law and make it uniform across India inevitably distorted or suppressed the lived plurality of Hinduism's regional and customary traditions. In the end, colonial law promoted an abstract, unified, and modernized form of religion we now refer to as 'Hinduism.'

Questions for Discussion

- What policy did the British adopt in 1772 with respect to the existing laws and religions of India? What were the consequences of that policy?
- How did the imposition of colonial law in India contribute to a more unified understanding and practice of Hinduism?
- What areas of Hindu religious practice were most affected by the legal changes that occurred under colonialism?
- What can we learn from the history of Hinduism and colonial law about the proper role of law and state governance in relation to religion?

Acknowledgments

The authors would like to thank Indrani Chatterjee for reading this chapter at a critical juncture and providing helpful suggestions, only some of which we were able to integrate.

Notes

1 'Gentoo' (from the Portuguese *gentio*) was an early term employed by British administrators and other Europeans to speak of the 'gentiles' or 'heathen' as opposed to the Muslims of South Asia.

2 There were exceptions. One senior pandit of the Chief Court of Appeal (Sudder Adalat) of Madras determined that in such cases the only thing that mattered was 'whether [the adopted girl] had been recognized by the said individual as her daughter, such recognition in the instance of dancing girls sufficing to constitute adoption without any formal act of adoption' (*Vencatachellum v. Vencatasamy*, S.U. Madras 65, 1856).

3 The story is too complex to be told here in detail (see Derrett 1968: 225–320).

Suggested Readings

Derrett, J. Duncan M. (1968). *Religion, Law and the State in India*. London: Faber.

Galanter, Marc (1989). *Law and Society in Modern India*. Delhi: Oxford University Press.

Lariviere, R. W. (1989). 'Justices and Panditas: Some Ironies in Contemporary Readings of the Hindu Legal Past.' *Journal of Asian Studies* 48, No. 4: 757–769.

Lubin, Timothy, Donald R. Davis, Jr., and Jayanth Krishnan, eds. (2010). *Hinduism and Law: An Introduction*. Cambridge: Cambridge University Press.

Mallampalli, Chandra (2010). 'Escaping the Grip of Personal Law in Colonial India: Proving Custom, Negotiating Hinduness.' *Law and History Review* 28, No. 4: 1043–1066.

Bibliography

Agnes, Flavia (2001). *Law and Gender Inequality: The Politics of Women's Rights in India*. Delhi: Oxford UP.

Appadurai, A. (1981). *Worship and Conflict under Colonial Rule: A South Indian Case*. Cambridge: Cambridge University Press.

Baltutis, Michael (2005). 'Recognition and Legislation of Private Religious Endowments in India Law.' In *Religion and Law in Independent India* 2nd ed. (pp. 443–467). Ed. R. E. Baird. Delhi: Manohar.

Brick, David (2010). 'The Dharmaśāstric Debate on Widow-Burning.' *Journal of the American Oriental Society* 130, No. 2: 203–223.

Cassels, Nancy Gardner (2010). *Social Legislation of the East India Company: Public Justice versus Public Instruction*. New Delhi: Sage.

Derrett, J. Duncan M. (1963a). *Introduction to Modern Hindu Law*. London: Oxford University Press.

——— (1963b). 'Justice, Equity and Good Conscience.' In *Changing Law in Developing Countries* (pp. 114–153). Ed. J.N.D. Anderson. London: George Allen & Unwin.

——— (1968). *Religion, Law and the State in India*. London: Faber.

Frykenberg, R. E. (2000). 'The Construction of Hinduism as a "Public" Religion: Looking Again at the Religious Roots of Company Raj in South India.' In *Religion and Public Culture: Encounters and Identities in Modern South India* (pp. 3–26). Eds. K. E. Yandell and J. J. Paul. Richmond, Surrey: Curzon.

Ganapathy Iyer, Pudukota (1905). *The Law Relating to Hindu and Mahomedan Religious Endowments*. Madras: Scottish Press.

Halhed, Nathaniel Brassey (1776). *A Code of Gentoo Laws*. London: [East India Company].

Hatcher, Brian A. (2012). 'Introduction.' In *Hindu Widow Marriage*. Trans. Brian A. Hatcher. New York: Columbia University Press.

Heimsath, C. H. (1962). 'The Origin and Enactment of the Indian Age of Consent Bill.' *Journal of Asian Studies* 21, No. 4: 491–504.

Jacobsohn, G. J. (2005). *The Wheel of Law: India's Secularism in Comparative Constitutional Context*. Princeton: Princeton University Press.

Kane, P. V. (1930–1962). *History of Dharmaśāstra*. 5 vols. Poona: Bhandarkar Oriental Research Institute.

King, Richard (1999). *Orientalism and Religion: Post-Colonial Theory, India and 'The Mystic East.'* London: Routledge.

Kishwar, Madhu (1986). 'Pro Women or Anti Muslim? The Shah Bano Controversy.' *Manushi* 32: 4–13.

Kumari, N.K. (1998). *History of the Hindu Religious Endowments in Andhra Pradesh*. New Delhi: Northern Book Centre.

Lariviere, R.W. (1989). 'Justices and Panditas: Some Ironies in Contemporary Readings of the Hindu Legal Past.' *Journal of Asian Studies* 48, No. 4: 757–769.

Majumdar, Rochona (2009). *Marriage and Modernity: Family Values in Colonial Bengal*. Durham: Duke UP.

Mani, Lata (1989). 'Contentious Traditions: the Debate on Sati in Colonial India.' In *Recasting Women: Essays in Colonial History* (pp. 88–126). Eds. K. Sangari and S. Vaid. New Brunswick: Rutgers UP.

——— (1998). *Contentious Traditions: The Debate on Sati in Colonial India*. Berkeley: University of California Press.

Moran, Arik (2014). '"The Rani of Sirmur" Revisited: *Sati* and Sovereignty in Theory and Practice.' *Modern Asian Studies* 49, No. 2: 302–335.

Narula, Smita (2010). 'Law and Hindu Nationalist Movements.' In *Hinduism and Law: An Introduction* (pp. 234–251). Eds. T. Lubin, D.R. Davis, Jr., and J. Krishnan. Cambridge: Cambridge University Press.

Oddie, G.A. (1995). *Popular Religion, Elites and Reform: Hook-Swinging and its Prohibition in Colonial India, 1800–1894*. New Delhi: Manohar.

Parker, Kunal M. (1998). '"A Corporation of Superior Prostitutes": Anglo-Indian Legal Conceptions of Temple Dancing Girls, 1800–1914.' *Modern Asian Studies* 32, No. 3: 559–633.

Presler, F.A. (1987). *Religion under Bureaucracy: Policy and Administration for Hindu Temples in South India*. Cambridge: Cambridge University Press.

Rocher, Rosane (2010). 'The Creation of Anglo-Hindu Law.' In *Hinduism and Law: An Introduction* (pp. 78–88). Eds. T. Lubin, D.R. Davis, Jr., and J. Krishnan. Cambridge: Cambridge University Press.

Sarkar, Tanika (1993). 'Rhetoric against Age of Consent: Resisting Colonial Reason and Death of a Child-Wife.' *Economic and Political Weekly* 28, No. 36: 1869–1878.

Spivak, Gayatri Chakravorty (1988). 'Can the Subaltern Speak?' In *Marxism and the Interpretation of Culture* (pp. 271–313). Eds. Cary Nelson and Larry Grossberg. Chicago: University of Illinois Press.

Sturman, Rachel (2010). 'Marriage and Family in Colonial Hindu Law. In *Hinduism and Law: An Introduction* (pp. 89–104). Eds. T. Lubin, D.R. Davis, and J. Krishnan. New York: Cambridge.

Stokes, Whitley (1887). *The Anglo-Indian Codes*. 2 vols. Oxford: Clarendon Press.

Sreenivas, Mytheli (2004). 'Conjugality and Capital: Gender, Families, and Property under Colonial Law in India.' *Journal of Asian Studies* 63, No. 4: 937–960.

Viswanathan, Gauri (2003). 'Colonialism and the Construction of Hinduism.' In *Blackwell Companion to Hinduism* (pp. 23–44). Ed. Gavin Flood. Oxford: Blackwell.

Williams, R.V. (2006). *Postcolonial Politics and Personal Laws: Colonial Legacies and the Indian State*. New Delhi and New York: Oxford University Press.

Part III
Movements and Relocations

7 Hinduism in Fiji, Mauritius, South Africa, and Trinidad

Anantanand Rambachan and Usha Shukla

This chapter will outline the present situation in the field of Hindu religious practice in the Diaspora—specifically the nineteenth-century diaspora of indentured Indians who were transported from India to mostly British colonies in the South Pacific (Fiji), Indian Ocean Islands, and adjacent African countries, as well as islands in and countries contiguous to the Caribbean. We encounter the stories of the Hindus of Fiji, Mauritius, South Africa, and Trinidad, focusing in particular on the descendants of the original nineteenth-century indentured laborers. It will become clear that each location has its own unique story to tell, shaped by such factors as the place of origin of Hindu migrants, the time and conditions of their emigration and the sociopolitical milieu of their 'new homelands' (Younger 2009).

The abolition of slavery worldwide in 1833, followed by the emancipation of slaves, created an enormous shortfall in the labor supply to the English plantation owners, other farmers and a variety of government services in all of these localities. The system of indentured labor was developed to address this shortfall, and, in time, it would become something like a 'new system of slavery' for many Indians (see Tinker 1974). Labor contracts for indentured male workers were generally issued for a period of five years (three years for women). At the end of this period, the laborers could choose to reindenture themselves, return to India, or take up some independent occupation. A significant proportion of migrant workers chose to return to India after completing the conditions of their contracts.

Mauritius was the first destination for Indian laborers, who began migrating there in 1834. It would also be the destination that received the largest number of migrants all told. Fiji was the latest of the destinations, with migration commencing in 1879 (see table on next page).

The factors influencing emigration were many. Circumstances in India created what is known as a 'push factor' that encouraged young and older men and women to venture across the 'black waters' (*kala pani*) to pursue a better life. In several instances, force was employed and misleading information provided by recruiting agents. Economic push factors were dominant reasons for emigration: poverty, famines, landlessness, and lack of employment made

Major Movement of Indentured Labor

Name of Colony	Years of Immigration	No. of Immigrants	Indian Population in 1969
Mauritius	1834–1900	453,063	520,000
British Guiana	1838–1916	238,909	257,000
Trinidad	1845–1916	143,939	360,000
Jamaica	1845–1915	36,412	27,951
Natal, South Africa	1860–1911	152,184	614,000
Suriname	1873–1916	34,304	101,715
Fiji	1879–1916	60,965	241,000

(Adapted from Lal, 2000: 75)

indenture a welcome proposition. Exploitation and abuse of women (especially young widows) in the patriarchal system also drove many hapless women to brave the challenges of indenture (Bahadur 2013). Some laborers migrated out of a love for adventure, while others were fleeing the hands of British law for their involvement in the 1857 uprising. In the main, however, emigrants were seeking to escape from the devastating effects of frequent famines in the North Indian provinces of Agra, Oudh, and Bihar. In many cases, industrious recruiters also advertised a number of what might be called 'pull' factors, including such things as the prospect of wealth, decent work conditions, and the opportunity for land ownership. Whether pushed or pulled, on the whole, migrants were hoping for a better life in new lands.

The principal ports of embarkation for new indentured laborers were Calcutta and Madras, although a good number also departed from Bombay. The majority of such laborers were drawn from the districts of the United Provinces and Bihar. Among the various North Indian dialects that traveled with these laborers into the diaspora, Bhojpuri (a dialect of Hindi) was the predominant one; it is still spoken by many elderly members of the North Indian community in places like Trinidad and South Africa, while both Bhojpuri and Hindi are still spoken in Fiji and Mauritius. Migrant workers from the south of India carried with them the languages of Tamil and Telugu to places like Mauritius, South Africa, and Fiji. In Fiji, the Tamil speakers were in the minority and arrived later. In time, Hindi became the *lingua franca* of all Indians.

While economic migrants often traveled with only meager belongings, all of them, whether from North or South India, carried with them significant elements of their religious tradition. These elements included aspects of what is sometimes referred to as the Great Tradition of Hinduism, centered on Sanskrit epic and ritualistic texts and intellectual or philosophical systems as well as a range of locally specific Little Traditions, which tended to be, regionally, quite diverse and were often only transmitted orally or through shared folk practices. Among the migrants were Brahmins, who represented the traditional repositories of Hindu learning and religious praxis. Additionally, following the rise of new Hindu organizations during the nineteenth century (like the Brahmo Samaj and Arya Samaj), representatives of new religious movements also found their way to the diaspora. As a result, diasporic Hinduism exemplifies the traces of both ancient Hindu values and traditions as well as the restructured approaches of these modern groups, which are sometimes labeled 'neo-Hindu' movements. This means that the expression of religious authority in diasporic Hinduism is diverse; local and international teachers, as well as traditional ritual specialists, all have roles to play. Meanwhile, the expressions of diasporic Hinduism flourish through a wide range of rituals, festivals, formal discourses, congregational worship, or literary and other artistic modes of expression. Descendants of the original indentured laborers feel a deep sense of pride and gratitude for the rich, religious heritage bequeathed to them by their ancestors who survived the physical, cultural, and economic challenges of the so-called *girmitiya* system (work taken on under the terms of a *girmit* or 'agreement'). Orthodox and reformed practices and beliefs persist and exist side by side in the diaspora.

Hinduism in the Diaspora

Hindu religious practices amongst communities long separated from India still closely resemble the traditions transported by the original migrants. Indentured laborers emigrated to the diaspora carrying with them their traditions, which took on particular valences in the diaspora. In most diaspora countries, the name 'Ramayana' refers not to the Sanskrit text composed by Valmiki but to the vernacular Ramacharitmanas of Tulasidas; hundreds of Tulasidas's verses and rhyming couplets in the Awadhi dialect of Hindi were committed to memory by North Indian migrants. As for the traditions contained in the Sanskrit texts, migrants relied mostly on the stories that had been passed on orally or by hand-written texts in their communities in India. Initially, printed texts were available only in very small numbers, in contrast to the present day when Indic texts are readily available in the diaspora, often with English translations. The wider availability of such printed texts has greatly facilitated new possibilities for understanding and practicing Hinduism in these countries. Apart from texts and stories, indentured laborers carried with them a range of worship and performance traditions, each again inflected in the tones and characteristics of their original home districts. The Satyanarayan Vrat Katha was recited in Sanskrit (generally learnt by rote) while expositions were given in various Hindi dialects. Today, the priests (most still Brahmins) are better trained, and, while reciting the text in Sanskrit, are likely to offer an English translation and commentary. The priests' embellishments to the Satyanarayan Vrat Katha have become something like hallmarks of local exposition. Ramlila performances in Trinidad, for example, creatively adapt dialogue and action to comment on local politics and other issues of contemporary concern. As with texts and performances, Hindus in the diaspora have also found ways to re-create and reconstruct the kinds of built spaces they required for temple ceremonies and other modes of congregational worship. Even with often very limited resources, Hindus in the diaspora found ways to preserve and transmit their traditions of worship.

Fiji

The Fiji *girmitiyas* left India at a time of political, cultural, and religious awakening. The *girmitiyas* tended to be drawn from rural peasantry in search of better opportunities (Lal 2000). The majority of them were firm in their beliefs and practices. As an example, we may refer to Brij Lal's account of his Aja, or paternal grandfather. In Fiji in the 1960s, he still maintained ancient practices of making water offerings to the Sun deity (*surya deva*), took the lead in discourses on the Ramayana and Bhagavata Purana, and led rituals for Satyanarayan Puja, Rama Navami, and Shivaratri and singing of *bhajans* (devotional songs). These are the typical, regular observances of devout Hindus of Hindi-speaking background.

Such Fijian Hindus, and other Indians, are descendants of the *girmitiyas* who arrived between 1879 and 1916. From 1931, other immigrants from India also settled in Fiji, contributing to the religious, cultural, and economic life of the people. The Fiji Hindus exhibit a sense of pride and ownership of their existence in Fiji. Their history has been characterized by struggle, resistance, confrontation, and contestation since the period of indenture, first against the colonial powers and later against the reformist the Arya Samaj because of its strong antiorthodoxy approach to certain Hindu rituals and beliefs. The core of the Fiji Indian population represents this ethos, and demonstrates their resilience in the face of new adversities, notably the political upheavals beginning in 1987. The Fijian Indian's adoption of Hindi, especially the local variant 'Fiji Hindi,' as the language of literary expression in all genres and communication, even with their indigenous Fijians (Kaibiti) compatriots, exemplifies their religiocultural tenacity.

As with indentured Indians throughout the diaspora, the Fijian Hindus did not receive support in their religious aspirations from the colonists or the government. The orthodox Sanatani Hindus were, on the other hand, challenged by the 'reformist' efforts of the Arya Samaj, which preached social equality and strict religious conformity to the ancient Vedas, to the exclusion of post-Vedic beliefs and practices. Such efforts, however met with little success, since even the government became wary of the Arya Samaj and its activism.

The majority of contemporary Fijian Hindus are of North Indian ancestry, with a smaller population of Tamils. The Tamils' specific ceremonies, e.g. fire-walking (Draupadi Amman), Kavady (Lord Muruga) and Karthigai Deepam, are observed at the largest South Indian Temple in the Pacific, at Nadi. They also celebrate other occasions such as Shivaratri, Rama Naumi, Krishna Janmashtami (birth of Krishna), and Diwali (festival of lights, marking the return of Rama to his capital, Ayodhya, after fourteen years in exile) with the other Hindus. Like all linguistic groups, Gujarati-speaking Hindus have their own distinct practices as well. Currently, there is a vibrant Hindu life in Fiji, with temples for regular worship and celebration of festivals like Diwali, Rama Naumi, etc. Home shrines are common and flags (Jhandi or Jhanda—to Hanuman in particular) are also visible in Hindu homesteads. Traditional, orthodox practices such as *murti puja* (worship through icons), and rites of passage such as birth, marriage, and death are widespread. The Arya Samaj is active, particularly in the educational field.

The Ramacharitmanas of Tulasidas is widely read and revered as the Fifth Veda in Fiji. The text received official recognition by the Fiji Courts as a scripture for official purposes and remains the authoritative religious text for Fiji Hindus. The elevation of the Ramacharitmanas to the status of Fifth Veda made the Arya Samaj's insistence on 'back to the Vedas' difficult to implement. The adoption of the Ramacharitmanasas as the Fifth Veda was championed by orthodox stalwarts such as Ram Chandra Sharma on the basis that the Fijian Hindus needed faith in a God whose experiences bore resemblance to their own rather than mere knowledge (Kelly 2001: 348). The identification of *girmitiyas* with Rama as fellow sufferer in exile is widespread, and is graphically illustrated by the Marga Geet (in Shukla 2011: 142). This powerful role of the Ramacharitmanas is felt in the moral, spiritual and anticolonial/antihegemonic struggles of the indentured Hindus. Ramayana recitals take place on Tuesdays and Fridays, with Ramayana Mandalis (groups) active in all Hindu communities. Rama Naumi (birth) is celebrated with great splendor. The offspring of the *girmitiyas* are continuing their religious traditions in the land of their birth with great dedication. The Ramacharitmanas and Rama Bhakti (devotion to Rama) provide ideal opportunities for communal worship (*satsang*). Such communal worship is a prominent feature of Hindu practice in diaspora communities.

Mauritius

The India Ocean countries of Madagascar and Mauritius are considered to be politically part of Africa. Madagascar has some Hindus, mostly in business. Mauritius constitutes the first modern Hindu diasporic community. Mauritian Hindus, of Bhojpuri, Tamil, Telugu, Gujarati, or Marathi extraction, brought the great/classical/brahmanical traditions and the little/vernacular/regional traditions. Reinforced by their languages, Hindu values and practices took root in Mauritius and continue to flourish today.

Mauritius exhibits the persistence and prevalence of traditional practices such as daily domestic and periodic pujas, observance of the major Hindu religious festivals, as well as rites of passage encompassing birth, marriage, and death. North Indians, particularly the Hindi/Bhojpuri speakers, observe Rama Naumi, Krishna Janmashthami, Shivaratri, Navaratri, Diwali, Holi, etc. Families host Shiva Puran and Satyanarayan Katha. The observance of fasts (*vrats*) as well as daily prayers in home shrines is common practice. Whilst major festivals are observed by most Hindus, some differ in name or significance. The Tamil community observes Kavady in honor of Lord Muruga, and fire-walking in honor of Draupadi. There are many temples representing the various lin-guistic groups and denominations. The ISKCON Temple preserves traditional temple practices and the Sanatan Dharma Temples Federation, which controls a number of temples, promotes the cause of the orthodox Sanatan Dharma. The Arya Samaj is one of the most active socioreligious organizations in Mau-ritius. Education and poverty eradication are the major 'extra ritualistic' activ-ities of the Arya Samaj in the country.

It is noteworthy that Mauritius is the only country in the world whose Par-liament researched, debated, and completed the construction of a Ramayana Centre in Mauritius through Act No.7 of 2001. Part of the motivation is that Rama's victory over Ravana is the victory of justice over injustice extended as the victory of the indentured laborers over their Colonial masters (Gopee 2003: 144). Rama is viewed as God incarnate and the Ramayana Centre is dedicated to upholding all the values and virtues of Rama and the Ramayana.

Hinduism in Mauritius is reinforced by the evolution of pilgrimage centers, sites such as the Mauritiuseshwar Nath Shiv Jyotir Lingam Mandir and the Ganga Talao, a lake sanctified as the Ganga, the sacred river of India. These holy places draw thousands of pilgrims from within Mauritius and adjoining countries. The faith and devotion of people create hierophants and centers of pilgrimage far away from the source of a specific religion. Mauritius has a close bond with India and is home to many religious organizations, local and international, as well as host to foreign scholars and gurus. Some of these are ISKCON, Arya Sabha, Sathya Sai Organization, Ramakrishna Mission, Mata Amritanandamayi, and Brahma Kumaris, with devotees across the linguistic divide. These supplement the work of the early organizations and temples. Political security and state support empower the Mauritian Hindus to flourish in their religio-cultural lives.

South Africa

Hinduism was first systematically introduced in the continent of Africa when *girmitiyas* from Calcutta and Madras landed in Durban in November 1860. South Africa has the largest concentration of Indians/Hindus outside India. Durban is the chief among South Africa's metropolitan areas (including Piet-ermaritzburg, Johannesburg, Pretoria, and Cape Town) that exudes the Hindu ethos throughout the year. The South African Hindus commenced temple building soon after completing their term of indentured service. Many Shiva, Mariamman, Lakshmi, and Vishnu temples were built by artisans trained in India. Examples would include the Shree Gopallal Temple in Verulam (1888), the Durban Hindu Temple (1898), the Mariamman Temple in Isipingo (1860s), and the Melrose Temple in Gauteng (ca. 1870s). Temple building continues as the community expands. The temple is the most important reli-gious destination after the home shrine. Priests, many of whom are India- or Sri Lanka-trained, perform the ritual worship at temples. Indian languages are closely linked with worship and scripture studies, and owe their continued existence to the flourishing of the religious tradition.

Radio and press releases, reports, and posters all draw attention to events such as Shivaratri, Holi, Rama Naumi, Hanuman Jayanti, and the New Year celebrations of the Hindi, Telugu, and Tamil communities in March/April. This is followed by Krishna Janmashtami, Navaratri, and Diwali observed by all Hindus. The birth festivals of Rama and Krishna create opportunities for the younger generation to participate in discourses and recitals in temples, halls, and radio, e.g. the Hindi station Hindvani. The major religious organizations such as Divine Life Society, Ramakrishna Mission, Chinmaya Mission, Sathya Sai Organization, and ISKCON observe most of the major festivals of the Hindu calendar. Denominational and linguistic boundaries are fading because of the pan-Hindu nature and appeal of the events as well as the multilinguistic membership of the organizations. The observation of Hanuman Jayanti by ISKCON emphasizes the broader Vaishnava and Hindu nature of its belief system. It explains the widespread worship of Hanuman as the 'great servitor of Lord Rama, the Supreme Personality of Godhead.' The popular Chariot Festival on the Durban Beachfront (based on the Jagannath Ratha Yatra of Puri, India) held every Easter weekend by ISKCON attracts thousands of people of all religio-cultural groups. The Durban Deepavali Festival organized by the South African Hindu Maha Sabha and sponsored by a major financial institution is also attaining iconic status. The Diwali festival is taking on a complete national character, and is hosted in other major centers, e.g. Cape Town and Johannesburg. Large numbers of Hindus and South Africans of other faiths attend these festivals and enjoy the broader cultural aspects of such celebrations in addition to the tradition-specific discourses and rituals. This is a growing feature of Hindu diaspora communities.

The Mariamman Festival during Easter at Isipingo, Durban likewise draws Hindus of all groups. The Kavady and fire-walking rituals are also spreading to all groups. The brahmanical goddesses Lakshmi, Saraswati, Parvati, Durga, and Kali enjoy equal status with the deities such as Mariamman, Gengaiamman, Draupadi, the major non-brahmanical mother deities. The three major denominations of Hinduism, viz the Vaishnavas, Shaivas, and Shaktas (goddess worship), are represented.

South African Hindus of all linguistic and denominational groups, including the Arya Samaj, observe their rituals and sacred occasions, daily prayers/rituals, including offering water to Surya (like Brij Lal's Aja in Fiji), periodic prayers like Satyanaryan Katha and Hanuman Jhanda, Surya Puran, Shiva Puran, Mariamman Prayers, Pitra Paksha, and Puratassi like the Mauritians and Fijians. In South Africa, Hindu praxis is highly visible, emphatic, and vigorous. The engagement with Rama devotion and recent trends in Hanuman and Shiva worship, with recitation of Chalisas (forty-couplet eulogies) and enormous statues built to Hanuman and Shiva in Durban and Benoni respectively, are significant. Tulasidasa's Ramacharitmanas, Hanuman Chalisa, Bajrang Baan, and the Hanuman Bahuk are drawing more devotees. In totality, Hinduism in present-day South Africa encompasses philosophy, devotion, and service.

South African Hindus exploit their freedom and economic empowerment to celebrate and propagate their culture. The existence of the religious organizations over the past fifty to sixty years, underpinned by institutions such as the Hindu Maha Sabha, Sanatan Dharma Sabha, Arya Samaj, South African Tamil Federation, Andhra Maha Sabha, and the Gujarati Parishad, ensure continuity and commitment as well as mend the financial, emotional, and physical ravages of apartheid. Scholars and teachers from South Africa and India have been regularly providing spiritual guidance to South African Hindus: a new trend is the advent of young Hindu missionaries from the western diaspora, Trinidad and the United States, who offer discourses on the Hindu texts and *bhajans*. The religious organizations and temples keep Hindus of all ages and groups informed and educated through their publications and programs. South African Hindus have experienced the elevating feeling of celebrating together. The annual Panchaupuja (Communal Prayers) observed in honor of Goddesses and other deities in many areas are still very well attended. The neo-Hindu movements emphasize unity and give all Hindus the opportunity to participate in religious activities.

Caste observation began to lose its relevance over the decades and is hardly adhered to these days. One even sees the emergence of non-Brahmin priests in some communities. The Arya Samaj has trained women priests and continues to do so. However, there are some who still prefer male Brahmin priests to perform their pujas. Many Hindu women deliver discourses on religion during *satsangs*, ceremonies, *pujas*, and festivals. Generally, devotees, irrespective of caste and gender, are allowed to worship in the shrines. Most parents accept marriages across castes. Prejudices at all levels appear to be less significant in the Hindu community today.

Hinduism in South Africa is vigorously expanding and it could eventually become an instrument of greater transformation on the continent, driven by dedication to serving humanity, enhancing access to education and health, as well as to promoting new avenues for spiritual guidance.

Trinidad

The historical facts of Hindu immigration to the Caribbean in the nineteenth and early twentieth centuries are well known and share much in common with other countries discussed in this chapter. Here also, India proved to be the most fruitful source of labor, both in terms of numbers and skills, and provided a steady stream from 1838, the year the first group of 396 Indians arrived in Guyana, until 1917, when Indian immigration was finally abolished. In roughly eighty years, 548,000 Indians journeyed to the West Indies under the official scheme. Of these, the majority (239,000) went to Guyana and Trinidad (143,939).

Some 75,547 (or 31.62%) of those who migrated returned to India from Guyana, and 33,294 (or 23.13%) of the migrants eventually returned from Trinidad. The important statistic is that 71% of those who made the arduous journey around the Cape of Good Hope and across the Atlantic Ocean chose to make their homes in the Caribbean. The current Hindu population in Trinidad is estimated to be 240,100 out of a total population of 1.3 million. This reflects a decline of 4.3% since 2000. The Hindu community in the Caribbean was the earliest in the western world and one of the earliest to find itself as a minority in an overwhelmingly western Christian majority. The challenges of this new context continue to this day.

Despite the isolation from India and an environment that was inhospitable, Hindus quickly sought to reconstitute the basic elements of their religion and way of life. In Trinidad, there is evidence that, by the 1860s, Hindu temples were constructed and major festivals celebrated. Hindu traditions, though subject to continuous challenge and change, have endured and thrived with remarkable persistence. There are many factors that explain the survival and persistence of the Hindu tradition in the Caribbean.

Among the early Hindu migrants to the Caribbean, as in Fiji, Mauritius, and South Africa were Brahmins, the traditional repositories of sacred learning and wisdom. These religious specialists, while laboring also on the sugar plantations, assumed leadership roles and played a vital role in the preservation and continuity of Hindu traditions. Their descendants continue to fulfill priestly roles in Trinidad and other islands. Another significant asset for the survival of Hinduism in the Caribbean is the traditional emphasis on the oral experience of scripture. Although most of the immigrants were illiterate, repeated exposure to scriptures ensured that they were familiar with the contents and had memorized large portions of texts. The two texts that sustained them were the Bhagavata Puraṇa and the Ramacharitamanas of Tulasidas. The Tulasidas version of the Ramayana, written in rhyming couplets, facilitated memorization and has become the most popular Hindu scriptural text in the Caribbean. Trinidad Hindus continue to look to this text as a source of moral values and religious instruction. Their familiarity with it and its accessibility are important reasons for a thriving religious culture. It is fair to say that the Ramayana occupies a status in Trinidad that is similar to the Bible and Quran for the Christian and Muslim communities. Many Hindus speak of Trinidad as 'Ramayana country.'

Although most of the Hindus in Trinidad are not fluent in Hindi, the text continues to be widely read and expounded. The recitation is usually done in Hindi, but the commentary and exposition are almost always in English. During any week of the year, expositions of the text occur in various locations throughout the island. These are well publicized and often broadcast on one of the many radio stations serving the Indian community. These sessions last from a week to nine days and are held in temples or in Hindu homes. These public expositions of the text are referred to as Ramayana Yajnas. Elaborate preparations are made for these readings and they are usually very well attended. Hindus in Trinidad look to this text as a source of moral values and religious instruction. Many important family events and life-cycle rituals are celebrated and marked by recitations of the Ramayana. It is quite common for the text to be read on the occasion of a birthday or wedding anniversary as well as in homes as a source of consolation when a family member dies.

The power and popularity of the Ramayana and its traditions in Trinidad are evident also in the importance of the festival of lights (Diwali) and the continuing performance of the play of Rama (Ramlila) in open-air theaters across the island. Diwali, in Trinidad, has a single narrative commemorating the triumphant return of Rama with his wife, Sita, and brother, Lakshmana, to the city of Ayodhya after his long exile and his defeat of the evil king, Ravana. Diwali is celebrated on a lavish scale in Trinidad and it is the occasion for a national public holiday. Newspapers publish special supplements focusing on the festival and on Hinduism, and the television and radio stations broadcast appropriate music, messages, and information throughout the day. Public celebrations, sometimes in the weeks leading up to the festival, are held at various venues in the island. In recent years, the major public celebration occurred in central Trinidad on lands donated by the government to a major local organization, The National Council for Indian Culture. During the week leading to the festival, Hindus and non-Hindus converge at this venue for a nightly feast of Indian song, music, dance, food, and educational displays. Local businesses set up display booths and charitable organizations make their services available. Almost every school and college, business, and state ministry in Trinidad has its own celebration. For Hindus in Trinidad, the festival is essentially religious in character. Most Hindus abstain from intoxicants and meat in the days leading up to the celebration and it is customary for families to worship God in the form of Lakshmi, the goddess of wealth and prosperity. Gifts, cards, and food are shared with friends and neighbors and, increasingly, many non-Hindus illumine their homes and share Indian meals with Hindu friends. As in South Africa, Diwali has become a national festival.

The 'Play of Rama' (*Ramlila*), an open-air reenactment of the story of the Ramayana, has a long history in Trinidad and the public interest in this drama has not wavered. During the month of October, thousands of Hindus gather each night at several established venues to witness the story of Rama's birth, marriage, exile, the abduction of Sita, the defeat of Ravana, and Rama's triumphant return to Ayodhya. Camps at both ends of the field represent the respective abodes of Rama and Ravana, and the story unfolds while narrators recite the text of Tulassdasa. The festival ends with the burning of a large effigy of Ravana. Other Hindu festivals widely celebrated in Trinidad include Shivaratri (the night of Shiva), the spring festival of Holi, referred to locally as *phagwah*, a ritual sea-bath during the eighth lunar month of the Hindu calendar (*kartikka*), and the birth anniversaries of popular avatars like Rama and Krishna.

In spite of the many public faces of the Hindu tradition in Trinidad, it has also maintained its domestic character especially in the practice of families maintaining a relationship with and served by the family priest. The success of this system, with the priest serving both as ritual specialist and family counselor, has contributed immensely to the preservation and vitality of the Hindu life in Trinidad. Most of the life cycle rituals (*samskara*) connected with birth, initiation, marriage, and death take place in Hindu homes.

Organizationally, the Hindu tradition in Trinidad reflects its diversity. The largest Hindu organization in Trinidad is the Sanatan Dharma Maha Sabha. This body was founded in 1949 and led by a legendary businessman, Bhadase Sagan Maraj (1920–1971). Under his leadership, the Maha Sabha, in the 1950s, launched a vigorous primary school building program in the agricultural areas and ensured the availability of a basic education for many Hindus. The administering of its schools, which now include high schools for girls and boys, still remains an important focus of the activity of this group. Although the medium of education is English and students are prepared for a national high school entrance examination, these schools offer a basic exposure to Hindu religion and culture and participate in competitive Hindu cultural programs where prizes are awarded for song, music, dance, dramatic performances, and knowledge of Hinduism. In addition to its educational projects, the majority of Hindu temples in Trinidad are affiliated with the Maha Sabha and it is also the organization in which the majority of Hindu priests in Trinidad hold membership.

The Arya Samaj movement, a reformist Hindu group, founded in India by Swami Dayananda Saraswati (1824–1883) was established in the early twentieth century in Trinidad through the work of Vedic missionaries. Like the Maha Sabha, this organization has also made significant contributions to primary education in Trinidad and many of its schools have earned a reputation for excellence and success in national examinations. As a Hindu reform movement, many of its doctrinal views are different from those advocated by the Maha Sabha and the relationship between the two organizations has been occasionally contentious. In recent years, however, relationships have been cordial, but the Arya Samaj has also grown weaker through declining membership and participation. It retains a visible presence largely through its educational institutions.

In more recent years, newer organizations have become active in the community. The Sathya Sai Baba Movement, established in the mid-70s, is one of the more vigorous new bodies. Its various centers, now scattered throughout the island, sponsor regular worship meetings (*satsangs*) consisting of devotional songs and chants and lectures on the life and teachings of Sathya Sai Baba (1926–2011). In addition to participation in *satsangs*, members engage in service-oriented activities of various kinds. Other Hindu-based groups include the International Society for Krishna Consciousness (ISKCON), Transcendental Meditation (TM), the Brahmakumaris, and the Chinmaya Mission.

The historical ability of the Hindu tradition to adapt and assimilate under changing conditions has clearly served it well in Trinidad. Its history, however, is not merely one of survival, but also of innovation and creativity. Congregational forms of worship have become a prominent feature of Hindu worship and most temples have regularly scheduled services on a Sunday morning consisting of chanting, ritual, and lecture. Traditional temple architecture has been modified for the purpose of collective worship. The shrine area, where icons (*murtis*) are housed, is now integrated with the larger congregational hall and worshippers sit directly facing the altar area. In the traditional Hindu temple, the shrine is usually set apart physically from the other spaces in the temple and only priests have access. Hindu temples in Trinidad allow all worshippers direct access to the *murtis* and are often surprised to discover that this is not possible in most temples in India.

Regional and linguistic differences have virtually disappeared and this has made possible the forging of a common Hindu identity. Except for the followers of neo-Hindu movements—for example, the International Society for Krishna Consciousness—Hindus in Trinidad rarely identify themselves as belonging to specific Hindu traditions such as Vaishnavism or Shaivism. They participate in what may be described as an ecumenical Hindu tradition, following a calendar and participating in festivals that celebrate the divine as Shiva, Vishnu, Durga, and Ganesha. Almost all the temples, even when dedicated to a specific form of God, celebrate events associated with other forms. While Sanskrit and Hindi remain the liturgical languages, they are increasingly used along with English translations and the medium of religious instruction is English.

Worship patterns and strategies for transmission of tradition that have evolved in Trinidad and, more broadly, in the Caribbean will be vital for the Hindu tradition in societies where Hindus exist as a minority. In the past forty years, for example, the migration of Hindus from the Caribbean to the United States and Canada has contributed to the vitality of Hinduism in these countries and some of the most successful temples, like the Vishnu and Devi Mandirs in Toronto, and the Shiva Mandir in Queens, New York, are those which reflect the Caribbean–Hindu heritage. These temples offer structured congregational forms of Hindu worship conducted in English that many find quite attractive.

Hindu priests in Trinidad are increasingly moving to a model of combining the generally separated roles of ritual specialist and religious teacher. Traditionally, Hinduism distinguished between the specialist in the performance of religious ritual and the teacher of wisdom. The first, referred as a *pujari* or *purohit*, was trained in the intricacies of domestic and temple ritual and served families or worked as temple priests. In the temples, they care for the particular icon (*murti*) or form of God to which the temple is dedicated, leading the daily round of worship, and the calendar of festivals associated with the deity. Temple priests assist devotees who visit, making offerings on their behalf and returning consecrated offerings to them as *prasada* or gifts of God. Temple and domestic priests serve the Hindu community in very important ways, helping to meet a variety of religious needs through leadership in matters of ritual. It is true also that they receive little or no theological training and are not expected generally to function as religious teachers or disseminators of wisdom. The teachers of wisdom (*guru* or *acharya*) received theological training and have the skills to interpret sacred texts and transmit religious teaching. The model of combining ritual and teaching has grown in importance in

Trinidad, influenced by the example of other religious communities and by a greater need for instruction in religious doctrine. It is a model that Hindu priests from Trinidad have taken to North America.

Caste, while not absent, is a minimal feature in the everyday life of Hindus in Trinidad. It features prominently in the selection of priests, with the Sanatan Dharma Maha Sabha insisting that only Brahmins are eligible to serve as priests. This position, however, is contested by other Hindu organizations that offer priestly training that is not bound by caste. Other features of caste, such as work exclusivity, conventions regulating marriage across caste barriers, inter-dining, and social relationships have almost disappeared. Trinidad and Caribbean Hinduism point to the possibility of a Hindu way of life without the hierarchy and rigidity of caste.

Conclusion

Our review of the Hindu tradition in Fiji, Mauritius, South Africa, and Trinidad highlights a continuing process of continuity, change, and innovation. Although Hindu traditions have managed to preserve their rich, historical diversity, the experience of diaspora Hinduism also attests to an emerging culture of Hindu ecumenism, characterized by a sharing of worship space, festivals, and rituals. The sheer distance from India as well as the challenges of being minorities in unfamiliar cultures have each been factors shaping this process. Increasingly, Hindu temples in the diaspora are not sectarian in nature, but serve the needs of a range of local Hindu communities. There seems to be more emphasis on what is shared and less on the preservation of regional and linguistic differences. Traditional temple architecture has likewise been modified in the diaspora to accommodate communal worship practices that now often occur in large halls facing open altars on which icons are located. Many Hindu temples in the diaspora have regularly scheduled worship on weekends that have a distinctly congregational character. There is, on the whole, greater lay participation in the administrative and liturgical life of Hindu temples.

Traditional features of Hindu life and culture are also undergoing change in the diaspora. While the practice of caste has not disappeared, its significance is declining and many diaspora temples have non-Brahmin priests. Other features of caste, such as work exclusivity, conventions regulating marriage across caste barriers, restrictions on inter-dining, and other social relationships, have largely disappeared. And while the sacred geography of India continues to have special significance for Hindus in the diaspora, such communities have come to develop their own sacred spaces and locations. The Ganga Talao in Mauritius is a prime example of a new place of Hindu pilgrimage.

We note also the emergence of the Ramacharitamanas of Tulasidas as the most prominent sacred text in all four locations. The multiple ways in which this text is used ritually and theologically makes for a fascinating study in continuity and innovation. In her own research, Usha Shukla has noted the importance of this text for shaping the common experience of exile that believers feel to be shared between Rama and Hindu indentured immigrants (2011). Related to the prominence of the Ramayana is the growing significance of Diwali as a national festival in all locations and participation by non-Hindus. And while developments in India continue to shape life in the diaspora, it is quite likely that, with the ease of travel and today's social media, diasporic Hindu communities will themselves become sources of change for Hindu life in India.

Summary

While Hindus have been traveling and living outside the subcontinent for at least a millennium, the modern era witnessed the largest flow of Hindu migrants to diverse regions of the globe. Propelled by the desire to escape trying conditions in colonial India, the promise of new wealth and opportunities in locations from the Pacific to the Caribbean, Hindu merchants, seamen, indentured laborers, saints, and devotional leaders have contributed to the emergence of Hinduism as a worldwide presence. This chapter has explored the conditions for migration to regions such as Fiji, Mauritius, South Africa, and Trinidad, while considering the ways in which the expression of Hinduism has involved a dynamic interplay between cultural continuity and modern innovation in styles of worship, belief, architecture, and social practice.

Discussion Questions

- What does the minimization of caste practices in the diaspora tell us about its significance in the Hindu tradition?
- What factors, historical and religious, explain the prominence of the Ramacharitamanas in the Hindu diaspora?
- What are the new strategies evolving in the Hindu diaspora for the transmission of tradition?
- What are the major challenges facing Hindus in the diaspora?
- How does the transformation of temple architecture in the diaspora reflect change and continuity?

Suggested Readings

Klass, Morton (1961). *East Indians in Trinidad*. New York: Columbia University.
Kumar, Pratap (2000). *Hindus in South Africa*. Durban: University of Durban-Westville.
Tinker, Hugh (1974). *A New System of Slavery: The Export of Indian Labour Overseas, 1830–1920*. London: Oxford University Press.
Vertovec, Stephen (2000). *The Hindu Diaspora*. London: Routledge.
Younger, Paul (2009). *New Homelands: Hindu Communities in Mauritius, Guyana, Trinidad, South Africa, Fiji and East Africa*. New York: Oxford University Press.

Bibliography

Bahadur, Gaiutra (2013). *Coolie Woman: The Odyssey of Indenture.* Chicago: University of Chicago Press.

Diesel, Alleyn (2005). 'The Suffering Mothers, the Hindu Goddesses as Empowering Role Models for Women.' *Alternation* (Special Edition) 2: 35–53.

Gopee, Neerunjun (2003). *Ramayana in Parliament.* Mauritius: Ramayana Centre.

Indranath, Indradev Bholah (2009). *Arya Samaj Aur Hindi Visva Sandarbha Mein.* Delhi: Star Publishers.

Kelly, John D. (1991). *A Politics of Virtue.* Chicago: University of Chicago Press.

——— (2001). 'Fiji's Fifth Veda: Exile, Sanatan Dharm, and Countercolonial Initiatives in the Diaspora.' In *Questioning Ramayanas: A South Asian Tradition* (pp. 329–351). Ed. Paula Richman. Berkley and Los Angeles: University of California Press.

Klass, Morton (1961). *East Indians in Trinidad.* New York: Columbia University.

Kumar, Pratap (2000). *Hindus in South Africa.* Durban: University of Durban-Westville.

La Guerre, John, ed. (1974). *Calcutta to Caroni: The East Indians of Trinidad.* St. Augustine: The University of the West Indies.

Lal, Brij V. (2000). *Chalo Jahaji.* Canberra: Australian National University.

Look Lai, Walton (2004). *Indentured Labor, Caribbean Sugar: Chinese and Indian Migrants to the British West Indies, 1838–1918.* Baltimore: Johns Hopkins University Press.

Mahabir, Noor Kumar (1985). *The Still Cry: Personal Accounts of East Indians in Trinidad and Tobago during Indentureship 1845–1917.* Ithaca: Calaloux Publications.

Niehoff, Arthur and Juanita (1960). *East Indians in the West Indies.* Milwaukee: Milwaukee Public Museum.

Shukla, U. D. (2002). *Ramacaritamanasa in South Africa.* Delhi: Motilal Banarsidass.

——— (2011). *Ramcharitmanas in the Diaspora: Trinidad, Mauritius and South Africa.* New Delhi: Star Publications.

Tinker, Hugh (1974). *A New System of Slavery: The Export of Indian Labour Overseas, 1830–1920.* London: Oxford University Press.

Vertovec, Stephen (2000). *The Hindu Diaspora.* London: Routledge.

——— (1992). *Hindu Trinidad: Religion, Ethnicity, and Socio-Economic Change.* Basingstoke: Macmillan.

Younger, Paul (2009). *New Homelands: Hindu Communities in Mauritius, Guyana, Trinidad, South Africa, Fiji and East Africa.* New York: Oxford University Press.

8   Hinduism in Britain

Maya Warrier

Between April and July 2007, a bull in West Wales became the symbol around which British Hindus rallied in defense of what was deemed the right of Hindus to practice their religion in the UK. The bull, named Shambo, belonged to a small, monastic community in rural West Wales that calls itself 'Skanda Vale' or the 'Community of the Many Names of God.' This community was founded by a Sri Lankan Hindu, Guru Subramaniam (1929–2007). His followers, the resident monks and nuns, are mainly individuals of European origin. Skanda Vale is devotionalist, or *bhakti* oriented; its practice centers on daily worship at shrines dedicated to deities in the Hindu pantheon. The pilgrims who visit Skanda Vale are mostly Hindu.

In the course of a routine test in April 2007, Shambo, whom the Skanda Vale residents had reared since his infancy, tested positive for bovine tuberculosis. Government officials deemed that, as a potential threat to the national herd (since tuberculosis is highly contagious), he had to be put to death. The monks and nuns at Skanda Vale questioned this decision. They offered to quarantine Shambo and restore him to health through medication. However, their appeals were to no avail. Deeply concerned for the life of their beloved bull, the monks and nuns launched a 'Save Shambo' campaign to rally support from the general public (Warrier 2010). In particular, they sought support from other British Hindus, arguing that the cow is sacred to Hindus, that cow protection is a fundamental principle of Hindu tradition, and that to violate this principle would be to violate the British Hindu community's basic right to practice its religion. Skanda Vale fought its case in court on these grounds. They made special appeal to Article 9 of the European Convention for the Protection of Human Rights and Fundamental Freedoms, which safeguards the freedom of all individuals to manifest their religion or belief, in private or in public, in worship, teaching, practice, and observance.

In response to Skanda Vale's call for support, spokespersons from various Hindu groups wrote to MPs, issued press statements, and raised awareness within their own as well as allied organizations about the Shambo crisis. In early July, in a highly symbolic move, the Skanda Vale authorities installed a *murti* (image) of the deity in front of Shambo's pen at the rear of the Skanda temple and commenced regular *puja* at what had now become Shambo's shrine. Government officials were at this point prevented from removing Shambo since to do so would mean desecrating what was demarcated as Hindu sacred space (Warrier 2010). The media reported furthermore that one of the UK's two key Hindu umbrella organizations, the Hindu Forum of Britain—which claimed to represent 700,000 British Hindus—had announced that, if necessary, 'the Hindu community' would form a human chain around the bull to prevent its capture. This lent the Shambo crisis ever more publicity and bolstered the notion that the so-called British Hindu community in its unified entirety was firmly behind the Skanda Vale campaign, even though, in fact, an online 'Save Shambo' signature campaign had raised only approximately 20,000 signatories, comprising less than 3% of Britain's total Hindu population (ibid).

In the end, Skanda Vale lost its battle, and Shambo was put to death. Not long afterwards, one lone Hindu voice arguing against the 'Save Shambo' campaign made itself heard. In an article published in the *New Statesman*, a leading figure in the second of Britain's two Hindu umbrella organizations, the Hindu Council UK, argued that the campaign had in fact compromised Hinduism's credibility in the British public domain. To seek special privileges for cows and bulls at Hindu temples while endangering the life of other British cattle, he argued, went against the Hindu principle of the sanctity of all life. This article unleashed a storm of comments and opinions in the *New Statesman* from Hindus who were clearly deeply divided over the question of whether or not the attempt to save Shambo's life was morally defensible. The debate effectively served to debunk the notion that there is a unified Hindu community in Britain with shared ideals and values (Warrier 2010).

The Skanda Vale episode highlights a crucial tension that lies at the heart of Hinduism as it has developed in Britain over the last half century. On the one hand, there is an impulse on the part of groups and organizations to forge a sense of Hindu unity, and to mobilize Hindus so that they may assert a shared public identity, work towards promoting Hindu collective interests, and defend their rights as a religious group. This impulse towards unification, which is particularly strong in the face of perceived threats, exists in tension with the considerable plurality and diversity of Hindu identities and worldviews at the grassroots. Hindus in Britain are divided by, among other factors, caste, sectarian affiliation, class, educational and professional status, regional and linguistic backgrounds, and the particular routes they have followed to Britain. To try and reconcile the multiplicity of perspectives, interests, and agendas in such a context is no easy task. Efforts at presenting a unified vision of Hinduism seldom go uncontested—there are always dissenting voices that challenge notions of what it means to be Hindu, and that challenge, furthermore, the legitimacy of particular spokespersons to speak on behalf of all British Hindus. In what follows, we will examine this crucial tension in greater detail.

The Passage to Britain

Hindus have been present in Britain right from the eighteenth century, in the early period often serving as domestic servants, sailors, and soldiers (Visram 1986). Originally, their numbers were extremely small and the majority of them returned to India after a contracted period of service. It was not until the middle of the twentieth century that the numbers of South Asian immigrants in Britain grew significantly. In the 1950s and early 1960s, a number of Indians, with a high proportion of Hindus among them, moved to Britain in response to the growing demand in British industry for cheap labor. The early migrants were mostly men between the ages of twenty and fifty. These new immigrants resided in groups defined by regional, religious and linguistic markers, and by kinship links. Many were from the north Indian state of Punjab, and a significant number from the western state of Gujarat. Over time, their wives and dependents joined them in their new home (Hinnells 2000).

During the 1960s, there was a fresh influx of South Asian immigrants, this time from East African countries where many had settled during the colonial period. They included entrepreneurs from Gujarat, laborers from Punjab, as well as Gujarati and Punjabi artisans. Some of these people were forced to leave their East African homes as a result of exclusivist Africanization policies introduced by the state (Hinnells 2000). Over the years, there has also been a movement to Britain of South Asians from other British ex-colonies such as Trinidad, Fiji, and Mauritius, as well as from Sri Lanka, particularly during the period of civil unrest there. Additionally, large numbers of educated professionals from across the Indian subcontinent have moved to Britain seeking employment in Britain's tertiary sector, perhaps most visibly as doctors and nurses in the National Health Service.

For the first time in 2001 (and then again in 2011), the census authorities in England and Wales collected information about the religious identities of the population. In the 2011 census, 817,000 people (1.5% of the total population of England and Wales) identified themselves as Hindus.[1] The capital city of London recorded the highest population of Hindus (about 5.5% of all Londoners), a number that had risen by 1% in the ten years since the 2001 census. Outside London, the highest proportion of Hindus was recorded in Leicester. These figures reflect a steady growth in the population of Hindus in Britain since the middle of the twentieth century.

The vast majority of Hindus in Britain today are of Gujarati origin, and a significant number are East African Gujarati. Punjabis comprise the second largest regional-linguistic group (Ballard 1994; Knott 2000; Vertovec 2000: 87–107). In addition to Gujaratis and Punjabis, there are growing numbers of Hindus in the UK who have migrated from other parts of India. Each such immigrant group has distinctive defining characteristics and is further differentiated in terms of class, caste, dialect, original locality, and route of migration to the UK. The diverse provenance of these multiple subgroups is often reflected in differences in their religious orientations and traditions, variations in religious festivals and domestic practices, and in styles and foci of worship.

Institutional development among Hindu groups in Britain took place very gradually (Bowen 1987; Vertovec 2000: 95–99). In the 1950s and 1960s, some loosely-knit associations were formed to organize, for instance, modest celebrations of Hindu festivals. In the 1970s, numerous and diverse regional-linguistic, sectarian, and caste associations developed; a significant number of these operate to this day in Britain's towns and cities. Many have been active in raising funds for establishing and running Hindu temples and centers. The establishment of temples has enabled the perpetuation and transmission of sociocultural and religious practices and orientations across successive generations of Hindus. Many of these temples have distinctive regional and sectarian orientations (Knott 2000; Vertovec 2000: 124–140); some are more broad-based and eclectic. Since the 1960s, there has also been a proliferation of caste-based associations, organized both locally and nationally, which hold regular gatherings, celebrate religious festivals, assist in the arrangement of marriages, and serve to maintain links with villages and caste and kinship networks in the Indian subcontinent (Ballard 1994; Knott 2000; Vertovec 2000: 87–107).

Hindus in Britain are often affiliated with one of a diverse range of sectarian traditions. Prominent in the British Hindu landscape are two Vaishnava groups, the Bochasanwasi Akshar Purushottam Sanstha (BAPS), which is one of three rival divisions of the Swaminarayan *sampradaya* or tradition of Gujarat, and the International Society for Krishna Consciousness (ISKCON) better known as the Hare Krishna movement, which attracts adherents from a range of different backgrounds, including, most visibly, persons of Western (rather than Indian) origin. One also finds in Britain Hindu followers of other sectarian traditions like the Arya Samaj, Radhasoamis, and Pushtimargis, and indeed followers of a very wide range of modern gurus (see Kim and Williamson, this volume).

The Perpetuation and Transmission of Hindu Traditions

The diversity of backgrounds of Hindus in Britain means that Hindu socioreligious practices vary significantly. The background-specific Hindu orientations and practices have tended to be transmitted from one generation to the next in the domestic sphere, mainly by the women in the household (McDonald 1987). This religious knowledge tends not to be centered on belief, but instead reflects the practice-centered nature of much of popular Hinduism. However, this practice orientation can present a problem for young British Hindus who are often at a loss when asked what the central 'beliefs' of their religion are. They often lack a conceptual framework within which to situate their practical knowledge and experience in ways that can make Hinduism comprehensible as a 'religion,' both to themselves and to outsiders. Partly in order to address this problem, a number of organizations in Britain began to offer classes for young Hindus in temples, community centers, schools, and private homes as a means for their more formal religious nurture (Jackson 1985; Jackson and Nesbitt 1986, 1993). Jackson (1985) notes that though these classes tend to differ in scope and content depending on the organization's regional, linguistic, caste, and sectarian origins, some of these ventures present young Hindus with a more unitary understanding of Hinduism, and provide them with the kind of conceptual framework and moral guidelines they would need in order to make the idea of Hinduism as a unified religion more comprehensible.

Awareness of the need for formal religious nurture of British Hindu youngsters has led to campaigns to establish a state-supported Hindu school in Britain. Initial campaigns to set up a proposed Vivekananda Hindu High School, which would nurture an ethos based on the universalistic Neo-Hindu message of Swami Vivekananda, proved unsuccessful (see Kanitkar 1979, cited in Vertovec 2000: 102). In 1992, the BAPS Swaminarayan group set up a Swaminarayan School in Neasden, in northwest London, across the road from the spectacular Swaminarayan temple. This temple, built in marble and limestone, is now a significant site for Hindu (not just Swaminarayan) worship and also a major tourist attraction. Financed and managed by the Swaminarayan group, the BAPS school delivers the British National Curriculum; additionally, it provides classes in Gujarati and lessons in Indian music and dance (Vertovec 2000: 102–103). It familiarizes students with the Swaminarayan scriptures and encourages them to participate in daily prayers as well as Hindu religious festivals. The Swaminarayan *sampradaya* or lineage is a Vaishnava tradition and though the school conveys a pluralistic understanding of Hinduism, it foregrounds Vaishnavism as central to Hindu belief and practice (ibid).

In the last few years, new initiatives to set up state-supported Hindu schools in Britain have met with success. It comes as no surprise that, given the high concentration of Hindus in London and Leicester, it was in these two cities that the first 'voluntary-aided' Hindu schools in the UK emerged.[2] The burough of Harrow in London (with the highest proportion of Hindus in the city) saw the establishment of the first Krishna Avanti Primary School in 2008. A second school, the Krishna Avanti Primary School in Leicester, was set up in 2011. Following this, two further schools emerged in London—a second one in Harrow and another in the London Burrough of Redbridge. All four schools are managed by the Avanti Schools Trust, which describes itself as 'a family of schools that share the ideals of educational excellence, character formation and spiritual insight.'[3]

These schools, like the one in Neasden, deliver the British National Curriculum. They claim to promote 'holistic, responsible lifestyles through a vegetarian diet, a curriculum that integrates yoga and meditation, and a built environment that actively fosters environmental concern.'[4] Sanskrit is taught in these schools, and the devotional practice of chanting the many names of god (*nama japa*), with a focus on Krishna, is encouraged. In a television interview for BBC4, the chairman of the school governing board of the first of these schools, Nitesh Gor, described the school project as resulting from growing grassroots demand from the Hindu community for faith school provision since the mid-1990s. The demand for a faith school reflects to some extent Hindus' anxieties about losing touch with religious traditions and the desire to inculcate religious values and ideals in their young. It also reflects their need for a tangible and comprehensible form of Hinduism 'that can be explained to outsiders as a respectable religion, that can be taught to their children in religious education, and that can form the basis for collective action' (van der Veer 1993: 42–43).

Hindu Umbrella Organizations

From the 1960s onwards, and particularly since the 1980s, a number of Hindu umbrella organizations have emerged in Britain, presenting an ecumenical form of Hinduism; these organizations recognize the variety and diversity of Hindu traditions, and occasionally seek to bridge the differences between them by organizing Hindu activities, campaigns, and celebrations that cut across the regional, linguistic, caste-based, sectarian, and other divisions. Two kinds of Hindu umbrella organizations operate in Britain. Those of the first kind stem from organizations promoting Hindu nationalism in India (see Kanungo, this volume); these promote what may be seen as the goals and aspirations of the Hindu right, which is to say a more assertive brand of 'Hindu-ness' (Hindutva). The second kind comprises homegrown British organizations that seek to speak for all British Hindus and often mediate between Hindu grassroots organizations and the state.

Though their roots can be traced to developments in colonial South Asia, Hindutva organizations have a tangible presence in many overseas Indian contexts. As in India, overseas they also operate through what is known as a family (*parivar*) of organizations. In Britain, that family includes the Hindu Swayamsevak Sangh (affiliated to the Rashtriya Swayamsevak Sangh in India) and the Vishwa Hindu Parishad (VHP) UK. Both of these organizations have had a presence in the UK since the late 1960s and both were especially active in the late 1980s and 1990s. This was not only a period when religious identity was becoming central to the British government's discourse on minority identities; it was simultaneously a period of intensive VHP-led political mobilization in India around a campaign to destroy the Babri mosque in Ayodhya. In the years since, VHP UK has intermittently played a high-profile role in Hindu-related campaigns in Britain. The National Hindu Students Forum, affiliated with the Hindu right, operates in the UK targeting university and college students, and Sewa International has been actively involved in raising funds for Hindu nationalist projects in India (Mathew and Prashad 2000; Jaffrelot and Therwath 2007). Zavos (2010a) notes that Hindu nationalist organizations operate vigorously at local and regional levels; at the national level, they often yield to homegrown Hindu ecumenical organizations. He argues, however, that while operating at local and grassroots levels, these rightwing groups generate what he calls a 'Hindutva effect' whose ideological influence often continues to be felt at the national level.

The most prominent of home-grown Hindu organizations in the UK are the National Council of Hindu Temples (NCHT), the Hindu Council UK

(HCUK), and the Hindu Forum of Britain (HFB), all of which 'project themselves as public authorities on Hindu-ness, and as the voice of a community of people with [. . .] common aspirations and contributions to make to public life' (Zavos 2009: 882). Registered as a charity in 1980, NCHT operates in an advisory capacity, helping groups to set up temples and providing resources on Hinduism and Hindu worship (Nesbitt 2006). Scores of temples in the different parts of the UK are members of this organization. The Hindu Council UK was set up in 1994 and registered in 1998. It lists over 400 member organizations on its website. The Council is closely related to the NCHT, and its purpose, according to its website, is 'to give the UK Hindus an effective voice on policy matters with the Government of the day whilst enhancing mutual understanding among the major faiths predominant in the UK.'[5] In 2004, the Hindu Forum of Britain came into being with a particular focus on community cohesion among British Hindus. It quickly assumed a position of relative predominance compared to the NCHT and HCUK, presenting a highly professional and dynamic face to British Hindus and to the government. While all three organizations evidence a concern to protect Hindu interests, the image each presents to the public is distinctive (Zavos 2009).

Multiculturalism and Representational Politics

In many ways, the mode of Hinduism's development in Britain is shaped by the multiculturalist policies of the government. In multicultural Britain, religion is a significant factor in the conceptualization of minority identity. It serves as a marker of ethnic identity and as a means for politically mobilizing individuals and groups. Since the mid-1990s, a UK-government initiative to promote interfaith relations and community cohesion has come to project religion as a vehicle for promoting such common public values as peace, nonviolence, and respect for one's fellows.

The language of religion and faith relations works within a 'world religions' paradigm. This results in a limited range of identity options—for instance, identity as a Hindu is recognized officially but not sectarian identity as a Vaishnava or caste identity as a Patidar. Particular religious identities are thus privileged, and others marginalized. The Religious Education syllabus used in schools in the UK demonstrates this point well—it enables the study of 'world religions' like Hinduism, but allows little or no room for the study of ISKCON or BAPS, both significant players in British Hinduism. If ISKCON is to be heard in the Religious Education arena, it must speak not just for Vaishnavism but for Hinduism as a whole (Warrier 2012).

Religions are presumed to have an internal coherence and structure and are conceptualized as bounded categories with clear lines demarcating them from other religions. There is the expectation that a few individuals from the religious 'community' can speak on behalf of the group as a whole. This is particularly problematic for Hinduism with its fuzzy boundaries, extreme internal diversity, and lack of a centralized authority structure. The more enterprising Hindus, harboring aspirations as community leaders, respond to the government's expectations, setting up and leading Hindu umbrella organizations. These leaders play a significant role in the negotiation of group identity and interest; they mediate between Hindus and the state, and they make Hinduism heard in the public sphere.

The Hindu Forum of Britain is a particularly telling example of an organization that has emerged directly in response to government initiatives and is shaped largely by the concerns of the government. It was in the early 2000s that the British government took up its 'community cohesion' agenda in earnest, with the aim of countering subversive strains in minority religions, and mediating difference by highlighting common values across religions (Zavos 2009, 2012). Religion was now seen as a means to stabilize and advance a liberal political culture, and the British government sought to work with religious groups to advance this agenda. The success of such engagement was seen to depend on the setting up of appropriate institutional structures at the community level. Religious organizations were required to have a written constitution, systems to allow members to influence decisions, and arrangements for involving women and young people. They were required to participate in local minority initiatives, and to come to the consultation table with a clear position previously agreed with a wide range of traditions and organizations within the community (Zavos 2009, 2012).

It was partly in response to this invitation from the government that the Hindu Forum was set up. As noted earlier, it projects an image of legitimacy and professionalism and operates within the framework of the government's community cohesion agenda, emphasizing 'community consultation,' 'capacity building,' and 'interfaith relations' (Zavos 2012: 85). A democratically elected National Executive Committee oversees its activities. This organization now plays a major role mediating between Hindu organizations and the state. It claims to represent, far more than its predecessors, the views and needs of British-born Hindus. It seeks to articulate Hindu identity in ways that are deemed appropriate to the official public sphere, governed by the logic of community cohesion (Zavos 2012: 83).

Organizations like the Forum are typically Janus-faced. One face looks towards the state and seeks to present some semblance of a unified cohesive Hindu front. The other looks towards the multiplicity of Hindu organizations, communities, and individuals at the grassroots, and seeks to foster a sense of unity within what is in reality an extremely diverse collective. One way in which ecumenical umbrella organizations often seek to forge a sense of unity across this diversity at the grassroots level is by arguing that Hindus are vulnerable when disunited and that they need to unite if they are to hold their own against threatening forces. These ideas have found expression through a range of HFB-backed campaigns to protect Hindu interests in the UK. One may discern, in all of this, crucial affinities with Hindu nationalist agendas and activities. The discursive and organizational strategies of Hindutva activists undeniably serve as useful resources in furthering British Hindu interests. This is not to say, however, that the political ends of British Hindu organizations like the Hindu Forum can be reduced to those of Hindutva; instead, we might say they are particular to the needs and concerns of politicized British Hindus negotiating their religious identity in a multicultural, multifaith British context.

A Strident, Assertive Hindu Consciousness

Two important points emerge from recent scholarship on the public face of Hinduism in Britain. First, such Hinduism is highly politicized; second, the politics of Hinduism in a place like Britain turn on grave anxieties, insecurities, and fears. One of the most visible aspects of this politicized Hinduism has been the spate of protests and campaigns that Hindus have launched in recent times.[6] A number of campaigns have been instances of groups fighting to protect their interests by demanding their freedom to practice religion as Hindus. This was the case with the 'Save Shambo' campaign outlined earlier, launched by the Skanda Vale community. This was the case also with ISKCON UK, which was embroiled in a protracted planning dispute with the local authority over the right to conduct public worship at its temple in Bhaktivedanta Manor in north London. It launched a public campaign, which gathered momentum in the 1980s and 1990s, galvanizing a number of Hindus and Hindu organizations to support its cause (Nye 2001). The respective groups chose to take recourse to laws protecting the religious freedoms of minority groups to practice their religion. Hindu umbrella organizations rallied to the support of the respective groups. The campaigns were strident and aggressive—this was an assertive form of Hinduism that borrowed from Hindutva's modes of expression.

A number of campaigns and protests have also had to do with seeking to assuage the 'hurt sentiments' of Hindus following allegations that particular objects, events, and/or actions were disrespectful to Hindus, and brought about a desecration of the Hindu sacred (Zavos 2008). Recently, Britain witnessed Hindus protesting against a Royal Mail Christmas stamp depicting an identifiably Hindu man and woman holding a blond baby Jesus, an image deemed to be disrespectful to Hindu sentiments (Zavos 2008). It has additionally seen Hindu activists protest against a line of footwear bearing images of Lord Ram (Raj 2009), against cakes decorated with images of Hindu deities, and against a newspaper image showing Ganesh drinking beer (Zavos 2008), all of which were interpreted as instances of the desecration of the Hindu sacred.[7] While it is tempting to see such campaigns as top-down orchestrations on the part of organizations claiming to represent Hindus, the reality is often far more complex than this (Zavos 2008; Warrier 2010). The performative aspect of these campaigns and protests is noteworthy; each of these can be seen as attempts to create and express something like a British Hindu 'community' through public performance (Zavos 2008). Yet, if we consider the actual number of Hindus participating in these campaigns it becomes quickly evident that they are a tiny minority of Britain's Hindu population. Clearly, there is a large, silent majority of Hindus who play no part in these politics. These individuals, we might surmise, are either unaware of, or disinterested in, such campaigns, or perhaps even quietly opposed to them.

The Public Visibility of Vaishnava Strands in British Hinduism

No account of Hinduism in Britain is complete without a discussion of the role of ISKCON, which, despite its founder's reluctance to define the organization as Hindu, has been a major player in the shaping of Hinduism in the UK context. As Steven Vertovec (2000: 101) notes, even though the leading figures in ISKCON are white converts, British Asians usually show great respect for the members of this organization, particularly their commitment to detailed rituals, their strict vegetarianism, and their knowledge of Sanskrit. One of the first temples to be inaugurated in Britain was the ISKCON temple opened in London in 1979 by the founder, A.C. Bhaktivedanta Prabhupada. Other ISKCON temples have been established since, and ISKCON is known to have played a significant role in the development of the National Council of Hindu Temples in its early years. An important aspect of ISKCON's many outreach activities, particularly since the 1990s, has been its close involvement with Religious Education in British schools. ISKCON Educational Services, which leads this activity, provides significant resources on Hinduism for educationists and school students in Britain (Warrier 2012). An important aspect of their program is the organizing of school visits to ISKCON temples.

ISKCON's ten-year legal battle with the local government over planning issues in relation to its temple in north London kept it very much in the limelight as far as British Hinduism was concerned. The developments relating to this case were covered extensively in the mass media, and ISKCON supporters keenly lobbied MPs demanding that Bhaktivedanta Manor be retained as a place for public worship (Nye 2001). This was one of the first major Hindu campaigns in Britain and, in some ways, set the tone for those that followed. ISKCON has been involved in a number of other campaigns since, one of the most recent being a campaign against Britain's Royal Society for the Prevention of Cruelty to Animals (RSPCA) in 2008, sparked by the decision of officials at RSPCA to put down an ailing cow housed at Bhaktivedanta Manor. After lobbying RSPCA and DEFRA for a year, ISKCON eventually received an apology from RSPCA for any offense caused by their actions (Warrier 2010: 274).

Since the mid-1980s, ISKCON has shown a readiness to engage with Hindu organizations in the UK and with the government. It brings several strengths to such work, including excellent organizational skills, the presence of articulate and efficient personnel within the organization, and multiple cultural competencies. In this respect, it becomes an important model for other Hindu organizations. Today, it plays a major role in the running of the government-aided Hindu faith schools that have come into being in the last few years, working as the faith partner and advisor of the Avanti Schools Trust. As a result, these schools are mainly Vaishnava in their orientation, as is evident from the official statement describing their ethos:

> By drawing on the teachings of Krishna Chaitanya, our School embraces a universal, inclusive approach to spirituality, aimed at rekindling a personal, loving and spontaneous relationship with the divine (Krishna).[8]

This Vaishnava and Krishna-centered focus in these schools is a clear reflection of ISKCON's significant involvement in their envisioning. Aspects of ISKCON's involvement can sometimes be contentious and often need negotiation. For instance, when the first Krishna Avanti Primary School in Harrow, London announced an admissions policy prioritizing the children of parents who were 'practicing Hindus,' it generated controversy over the definition of 'practicing Hindu.' Among the criteria announced by the school authorities was the practice of vegetarianism (central to ISKCON devotionalism). This met with considerable opposition, particularly from the UK Hindu Council, whose representatives argued that very small numbers of Hindus observe vegetarianism, and that this criterion disqualified the vast majority of Hindus in the UK. The school was forced to change its definition of a practicing Hindu and therefore to change its admissions criteria. The school now understands 'practicing Hindus' to refer to individuals who worship regularly at Hindu temples and thus applicants are required to provide a written statement to this effect from temple priests. It is noteworthy that the notion of the practicing Hindu remains narrowly focused on the devotional (and temple- and ritual-centered) aspects of Hinduism.

Over a decade ago, Malory Nye (2001) noted that Hinduism in the UK was getting increasingly 'Iskconized.' This trend has certainly continued. This public prominence of ISKCON does not mean, however, that Hinduism in Britain as such is getting homogenized. In the last two decades, the Vaishnava strands may have been particularly visible in public, but alongside these a whole range of other Hindu traditions continue to flourish. There are major Shaiva as well as eclectic and broad-based temples in Britain, and inevitably Hinduism remains at the grassroots as diverse as ever. Hindu organizations, if they are to receive support at the grassroots, are inevitably forced to accommodate this diversity and difference. Though some groups may seek to give Hinduism in Britain a semblance of coherence and neatness, Hinduism itself keeps spilling out of all orderly paradigms and frameworks; it remains stubbornly messy, defying definition, and eluding any attempt at disciplining. It may be that this indeterminacy, this elusiveness, continues to contribute to deep-seated anxieties among sections of Britain's Hindu population.

Conclusion

It is more than half a century since Britain became home to a fairly sizeable Hindu population. Over this period, the immigration of Hindus from new backgrounds and the gradual setting up of a range of Hindu societies and institutions has added new threads and colors to the rich tapestry of British Hinduism. The growing numbers of British-born Hindus, some of whom now play leading roles in new organizational initiatives like the setting up of the Hindu Forum and the establishment of Hindu faith schools, have introduced subtle changes in the textures and patterns of this tapestry. Additionally, changes in the state's perception of the place of minority religions in Britain, along with state initiatives in the last two decades to engage with organizations and spokespersons from different faith groups, have given Hinduism a new public face as well as new inflections and meanings. Different aspects of Hinduism are thrown into relief at different points in time even as the sociopolitical contexts in Britain (and beyond) continue to alter. Hinduism in Britain is dynamic and poly-vocal, and reflects all the diversity and versatility characteristic of the religion in its place of origin.

Summary

The story of Hindus and Hinduism in Britain as it has developed over the last six decades demonstrates the following features. Hinduism at the grassroots is marked by significant diversity in its forms, practices, and orientations both in the private, domestic sphere and in the range of local institutions that have mushroomed based on caste-based, linguistic, sectarian, and regional divisions. This diversity exists in tension with efforts at the national level to unify British Hindus and British Hinduism. A range of ecumenical Hindu organizations have emerged claiming to represent *all* British Hindus. These organizations work to generate a Hindu identity and consciousness that transcends the many differences evident at a grassroots level. The multiculturalist and multifaith policies of the government have served to legitimize some of these organizations and their leaders. The 'British Hindu' consciousness that the national-level organizations seek to generate tends to be highly politicized, and often can be assertive and strident. Additionally, at the national level some sectarian groups, notably ISKCON, have come to play a major role in the shaping of this consciousness. A largely Vaishnava temple-based form of Hinduism would seem to be on the ascendant currently, a trend actively promoted through ISKCON's activities in the political and educational spheres.

Discussion Questions

- This volume contains discussions of Hinduism's development in different contexts outside India. How does the development of Hinduism in Britain compare with that in the United States? What are the similarities and differences? And how does Hinduism in these two contexts compare with Hinduism in Fiji, Africa, and Trinidad?
- Hinduism is often understood as an 'ethnic' religion rooted in India and centered on Indian sacred geography. To what extent do you think the idea of India as the sacred homeland is significant in the development of Hinduism in Britain?
- What are the similarities and differences between Hinduism in Britain today and Hindutva or Hindu nationalism as it has emerged in India since the 1980s? What role do you think the ideology and practices of Hindutva have played in the development of British Hinduism?

Notes

1 'Religion in England and Wales 2011,' published by the Office for National Statistics, December 11, 2012. Retrieved on July 20, 2013. http://www.ons.gov.uk/ons/dcp171776_290510.pdf
2 A 'voluntary aided' school in England or Wales is a state-funded school in which a foundation or trust (usually a religious organization) may own the school site and buildings and contribute to building costs. The foundation or trust provides the vision and the goals for the school and usually exerts a substantial influence in the running of the school.
3 http://www.avanti.org.uk/section.php?section=47#.UfDqguByHdk (July 25, 2013)
4 ibid.
5 http://www.hinducounciluk.org/about-us (July 20, 2013).
6 A number of scholars have noted the same underlying anxieties in the case of Hinduism in the United States—see for instance Lal 1999, 2003; Chaudhuri 2012.
7 There have been a similar string of Hindu protests and campaigns in the United States, widely reported in the news and scrutinized in academic literature. Among the more prominent ones are protests against psychoanalytical interpretations of Hindu mythological stories by academic scholars, the campaigns against the depiction of Hinduism in school textbooks in California in 2005–2006 and in Virginia before that, and protests against the use of images of Hindu deities for marketing products ranging from toilet seat covers to burgers (see Bose 2008, Khanduri 2012).
8 http://www.avanti.org.uk/kapsharrow/sub_section.php?section=2&sub=1 (July 20, 2013)

Suggested Readings

Ballard, R., ed. (1994). *Desh Pardesh: The South Asian Presence in Britain*. London: Hurst.
Burghart, R. (1987). *Hinduism in Great Britain*. London: Tavistock.
Vertovec, Steven (2000). *The Hindu Diaspora: Comparative Patterns*. London: Routledge.
Zavos, John (2009). 'Negotiating Multiculturalism: the Organisation of Hindu Identity in Contemporary Britain.' *Journal of Ethnicity and Migration Studies* 35, No. 6: 881–900.
——— (2010). 'Situating Hindu Nationalism in the UK: Vishwa Hindu Parishad and the Development of a British Hindu Identity.' *Journal of Commonwealth and Comparative Politics* 48, No. 1: 2–22.

Bibliography

Ballard, R., ed. (1994). *Desh Pardesh: The South Asian Presence in Britain*. London: Hurst.
Bose, P. (2008). 'Hindutva Abroad: The California Textbook Controversy.' *The Global South* 2, No. 1: 11–34.
Bowen, D. (1987). The Evolution of Gujarati Hindu Organizations in Bradford.' In *Hinduism in Great Britain* (pp. 15–31). Ed. R. Burghart. London: Tavistock.
Burghart, R., ed. (1987). *Hinduism in Great Britain*. London: Tavistock.
Chaudhuri, A. (2012). 'American Hindu Activism and the Politics of Anxiety.' In *Public Hinduisms* (pp. 324–347). Eds. J. Zavos et al. London and New Delhi: Sage.

Coward, H., J.R. Hinnells, and R.B. Williams, eds. (2000). *The South Asian Religious Diaspora in Britain, Canada and the United States*. New York: State University of New York Press.

Hinnells, J.R. (2000). 'South Asians in Britain—Introduction.' In *The South Asian Religious Diaspora in Britain, Canada and the United States* (pp. 1–12). Eds. H. Coward, J.R. Hinnells, and R.B. Williams. New York: State University of New York Press.

Jaffrelot, C. and I. Therwath (2007). 'The Sangh Parivar and the Hindu Diaspora in the West: What Kind of Long-Distance Nationalism?' *International Political Sociology* 1: 278–295.

Jackson, R. (1985). 'Hinduism in Britain: Religious Nurture and Religious Education.' *British Journal of Religious Education* 6: 141–146.

Jackson, R. and E. Nesbitt (1986). 'Sketches of Formal Hindu Nurture: Hindu Supplementary Classes in England.' In *World Religions in Education* (pp. 25–29). London: Commission for Racial Equality.

——— (1993). *Hindu Children in Britain*. Stoke on Trent: Trentham.

Khanduri, R. (2012). 'Does This Offend You? Hindu Visuality in the United States.' In *Public Hinduisms* (pp. 348–364). Eds. J. Zavos et al. London and New Delhi: Sage

Knott, K. (1986). *Hinduism in Leeds: A Study of Religious Practice in the Indian Hindu Community and Hindu-Related Groups*. Leeds: Community Religions Project, University of Leeds.

——— (2000) 'Hinduism in Britain.' In *The South Asian Religious Diaspora in Britain, Canada and the United States* (pp. 89–108). Eds. H. Coward, J.R. Hinnells, and R.B. Williams. New York: State University of New York Press.

Lal, V. (1999). 'The Politics of History on the Internet: Cyber-Diasporic Hindus and the North American Hindu Diaspora.' *Diaspora: A Journal of Transnational Studies* 8, No. 2: 137–172.

——— (2003). 'India in the World: Hinduism, the Diaspora, and the Anxiety of Influence.' *Australian Religious Studies Review* 16, No. 2: 19–37.

Mathew, B. and V. Prashad (2000). 'The Protean Forms of Yankee Hindutva.' *Ethnic and Racial Studies* 23, No. 3: 516–534.

McDonald, M. (1987). 'Rituals of Motherhood among Gujarati Women in East London.' In *Hinduism in Great Britain* (pp. 50–66). Ed. R. Burghart. London: Tavistock.

Nesbitt, E. (2006). 'Locating British Hindus' Sacred Space.' *Contemporary South Asia* 15, No. 2: 147–164.

Nye, M. (1995). *A Place for Our Gods: The Construction of a Temple Community in Edinburgh*. Richmond: Curzon.

——— (2001). *Multiculturalism and Minority Religions in Britain: Krishna Consciousness, Religious Freedom and the Politics of Location*. London: Routledge Curzon.

Raj, D. (2000). ' "Who the Hell Do You Think You Are?" Promoting Religious Identity among Young Hindus in Britain.' *Ethnic and Racial Studies* 23, No. 3: 535–558.

——— (2009). 'Hindu Protest in London-Stan: Lord Ram's Modern Transnational Epic Journey.' Paper presented at seminar on 'Hindu Transnationalisms: Origins, Ideologies, Networks.' Rice University, 20–21 November, 2009.

van der Veer, P. (1993). 'The Foreign Hand: Orientalist Discourse in Sociology and Communalism.' In *Orientalism and the Postcolonial Predicament* (pp. 23–44). Eds. C.A. Breckenridge and P. van der Veer. Philadelphia: University of Pennsylvania Press.

Vertovec, S. (2000). *The Hindu Diaspora: Comparative Patterns*. London: Routledge.

———— (2004). 'Migrant Transnationalism and Modes of Transformation.' *International Migration Review* 38, No. 3: 970–1001.

Visram, R. (1986). *Ayahs, Lascars and Princes: Indians in Britain 1700–1947*. London: Pluto Press.

Warrier, M. (2010). 'The Temple Bull Controversy at Skanda Vale and the Construction of Hindu Identity in Britain.' *International Journal of Hindu Studies* 13, No. 3: 261–278.

———— (2012). 'Krishna Consciousness, Hinduism and Religious Education in Britain.' In *Public Hinduisms* (pp. 463–486). Eds. J. Zavos et al. London and New Delhi: Sage.

Zavos, J. (2008). 'Stamp It out! Disciplining the Image of Hinduism in a Multicultural Milieu.' *Contemporary South Asia* 16, No. 3: 323–337.

———— (2009). 'Negotiating Multiculturalism: the Organisation of Hindu Identity in Contemporary Britain', *Journal of Ethnicity and Migration Studies*, 35, 6: 881–900.

———— (2010a). 'Situating Hindu Nationalism in the UK: Vishwa Hindu Parishad and the Development of a British Hindu Identity.' *Journal of Commonwealth and Comparative Politics* 48, No. 1: 2–22.

———— (2010b). 'Diaspora Consciousness, Nationalism, and "Religion": The Case of Hindu Nationalism.' In *The Call of the Homeland: Diaspora Nationalisms, Past and Present* (pp. 323–344). Eds. A Gal, A. S. Leoussi, and A. D. Smith. Leiden and Boston: Brill.

———— (2012). 'Hindu Organisation and the Negotiation of Public Space in Contemporary Britain.' In *Public Hinduisms* (pp. 70–89). Eds. J. Zavos et al. London and New Delhi: Sage.

9   Hinduism in the United States

Prema Kurien

There are no official figures on how many Hindus there are in the United States. The US government does not collect data on religion, but surveys conducted by other organizations can provide us with good estimates. According to the Global Religious Landscape study (Pew Forum 2012a), there were 1,790,000 Hindus in the United States in 2010, mostly from India. While Hindus comprise over 80% of the population of India, due to large proportions of Indian Christians and Sikhs in the United States, Hindus make up only 51% of Indian Americans (Pew Forum 2012b). There are now over 1,500 Hindu American temples and centers (Briggs 2011) not to mention several thousands of local Hindu organizations scattered across the country. While it can be said that Hinduism has become established in the United States, it is best not to think of it as something transplanted wholesale from India to the United States. Rather, Hindu organizations, practices, and interpretations have been modified and reworked as the religion has been institutionalized in the American context.

This chapter addresses two central issues. First, it examines some of the challenges that Hindu Americans have had to face during the process of institutionalizing Hinduism in the United States, addressing along the way the issue of how and why Hinduism and Hindu organizations have come to be modified in the process. Second, it explores the kinds of concerns that ordinary Hindus and Hindu leaders have experienced with respect to how Hinduism is both perceived and represented in the United States. In this context, the chapter will explore particular attempts to contest certain negative characterizations of Hinduism. I focus in particular on two types of Hindu organization: those that help Hindus re-create, practice, and transmit their religion and cultural traditions, and those that act as the public representatives of Hindu Americans. What I have to say draws on eight years of field research and interviews between the mid-1990s and the early 2000s. In this research, I focused on a range of Hindu Indian American organizations: *satsangs* (local worship groups), *bala vihars* (educational groups for children), temples, Hindu student organizations, and Hindu umbrella groups. My research also includes ongoing research on the activities of various Hindu American advocacy organizations and their leaders. To maintain confidentiality, I use pseudonyms throughout for the local organizations and members.

Re-creating Hinduism in America

Unlike most other established religions, Hinduism does not have a founder, an ecclesiastical structure of authority, or a single canonical text or commentary. Consequently, in India, Hinduism largely consists of an extraordinary array of practices, deities, texts, and schools of thought. It is also a religion that tends to stress proper behavior (orthopraxis) over proper theological belief (orthodoxy). For these reasons, the average Hindu immigrant is often unable to explain the 'meaning' of Hinduism and its 'central tenets.' Of course, this is something that she or he is repeatedly asked to do in the American context. A variety of Hindu organizations have developed to address the needs of immigrants and their children in the United States.

Some of these organizations, such as *bala viharas* are unique to the US context, while others such as the *satsang* represent modifications from common Indian patterns. *Bala vihars* arose in the United States as a means to provide religious education for children. Such instruction may often also include both language training and classes in Indian history. These *bala viharas* are largely a diasporic invention. By contrast, *satsang* groups represent something like the local articulation of an Indian model. Such groups typically meet once or twice a month. During the meetings, lay members will perform *puja* (worship), offer prayers, perform chants, the sing *bhajans* (devotional songs), and, frequently, engage in a discussion of sacred texts. Insofar as many Hindu devotional movements have emphasized forms of group worship through meetings like the *satsang*, in India it is also true that many Hindus worship as families or as individuals; Hinduism does not require either group meetings or even attendance at temple worship. It is therefore worth noting that many Hindu immigrants continue such home-based religious practices and family rituals in the United States. Home shrines of Hindu Americans may consist of a whole room set aside for worship, an elaborate shrine cabinet with images of deities and other sacred objects, or merely a few pictures or images in a closet or arranged on the kitchen counter. But given the nature of diasporic life, Hindu immigrants have tended to experience a need for the sense of community. As such, many will also participate in congregational forms of worship like the *satsang*.

The teaching of Indian culture and values to children is an important reason for the popularity of community gatherings and constitutes the primary reason for the creation of *bala vihars*. In India, children 'breathe in the values of Hindu life' (Fenton 1988: 127). In the United States on the other hand, parents realize that unless they make a deliberate effort, children will never learn what being Hindu or Indian means. Although quick to appreciate the economic and educational benefits they obtain through immigration to countries like the United States, Indian immigrants also tend to be critical of many aspects of American culture and society. They experience their new home as characterized by unstable families, lack of close community ties, sexual promiscuity, violence, drug and alcohol abuse, and teenage delinquency. Hindu immigrants to the United States also face negative racial, cultural, and religious stereotypes. Living in isolation from the larger supportive networks of relatives and friends they were accustomed to in India has meant that Hindus in the United States have been eager to re-create forms of community and to carry on important ethnic and religious traditions. Institutions like *bala vihars* and *satsangs* capitalize on the expertise of knowledgeable people within the community and help children and parents deal with many of the issues they confront in their everyday lives. Such gatherings also benefit from the participation of an increasing number of retirees and older immigrants who have more leisure time to spend on congregational activities.

Describing his motivation to form an association, the founding president of one *satsang*, the Kerala Hindu Organization (KHO), Ravi Menon told me: 'My idea was to develop a support group for Hindu Malayalees.[1] Christians have the church as a support group, Hindus don't have anything.' Other members of the KHO executive committee echoed Mr. Menon's views. During my first meeting with members of the committee Hari Ramanan commented: 'Growing up as Hindus in a Judeo-Christian environment can be difficult. There are so many misconceptions here about Indians and Hindus. People ask us about the cows roaming the streets—they think we are all vegetarians, that India is full of snake charmers. A few of us, not all, feel a sense of being persecuted as non-Christians.' He said that one of the reasons for the creation of the KHO was as a means to correct such misconceptions. Priya Ramachandran, another executive member continued: 'We are not fanatics but being a Hindu organization, we believe very strongly that the Hindu religion and faith should be preserved forever. We believe that Hindu values have a big role to play in the future world and we are all proud of being Hindus.' Other organizations trace their origins more specifically to the desire to cater to the needs of children. This is true of the Tamil *bala vihar*.[2] Vivek Iyer, one of the founders of the Tamil *bala vihar* said his goal was to impart cultural and moral values to Hindu children in the United States when they were young. After this, he felt they would be 'set for life.'

In my research, I have found that both the *satsang* and the *bala vihar* have been successful in creating close-knit groups that can act as something like an 'extended family.' They help members deal with the very practical issues of relocation and settlement as well as with any number of problems they face as immigrants in a new country. Parents involved in both the *satsang* and the *bala vihar* also felt that their children had benefitted a great deal from the organizations. In the absence of the kinds of residential concentration typical among other immigrant groups (such as Italian Americans or Polish Americans), the *satsangs* and *bala vihars* of Indian Americans are often the only place where the members are free to interact with other members of their religious community. Through their activities, second-generation children are socialized into their Indian–American identity and are encouraged to meet other young people who can provide peer support. Children involved in such organizations told me that 'it is really hard growing up here as both Indian and American.' One difficulty is thought to stem from the different expectations Indian parents have for their children when compared with their American counterparts. Another comes in the form of the kinds of racism and ethnocentrism Hindu children may experience while growing up. *Bala vihar* sessions help children talk through their struggles and provide them with strategies for balancing their Indian and American identities.

The beneficial effect that a *bala vihar* can have on youngsters is eloquently described by Hema Narayan who wrote an essay for school on the topic of diversity that won a national prize. Initially, she wrote, she struggled to 'fit in' by trying to be like her classmates and by rejecting her Indian identity. Over time, as she began to learn more about the richness of her heritage from her parents and the *bala vihar*:

> I became more confident and sure of myself. With a wealth of knowledge by my side, I felt strong. I stood up to my classmates and introduced them to my beliefs. To my surprise, they stopped mocking me, and instead, wanted to know more. . . . I felt a sense of belonging, but not sameness, as though I were an individual piece adding color to the complete picture. I could fit in but still be different.

While many teenagers felt that a *satsang* like KHO 'was an organization for adults,' they also acknowledged that the group had helped them indirectly by putting them in contact with adults and other children from the community. 'It made me finally comfortable as an Indian. I realized that there were many other people out there who are like me, who talk like me and that I am not by myself,' elaborated Mohan, one of the teenage boys involved in the *satsang*.

In my research, I was interested in the ways in which both the *satsang* and the *bala vihar* adapted Hindu practices and interpretations to fit the American context. Sometimes these adaptations were made in an attempt to find common ground among Hindus from a variety of subtraditions. At other times, the goal was to let children of Indian origin know 'that our heritage is not a hindrance but a help.' The KHO started a Bhagavad Gita discussion period (modeled on Bible study sessions). In many of the *bala vihar* sessions I attended, concepts such as 'family values' and a good 'work ethic' were the focus of discussion. Overall, the goal of such sessions seemed to be to show children how Hindu values were important and remained relevant in dealing with the daily problems of their lives in the United States.

For instance, one session featured discussion of a traditional Hindu story featuring a figure known as the *pativrata* or 'ideal wife.' The story told of a loving wife who, through devotion to her husband, was able to amass greater spiritual power than a religious mendicant who had performed severe austerities for many years. The moral of the story was that the earthly duty of a wife toward her husband was more important for women than even their spiritual obligations and that this devotion could procure them supernatural powers. Kalpana Subramanian, who narrated this story, concluded triumphantly that for this reason, 'women actually have a better deal since men do not have this power.' She then hastened to add, 'but this is not because women are seen as dumb or passive but precisely because they are capable.' Kalpana went on to emphasize that the duty of the wife was not merely one-sided because men also had an obligation to look after their wives. She also emphasized that the duty of the *pativrata* did not mean that women should be submissive. In order to illustrate her argument, she gave several examples selected from the Hindu epics of loving husbands and assertive women. I was struck by the fact that Mrs. Subramanian's presentation and interpretation of the story and its moral were considerably different and more egalitarian than more traditional understandings of the concept of *pativrata* in India. In the latter case, the ideal wife is thought to be the one who worships her husband as God, puts his interest above hers in all situations, and does everything she can to fulfill his every desire.

Through my research, I also realized that Hindu organizations like *satsangs* and *bala vihars* provided important mechanisms through which Indian Americans were able to maintain and reproduce their socioeconomic status. Apart from providing a setting in which to establish professional contacts and identify resources to help the immigrant generation succeed in their jobs, I found that most of the college-going youngsters in both kinds of group had plans to attend premier educational institutions. Not only was education strongly emphasized by parents and relatives, but being part of a group such as the KHO and the Tamil *bala vihar* provided both children and parents with the concrete resources and knowledge to achieve educational success. Information regarding the process of selecting high schools, summer programs, extracurricular activities, SAT coaching classes, as well as test preparation and test-taking strategies, what to emphasize in personal statements, and how to go about the admission and financial aid process was available within the group and was often also exchanged over monthly dinners and over the phone.

Hindu student organizations represent another diasporic invention in the United States. Several of the youngsters I talked to indicated that it is often in college that issues of identity become important, particularly for minority groups. Faced with the fact of multiculturalism on college campuses, minority students find it necessary to be able to articulate 'who we are and what we are about.' Hindu student organizations provide the second generation (and sometimes Hindu students from India) a forum in which they can discuss these sorts of issues in a safe space. Now prevalent in many of the universities and college campuses around the country, Hindu student organizations offer counterparts to the kinds of campus religious organizations popular among other communities and denominations. Campus groups generally meet at least a few times a semester (some of the more active organizations meet weekly) for discussions about various Hindu and Indian concepts and practices, presentations on various aspects of the religion by knowledgeable Hindus in the community, and to celebrate Hindu festivals. Hindu student groups also organize periodic trips to local temples and other Hindu venues. Many Hindu student organizations are specific to their particular campuses, but there is also an important national organization, the Hindu Student Council, which was formed in 1990. The meetings of the Hindu Student Council chapter that I studied were organized and moderated by the two young women who served as cochairs for the year. They would introduce a topic for a session by summarizing an article or by identifying a central issue and would then facilitate discussion among members. Topics treated in the semester that I attended included 'the Hindu male,' discussion of an article (downloaded from the Internet) entitled, 'Why I am not a South Asian,' the concept of 'desire' in the Gita, 'nationalistic dharma,' a discussion of Genre magazine's write up on homosexuality in Hinduism and its decision to feature a depiction of Lord Krishna on the cover, and a presentation on the RSS (*Rashtriya Swayamsevak Sangh*, a Hindu nationalist organization in India) by some local Hindu activists (see Kurien 2005).

As mentioned, Hindu temples have by now mushroomed all over the United States. Since the Hindu temple is considered to be a dwelling place for deities in the world of man, great care is taken in its construction. Precise mathematical rules laid out in ancient Hindu architectural texts known as *Shastras* and *Agamas* govern the geometry of the ground plan, the dimensions, shape and placement of the structure, the proportions of the different parts of the temple, and the size of the *murti* (image). Traditional temple architects (*sthapati*) in India follow these architectural texts when designing temples, and it should be noted that all the major temples in the United States have been designed by well-known Indian temple architects. Local Hindu engineers in the United States donate their time and expertise to make sure the new structures satisfy local building codes.

One distinctive feature of American Hindu temples is that many of them, particularly the ones that were first established in the United States, tend to be more 'ecumenical' than temples in India (Williams 1992: 239). In India, many temples are devoted to a single regional deity and often the local language is used for rituals and worship. Because of the enormous expense involved when constructing a temple in the United States, typically diverse Hindu groups join together to raise the necessary funds. As a result, many American Hindu temples often house the major Indian deities (such as Shiva and Rama) while also enshrining deities from regional or specific sectarian traditions (such as Murugan). Rituals and worship in ecumenical temples are generally conducted in Sanskrit. But in the American context, there often is a greater emphasis on understanding. The meaning of religious performances are frequently explained in Hindi or English for the benefit of the temple's eclectic audience. It is interesting to note that many temples around the country have been able to overcome long-standing tensions between the two major Hindu theological traditions in India—the *Vaishnavite* (devotees of Lord Vishnu and his *avatars*) and the *Shaivite* (devotees of Lord Shiva and his retinue)—by constructing shrines to both Lord Vishnu and Lord Shiva within the same temple. And yet it would seem few temples have been able to overcome the cultural and religious divide between north and south Indian traditions, which differ in terms of building styles, rituals, worship customs, language, and ritual chants. As a result, worshipers from one tradition may not always feel at home in temples belonging to the other tradition. Consequently, separate north Indian and south Indian temples are generally constructed in the United States.[3]

As religious institutions become de facto ethnic institutions, American temples also become cultural and social centers for Hindu Americans. In this they perform a range of services not typically performed by temples in India. Apart from classes on Hinduism, many temples offer classes on Indian language, music, and dance and may have a central hall where dance, drama, and music recitals are regularly performed. Many temples now schedule their major weekly *pujas* over the weekend for the convenience of the devotees. This promotes greater congregationalism of temple worship in the United States when compared to India.

The American environment also affects the important issue of temple administration. The Hindu temple in the United States is founded as an American corporation and a nonprofit organization and is consequently bound by the legal rules applicable to such entities. In accordance with these rules, temples must have a 'general body' and a 'board of directors.' Thus they are required to develop 'membership lists.' This means that members of the temple must hold elections to choose members of the board of directors. None of these are traditional practices in India. Such requirements can lead to significant disputes over who constitutes a 'member' of a temple and who is in fact a 'Hindu.' The position of wealthy donors to the temple may become another source of dispute since the norms of 'custom and usage' governing both symbolic and material temple transactions that apply in India are not officially recognized in the United States. Thus, rights of ritual precedence during worship and control over trusteeship can become contentious issues in American temples; on occasion, disputes over these issues give rise to legal conflicts (Kurien 2006a).

The status and role of Hindu temple priests in the United States are also affected in many ways by the American context. Official rules regarding visas regulate the terms under which Hindu officiants arrive in the country, what their relationship should be to the temple that employs them, and how long they must reside in the United States before a temple can sponsor them for a green card. Once again, the ecumenism of major Hindu American temples also means that priests who specialize in particular theological traditions (e.g. *Vaishnavism* or *Shaivism*) may have to be willing to learn several new rituals and chants and officiate in temples belonging to opposing traditions. In addition, priests may have to learn to drive in order to be able to visit private residences to conduct home ceremonies. Finally, unlike the Indian context, Hindu priests in the United States are often required to be able to 'explain' to the audience the meaning of the rituals they perform. This is especially important for second-generation American members and for non-Hindu visitors. Some priests are also expected to act as counselors and advisors to temple visitors. For all these reasons, the priests I interviewed pointed out that the demands on Hindu priests in the United States were far greater than in India.

In addition to 'ecumenical' temples, there are also sectarian temples like the temples of the *Bochasanwasi Akshar Purushottam Sanstha* (BAPS), a Vaishnava *sanstha* (subsect) from the state of Gujarat, organized around the figure of a divine guru and succession of charismatic leaders. Although BAPS members comprise only about 5% of the population of Gujarat and constitute only a small percentage of Hindus in the diaspora, they have often become the public face of Hinduism, particularly in the West. Some of the largest, costliest, and most ornate temples outside India have been built by this group, largely through the volunteer labor of its devotees. As a congregational group, the temple plays a different religious role in BAPS worship and communal activity than it does for the kinds of Hindu worshipers discussed above. In addition to being the house of God, the BAPS temple is also the space where the religious community meets to learn about their sacred scriptures and their Lord (known as Swaminarayan), to hear about the activities of their current guru Pramukh Swami, and to perform those public rituals that are central to their faith. As a congregational sect organized around a central figure, the BAPS temple is able to create community and to provide for transmission of religion to adults and children in a much more systematic way than temples predicated on more traditional models. In this respect, sectarian temples like those of BAPS operate analogously to *satsangs* and *bala vihars*.

Representing Hinduism and Hindu Interests in America

In addition to the organizations mentioned above, there are also a variety of Hindu American advocacy organizations whose goal is to act as public representatives and protectors of Hinduism and Hindus in the United States. These advocacy groups are pan-Hindu or umbrella organizations that aim to unite and represent Hindus from a variety of traditions and regions of India. In India, the major Hindu umbrella groups are interlinked and known collectively as the *Sangh Parivar*, or the family of (Hindu) organizations. These offer politicized expressions of what is often referred to as Hindutva ideology, first developed during the colonial period and deployed to mobilize Indians around a collective Hindu nationalist ideology. Some Hindu American umbrella organizations are branches of *Sangh Parivar* organizations even if they often claim to be 'independent' organizations in the United States. There are also a large number of other Hindu umbrella organizations, both regional and national, that are not directly connected with the ideology or programs of the *Sangh Parivar*. Some of these organizations identify themselves as 'Hindu,' but there are also other labels adopted by those groups in their attempts to promote Hinduism. For instance, many Hindus interested in challenging what they took to be the dominant portrayal of their religion and culture in the scholarly academy mobilized under an 'Indic' identity in the 1990s and early 2000s. The emphasis of these Indic groups is in promoting 'authentic' South Asia understandings of Hinduism. Other Hindus chose to emphasize the distinctiveness of Hinduism by contrasting it with the Abrahamic religions (e.g. Judaism, Christianity, and Islam). We could say these groups organized around a 'Dharmic' identity, where the uniting emphasis was located in some understanding of Hinduism as eternal *dharma*. We may also identify several 'Vedic' organizations, which promote the scriptural roots of true Hinduism.

One of the most respected contemporary sources of authority on Hinduism outside of India from the 1990s has been the Hindu periodical *Hinduism Today* published by the Himalayan Academy of the Kauai Monastery in Hawaii. However, perhaps the best-known and most active Hindu umbrella organization in the United States is the Hindu American Foundation (HAF), which was formed in 2003. The HAF is also the first Hindu umbrella organization to have a professional organizational structure and full-time staff. It is headquartered in the nation's capital, a location that has allowed the HAF to become well integrated with governmental and policy offices and to attain greater national visibility. HAF activists gain additional visibility through their regular contribution to online publications such as the *Huffington Post*, Patheos.com, the 'On Faith' section of the online edition of the *Washington Post/Newsweek*, as well as the Indian e-newspaper, DailyPioneer.com.

In the United States, immigrant mobilization around religion to promote recognition and greater inclusion within the religious fabric and identity of the nation has a long tradition, from the mobilization of Irish and European Catholics in the nineteenth century to the activism of Jews in the twentieth century. This pattern, together with the legitimization provided by contemporary multiculturalism spurred Hindus to mobilize in an effort to correct misperceptions about their religion and to obtain greater recognition and respect. Hindu American leaders frequently draw a parallel between the struggle of Hindus in this regard and that of Jews in the United States. Following the pattern of American Jews, one of the first types of organizations that Hindu Americans formed that was explicitly oriented toward the wider American society were antidefamation groups. In 1997, the Vishwa Hindu Parishad of America (VHPA), an umbrella group affiliated with the Vishwa Hindu Parishad (VHP; part of the *Sangh Parivar* organization in India), formed the group American Hindus against Defamation (AHAD). This group has as its goal the aggressive defense of Hinduism against defamation, commercialization, and misuse. The organization has been involved in several successful protest campaigns against the use of Hindu deities, icons, and texts by American businesses and the entertainment industry. The success of AHAD was followed by the formation of several other antidefamation groups around the country. Following in this tradition, the HAF mobilizes whenever Christian evangelical leaders or US politicians are reported to have made anti-Hindu statements. HAF members are also active around incidents of discrimination and attacks on Hindus on a global scale through their annual report on Hindu Human Rights, which draws attention to assaults and indignities faced by Hindus in countries where they are a minority.

Due to the lack of recognition and understanding of Hinduism in the United States, the negative stereotypes faced by Hindus, and the absence of a compulsory religious education in American public schools, an important task facing Hindu American organizations has been to educate Americans about Hinduism. For instance, the website of the HAF offers a number of resources, including a link to 'Hinduism 101,' a Q&A booklet that explains the central briefs and practices of Hinduism, and a media tool kit detailing the top five 'misrepresentations' of Hinduism in the US media. Since 2009, they have also distributed pocket-sized 'Hinduism 2 Go' cards for use at interfaith gatherings and other events. In the process, an encapsulated, rather intellectualized Hinduism is promoted, which is in many respects very different from the diversity of on-the-ground ritual practices and caste observances characteristic of everyday Hinduism in India.

Many American Hindu groups like the HAF proclaim 'tolerance' and 'pluralism' as the 'essence of Hinduism' (see the website for HAF). One verse in particular from the Rig Veda is routinely cited by way of substantiating this claim: 'truth is one, sages call it by different names' (Rig Veda 1.164.46). At the same time, Hinduism in the United States is explicitly compared to the Abrahamic religions. Here too, American Hindu leaders frequently contrast the purported inclusivity of Hinduism with what they take to be the exclusivity of Abrahamic traditions, especially Islam and Christianity (see Shukla 2010). Many Hindu American leaders also refer to Hinduism as *sanatana Dharma* (eternal faith) in order to make the point that it is the most ancient and universalistic of all religions. They counter the negative American image of Hinduism as something primitive by arguing that contrary to American stereotypes, Hinduism is actually very sophisticated and scientific. Evidence to support this portrayal include the claim that Hindus recognize the history of the universe to be billions of years old and other claims about ancient Indian advances in astronomy, mathematics, metallurgy, and physics. Hindu American groups have also been active in interfaith forums and discussions around the country to promote a similar 'Dharmic' perspective on religion.

Hindu American leaders and groups have also focused on gaining public recognition of Hinduism as an American religion (see Image 9.1). In September 2000, despite opposition from conservative Christians, Indian American lobby groups were successful in having a Hindu priest open a session of Congress for the first time, an achievement reported with great pride in Indian-American newspapers and websites.[4] Further proof of the official recognition of Hindu Americans came a month later when President Bill Clinton issued a proclamation from the White House wishing Indian Americans a Happy Diwali (the 'festival of lights,' an important Hindu festival). Subsequently, President George Bush institutionalized the practice of having Diwali celebrated in the White House (although he did not himself attend), while President Obama has personally made a point of attending the celebration since 2009 (except in 2010 when

Figure 9.1 Secretary of State John Kerry greets Hindu priest at US State Department
Diwali celebration

he participated in a Diwali celebration in India). In the fall of 2007, at the urging of the HAF, the Senate and the House of Representatives passed resolutions (written with the input of the HAF) recognizing the significance of the festival of Diwali (Shukla 2008: 27). These activities have served to bring Hinduism to the attention of a wider group of Americans. No doubt as a result of such Hindu American activism and the rising public profile of Hindu Americans in administrative circles, President Obama included Hindus in his first inaugural address when he described the United States as 'a nation of Christians and Muslims, Jews and Hindus, and non-believers,' a description which overjoyed Hindu Americans as this was the first time they were officially recognized as forming part of the American religious canopy.

Finally, Hindu American leaders have been very active in the educational arena to challenge the presentation of their religious histories and traditions in school textbooks and within American academia (Kurien 2007b). The HAF and other Hindu groups have mobilized to demand a positive portrayal of Hinduism in school textbooks seeking a kind of parity with the treatment of other religions. They have been involved in such activism in Virginia, California, and Texas, including a long-drawn-out legal battle against the California State Board of Education (see Reddy 2012 for details). Hindu American groups and leaders also charge that, unlike their treatment of Abrahamic religions, Western academic scholars of Hinduism tend to focus on sensationalist, negative attributes of the religion and represent it in a demeaning way that is disrespectful to the sentiments of practitioners (see Sippy 2012 for a discussion).

Many of these critical perspectives were published in a volume, *Invading the Sacred: An Analysis of Hinduism Studies in America* (Ramaswamy et. al 2007), which went on to be discussed at various Hindu meetings in India and the United States. One particular Hindu American leader, Rajiv Malhotra, who was the sponsor behind the publication of *Invading the Sacred*, has been writing and speaking about these issues since the year 2000. Although he is not an academic, he is nonetheless frequently present to observe meetings of the American Academy of Religion (AAR). Malhotra has also written several newspaper articles (see Kurien 2007a and 2012 for more details) and at least two books, *Breaking India: Western Interventions in Dravidian and Dalit Faultlines* (Malhotra and Neelakandan 2011), and *Being Different: An Indian Challenge to Western Universalism* (Malhotra 2011). His arguments have been widely discussed in both popular and academic circles (e.g. see Larson 2012).

Conclusion

While Hinduism is generally transmitted informally in India, Hindu Americans realized that more formal institutions and mechanisms were needed to accomplish this task in the United States. In addition to practicing and reproducing Hinduism, local Hindu organizations also serve to create community; provide professional, educational, and economic support; understand and articulate identity; and provide a shelter from the racism and cultural misunderstanding that Hindus encounter in the wider society. The American context has occasioned changes in traditional organizations like *satsangs* and temples, and has led to the development of new institutions such as *bala vihars* and Hindu student groups. At the same time, Hindu umbrella organizations have arisen in the United States to define Hinduism and represent Hindu interests. Spokespersons for Hinduism in the United States define the distinctiveness of Hinduism with respect to other religions, defend the religion from misrepresentations and criticism, and seek to have Hinduism recognized as an important contributor to the American religious fabric. Through these organizations, Hindu Americans have been playing a significant role in reshaping the contours of religion, society, and politics in the United States (see also Kurien 2006a, 2006b). As Hindu Americans continue their work to integrate into the American religious landscape, we can expect to see the religion change in new and fascinating ways.

Summary

This chapter focuses on five types of organizations through which Hinduism has been institutionalized in the United States: *satsangs, bala vihars*, Hindu student organizations, temples, and umbrella groups. In addition to congregational forms of worship and formal mechanisms to transmit culture and religion to the younger generation, there are also organizations to unite Hindus and represent their interests. This chapter also describes several of the practices and interpretations that are characteristic of American Hinduism and shows how the formation and development of an American Hinduism has been shaped by the social, legal, and political context in the United States. Finally, this chapter addresses some of the ways in which Hindus have become visible and consequential actors within the American religious landscape as a result of these organizations. American Hindu leaders want Hinduism to be recognized and respected as a global religion and—in view of the large number of adherents in the United States—as a genuinely American religion as well.

Discussion Questions

- In what ways has Hinduism been transformed in the United States?
- How have these changes been prompted or shaped by the American context?
- What are some of the ways in which Hindus have become visible and consequential actors within the American religious landscape?
- Recall what you have learnt about Hinduism in school and college. Do you think Hinduism was presented negatively in comparison with other religious traditions? Explain.

Notes

1 Malayalam is the language spoken in the state of Kerala.
2 Tamil is the language spoken in the south Indian state of Tamil Nadu.
3 As part of my research, I studied both a more 'ecumenical' south Indian temple and a 'sectarian' north Indian temple, both located in Southern California.
4 A Hindu priest was also invited to open a Senate session in July 2007, but his prayer was disrupted by Christian demonstrators.

Suggested Readings

Dempsey, C. (2005). *The Goddess Lives in Upstate New York: Breaking Convention and Making Home at a North American Hindu Temple*. New York: Oxford University Press.
An examination of a temple in upstate New York, including a description of the roots of the practices as well as a discussion of how the temple is and is not typical of North American Hinduism.
Joshi, K. (2012). 'Religion in the Lives of Second-Generation Indian American Hindus.' In *Race, Ethnicity, and Religion among the Latino and Asian American Second Generation* (pp. 241–258). Eds. C. Chen and R. Jeung. New York: New York University Press.
A sociological examination of two waves of Hindu immigrants in America, focusing on the intersection between their religious and ethnic identities.
Kurien, P. (2007). *A Place at the Multicultural Table: The Development of an American Hinduism*. New Brunswick: Rutgers University Press.
Examines Hinduism in America as distinctly multicultural, discussing popular Hinduism, official Hinduism, and the connection between the two.

Zavos, J., P. Kanungo, D. S. Reddy, M. Warrier, and R. B. Williams, eds., (2012). *Public Hinduisms*. Thousand Oaks: Sage Publications Inc.
A collection of essays examining how Hinduism becomes public and the ramifications of becoming public both to the societies where this happens and for the traditions themselves.

Bibliography

Briggs, D. (2011). 'First Hindu Census Reveals Quiet Growth in U.S.' *Association of Religion Data Archives*. Retrieved May 20, 2013. http://blogs.thearda.com/trend/featured/first-hindu-census-reveals-quiet-growth-in-u-s/

Eck, D. L. (2001). *A New Religious America: How a 'Christian Country' Has Now Become the World's Most Religiously Diverse Nation*. San Francisco: Harper Collins Publishers.

Fenton, J. Y. (1988). *Transplanting Religious Traditions: Asian Indians in America*. New York: Praeger.

Kibria, N. (2006). 'South Asian Americans.' In *Asian Americans: Contemporary Trends and Issues* (pp. 206–227). Ed. P. G. Min. Thousand Oaks: Pine Forge Press.

Kurien, P. (2004). 'Multiculturalism, Immigrant Religion, and Diasporic Nationalism: The Development of an American Hinduism.' *Social Problems* 51, No. 3: 362–385.

—— (2005). 'Being Young, Brown, and Hindu: The Identity Struggles of Second Generation Indian Americans.' *Journal of Contemporary Ethnography* 34, No. 4: 434–469.

—— (2006a). 'Multiculturalism and 'American' Religion: The Case of Hindu Indian Americans.' *Social Forces* 85, No. 2: 723–742.

—— (2006b). 'Mr. President, Why Do You Exclude Us from Your Prayers? Hindus Challenge American Pluralism.' In *A Nation of Religions: The Politics of Pluralism in Multireligious America* (pp. 119–138). Ed. S. Prothero. Chapel Hill: University of North Carolina Press.

—— (2007a). *A Place at the Multicultural Table: The Development of an American Hinduism*. New Brunswick: Rutgers University Press.

—— (2007b). 'Redefining Americanness by Reformulating Hinduism: Indian Americans Challenge American Academia.' In *Race, Nation, and Empire in American History* (pp. 307–334). Eds. J. T. Campbell, M. Guterl, and R. Lee. Chapel Hill: University of North Carolina Press.

—— (2012). 'What is American about American Hinduism? Hindu Umbrella Organizations in the U.S. in Comparative Perspective.' In *Public Hinduisms* (pp. 90–111). Eds. J. Zavos, P. Kanungo, D. S. Reddy, M. Warrier, and R. B. Williams. Thousand Oaks: Sage Publications.

Malhotra, R. (2011). *Being Different: An Indian Challenge to Western Universalism*. New Delhi: HarperCollins.

Malhotra, R. and A. Neelakandan (2011). *Breaking India: Western Interventions in Dravidian and Dalit Faultlines*. New Delhi: Amaryllis.

Mathew, B. and V. Prashad (2000). 'The Protean Forms of Yankee Hindutva.' *Ethnic and Racial Studies* 23, No. 3: 516–534.

Larson, G. J. (2012). 'The Issue of Not *Being Different* Enough: Some Reflections on Rajiv Malhotra's *Being Different*.' *International Journal of Hindu Studies* 16, No. 3:311–322.

Narayanan, V. (1992). Creating South Indian Hindu Experience in the United States. In *A Sacred Thread: Modern Transmission of Hindu Traditions in India and Abroad* (pp. 147–176). Ed. R. B. Williams. Chambersburg: Anima Publications.

Pew Forum (2012a). 'The Global Religious Landscape: A Report on the Size and Distribution of the World's Major Religious Groups as of 2010.' Pew Forum on Religion and Public Life, December 18. Retrieved December 27, 2012. http://www.pewforum.org/global-religious-landscape.aspx

———— (2012b). 'The Rise of Asian Americans.' Pew Social and Demographic Trends, Pew Research Center Report. Retrieved June 22, 2012. http://www.pewsocialtrends.org/2012/06/19/the-rise-of-asian-americans/

Portes, A. and R. Rumbaut (2006). *Immigrant America: A Portrait.* 3rd ed. Berkeley: University of California Press.

Rajagopal, A. (2000). 'Hindu Nationalism in the United States: Changing Configurations of Political Practice.' *Ethnic and Racial Studies* 23, No. 3: 467–515.

Rajghatta, C. (2002). 'India Tops China in Student Inflow to U.S.' *India West.* A 35.

———— (2009). 'Indian Students in US Cross 100,000 Mark.' *Times of India,* November 18. Retrieved May 21, 2011. http://timesofindia.indiatimes.com/world/us/Indian-students-in-US-cross-100000-mark/articleshow/5240338.cms#ixzz0xMMeDJFt

Ramaswamy, K., A. de Nicolas, and A. Banerjee, eds. (2007). *Invading the Sacred: An Analysis of Hinduism Studies in America.* New Delhi: Rupa & Co.

Reddy, D.S. (2012). 'Hindu Transnationalisms: Organisations, Ideologies, Networks.' In *Public Hinduisms* (pp. 309–323). Eds. J. Zavos, P. Kanugo, D. Reddy, M. Warrier, and R. B. Williams. Thousand Oaks: Sage Publications.

Shukla, A. (2010). 'Exclusivists versus Pluralists: Very Different Paths to the One Truth.' Retrieved May 21, 2011. http://newsweek.washingtonpost.com/onfaith/panelists/aseem_shukla/2010/07/the_question_posed_here_on.html

Shukla, S. (2008). 'Hindu American Political Advocacy.' *Swadharma* 3. Retrieved May 21, 2011. www.swadharma.org/public/Swadharmav3.pdf.

Sippy, S. (2012). 'Will the Real Mango Please Stand Up? Reflections on Defending Dharma and Historicising Hinduism.' In *Public Hinduisms* (pp. 22–44). Eds. J. Zavos, P. Kanungo, D. Reddy, M. Warrier, and R. B. Williams. Thousand Oaks: Sage Publications.

Vertovec, S. (2000). *The Hindu Diaspora: Comparative Patterns.* London and New York: Routledge Press.

Waghorne, J. P. (1999). 'The Hindu Gods in a Split-Level World: The Sri Siva-Vishnu Temple in Suburban Washington, D.C.' In *Gods of the City: Religion and the American Urban Landscape* (pp. 103–130). Ed. R. Orsi. Bloomington and Indianapolis: Indiana University Press.

Williams, R. (1988). *Religions of Immigrants from India and Pakistan: New Threads in the American Tapestry.* Cambridge: Cambridge University Press.

———— (1992). 'Sacred Threads of Several Textures.' In *A Sacred Thread: Modern Transmission of Hindu Traditions in India and Abroad* (pp. 228–257). Ed. R. Williams. Chambersburg: Anima Press.

Part IV
Networks of Meaning

10 Modern Monks and Global Hinduism

Timothy S. Dobe

'Up, India, and conquer the world with your spirituality!' Swami Vivekananda (1863–1902), perhaps Hinduism's most famous modern monk, issued this challenge to his fellow Indians and provided a personal example of spiritual conquest when he became a major sensation at Chicago's 1893 Parliament of World Religions (see Image 10.1). In his public lectures before the Parliament, Vivekananda not only defended Hinduism against its Evangelical Christian critics, he just as importantly won over an American audience craving spiritual truths from 'the East.' Building on his success, Vivekananda went on to establish the Vedanta Society, the first Hindu religious organization to spread across the western world. Through his personal charisma and the institutional support of the new society, Vivekananda helped ensure that his particular interpretation of Vedantic Hinduism would become dominant well into the twentieth century and beyond (Jackson 1994). Notwithstanding Vivekananda's unique accomplishments, he was by no means the only modern Hindu monk to yoke his status to the task of sanctioning a particular vision of Hinduism. As this chapter will demonstrate, modern Hinduism has been promoted and represented by a number of celibate ascetics, world-renouncing monks, and saffron-robed *sadhus*.

We might of course see such figures as continuing India's ancient spiritual tradition, indeed, as capturing the very timeless essence of Hinduism itself. In this view, their authentic spirituality remains untainted by and superior to the materialism of the modern west. Alternatively, we might see modern monks as quite different from their premodern ancestors, highlighting the ways modernity and colonialism transformed traditional practices. What have monks, who have supposedly renounced the world, after all, got to do with World Fairs, global spiritual 'conquest,' or, as we will see, the (masculinized) Indian nationalism they so often trumpeted?

Both of these interpretations, however, may rely too heavily on a strict opposition between 'tradition' and (western) 'modernity' that scholars increasingly have come to question and rethink. Is it adequate to imagine the former only as resisting the latter or to see the latter only as transforming the former, for good or ill? If we do not assume a strict binary of tradition and

Figure 10.1 Swami Vivekananda

modernity, I suggest below, modern monks can show us important, if unexpected, convergences between Hindu asceticism (in whatever period) and (western) modernity as usually conceived: media-savvy self-presentation, individualism, and protest are central in both contexts. In this chapter, I will draw examples of each of these features from my research on the modern Hindu monk Rama Tirtha (1873–1906) and the Indian Christian convert and *sadhu*, Sundar Singh (1889–1929), set in the context of wider trends represented by better-known figures such as Vivekananda. While an Indian Christian figure may seem tangential to modern Hinduism, his example helps to show how deeply intertwined the two traditions, in fact, were.

Monkish Mimesis between and beyond Modernity and Tradition

Perhaps surprisingly, many scholars have stressed the effects of colonialism on modern Hinduism so much that they have interpreted even modern monks in terms of the imitation (*mimesis*) of western models, rather than seeing them as traditional or as simply spiritual. The appeal of Hindu monks in a modernizing world can, for example, be understood by applying ideas from the German sociologist, Max Weber, who saw Europe's move away from medieval Catholic monasticism to an 'inner-worldly asceticism' as crucial for capitalist modernization (Weber 1985). That is, unlike Catholic monastic isolation, Puritans now worked to transform the world according to God's will and to confirm their own 'elect' status through self-disciplined professional work and accumulation of wealth. As a model in colonial India, this meant that, in contrast to earlier 'world-negating,' jungle-dwelling holy men, modern monks such as Vivekananda now founded institutions, pursued social reform, and developed new relationships with householders (nonascetics) as the latter emerged as a 'middle class' (Miller 1999; Sarkar 1992; Hatcher 2008). For some scholars, even such major transformations did not follow western precedents far enough: modern Hindus failed to become fully autonomous individuals because the philosophy promoted by modern monks (Vedanta) viewed the individual as unreal (*maya*) and produced a 'fragile . . . ego' (Bharati 1970). Worse still, modern Hindu 'monasticism'—along with a sense of sin, guilt, and repentance—might be seen not only as limited but as essentially defensive, a mere 'imitat[ion]' of Christianity based in Hindu insecurity and leading to antimodern fundamentalism (Copley 2000: 9).

As postcolonial scholars have pointed out, however, such transformations need not be seen as failures at, or (relative) successes in modernization, but in terms of imposed foreign models in need of deconstruction. Thus, modern Hinduism has been seen as too Christianized (Nandy 1989) or homogenized as a 'textualist/world religion,' (King 1999: 68) or shaped by 'Orientalist epistemology' (Hansen 1999: 67) and contrasted with earlier Hindu diversity and tolerance. Ashis Nandy links such impositions directly with Vivekananda and, the founder of the Arya Samaj and *brahman* monk (*sannyasi*), Dayanand Saraswati (d. 1883). Both, he claims, tried to 'Christianize Hinduism . . . with an organized priesthood, church and missionaries; accept[ed] the idea of proselytization and . . . the concept of The Book following the Semitic creeds (the Vedas and the Gītā); . . . and this-worldly asceticism borrowed . . . partly from

Calvinism' (Nandy 1989: 25). Mimetic models contain a strong, gendered dimension as well. Since colonialists often represented themselves as the manly rulers capable of making effeminate Indian men more civilized, Indians often touted their manliness to prove them wrong. Accordingly, Revathi Krishnaswamy describes modern Hinduism as a 'religion in the image of a muscular, monotheistic, heterosexual, masculine Protestantism,' linked with 'The Book' and 'an order of monks' (1998: 44–45). Vivekananda's own saying that Hindus could understand the *Bhagavad Gita* 'with biceps' and by eating beef (qtd. in Sil 1997: 53) makes this point well.

Yet these same transformations, including Victorian gender and other norms, were key to the rise of Indian anticolonial resistance centered on the figure of the holy man. The Indian appropriation of the 'affirmative Orientalism' of nineteenth-century European Romanticism, which imagined the East as a land of sages, mysticism, and otherworldliness enabled Vivekananda to turn the ascetic holy man into a 'heroic' ideal that could champion Indian superiority even amidst colonial rule (Chowdury-Sengupta 1996)—thus linking spirituality with ideas of global 'conquest,' as in the quote that begins this chapter. Ancient ascetic ideas about celibacy as a source of spiritual power (*tapas*), for example, were harnessed anew to argue that spirituality could equip Indians with the strength necessary to fight British rule as '*karmayogis*'—holy men (*yogis*) engaged with social and political action (*karma*). Arguably, the creation of an imagined sphere of 'spirituality' outside of the realm of direct colonial control allowed subordinated Indians to experience a kind of sovereignty that led to nationalist politics itself (Chatterjee 1993).

Such unexpected twists and turns of colonial history and religion have challenged scholars to go beyond simple contrasts (binaries) of modernity (Europe) and tradition (India) in search of new ways of describing transcultural dynamics. These models have included, among others, subaltern autonomy from and rebellion against western rule (Guha 2002); colonialism as a 'contact zone' in which colonizers and colonized encounter each other in diverse ways and times (Pratt 2007); an 'interactional' history in which western modernity depends on religion and colonialism even as secularity emerges from India (van der Veer 2001; Viswanathan 1998); notions of hybridity as a 'third space' for cultural mixings and complex, subversive Indian agency (Bhabha 1994); and the idea that the modern and premodern might share enough to overlap or 'converge,' raising questions about how different they were in the first place (Hatcher 2001). Most recently, even some postcolonial critiques have themselves been critiqued for the way they keep the west at the center of, and thus Indians always responding to, an essentially imperial story (Pennington 2007; Pinch 1999). One emerging result of newer, more dynamic models is that continuities between precolonial and colonial Indian religious traditions can help us explore how 'older notions' connected with religion 'continued to shape everyday experience' (Mir 2010: 124; cf. Yelle 2012), indeed, much as was suggested of the 'traditional' ascetic roots of Gandhi's modern, political charisma some time ago (Rudolph and Rudolf 1983) and has now been extensively documented (Amin 1988).

Media-Savvy Monks, the War of Images, and Sacred Vision

Vivekananda's well-known poster from the Chicago Parliament is just the tip of an image-rich iceberg representing Indian holy men and Hinduism more generally from the colonial period. Focusing on visual images of modern monks allows us to explore convergences between modern media and religion in the relatively neglected context of asceticism. More importantly, perhaps, since portraits were often made and circulated by the holy men themselves, these sources can give us a better sense of the individual choices, lives, and strategies that produced them. How did older Indian traditions of sacred sight (*darshan*) provide resources for Indians to actively engage modern media, utilizing it to represent themselves and to embody notions of religious perfection and to attract an audience? The fact that Sundar Singh and Rama Tirtha so often posed for formal and informal portraits and, in fact, often sent photos of themselves to their devotees (see Image 10.2) suggests a high degree of self-consciousness about the importance of images of themselves. It suggests they were media-savvy.

The first thing to point out about all three images is simply how attractive they are. Vivekananda's regal yet almost confrontational stance provides a clue as to how the appeal of such pictures worked in the historical context of the turn of the twentieth century. The particular beauty of images of modern monks came as a startling contrast to the flood of drawings, photos, and postcards of Indian holy men that had dominated earlier western imagery and imaginations. For most Orientalist scholars and Christian missionaries of the nineteenth century and before, Indian holy men were the human equivalent to the 'much maligned monsters' or 'idols' of Hinduism, providing one of

Figure 10.2 Sadhu Sundar Singh

the most vivid examples of heathenism (Mitter 1977). The visual ugliness or strangeness of Indian ascetics in such pictures encoded, for westerners, their many unappealing features: 'self-torture,' idleness, sexual promiscuity, super-stitious claims of miraculous powers (*siddhis*), the arrogance of gurus demand-ing worship. Often, such missionary images served to associate Hindu ascetics with the negative associations conjured for non-Indians by such terms as the Islamicate word *fakir*, or its close Hindu cousin, *yogi*. Their wide dissemination in Europe and America under such headings—and under the term 'saint'—revealed and reinforced modern Protestant distaste for the 'monasticism' of medieval Catholic Europe.

In contrast, these newer, self-circulated photographs provided counterim-ages of holy men by adopting the conventions of western portraiture to con-vey images of noble, mystical, self-denying sages (Beckerlegge 2008). Rama Tirtha's portrait, for example, infuses this sense of Eastern spirituality with a bucolic vision that strongly evokes European Romanticism. Such emerging affirmative, if Orientalizing, views provided an opening for Indian ascetics to gain a new hearing that, quite literally, depended on their producing a new image. At the same time, suspicions of Indian *yogis* and *fakirs* led to modern monks stressing an elite aura of ancient, and upper-caste traditions and dis-tancing themselves from more vernacular traditions, including the contorted bodies of *yogis* (Singleton 2010), and the many Indian Islamic (Sufi) holy men, the original *fakirs* themselves. The nakedness of *yogis*, or the white, blue, and green robes of Sufis, would disappear as saffron became evermore synony-mous with Indian *gurus*. Through such examples, we can see that although modern (western) religion and modern Hinduism have often been described as privatized, scripturalized, or belief centered, both were simultaneously satu-rated with material objects and visual practices. The saffron robes of holy men played a key role within a wider 'iconomachy,' a war of images (Morgan 2005: 12), which often gained their power from western contexts of image produc-tion and visual consumption.

Thus, the myriad of photographs, portraits, posters, and illustrated pam-phlets that include images of holy men provide rich sources for recent conver-sations among scholars about the connections between modern Hinduism and modern media (Babb and Wadley 1995). Overall, scholarship on devotional posters, comic book mythology, and popular TV series (Pinney 2008, McLain 2009), for example, has demonstrated not only the compatibility of modern media and many longstanding Hindu beliefs and practices, but also their mutual reinforcement. Even understanding the latest Bollywood box-office smash requires attention to ancient Sanskritic notions of emotion and drama, the narrative patterns of medieval epics, and the visual and material practices of contemporary worship (Dwyer 2006).

In this sense, the very aspects of holy man traditions that so many west-erners found objectionable can be said to have provided excellent training for negotiating the modern world of western religion and its various media. For the divine status, miraculous power and veneration of Indian holy men and women are all closely connected to the worship of 'idols' (*murtis*) so central to Hinduism past and present. In this religious idiom, Hindus interact with the gods and goddesses through vision, the divine sight (*darshan*) that devotees 'take' from the embodied, material deities who also 'give' it through their active blessing (*prasad*). Rather than a simple perception of an external image, the framework of *darshan* imagines vision itself in terms of a material give and take, an exchange of substances through the eyes (Eck 1998), in which the line between self and deity is blurred or even obliterated (Lutgendorf 2006: 232). The common gathering of holy men at Hindu temples, sometimes themselves sitting in the very places reserved for deity statues, makes it clear that living ascetics are equally sites of *darshan*. The visual power of Indian holy men has taken on further resonance from Islamic notions of the powerful, protective gaze (*nigah*) or highly charged glance (*nazar*) of the ascetic saint (*faqir*) (Lutgendorf, ibid). More concretely still, the myriad painted adornments, sartorial styles and symbolic objects of holy men carry a range of meanings and functions, including divine embodiment, intersectarian negotiation of identity, hierarchical differentiation of ascetic achievement or commitment, and condensations of elaborate theological debate (Olivelle 1986). Each of these aspects of ascetic practice and identity have long lent themselves to an equally rich variety of roles of performance: the ascetic holy man is miracle worker; materializer of divine blessing, power, and protection; healer; storyteller; singer; spiritual noble holding court; and scholar in learned public debate.

The importance of the visual in premodern and modern Hindu ascetic traditions helps us see that modern media such as the photographic portrait, the global lecture circuit, and the varied costumes they required became a part of the expansive and creative repertoire of the modern monk. Rather than bringing disenchantment, photographs of gurus multiply, transferring charisma through global networks evermore into our own day (Aravadamudan 2006: 226). Were the powerful traditional religious experiences of the *darshan* of a holy man and, for example, the modern construction of Hinduism through widely circulated imagery really all that different? I turn now to an example of the 'iconicity' of emerging Protestant biblical art (Morgan 2005) and the Indian Christian holy man, Sundar Singh, to pursue this question.

Indian Christians, Neo-Hindu Holy Men, and the Oriental Christ of the West

I got my first on-the-ground sense of the importance of images to modern Indian religion when I saw the portrait of Sundar Singh, an Indian Christian *sadhu*, as I walked into the teachers' break room of Henderson Memorial Girls School in north India. As the paper-cut lotus flower placed in front of the photo showed, Singh is still honored by many Indian Christians today for loving Jesus in a truly Indian style, that of the Hindu ascetic. Since I was writing a dissertation on him, I took this as a confirmation of the importance of 'my' figure, of the relevance of the ancient Hindu spiritual traditions, and that Hindu-style monks were even important to today's Indian Christians.

It took me some ten more years to realize, however, that the picture also bears a striking resemblance to the twentieth century's most widespread western image of Jesus, the American painter Warner Sallman's *Head of Christ*. This similarity is an important clue to Sundar Singh's popularity not only among Indian Christians, but also on his tours in Protestant America and Europe. For by the time of his tours, western Christians had seen their Bibles illustrated as an 'Oriental' book for some decades, the turbans, robes, long hair, and 'olive' skins of figures in biblical paintings resulting from the archeological and historical work of nineteenth-century biblical scholars. It was not so surprising then that Sundar Singh, who always toured in a turban, saffron robe, and sandals, and whose photographs often sold out at his events, was hailed by many as the closest thing western Christians had to a living picture of Jesus. Stories of children—and at times adults—actually mistaking him for Christ became a standard feature of his travels. It is even possible that press coverage and images of Sundar Singh's 1920 tour in America might have influenced Salman's own early 1924 sketch for his best-known painting of Christ, since Singh visited Moody Bible Institute in Chicago, where Salman had recently graduated.

As is clear from the above, the Orientalized biblical imagination that Sundar Singh's looks and dress evoked so powerfully also had a second source: the very spiritual conquest pioneered two or three decades earlier by modern Hindu monks, such as Swami Vivekananda, and his friend, Swami Rama Tirtha. After all, they reminded their audiences that if Jesus was an Oriental and the Bible an Oriental book, then Hindus naturally understood them both better than western Christians could hope to do. As Keshub Chandra Sen understood it, his 'flowing robes' showed that Christ himself was a Hindu *sadhu* or even a *yogi*, a connection cemented visually in the many appearances by and pictures of modern Hindu monks in just such 'Jesus-like' robes. The link took on doctrinal dimensions as well: Rama Tirtha argued that the wisdom of the Bible, and especially of Jesus' message, was only a 'faint echo' of the ancient Hindu scriptures, the Veda, and their philosophical tradition, Vedanta. When Jesus said 'I and my Father are one,' he was merely repeating the truth of the divinity of the soul (*atman*) that Hindus had known for thousands of years. His resurrection too was based on techniques long known to Indian holy men in the Himalayas, where Jesus likely learned them when he visited India as a young man. In this way, modern Hindu monks helped create yet one more 'American Jesus' (Prothero 2003: ch. 6), who also happened to be Indian.

If Jesus, the Bible, and 'true' Christianity, assumed by so many to be fundamentally western, could be claimed as Oriental by modern Hindu monks through their robes and their Vedantin Christ, so too could modern science. Before becoming a monk, Rama Tirtha had been a mathematics professor in Lahore, a fact he was fond of pointing out to his American audiences. As modern men of science, he argued, we should never blindly accept religious dogma, but should confirm the truth of religious claims for ourselves. What we would find through our own experience, he predicted, would be Vedanta; for, rather than a 'religion,' it is nothing less than the 'science of the soul.' Here, too, Rama took pains to look the part he preached, not of the Oriental monk this time, but of the scholar: he brought his graduate robes, his cap and gown, as it were, with him all the way from India so that he could wear them for public lectures and for his American portrait.

Individualism, World Renouncers, and Autobiography

While science and photography are common indicators of what counts as 'modern,' some scholars describe modernity more specifically with reference to a more internal ideal: the autonomy of the individual (Keane 2007). What distinguishes modern western society from others, in this view, is the value placed on the individual and his or her freedom, an idea at the heart of political liberalism, democracy, and human rights. Crucially, the individual's freedom can be measured by a person's rejection of the authority of external, often hierarchical, sources. From Martin Luther's stance against papal authority to Immanuel Kant's definition of Enlightenment as 'daring to know' (*sapere aude*) *for oneself*, an essential part of being modern in this sense is to think, speak, and reason independently and to have the recognized right to do so. In this view, of course, India has often been seen as lacking this specifically western type of individualism.

What then to make of Rama Tirtha's repeated challenges to his western audiences to stop relying on the authority of others for their religion, to be more scientific, more free? Indeed, in his view, the majority of the world religions' followers are little more than tradition-bound slaves, since they relied on the outdated answers offered by religious founders and holy men:

> Sell not your liberty to Buddha, Jesus, Mohammad or Krishna. If Buddha taught that way or Christ taught this way, or if Mohammad taught in some other way, it was all good and all right for them; they lived in other times. . . . But you are living today; you shall have to judge and scrutinize and examine matters for yourselves. Be free, free to look at everything by your own light. (Tirtha 2002, *IWGR*: vol. 1, 125)

Thus, a Hindu monk challenged his western audience to live up to their own often-touted modern ideals, to take religious freedom more seriously. In this sense, individualism demands that not even the most revered figures of the world religions are spared—in fact, they are especially the problem. For, in addition to his stress on the freedom of the individual, Rama Tirtha's emphasis on the *present* as requiring new religious answers than those of the past marks him as particularly *modern*. Put simply, the religion of modern westerners showed that they simply had not caught up with the times.

If such a combination—a 'traditional' guru dramatically invoking cutting edge modern values of individualism—still might strike us as surprising, it surely had similar effects in Rama Tirtha's own day, when the 'Orient' tended to signify all that was nonmodern. Yet, as suggested above, the theme of individualism in Rama Tirtha's message can be seen as deeply rooted in his own Indian tradition of world renunciation, rather than merely reflecting his English-language education or scientific temper. As Louis Dumont's famous essay (1960) on Indian monks suggested long ago, the renouncer is the one figure who, in a society taken to value the group over the individual, pursues his own ends to the exclusion of the duties of caste, family, and community. The wandering holy man rejects the hierarchical religious order, standard notions of caste and ritual purity, and the social institutions that define the lives of householders, if not exactly to 'find himself,' then, in a close Advaitin analogue, to find his true *self*.

Although there have been important critiques of Dumont's analysis of Indian society, caste, and individuals (Dirks 2001), recent studies of South Asian autobiographical writing suggest he was on to something in identifying a kind of renunciatory individualism. In particular, analyses of South Asian texts from the 'secret biographies' of Tibetan adepts (Gyatso 1999) and the confessional life story of a Baul guru (Openshaw 2010) have shown that it may be monks who best prove that the western individual is not in fact so unique after all. Women's autobiographies in particular show the importance of premodern religious communities and models in inspiring the telling of life stories (Sarkar 2006; Malhotra 2012). Indeed, even Brahminical Sanskrit scholars who defended dominant social 'tradition' (*dharma*) in colonial times felt themselves enough 'individuals' to tell their own, particular life stories in ways that conform to conventions of 'autobiography.' Such texts offer striking examples of the 'convergence' of Indian and so-called modern colonial genres and sensibilities (Hatcher 2001).

It is not then so surprising to learn that Rama Tirtha and Sundar Singh wrote autobiographical texts, joining the example of other colonial monks famous in their own region of Punjab, such as Dayananda Sarasvati. Close reading of these texts confirms the idea that, rather than remaining silent about themselves as they are often said to, renouncers have instead been quite effusive about them, exhibiting a substantial self-consciousness and challenging the idea that India lacks 'individuals.' At the same time, the texts raise interesting interpretive questions. When Rama Tirtha wrote about his own life, why did he use the third instead of the first person, referring to himself as 'Rama' rather than 'I'? What is the relationship between the prose he uses to describe his ascetic wanderings and the Hindu and Islamic mystical poems he quotes that break up the narrative again and again? Might his choice to write about his life in fragmented 'installments,' publishing separate accounts serially in a journal rather than in a single, self-contained book, be a kind of narrative technique for ascetic deconstruction of the ego? What do we make of passages where he addresses European philosophers such as John Stuart Mill and David Hume as he wanders in the Himalayan heights?

Much of Sundar Singh's earliest autobiographical texts focus on his meeting with a naked, long-haired, over three-hundred-year-old *rishi* (Hindu holy man or seer) living in a Himalayan cave on the sacred mountain of Lord Shiva, Mt. Kailash. Incredibly, however, this figure was a Christian and was later said to be a part of a secret order of Indians who preached the 'true Vedanta' of Christ, used their own Sanskrit Bible and lived like Hindu monks. More particularly, they traced their lineage (*sampradaya*) to both the great Advaitin philosopher Shankara and to Jesus's visits to India. Such stories, fascinating for their mixing of Christian and Hindu elements, raise questions about whether Christian conversion is best understood as the conversion of an individual to a 'foreign' religion or as the conversion of Christianity itself within an individual's layered and local religious idioms. These stories might also suggest that ascetic individualism requires reimagining oneself in relationship to powerful others, especially identities shaped by the authority of lineage (Metcalf 2007: 74). Quite different from these early texts and tales of wanderings and meetings, Sundar Singh's writings from around 1918 focused on the story of his own conversion. This new life story offered a dramatic tale of his own near-suicide as a teenage boy and Christ's supernatural appearance to save him, echoing details of both the famous conversion narrative of St. Paul in the Book of Acts and stories of Hindu saints who compel a deity to appear by threatening suicide. While such shifts clearly suggest an individualistic tailoring of a life story to appeal to multiple audiences, they also give evidence of the extent to which a 'conversion to modernity' (van der Veer 1996) could remain polyvalent, layered with multiple levels and pluralistic sources of religious imagination.

Finally, at least two other famous modern Indian leaders and their autobiographies call for a brief mention, namely, Yogananda's *Autobiography of a Yogi* and Mahatma Gandhi's *My Experiments with Truth*. These leaders and their texts could of course represent the spiritual-modern dichotomy we started with: we could celebrate Yogananda's spirituality over against modern materialism and analyze Gandhi's politicization of religion. Yet things were not so neatly divided in either case: Gandhi's political success as an anticolonial figure not only depended in large part on his appearance as a *sannyasi* but also on his own ascetic beliefs and practices; the British secret service was spying on Yogananda as he toured the west, suspicious of yet another of those they termed 'political *sannyasis*.' Thus, these two ascetic individuals—one a symbolic monk and the other literally so—were confident and self-aware enough to write their own life stories, confident and aware enough to appear as or to be a threat to various forms of western dominance.

Modern Monks and Colonial Critique

As scholars working on imperial history have pointed out, modern ideals of scientific objectivity, individualism, democracy, and free expression (media) have an uncomfortably close relationship with the history of western imperial expansion, racism, and colonial domination (van der Veer 2001). As Mill argued, it is precisely the ideal of freedom that required that the British severely limit the actual freedom of their colonial subjects, who, like children, were not yet mature enough for independence. This immaturity was of course often documented by colonial knowledge through its own construction of Hinduism, in which Hindus were thought, at best, to 'childishly' worship idols, for example. In the specific context of colonial dominance in India then, modern monks not only embody the centrality of religion to modernity, but are also among the leading critics of the darker side of modernity itself. Gandhi's rejection of 'modern civilization' in his manifesto *Hind Swaraj*, for example, echoes the shaper edges of Vivekananda's characterization of the East as a land of spirituality (Gandhi 2009). In this way, religious language functions not merely as a criticism of 'materialism' in the universal sense of greed in the abstract but as a form of specific, cultural critique and protest. More positively, perhaps, the critique of authority central to both Protestantism and the Enlightenment might be said to offer important precedents and norms for contemporary protest.

The western speeches of Rama Tirtha and Sundar Singh make it clear that their own religious vision and ascetic practice inspired protest against colonial domination. They attacked ideas of western superiority and the linking of Christianity with modern Euro-American progress. In one lecture, Rama Tirtha directly responded to the idea that Christianity was the cause of European progress, superiority, and tolerance, a common idea at the time. In response, he retells an alternative Enlightenment history as a progressive secularization:

> If all the civilization and all the scientific progress were to be attributed to Christianity, then please let us know when Galileo made that little discovery, how was he dealt with by Christians? . . . Huxley, Spencer and Darwin lived in the very teeth of your Christianity. Their discoveries and progress and independence of spirit were not engendered and encouraged by Christianity; they are living in spite of all the crushing influences of Christianity. . . . From the very beginning all progress has been made in spite of Christianity and not by Christianity. . . . If there were something in Christianity which would remove slavery, why did not Christianity remove slavery during the previous 1700 years? . . . If you ascribe good things to Christianity then [the] inquisition, the burning of witches, guillotine—and you know what [the] inquisition is, it reigned supreme even in San Francisco at one time . . . to what are these to be ascribed? (Tirtha 2002, *IWGR*: vol. 3, 118–119)

It was of course the realization of one's own divinity taught by Vedanta that, in Rama Tirtha's view, fostered the 'independence of spirit' that could aid scientific progress. In stark contrast, the submission to a God separate from oneself inculcated by Christianity led directly to colonialism. For, as he told it, early Christian influence in India had not only (incredibly enough) introduced 'idolatry' there, it brought with it the very spirit of submission that made colonialism possible:

> The religion which wants us to look down upon the Self and condemn the Self and call ourselves worms, vermins, wretches, slaves, sinners, was imported into India [from Europe] when it became the religion of the masses[;] there began the fall of India. . . . [Thus] they were made slaves. By whom? They were made slaves by God, you say. Has God any shape? Has God any figure? This God in His shapeless form could not come and rule them. God came. What God? The Light of lights, the White One. The White One came in the fair skin of Englishmen and made them slaves; thus it was. It was misunderstood Christianity . . . that wrought the downfall of India. (Tirtha 2002, *IWGR*: vol. 3, 120–121)

In these passages, Rama Tirtha weaves together the three themes considered here—media savvy, individualism, and protest. His rhetorical use of dramatic tales of medieval Roman Catholic persecution, the charged imagery of 'idolatry,' and the very skin color of colonialism itself suggest his skill with the narrative, material, and visual registers at the core of modern media such as the popular press. By citing heroes of modern progress as Galileo and Darwin, he appropriates iconic figures of western individualism for him and his audience, as it were, to share. And, finally, by framing colonialism as a form of white religion with a white, slave-keeping God, Rama Tirtha evokes the single most powerful narrative of protest of recent American decades: abolition.

Sundar Singh's western audiences were drawn from largely missions-related Protestant circles, rather than Rama Tirtha's eclectic mix of 'free-thinkers,' Orientalizing theosophists and disaffected or unconventional Christians. It is perhaps understandable then that he downplayed politics and criticism of western colonialism and, when he offered critique, did so in the indirect idioms of his own Christian devotion. When the Day of Judgment comes, he told the crowds that filled European and American churches to hear him, the heathen idolaters will fare better than westerners; for it is the latter who, like Judas, once knew Christ but have betrayed him. In Europe and America, military and economic power weigh down the spirit, bringing divine justice through the suffering of WWI, whereas the so-called heathen idols and temples of India radiated an upward spiritual 'pull' toward higher things. After all, worshipping idols is certainly better than worshipping oneself, as westerners do. Put simply, westerners had white skins, but black hearts. And when Indian hearts became Christian, they yielded a whole new crop of brave martyrs for the faith, whose stories Sundar Singh told on his tours as a contrast to the 'easy' lives of western missionaries in India. That such religious language and comparisons implied a political critique of the west expressed in Christian idioms is made clearer by Sundar Singh's friendship with Gandhi and his sympathy for Gandhi's anticolonial program of noncooperation. Similarly to Rama Tirtha, Sundar

Singh proved masterful at evoking a dramatic and visual imagination and providing a heroic (Indian) Christian individualism, playing with the language of color upon which so much of colonialism was built.

Protest and critique too, like visual culture and individualism, have rich histories among Indian ascetics. The critical perspectives of Buddhists, Jains, and radical Shaiva and Tantric yogis, among many others, have yielded sharp criticism of mainstream, householder society and created alternative social institutions and spaces. In Romila Thapar's (2007) terms, South Asian history demonstrates the simultaneously critical and social authority of the renouncer, a view strengthened and diversified by recent research on the worldly roles of precolonial Hindu, Sikh, and Muslim holy men (Pinch 2006; Oberoi 1994; Eaton 1996). Such material contexts extend right down to the level of the renouncer's individual body, where ascetic practice and critique deconstruct social meaning and management through clothing, hair, bodily fluids, and sexual practice (Olivelle 1995). This deconstruction simultaneously clears the way for a more constructive refashioning of the self through new subjectivities shaped by submission to tradition (Flood 2004). In addition to the verbal critiques of the west offered by modern monks such as Vivekananda, Rama Tirtha, and Sundar Singh, their self-representation through the media can also be seen in terms of longstanding ascetic de- and reconstruction of the body, a defiant reclamation of Indian bodies that colonialism tried to define, shape, and control.

Conclusion: From Convergence to the Coincidence of Opposites

The above discussion might still be read as mostly about the *effects* of colonialism or western imperialism on modern Hinduism. If modern monks were media savvy, for example, it was only the coming of technologies such as photography that made such savvy possible in the first place. At first glance, it seems especially counterintuitive to think of Hindu asceticism as something that would lead to this kind of *recognition* of modernity as familiar. After all, the institution of the *guru* is still often seen as the very antithesis of modern ideals of autonomy (Smith 2003) and the widespread involvement of 'saints' (*sannyasis*) in right-wing Hindutva politics seems to violate western notions of secularity. If so, the binary of asceticism as pure spirituality against modern materialism, on the one hand, or of colonial monks' radical modernizing transformation on the other hand, will likely remain the dominant views. Yet, dynamic transcultural models of colonial encounter, such as notions of hybridity and the idea of convergence, emerging in some recent scholarship, ask us to consider and experiment with new interpretive possibilities. Might there be enough *similarity* between modernity and traditional Indian religion to show that features of the modern taken to be quintessential are not so unique after all? In fact, modern Hindus—as well as Indian Christians, Muslims, and others—may have chosen certain aspects of western formations to engage with, take on, or highlight precisely because of the gripping sense of affinity they felt for them.

If, as I have suggested, Dumont's interpretation of Hindu renouncers as India's paradigmatic 'individuals' was on the right track, convergence starts to make more sense. Rama Tirtha, for one, certainly thought of his own asceticism, and of Vedanta, in terms of a kind of radical freedom and autonomy that most westerners fell far short of. Indeed, as noted above, recent scholarship on South Asian autobiography suggests a similar overlap of sensibilities between renunciation and individualism, as do recent studies of women's pursuit of renunciation to carve out autonomous social spaces amidst patriarchy (Khandelwal 2004). Sundar Singh, a Christian, seems to exemplify characteristically 'Indian' or 'Hindu' traits, which at the same time had powerful effects among western Protestants. In these ways, consideration of Hindu traditions of sacred sight (*darshan*) in ascetic contexts, ascetic critique, and bodily re/deconstruction, however briefly examined here, opens up provocative spaces to rethink the modern. In what ways is the power of modern media itself a form of the sacred? Do ascetic practices such as celibacy provide critical space for 'thinking otherwise,' sites that Foucault describes as *heterotopias* (Aravadamudan 2006)? If we pursue such questions further, we may find that we move beyond convergence and approach something like the coincidence of opposites, where things that seemed mutually exclusive actually coinhere.

Summary

This chapter presents two colonial Indian holy men, the Hindu, Rama Tirtha (1873–1906), and the Christian convert, Sundar Singh (1889–1929), in light of the formative example of and patterns associated with Swami Vivekananda (1863–1902). Through an exploration of Indian holy men and scholarship on colonial encounter, the chapter argues that these figures exemplify the convergence rather than contrast of the modernity and tradition. Specifically, Rama Tirtha and Sundar Singh's media-savvy actions, individualism, and anticolonial protest—seemingly 'modern' features—cannot be separated from Hindu practices of divine vision (*darshan*), renunciation, and ascetic de/reconstruction of the body, features often identified as antithetical to modernity. The power of these latter dimensions during these men's tours in America and Europe raises interesting questions about the visual and material dimensions of supposedly 'inward' or 'belief-centered' western religions such as modern Protestantism.

Discussion Questions

*   What terms should we use to describe figures like Vivekananda, Rama Tirtha and Sundar Singh? Consider options including English terms, such as saints, holy men, heroes, or missionaries and Indian terms, such as *sannyasi, guru, yogi,* and *fakir.*

- Compare and contrast different kinds of images—Hindu 'idols,' modern photography, postcards of Indian holy men, popular cinema, and websites. Are any inherently more religious than others?
- Has reading about the modern encounter of Christianity and Hinduism changed your view of either religion? Do you see parallels or differences with respect to how the two religions have responded to the challenges of modernity?

Suggested Readings

DeNapoli, Antoinette (2014). *Real Sadhus Sing to God: Gender, Asceticism, and Vernacular Religion in Rajasthan*. New York: Oxford.
This recent ethnography explores the living traditions and communities of asceticism in India today, bringing holy women and their devotees to life through interviews, fieldwork, and, most importantly, their emphasis on performance.
Michael Dodson and Brian Hatcher, eds. (2012). *Trans-colonial Modernities in South Asia*. New York: Routledge.
Offers an overview of models for thinking about modernity, emphasizing how it has always 'exceeded the grasp' of colonial powers, with multiple meanings worked out in very 'local' contexts.
Singleton, Mark (2010). *Yoga Body: The Origins of Modern Posture Practice*. New York: Oxford University.
A readable introduction to the field of modern yoga studies, exploring long-neglected historical contexts such as early western and Indian anti-yoga and anti-ascetic bias, modern western gymnastics and dance, the YMCA, and Indian nationalism.
van der Veer, Peter (2001). *Imperial Encounters: Religion and Modernity in India and Britain*. Princeton: Princeton University Press.
An attempt to move beyond Orientalist constructions of East and West, exploring nationalism, religion, and radical spirituality in England and India.

Bibliography

Amin, Shahid (1988). 'Gandhi as Mahatma: Gorakhpur District, Eastern UP 1921–2.' In *Selected Subaltern Studies* (pp. 288–350). Eds. Ranajit Guha and Gayatri Chakravorty Spivak. Delhi: Oxford University Press.
Aravamudan, Srinivas (2006). *Guru English: South Asian Religion in a Cosmopolitan Language*. Princeton: Princeton University Press.
Babb, Lawrence and Susan Wadley, eds. (1995). *Media and the Transformation of Religion in South Asia*. Philadelphia: University of Pennsylvania.
Beckerlegge, Gwilym (2008). 'Svāmī Vivekānanda's Iconic Presence and Conventions of Nineteenth-Century Portraiture.' *International Journal of Hindu Studies* 12: 1–40.
Bhabha, Homi (1994). *The Location of Culture*. New York: Routledge Press.
Bharati, Agehananda (1970). 'The Hindu Renaissance and its Apologetic Patterns.' *The Journal of Asian Studies* 29: 267–287.
Butler, William (1891). *The Land of the Veda: Being Personal Reminiscences of India*. New York: Hunt & Eaton.
Chatterjee, Partha (1993). *The Nation and Its Fragments: Colonial and Postcolonial Histories*. Princeton: Princeton University.

Chowdury-Sengupta, Indira (1996). 'Reconstructing Spiritual Heroism: The Evolution of the Swadeshi Sannyasi in Bengal.' In *Myth and Mythmaking, Collected Papers on South Asia* (124–142). Ed. Julia Leslie. Surrey: Curzon.

Copley, Anthony, ed. (2000). *Gurus and Their Followers: New Religious Reform Movements in Colonial India.* New Delhi: Oxford University.

Dirks, Nicholas (2001). *Castes of Mind: Colonialism and the Making of Modern India.* Princeton: Princeton University.

Dumont, Louis (1960). 'World Renunciation in Indian Religions.' *Contributions to Indian Sociology* 4: 33–62.

Dwyer, Rachel (2006). *Filming the Gods.* New York: Routledge.

Eaton, Richard M. (1996). *The Rise of Islam and the Bengal Frontier, 1204 1760.* Berkeley: University of California Press.

Eck, Diana (1998). *Darshan: Seeing the Divine in India.* New York: Columbia University.

Flood, Gavin (2004). *The Ascetic Self: Subjectivity, Memory and Tradition.* Cambridge: Cambridge University Press.

Gandhi, Mohandas K. (2009). Hind Swaraj *and Other Writings.* Ed. Anthony J. Parel. New York: Cambridge University Press.

Guha, Ranajit (2002). *Elementary Aspects of Peasant Insurgency in Colonial India.* New York: Oxford University.

Gyatso, Janet (1999). *Apparitions of the Self: The Secret Autobiographies of a Tibetan Visionary.* Princeton: Princeton University.

Hansen, Thomas B. (1999). *The Saffron Wave: Democracy and Hindu Nationalism in Modern India.* Princeton: Princeton University Press.

Hatcher, Brian (2001). 'Sanskrit Pandits Recall Their Youth: Two Autobiographies from Nineteenth-Century Bengal.' *Journal of the American Oriental Society* 121: 580–592.

——— (2008). *Bourgeois Hinduism, or Faith of the Modern Vedantists: Rare Discourses from Early Colonial Bengal.* New York: Oxford University.

Jackson, Carl T. (1994). *Vedānta for the West: The Ramakrishna Movement in the United States.* Bloomington: Indiana University.

Keane, Webb (2007). *Christian Moderns: Freedom and Fetish in the Mission Encounter.* Berkeley: University of California.

Khandelwal, Meena (2004). *Women in Ochre Robes: Gendering Hindu Renunciation.* Albany: SUNY.

King, Richard (1999). *Orientalism and Religion: Post-Colonial Theory, India and 'The Mystic East.'* London: Routledge.

Krishnaswamy, Revathi (1998). *Effeminism: The Economy of Colonial Desire.* Ann Arbor: The University of Michigan.

Lutgendorf, Philip (2006). 'Is there an Indian Way of Filmmaking?' *International Journal of Hindu Studies* 10: 227–256.

Malhotra, Anshu (2012). 'Panths and Piety in the Nineteenth Century: The Gulabdasis of Punjab.' In *Punjab Reconsidered: History, Culture and Practice* (pp. 189–220). Eds. Anshu Malhotra and Farina Mir. New Delhi: Oxford University Press.

McLain, Karline (2009). *India's Immortal Comic Books: Gods, Kings, and Other Heroes.* Bloomington: Indiana University.

Metcalf, Barbara (2007). *Islamic Contestations: Essays on Muslims in Pakistan and India and Pakistan.* New Delhi: Oxford University.

Miller, David (1999). 'Modernity in Hindu Monasticism: Swami Vivekanand and the Ramakrishan Movement.' In *Ascetic Culture: Renunciation and Worldly Engagement* (pp. 111–126). Ed. K. Ishwaran. Boston: Brill.

Mitter, Partha (1977). *Much Maligned Monsters: A History of European Reactions to Indian Art.* Chicago: Chicago University Press.

Mir, Farina (2010). *The Social Space of Language: Vernacular Culture in British Colonial Punjab.* Berkeley and Los Angeles: University of California.

Morgan, David (2005). *The Sacred Gaze: Religious Visual Culture in Theory and Practice.* Berkeley: University of California.

Nandy, Ashis (1989). *The Intimate Enemy: Loss and Recovery of Self under Colonialism.* New Delhi: Oxford University.

Oberoi, Harjot (1994). *The Construction of Religious Boundaries: Culture, Identity and Diversity in the Sikh Tradition.* New Delhi: Oxford University.

Olivelle, Patrick (1986). *Renunciation in Hinduism: A Medieval Debate.* Vienna: E.J. Brill.

——— (1995). 'Deconstruction of the Body in Indian Asceticism.' In *Asceticism* (188–210). Eds. Vincent Wimbush and Richard Valantasis. New York: Oxford University.

Openshaw, Jeanne (2010). *Writing the Self: The Life and Philosophy of a Dissenting Bengali Baul Guru.* New York: Oxford University.

Pinch, William (1999). 'Same Difference in India and Europe.' *History and Theory* 38, No. 3: 389–407.

——— (2006). *Warrior Ascetics and Indian Empires.* Cambridge: Cambridge University.

Pinney, Christopher (2008). *The Coming of Photography in India.* London: British Library.

Pennington, Brian K. (2007). *Was Hinduism Invented? Britons, Indians and the Colonial Construction of Religion.* New York: Oxford University Press.

Pratt, Mary Louise (2007). *Imperial Eyes: Travel Writing and Transculturation.* 2nd ed. New York: Routledge.

Prothero, Stephen (2003). *American Jesus: How the Son of God Became a National Icon.* New York: Farrar, Strauss and Giroux.

Rudolph, Susanne H. and Lloyd I. Rudolph (1983). *Gandhi: The Traditional Roots of Charisma.* Chicago: University of Chicago Press.

Sarkar, Sumit (1992). 'Kaliyuga, Chakri and Bhakti: Ramakrishna and His Times.' *Economic and Political Weekly* 29: 282–357.

Sarkar, Tanika (2006). 'A Book of Her Own, a Life of Her Own: The Autobiography of a Nineteenth-Century Woman.' In *Cultural History of Modern India* (pp. 32–64). Ed. Dilip M. Menon. New Delhi: Social Science Press.

Sil, Narasingha (1997). *Swami Vivekananda: A Reassessment.* London: Associated University.

Singh, Sundar (1989). *The Christian Witness of Sadhu Sundar Singh: A Collection of His Writings.* Ed. T. Dayanandan Francis. Madras: The Christian Literature Society.

Singleton, Mark (2010). *Yoga Body: The Origins of Modern Posture Practice.* New York: Oxford University.

Smith, David (2003). *Hinduism and Modernity.* Malden: Blackwell Publishing.

Tirtha, Rama (2002). *In the Woods of God Realization* (IWGR), Vol. 1–7. Lucknow: Swami Rama Pratishthan.

Thapar, Romila (2007). *Cultural Pasts: Essays in Early Indian History.* New Delhi: Oxford University Press.

Yelle, Robert (2012). *The Language of Disenchantment: Protestant Literalism and Colonial Discourse in British India.* New York: Oxford University Press.

van der Veer, Peter, ed. (1996). *Conversion to Modernities: The Globalization of Christianity.* New York: Routledge.

——— (2001). *Imperial Encounters: Religion and Modernity in India and Britain.* Princeton: Princeton University Press.

Viswanathan, Gauri (1998). *Outside the Fold: Conversion, Modernity, and Belief.* Princeton: Princeton University Press.

Weber, Max (1985). *The Protestant Ethic and the Spirit of Capitalism.* New York: Routledge.

11 Modern Yoga and Tantra

Lola Williamson

The Hindu American Foundation (HAF) is an organization dedicated to ensuring 'an accurate understanding of Hinduism as a living tradition' (according to the HAF website, http://www.hafsite.org). In 2010, the HAF contacted the editors of *Yoga Journal*, a magazine that promotes yoga practice and philosophy and boasts over a million subscribers. The HAF wrote to inquire why the journal never made any reference to Hinduism. The reply they received was both short and pointed, 'Hinduism comes with too much baggage.' This reply prompted the HAF to launch a campaign designed to reclaim yoga for Hinduism. The campaign was dubbed 'Take Back Yoga,' a phrase that clearly communicates a fear that yoga has been hijacked from Hinduism by commercial interests. Such a concern can also be heard in the comments of Aseem Shukla, a cofounder of HAF, in a *Washington Post* blog claiming that Hinduism is the victim of 'the facile complicity of generations of Hindu yogis, gurus, swamis, and others that offered up a religion's spiritual wealth at the altar of crass commercialism' (2010).

The HAF also weighed in on a recent court case brought against the Encinitas Unified School District alleging that a thirty-minute exercise program offered to first graders represented indoctrination into Hinduism. When Judge John S. Meyer ruled in favor of allowing the program to continue, his decision was praised by HAF Director, Suhag Shukla, for making it clear that what was being taught in the public schools was not 'authentic yoga.' Shukla seemed less impressed by the constitutionality of the decision than by Judge Meyer's recognition that for yoga to be truly Hindu it had to represent, in her words, 'a holistic path for spiritual growth' (2013).

Cases like these raise a number of questions. Is it true that yoga has been pulled away from its Hindu roots? Does *Yoga Journal*, with its glossy ads for 'ToeSox' (featuring a naked female model) and its articles on mini-meditations for a fast-paced, work-a-day world, bear any resemblance to the life of matted-haired, ascetic yogis in India? If not, why do we use the same words to describe such unrelated phenomena? After all, most people who practice yoga do not think that they are doing something necessarily 'Hindu.' Do ancient yogic practices and the texts associated with them relate to the contemporary transnational yoga scene? Does the 'Take Back Yoga' movement have it right? If so, just what makes yoga authentic? This chapter attempts to address all of these questions by exploring the roots and genesis of modern yoga and tantra.

Along the way, we will explore the various ways yoga and tantra have been adapted and promoted, calling attention to the different ways in which they draw upon Hindu religion and philosophy.

Defining Yoga and Tantra

An argument can in fact be made against the HAF's view of yoga as unambiguously grounded in a religion called Hinduism. Such a view conveys a misleading sense of the unity of both yoga and Hinduism. The latter two terms have been endlessly constructed and reconstructed; each contains diverse strands drawing on multiple *sampradayas* (schools or orally handed-down instructions). One might even suggest that yoga itself arose from traditions of tantra that had originated in opposition to Hinduism (or more properly, Brahmanism), notably its concerns about purity, pollution, and caste. This suggests that it is not merely facile but incorrect to link yoga to one univocal tradition. Varieties of yoga can be found in the Jain, Buddhist, and even South Asian Islamic traditions; furthermore, within each of these religious traditions, different types of yoga can be identified. To complicate matters further, some strains of yoga have arisen outside of India. One Iranian text on meditation and breath control from the fourteenth century 'circulated in Arabic, Persian, Ottoman Turkish, and Urdu versions from the seventeenth century onward, in Persia, Turkey, and North Africa as well as in India' (Ernst 2012: 133). Similarly, contemporary iterations of yoga and tantra in the modern globalized context exemplify further adaptations as yoga and tantra migrate into new cultural contexts and find themselves competing in the marketplace of New Age spiritual technologies.

Since 'yoga' is a Sanskrit term, we might think it makes sense to turn to a Sanskrit dictionary for a good definition. Unfortunately, the dictionary is not much help since 'yoga' has more meanings than almost any word in the Sanskrit language (see White 2012: 1–23). For the purposes of this chapter, it will be most useful to adopt a rather classical understanding of yoga as 'the raising and expansion of consciousness' (White 2012: 8). We need to distinguish yoga from the more properly cross-cultural phenomenon known as 'Modern Yoga.' Elizabeth De Michelis defines Modern Yoga 'as a technical term to refer to certain types of yoga that have evolved mainly through the interaction of Western individuals interested in Indian religions and a number of more or less Westernized Indians over the past 150 years' (2004: 2). Within Modern Yoga, De Michelis identifies four subdivisions: Modern Psychosomatic Yoga, Modern Denominational Yoga, Modern Meditational Yoga, and Modern Postural Yoga. The first two forms are distinguished from one another by the degree to which they adhere to precise, doctrinal restrictions; the second two share an emphasis on either physical or mental practice. While some overlap exists between these categories, this typology provides a useful starting point for our discussion.

As suggested earlier, yoga is closely tied to tantra. At one level, the term 'tantra' is applied to texts that were written from 500 CE to 1,500 CE as well as to the various practices associated with these texts. Although these tantric texts (or tantras) are quite different from one another, certain themes tie them together, including the use of *mantra* (sacred sound), *mandala* (sacred design), meditation, guru, initiation, and ritual (Wallis 2012: 35). Stepping back from the texts, André Padoux offers a broad definition of tantra as 'an attempt to place *kama*, desire, in every sense of the word, in the service of liberation . . . not to sacrifice this world for liberation's sake, but to reinstate it, in varying ways, within the perspective of salvation' (qtd. in White 2003: 15). It is important to note that desire and salvation both find a place in this definition. This has occasioned some misunderstandings in the modern era.

As Hugh Urban points out, Orientalist scholars often focused on one or the other of the two extremes of tantra. Talboys Wheeler wrote in 1874 that tantra is a cult in which 'nudity is worshipped in Bacchanalian orgies which cannot be described.' In contrast, Sir John Woodroffe, whose work did much to popularize tantra for Westerners, referred to tantra as a 'noble and orthodox tradition'; in fact, he wrote, it is 'nothing but the Vedic religion . . . trying to reassert itself.' (qtd. in Urban 2003: 6). In light of the varying understandings of tantra, we can say that both historical and contemporary attempts to understand the tradition often reveal more about the bias of the historian than about tantra itself.

Because of the complex semantic history of the terms yoga and tantra, it is necessary to delimit our topic by focusing on those types of yoga and tantra that share common concerns and terminology. One such shared idea is that a subtle or spiritual body operates beneath the physical body. Yogic and tantric systems propose that within this subtle physiology lies a vast complex of conduits, called *nadis*, through which *prana*, a subtle life energy, flows. *Nadis* are said to converge at centers, or *chakras*, located in the subtle-body equivalent of the spine. *Mantras* (sound vibrations), visualization, concentration, *pranayama* (breath control), and *asana* (physical postures) are all used in yogic and tantric systems to awaken the *kundalini*, a latent spiritual power that is said to lie coiled in the *chakra* at the base of a major *nadi*. This *nadi*, running parallel to the spine, serves as a central channel called the *sushumna*. Once awakened, the *kundalini* travels through the *sushumna* to the uppermost *chakra*, resulting in a state of unity, or Self-realization. This unity is the goal of both yoga and tantra and is understood as a return to one's innate purity and perfection, known as *moksha* (here understood as freedom from limitation).

With this shared concern in mind, we might say that the local YMCA yoga class does bear a faint resemblance to historical practices of yoga insofar as it teaches students to join breath to movement, and recognizes in some fashion that controlling breath is a key to accessing the subtle body. The yoga class also provides more concentrated mental focus than might be found in other sorts of secular exercise classes. If music is used in such a yoga class, it will typically be quiet and soothing and will be intended to lead students toward the goals of calmness and inwardness. Tantric philosophy may also find its way into contemporary yoga since worldly enjoyment is not typically viewed as a distraction from spiritual peace. In tantra, the body is not something to be transcended, but is instead to be transformed into divinity.

Roots of Yoga and Tantra: Premodern and Early Modern Periods

What are the premodern sources of today's Modern Yoga? Certainly, the practices of meditation, *pranayama*, and *asana* (as seated posture) must all be considered since they are important today and were also integral to premodern Hindu, Buddhist, and Jain texts. One such text is the *Yoga Sutra* attributed to Patanjali, which offers a compendium of the different understandings of yoga at the time it was compiled around the first centuries of the Common Era. It is important to examine the *Yoga Sutra* because yoga revivalists in the early twentieth century sought to link their teachings directly to the text and this understanding remains widespread. The text of the *Yoga Sutra*, together with an early commentary, the *Yoga Bhashya* (c. fifth to sixth centuries CE), is often viewed as the source for 'classical yoga.' In this sense, yoga comprises one of the six *darshanas*, or viewpoints, of classical Hindu thought. Included in the *Yoga Sutra* is a discussion of *ashtanga*, or eight-limbed, yoga. This consists of a series of ethical precepts, *pranayama* and *asana*, as well as the stages of meditation—from withdrawal of the senses to final *samadhi* (total absorption).

Philosophically, the *Yoga Sutra* relies to a great extent on the related *darshana* known as Samkhya. Samkhya is a dualistic philosophy based on the division of reality into *purusha*, which is unmanifest and transcendent, and primal nature, or *prakriti*, which is the material source of the universe. The goal of classical yoga is to experience the separation of these two, a goal which has little in common with the union sought by practitioners of tantra and later forms of yoga. While the various yogic practices discussed in the *Yoga Sutra* are adopted in later tantric and yogic texts, the dualistic philosophical framework is not.

A major subject of the *Yoga Sutra* is *siddhis*, supernatural powers that are said to accrue to the practitioner through the practice of yoga. These *siddhis*—such as understanding the language of animals, bilocating, flying, walking on water—are not a part of contemporary yoga (unless one considers the 'TM-sidhi' program of the Maharishi Mahesh Yogi's Transcendental Meditation movement). The *siddhis* taught in the *Yoga Sutra* do not form an integral part of Modern Postural Yoga. It was not until the development of classical tantra, with its emphasis on psychophysical techniques for raising the subtle energy of *kundalini* that some of what we associate with Modern Postural

Yoga—such as body postures and hand gestures (*mudras*)—begin to come to the forefront.

Tantra, with its emphasis on the complex physiology of the subtle body developed within the religious tradition of Shaivism; its earliest scriptures were composed between the fifth and seventh centuries CE. Unlike Samkhya, most tantric traditions embrace a non-dual view of reality in which one divine consciousness 'projects within its awareness a vast multiplicity of apparently differentiated subjects and objects' (Wallis 2012: 55). During the period of classical tantra (ca. 800–1200 CE), strong patronage supported the elaboration of a range of tantric practices and philosophies along a continuum from external practices associated with blood offerings, bodily fluids, and ritual intercourse on the one hand to more interior, meditative forms of practice on the other. At the former extreme were found the sexual rites emphasized in what is known as Kaula Tantra (see White 2000: 12).

Following the earliest period of its development, during which tantric scriptures were believed to be a direct revelation from Shiva (male personification of energy) or Shakti (female personification of energy), a period of exegesis (commentary and explanation) ensued in the area of Kashmir. The most important philosopher of this time period was Abhinavagupta (ca. 950–1020), who wrote the *opus magnum* of tantra, the *Tantraloka*.

From around 1200 and well into the early modern period, we see the intermingling of disparate tantras, each originally centered on a particular guru. This was a period of decline for tantra as the advent of Muslim rule changed the systems of patronage that had hitherto supported tantric practice. Unlike earlier tantric practice which had emphasized householders and had therefore included female practitioners, tantra increasingly became the purview of wandering male ascetics, many of whom performed magic tricks in order to make a living. Likewise, more antinomian Kaula-influenced practices also proliferated, which challenged the norms of Brahmanical orthodoxy. Overall, the number of female practitioners decreased while the quest for *moksha* (transcendent freedom) was transformed into various attempts at attaining worldly power and *siddhis*. It was during this period that tantra acquired a 'bad name' (Wallis 2012: 308–311).

It was during this same period that a type of yoga called *hatha-yoga*, based in significant ways on tantra, yet practiced without *mantras*, grew in importance. The celebrated teacher Goraksha of the Nath lineage is often considered the father of *hatha-yoga*. The *Hatha Yoga Pradipika* (fifteenth century) is a central text that outlines many of the psychophysical techniques of earlier tantric literature. This text has been influential within Modern Postural Yoga as well, since it discusses sixteen different postures. Several other texts on *hatha-yoga* were also composed, but they often lacked the sophistication and philosophical support one finds in the earlier tantric texts. During the premodern period, the figures of the tantrika and the yogi were at times idealized for their spiritual attainments and at other times feared for their mastery of supernatural powers.

To this day, parents in rural India and Nepal will scold their children by warning them that a yogi will come and take them away (White 2012: 18).

Late Modern Period: Eighteenth – Early Twentieth Centuries

Yoga, in contemporary times, has gained remarkable prestige. Studies on the effects of meditation are conducted at major universities and medical research centers, such as the National Institutes of Health. Yoga has been incorporated into secular models of exercise, and doctors and mental health professionals recommend meditation and yoga to their patients. Furthermore, yoga has contributed to the popular concept of 'spirituality' in countries around the globe. How is it that something once viewed in India as potentially antisocial has come to be embraced so wholeheartedly in the present day? The answer lies in three developments that occurred during the colonial period and shortly afterward. The first came about through processes of acculturation as Hindus sought ways to reform their religion in order to bring it into line with the perceived demands of modern rationalism—reforms that included blending Western liberal religious traditions and modern esoteric movements with traditional Hindu concepts. The second involved a massive physical culture movement that swept through Europe and America in the early twentieth century and—as a result of colonialism—through India as well. The third development occurred as a few Indians, most notably Swami Kuvalayananda, performed scientific experiments aimed at proving the existence of the subtle body.

The period of British colonial rule prompted patterns of acculturation among Indian (and particularly Bengali) intellectuals who were educated in British schools. In response to Christian missionary criticisms of Hinduism, these Bengali intellectuals sought to formulate rational interpretations of Hinduism that eliminated what were seen as its problematic deities and superstitions. Such intellectuals reasoned that a reformed Hinduism might not only compete with Christianity but more importantly appeal to modernizing Hindus, not to mention sympathetic audiences outside the Hindu fold.

One such reformer, Rammohan Roy (1772–1833), established the Brahmo Samaj in 1828 after initially being drawn to the rational outlook and moral teachings of Unitarianism. While the Brahmo Samaj drew on Hindu texts and spiritual philosophies, it was also influenced by Western movements such as Unitarianism and Transcendentalism. Ironically, modern Unitarianism and Transcendentalism (as associated with the likes of Thoreau and Emerson) had themselves felt the influence of Hindu ideas. In an attempt to capture this complex interplay between Indian and Western thought, the scholar Agehananda Bharati coined the concept of 'the pizza effect.' He argued that while the Italians had enjoyed eating a dish of flatbread with tomato sauce, it was only after Italian immigrants to America elaborated that dish into a large pie with tomato sauce and various toppings that it came to acquire a new life back in Italy as what we today call 'pizza' (Bharati 1970). The development of Modern Yoga is similar; it has gathered layers of accoutrements and a complex register of associations as it has come in contact with different cultures.[1]

Bharati actually coined the concept of the 'pizza effect' when pondering the life and teachings of Swami Vivekananda (1863–1902), who had earlier in his life been a member of the Brahmo Samaj. Along with the general trend of Bengali reform, Vivekananda thought that religion must accord with rationalism and scientific inquiry as well as be nonsectarian. Based on an experience he had in which he perceived everything to be a manifestation of God, he settled on *advaita* (non-dual) *vedanta* as the supreme philosophical system to promote his vision. While Vivekananda's yoga was not the Postural Yoga that is so popular today, his attempts to universalize yoga helped to decouple its meaning from the particulars of Hindu practice and Brahmanical authority, which only helped support its globalization. For Vivekananda, yoga represented a rational process of self-inquiry that promised to yield the same outcome for everyone: Self-realization. His presentation of yoga as rational foreshadowed the pragmatic and antimystical elements in much of Modern Yoga.

During the time Vivekananda spent in the United States, beginning with his appearance at the World Parliament of Religions held in Chicago in 1893, his own views were influenced by 'harmonial religion,' defined by S. Ahlstrom as encompassing 'those forms of piety and belief in which spiritual composure, physical health, and even economic well-being are understood to flow from a person's rapport with the cosmos' (1972: 1,019). Harmonial religion, in turn, was intertwined with American New Thought, Christian Science, and Swedenborgian teachings, not to mention mesmerism (known today as hypnotism). Each of these, in their way, aim at developing inner power and spiritual force. In this respect, Vivekananda discovered in mesmerism the idea of a 'vital fluid,' believed to flow within subtle channels in the human body and to connect human beings to one another and the cosmos and he related this vital fluid to the yogic concept of *prana*, which forms a central concept in his book, *Raja Yoga* (see De Michelis 2004: 160–163).

A second major factor in the development of Modern Yoga was a dramatic international focus on health and the physical body around the turn of the twentieth century. In 1896, the same year that Vivekananda's *Raja Yoga* was published, the first modern Olympic Games were held in Athens, Greece. From the late 1800s to the 1930s, enthusiasm for athletic training swept through much of the world causing a 'shared global grammar' of 'somatic nationalism' (Uberoi 2006, qtd. in Singleton 2010: 82). Among Christians, the combination of manliness, morality, patriotism, and faith was sometimes dubbed 'Muscular Christianity.' It is worth noting that before this physical culture movement, English-speaking yogis and gurus, such as Vivekananda, never mentioned *hatha-yoga*. In fact, the practice had pretty much disappeared in India until T. Krishnamacarya (1888–1989), who might be called the father of

Modern Postural Yoga, decided to study it. He had to travel to Tibet to receive his training. Only when the Theosophical Society (an East/West conglomerate religion) began to publish texts connected to *hatha-yoga* did interest in physical yoga return to India (White 2012: 21).

The discourse and practices of British colonialism had played a part in yoga's disappearance. British Orientalists viewed Indian religious life as having slowly devolved since a purported Golden Age during the Vedic era. They often pointed to tantra and yoga as examples of the depravity of Indian religious customs. As it turns out, though, the British may also have indirectly fostered the resurgence of yoga in India. The British promulgated the myth of Indian effeminacy as a way to justify their 'manly' rule. In this narrative, Indians were weak and feeble. Colonized Indians tended to internalize such criticism, even as some, like Vivekananda, began to call for a return to Indian manliness. Around the turn of the century, we notice Indian men beginning to seek out such so-called masculine activities as body-building, wrestling, and the military (Singleton 2010: 95).

In the end, then, Indians employed the very masculinity the British had hoped to instill in their subjects as a tool for subverting the colonialist project. Yoga training became, among other things, a tool to coordinate violent resistance of the British. In the 1930s, for example, the teacher Tiruka (aka Raghavendra Rao) traveled around India gathering techniques that could be disseminated to freedom fighting 'yogis.' Tiruka's exploits exemplify the sometimes close relationship between nationalism and the development of yoga (Singleton 2010: 103–104).

But postural yoga was on the rise for other reasons as well. Both the British and the Indians attempted to combine elements of gymnastics and yoga in order to create a physical counterpart to yoga philosophy. Such developments prepared the ground for a number of modern postural teachers such as Krishnamacarya, Kuvalayananda, and Yogendra to revolutionize yoga. In 1930, Kuvalayananda began to train yoga teachers in a process almost like mass production, which has grown exponentially to the present day. The development of Modern Postural yoga is especially associated with Krishnamacarya and his students. His system, developed at the Mysore Palace, combined *hatha-yoga* techniques with British military calisthenics and southwestern Indian forms of wrestling and gymnastics (Sjoman 1996, in White 2012: 21). The students of his three main disciples—B.K.S. Iyengar, K. Pattabhi Jois, and T.K.V. Desikachar—created what is now a global, physical yoga phenomenon.

At the same time that interest in the physical body was on the increase, some western Orientalists became fascinated with the idea of the subtle body. Most notably, Sir John Woodroffe (1865–1936), aka Arthur Avalon, studied tantric texts and wrote extensively about the subtle body and psychophysical techniques for raising *kundalini*. Around this time, Kuvalayananda (1883–1966) began conducting scientific research in order to prove that the psychophysical techniques described in yogic and tantric texts were actually effective. He was less interested in the health benefits of yoga than in proving the existence of a subtle body and his curiosity was piqued when he met a yogi who was able to perform miracles. As Kuvalayananda saw it, if these miracles were possible, then they must be based on natural laws. Joseph Alter has pointed out that Kuvalayananda could have ignored science and simply aimed at a reformation of Hindu philosophy; or he might have chosen to study the physiological benefits of yoga. What he did instead was to use the categories and techniques of Western science to translate the philosophy of yoga into pragmatic terms. In the process, he helped make yoga universal (Alter 2004: 77, 102).

Such scientific experiments served to further separate modern yoga from the classical and premodern religions and culture of India, even as they promoted the existence of a 'something more' that differentiated yoga from mere physical exercise. In the end, it is the combination of the universalizing of yoga accomplished by the religious reformers, the work of the physical culture movement, and the scientific investigation of the subtle body that set the stage for an unprecedented globalization of yoga. And this brings us to the contemporary yoga scene.

Postmodern/Contemporary Yoga and Tantra

I once interviewed an Indian immigrant to the United States who had ignored his Hindu roots until he read a book called *Be Here Now* by former Harvard professor, Richard Alpert. After experimenting with psychedelic drugs, Alpert had gone to India where he met his guru, Neem Karoli Baba, and received his new name, Ram Dass. After reading *Be Here Now*, my interviewee decided to reconnect with his Hindu heritage. I relate this story because it aptly exemplifies the globalization of yoga and tantra. An Indian man returns to his roots after being inspired by an American who was, in turn, inspired by an Indian guru. Here is a wonderful example of the pizza effect!

How does one begin to describe the complicated intercultural evolution of ideas and practices that is occurring today? Global guru movements that focused on meditation took off in the 1960s, and yoga focusing on the physical body skyrocketed by the 1980s. Many of these movements might be characterized as Denominational Yoga, each group trying to distinguish itself from the next by seeking patents on ancient terms and practices, as if they were invented yesterday. Recently, there are signs that this trend may be changing; we notice greater openness and fluidity. A new trend is mounting toward what might be called Psychosomatic Yoga, which focuses more on practice and less on authoritarian dogmatism. It may prove helpful to review some of these more recent developments.

While some movements, notably those associated with Kundalini Yoga, have presented yoga and tantra as a seamless whole, others have tended to stress one over the other. Indeed, some yoga groups deliberately sought to disassociate Hindu tantra from their stated mission in order to ensure greater acceptance. But this turned out to be a rather tricky business since virtually all of the gurus who established global movements had been influenced by tantra (see Williamson 2010: 55–131). The sanitization had already begun at the very inception of global yoga with Vivekananda, who rarely mentioned his tantric guru, Ramakrishna, to American audiences; his nearly illiterate guru seemed almost an embarrassment to him. Likewise, Paramahansa Yogananda, who came to America in 1920, never taught *hatha-yoga*, but instead promoted a series of exercises which included tensing and releasing particular muscles, self-massage, and marching in place.

Maharishi Mahesh Yogi, founder of the Transcendental Meditation movement, went even further in removing any uncomfortable associations with Hinduism. In fact, he never used the word 'Hinduism.' Like the British Orientalists before him, he prioritized things Vedic, combining the Veda with the language of science to lend greater legitimacy to his teachings. Rather than yoga, tantra, or Hinduism, what Maharishi taught was 'Vedic Science' or the 'Science of Creative Intelligence.' As Transcendental Meditation (TM) rose to prominence in the 1960s and '70s, former hippies shed their tattered jeans and t-shirts; suddenly the men donned business suits and the women put on conservatively-styled dresses, all in an attempt to legitimize the new science.

In other guru movements, tantra was not merely discussed; it was touted as the fastest way to Self-realization. These groups offered various forms of what may be called Guru Yoga, in which liberation is attained through unquestioning devotion to the guru. In De Michelis's terminology, these represent the more extreme forms of Modern Denominational Yoga. Bhagvan Shree Rajneesh, later known as Osho (1931–1990), for example, was an Indian philosophy professor turned guru; he taught first to Indians, later to Westerners, and, in his final days, to an affluent international community of followers in India. There was no need to shed one's jeans with Rajneesh, unless it was for an orgy. Rajneesh preached a new tantra, one that allowed him to possess a fleet of ninety-three Rolls Royces and his followers to continue the hippie-style free love they had come to know before finding the spiritual sanction it required. Then there was Bubba Free John, (birth name, Franklin Jones), later known as Adi Da (1939–2008). Adi Da was a 'crazy wisdom' teacher; he intentionally used shocking and antinomian means to 'wake up' his disciples. Sexual tactics were particularly prominent as he urged his followers to engage in orgies and to switch partners. He himself had nine 'wives.' His stated purpose was to help people overcome habits that kept them stuck in conventional modes of thought and prevented openness to the divine. These tactics are all somewhat in line with the more extreme Kaula practices found within premodern and early modern tantra.

Modern Postural Yoga groups focus on the physical body, giving only a nod to meditation. Tracing the genealogy of the global postural movement known as Anusara Yoga, however, provides an example of the complex ways different types of yoga, tantra, and other New Age phenomena have tended to intersect in the world of contemporary yoga. John Friend, the founder of Anusara Yoga, studied under a plethora of teachers and traditions that drew from Western esoteric teachings (New Thought, Theosophy, Wicca), Modern Postural Yoga (Iyengar, Desikachar, Pattabhi Jois, Indra Devi), world religions (Sufism, Buddhism, Hinduism), and various gurus and their organizations (Paramahansa Yogananda and Self-Realization Fellowship, Gurumayi and Siddha Yoga). All of these influenced his presentation of yoga. After teaching Iyengar Yoga for a number of years, he developed new features that allowed him to distinguish himself from his teacher. We could even say that creating a 'style' that has unique features is a key theme within Modern Postural Yoga. It allows a teacher to trademark a name and take advantage of opportunities for capitalist entrepreneurship. In Friend's case, it also allowed him to place greater stress on tantric philosophy and tantric texts rather than what one finds in Iyengar's system, which foregrounds the *Yoga Sutra*.

From time spent teaching in *ashrams* of the Siddha Yoga movement, Friend learned about tantra and particularly Kashmir Shaivism. At one such *ashram*, Friend became part of a Teachers and Scholars Department, where he befriended swamis and scholars of Hinduism and tantra. From 2008 to 2012, he organized large gatherings of Anusara Yoga practitioners and also participated in a series of *Yoga Journal* conferences; his classes drew such a crowd that his image needed to be projected onto screens throughout the room. The Anusara Yoga movement was also prominent at music festivals, such as Wanderlust. Through such workshops, conferences, and festivals, Friend began tightening the association of Anusara Yoga with tantra by arranging for former swamis of Siddha Yoga and scholars of Hindu tantra to speak and offer classes. Those seeking certification as an instructor of Anusara Yoga are in fact strongly encouraged to study with any one or all of these teachers (Williamson 2013). The evolution of Anusara Yoga is just one instance of the dynamic intertwining of tantra and yoga and seems to suggest one direction in which yoga and tantra will continue to grow globally.

This growth comes with ethical challenges. Yogic and tantric systems, so closely tied to concepts of enlightenment and perfection, depend upon significant power differentials. The belief that a guru has attained a superhuman level of awareness, perhaps even omniscience, can inspire unquestioning or naive attitudes among a guru's followers. Such attitudes, combined with the view that the guru 'tests' his or her disciples in order to help them along the path, has led to problematic institutional and personal relationships. Sexual, financial, and physical abuses have plagued many modern movements, usually of the more professedly 'authentic' types in which yoga is taught as a complete system that includes the belief in enlightenment. Because the guru wields such tremendous power, bringing abuses to light requires a long and painstaking process when it is even attempted.

Another challenge is posed by the commodification of these systems. One thinks primarily of Postural Yoga, though it is not unique in this regard. According to statistics from the North American Studio Alliance, $27 billion were spent on yoga products in the United States alone in 2012. They also report that 44% of those who practice yoga in the United States make over $75,000 a year. Yoga retreats are generally for those who have enough wealth to afford them and enough leisure time to attend them. Whether in India or the West, yoga classes and weekend or longer retreats are geared toward middle- and upper-middle class practitioners. Furthermore, it is a subject of some debate whether these movements promote strong communities that support the needs of members or that engage with larger social issues. Jeremy Carrette and Richard King have provided a searing critique of this aspect of yoga and other New Age spiritualities. According to them, rather than helping to overcome conventional, ego-driven lives, Modern Yoga only reinforces individualism and conformism (Carrette and King 2005: 117).

On the other hand, it could be argued that yoga is having a positive influence on modern society, allowing an avenue for people to slow down and value calmness and silence in the midst of today's hectic lifestyle. The worldwide yoga movement provides incentives to develop healthier eating habits and to refrain from smoking or using recreational drugs as well as to reduce mindless television or Internet use. It should also be noted that attempts are being made to remedy the disparity between the yoga haves and have-nots. More and more yoga studios are offering free community classes at least once a week. Although it is too soon to tell, attempts to bring yoga into schools may have a positive effect on the school environment.

Conclusion

With this brief overview of the history of yoga and tantra, we are in a better position to answer the questions posed at the opening of this chapter. What is authentic yoga? If postures and breathing are extracted from the 'holistic path for spiritual growth,' should we call modern postural systems something else? I tend to agree with the HAF assertion that there is a difference between those who have been raised in a Hindu religious environment and those who take on only those aspects of the tradition that suit their needs. For this reason, I like to use the term 'Hindu-inspired' rather than 'Hindu' to describe movements of what I call Modern Meditational Yoga (see Williamson 2010). Even the most apparently Hindu of these emerge from a complex process that commenced with the efforts of reformers like Rammohan Roy and Swami Vivekananda. These reformers were influenced by Western ideas, including those found in forms of nineteenth-century 'harmonial religion' that emphasize the interconnectedness of mind, body, spirit, and outer reality—including economic well-being. Modern Yoga, as De Michelis has asserted, is clearly the result of the collaborative efforts of Indian Hindus and Westerners.

If we look at Modern Postural Yoga, we can say that it draws even less on Hindu ideas than Modern Meditational Yoga. One might agree with HAF that purely fitness-oriented yoga classes such as Power Yoga ought to be called something else. But what about that sixth-grader in a California public school who is taught 'crisscross applesauce'? The name is funny, but in the end, the student is learning a traditional *asana* for meditation, and may feel just a little bit more peaceful as a result? It may not look like 'authentic yoga,' but one could argue that it is yoga all the same, since its intent is to bring balance, calmness, and joy to students' lives. It may not be Hindu, but then again some Modern Postural yoga systems draw heavily on Hindu texts and traditions. Those training to become teachers are tested not just on their knowledge of postures, but on their knowledge of texts like the *Yoga Sutras* and the *Bhagavad-gita*. Thus, Chandra, an Indian taking Postural Yoga classes who was interviewed on National Public Radio stated: 'The vast majority of yoga teachers have studied more Hinduism than I have or my parents have. I am learning more about the meanings of the *shlokas* [verses from Hindu texts] and the intention of Hinduism than I ever knew as a kid growing up, being taught from my community' (qtd. in Roy 2010).

To aid our understanding of what constitutes authentic yoga, we might turn to another HAF representative, Sheetal Shah, who argues that yoga is a 'lifestyle' and a 'philosophy.' If truthfulness, nonviolence, and purity are not integral to the yoga package, she states, then 'the lifestyle of yoga has been lost' (qtd. in Adler 2012). To be sure, *satya* (truthfulness), *ahimsa* (nonviolence), and *saucha* (purity) are part of classical yoga's eightfold path, and are ethical precepts worthy of following. But the idea that some pristine ideal of yoga has been lost may in the end pull spokespersons like Sheetal into the same kind of mythologizing that leads Christians to bemoan the loss of 'family values' in America. The sentiments are understandable and the values are laudable, but what exactly has Hinduism lost? And when did this loss occur? Was it back in the premodern era when yogis began to be feared for their powers? Was it during the period when the *Yoga Sutras* were composed, a portion of which enumerates the very *siddhis* (powers) that have caused some to fear or mistrust yogis? By contrast, if authentic yoga is a holistic system, should it not include renunciation of the world, which was fundamental for groups like the Nath yogis who followed Gorakhnath? Should it incorporate such practices as *basti*, in which water is drawn into the colon through the anus while performing *nauli*, a rolling of the abdominal recti? Such are, after all, long-attested techniques for perfecting yogic purity.

The point is that what is considered useful for spiritual advancement varies considerably over time. Perhaps we should focus less on the question of whether yoga is authentic and more on the ways individuals today view the benefits and hazards of contemporary yoga systems. The global community of yoga practitioners could join together to question the commercialism surrounding yoga to examine the problem of authoritarianism and abusive behavior. Those who practice yoga could put more effort into making it available to people who do not have the resources to pay for classes and retreats. These are worthy discussions that yogis of all varieties Hindu, Christian, Jewish, or atheist could fruitfully engage in.

Summary

The use of the word 'yoga' today often conjures up pictures of athletic prowess rather than a holistic path for spiritual development. This chapter began by calling attention to concerns raised by the Hindu American Foundation with respect to yoga, namely that the current popular emphasis on yoga as a mode of physical fitness is not yoga at all, and that yoga as popularly understood today is divorced from its foundations in the Hindu religion. To analyze such concerns, we explored the ways in which yoga has been variously understood during different historical eras. Among other things, it turns out that far from being identical with orthodox Brahmanical Hinduism, in premodern South Asia, yoga forged significant links with tantric traditions, many of which arose in opposition to the orthodox or conventional Hinduism of the time. Furthermore, as yoga developed during the colonial era and into the present, it has often acquired other levels of meaning and significance such that, today, it is increasingly universalized and secularized. What we discover is that, despite attempts to preserve the essence of yoga as singularly 'Hindu,' it is in fact impossible to identify a pure and authentic yoga.

Discussion Questions

- What is the relationship between yoga and tantra?
- In what ways are modern yoga and tantra different from premodern versions of these practices and philosophies? How did developments in the early modern period enable such changes?
- How would you define an authentic religious tradition? Is the concept useful?
- Do you find it useful to draw a line between yoga as religious/spiritual and yoga as secular?

Note

1   Alternatively, one can speak of acculturation; see Williamson 2010: 23–25.

Suggested Reading

Singleton, M. (2010). *Yoga Body: The Origins of Modern Postural Practice*. New York: Oxford University Press.
Considers the roles that Indian nationalism, European bodybuilding, and women's gymnastics play in the development of Modern Postural Yoga.
Syman, S. (2010). *The Subtle Body: The Story of Yoga in America*. New York: Farrar, Straus and Giroux.
Offers an engaging history of the topic, highlighting early advocates such as Henry David Thoreau and Margaret Woodrow Wilson.
Urban, H. (2003). *Tantra: Sex, Secrecy, Politics, and Power in the Study of Religion*. Berkeley and Los Angeles: University of California Press.

Examines ways in which Tantra is imagined in different cultural contexts.

Wallis, C. D. (2012). *Tantra Illuminated: The Philosophy, History, and Practice of a Timeless Tradition*. The Woodlands: Anusara Press.

Provides a clear exposition of the complex field of classical Tantra, with a focus on nondual Shaiva Tantra.

Williamson, L. (2010). *Transcendent in America: Hindu-Inspired Meditation Movements as New Religion*. New York and London: New York University Press.

Provides a history of the globalization of Modern Meditational Yoga and Tantra, drawing significantly on experiences of American practitioners.

Bibliography

Adler, Margot (2012). 'To Some Hindus, Modern Yoga Has Lost its Way.' Morning Edition, National Public Radio, April 11. Retrieved July 5, 2013. http://www.npr.org/2012/04/11/150352063/to-some-hindus-modern-yoga-has-lost-its-way

Ahlstrom, S. E. (1972). *Religious History of the American People*. New Haven: Yale University Press.

Albanese, C. L. (2005). 'Sacred (and Secular) Refashioning: Esalen and the American Transformation of Yoga.' In *On the Edge of the Future: Esalen and the Evolution of American Culture* (pp. 45–79). Eds. J. Kripal and G. Shuck. Bloomington: Indiana University Press.

Alter, J. (2004). *Yoga in Modern India: The Body between Science and Philosophy*. Oxford: Princeton University Press.

Bharati, Agehananda (1970). 'The Hindu Renaissance and its Apologetic Patterns.' *Journal of Asian Studies* 39, No. 2: 267–287.

Biernacki, L. (2007). *Renowned Goddess of Desire: Women, Sex, and Speech in Tantra*. New York: Oxford University Press.

Buhnemann, G. (2007). *Eighty-four Asanas in Yoga: A Survey of Traditions (with Illustrations)*. New Delhi: D.K. Printworld.

Carrette, Jeremy and Richard King (2005). *Selling Spirituality: The Silent Takeover of Religion*. New York: Routledge, 2005.

De Michelis, E. (2004). *A History of Modern Yoga: Patañjali and Western Esotericism*. New York: Continuum.

Eliade, M. (2009). *Yoga: Immortality and Freedom*. 2nd ed. Princeton: Princeton University Press.

Ernst, Carl (2012). "A Fourteenth-Century Persian Account of Breath Control and Meditation." In *Yoga in Practice* (pp. 133–139). Ed. David G. White. Princeton: Princeton University Press.

Feuerstein, G. (2003). *The Deeper Dimension of Yoga*. Boston: Shambhala Press.

——— (1998). *Tantra: The Path of Ecstasy*. Boston: Shambhala Press.

Gleig, A. and L. Williamson, eds. (2013). *Homegrown Gurus: From Hinduism in America to American Hinduism*. Albany: State University of New York Press.

Newcombe, S. (2009). 'The Development of Modern Yoga: A Survey of the Field.' In *Religion Compass* 3, No. 6: 986–1002.

Padoux, A. (2004). 'Tantrism.' In *Encyclopedia of Religions* (vol. 14, p. 273). Ed. M. Eliade. New York: Macmillan.

Roy, S. (2010). 'Yoga: A Positively Un-Indian Experience.' National Public Radio, December 29. http://www.npr.org/2010/12/29/132207910/yoga-a-positively-un-indian-experience.

Samuel, G. (2008). *The Origins of Yoga and Tantra*. Cambridge: Cambridge University Press.

Shukla, A. (2010). 'The Theft of Yoga.' On Faith Blogs. *The Washington Post*. April 18. Retrieved July 5, 2013. http://newsweek.washingtonpost.com/onfaith/panelists/aseem_shukla/2010/04/nearly_twenty_million_people_in.html

Shukla, S. (2013). 'Ruling in Encinitas Affirms HAF's Take Back Yoga Project.' American Hindu Foundation Website. July 3. Retrieved July 5, 2013 http://www.hafsite.org/Ruling_Encinitas_Affirms_Take_Back_Yoga

Singleton, M. (2010). *Yoga Body: The Origins of Modern Postural Practice*. New York: Oxford University Press.

Strauss, S. (2005). *Positioning Yoga: Balancing Acts across Cultures*. Oxford and New York: Berg.

Syman, S. (2010). *The Subtle Body: The Story of Yoga in America*. New York: Farrar, Straus and Giroux.

Urban, H. B. (2003). *Tantra: Sex, Secrecy, Power, and Politics in the Study of Religion*. Berkeley and Los Angeles: University of California Press.

Wallis, C. D. (2012). *Tantra Illuminated: The Philosophy, History, and Practice of a Timeless Tradition*. The Woodlands: Anusara Press.

White, D. G., ed. (2000). *Tantra in Practice*. Princeton: Princeton University Press.

——— (2003). *Kiss of the Yogini: 'Tantric Sex' in its South Asian Contexts*. Chicago: The University of Chicago Press.

———, ed. (2012). *Yoga in Practice*. Princeton: Princeton University Press.

Williamson, L. (2010). *Transcendent in America: Hindu-Inspired Meditation Movements as New Religion*. New York and London: New York University Press.

——— (2013). 'Stretching toward the Sacred: John Friend and Anusara Yoga.' In *Gurus of Modern Yoga* (pp. 210–236). Eds. Ellen Goldberg and Mark Singleton. New York: Oxford University Press.

12 Renunciation and Domesticity

Meena Khandelwal

When I arrived in the pilgrimage town of Haridwar in 1989, as a graduate student eager to research Hindu renouncers, or *sadhus*, I did not grasp why so many Indians I met were unenthused about my plans. I had prepared for years in order to conduct this research, learning Hindi, reading scholarship, and working to obtain research funding. But everyone I spoke with, whether relatives, friends, or the middle-class urbanites I met, wondered why I would want to come all the way from America to live among Hindu renouncers. Many presumed that sadhus were aged, somber, and just plain boring. Moreover, for me to conduct research, I would have to live in Haridwar, a pilgrimage town where people get up at dawn and turn in by 9:00 pm, a place where the sale of alcohol, meat, and even eggs is illegal. Wouldn't I rather find some research project in the city and enjoy all its comforts and pleasures, including nightclubs and a more exciting social life?

Actually the lack of enthusiasm I encountered was not merely due to the perception that Haridwar was a dull place to live; it also reflected a pervasive skepticism toward sadhus and the ashrams where they reside.[1] Sadhus are people, mostly men, who have renounced worldly life and aim to achieve spiritual enlightenment through ascetic practices. Freed from the constraints of ordinary social rules and expectations, they are thought to have ample opportunity for corruption. While everyone I met during my research claimed to know a sadhu who was the real deal, a true saint worthy of reverence, they also believed that most were not to be trusted and that westerners were particularly naïve in this regard. That I was young, female, and American only enhanced their anxieties.

Another reason for the raised eyebrows was my own status as a 'girl' engaged to be married; my wedding was scheduled to take place at the very beginning of my research project. Marriage remains the most important lifecycle rite for Hindus, because it promises to transform a child into an adult and to ensure his or her future security and happiness. Rituals, generally speaking, express widely shared cultural values in symbolically condensed form such that they are felt viscerally by those in attendance. Hindu weddings, in particular, last multiple days, and reaffirm overall central values related to kinship, fertility, health, beauty, and material prosperity. Both in real life and in the cinematic narratives of Bollywood, the married couple is treated as firmly embedded within family and community. Thus, a proper wedding celebration is a loud, public affair; there may be fireworks and often a brass band will lead the wedding procession through the streets. Large numbers of extended kin and community members typically attend such events; invitation lists are maximized rather than highly selective. This emphasis on public display means that a marriage conducted secretly will often be condemned because elopement signals the couple's separation from community and their blatant disregard for parental wishes (Mody 2006). As for the sadhus I had begun to meet in Haridwar, there was no question of inviting them to my wedding in Mumbai. Sadhus do not attend weddings. In fact, as the very emblem of domestic life, weddings are at odds with the values of renunciation.

If the etiquette about whom to invite to my wedding was straightforward, other decisions were not. Returning to Haridwar after the celebrations, I faced a dilemma: What should I wear? The atmosphere inside of ashrams is generally quiet, austere, and aesthetically simple.[2] Once again, married life exists at the opposite end of the spectrum. A Hindu bride is said to embody Lakshmi, the beautiful and elaborately adorned goddess of wealth and good fortune. As a new bride, it was proper, auspicious, and morally sound for me to don bright reds, greens, and yellows and to wear jewelry as showy as our family wealth allowed; such attire is not merely a *symbol* of happy domesticity but also *creates* it. Aesthetics are central to Hindu devotional practice and worship. Moreover, the emotion of *sringara* (love between a man and woman, attraction, beauty) is central to Indian classical art forms, such as dance (Srinivasan 2011). A bride not suitably adorned is the object of pity. Should I emulate the goddess Lakshmi or take my cue from other ashram residents who view the pleasure of *sringara* as fleeting and illusory?

After my wedding, new dilemmas emerged. Just when my attention should have been focused on cooking food (or supervising its cooking), pleasing my husband, making myself beautiful, longing for children, building relationships of respect and trust with newly acquired in-laws, and, yes, having fun, I instead returned to Haridwar with my husband in lieu of a romantic honeymoon. It was odd, even unseemly, for me, at this youthful stage of life, to want to live among celibate renouncers (even female ones), to wear the simplest of clothing, minimal jewelry, and no make-up and to seek out solitude rather than the bustle and chatter of Indian familial life. Some worried that I might be harmed by some rascal posing as an ascetic. Others worried that I might be inspired to *become* a sadhu, which is another way of losing a family member. My presence created dissonance, and the irony was a perpetual subject of jokes. More seriously, though, the awkwardness of my situation spoke to the long-standing debate between two life orientations that play out in scripture, myth, ritual, popular culture, and the lives of actual people, both past and present. Hinduism offers reasonable arguments in favor of domestic life and for opting out of it.

The Good Life

Domestic space is the locus par excellence of the happiness and well-being so central to Hindu notions of 'the good life' (Madan 2010). A 'house' refers to a physical structure, while 'household' refers to the commensal group that eats from the same hearth. Thus, two brothers who occupy with their wives and children two different apartments in an urban high-rise constitute a single 'household' if they share meals cooked in one kitchen (Khare 1976). In such arrangements, children and adults move freely back and forth between units—no invitation required. 'Family' is an even more diffuse unit that commonly extends beyond households, cities and even countries (Seymour 1999; Singh 2006). The household has both structural and moral importance in Hindu society, and 'the householder' (m. *grihastha*, f. *grihasthi*) is a culturally elaborated figure often defined in opposition to the sadhu. Researchers also use terms relating to domestic life differently. Economists tend to theorize 'household' (unit of residence), which is more amenable to quantitative analysis, while 'family' involves intimate human relationships and is preferred by qualitatively oriented anthropologists and sociologists (Jain and Banerjee 2008). Scholars of religion tend to focus on the category 'householder' because of its elaboration in Hindu scripture, ritual, and myth.

That the relationship between 'household' and 'renunciation' has intrigued western scholars is evidenced by decades of debate on this topic. This debate has been shaped by Louis Dumont's controversial claim (1980) that the two exist in dialectical opposition to one another; this claim gained wide currency in the field of Indology, as evidenced by the work of Jan Heesterman (1985). Working largely from sacred texts and concerned with abstract structures of civilization writ large, both Dumont and Heesterman posited a radical and unresolvable ideological conflict between the social world and otherworldly renunciation. Even if other scholars pointed to ways in which Indian thought has attempted to resolve this apparent contradiction (see O'Flaherty 1981), the general householder–renouncer opposition has been central to Indological and anthropological understandings of Hindu culture. This framework implied a whole set of analogous binaries such that the male world of otherworldly asceticism was opposed to the female world of this-worldly domesticity. Subsequent work has shown that such stark oppositions oversimplify the treatment of renunciation in classical ethical codes (Olivelle 1984) and never really describe life as actually lived. For example, ethnographic research has shown the many ways in which the competing pulls of domesticity and ascetic withdrawal constitute not absolute opposition but rather a more nuanced distinction or tension (see Van der Veer 1987; Narayan 1989; Gold 1989; Hausner 2007). Other scholars, by focusing on gender, have further deconstructed the assumption that renunciation is always masculine and defined in opposition to domestic life in some absolute way (Alter 1992, 1994; Sinclair-Brull 1997; Roy 1998; Khandelwal 2004; Pechilis 2004; DeNapoli 2009).

Hindu (and Indian) families tend to be large and diffuse entities in which the conjugal couple is not privileged over all other kinship relationships. In most western contexts, heterosexual 'nuclear' families are idealized, even if not normative, and adult children marry to establish 'their own' families distinct from those of their parents. According to dominant Hindu culture, marriage adds to a larger familial unit. At the same time, and somewhat paradoxically, the heterosexual couple is necessary for the social reproduction of the (patrilineal) family, hence the intense social pressure to marry. The fact that today most educated, English-speaking young Indians opt for some version of arranged marriage speaks to the continuing importance of familial involvement in a matter too important to be left to the fickleness of youthful infatuation, even as romantic love and companionship are accommodated as part of marital aspirations (Mody 2006; Sharangpani 2010). Thus, Hindu society's dominant vision of a good life—'good' in the dual sense of emotionally satisfying and morally sound—is to marry with parental approval, earn sufficient money to meet social and ritual obligations, and raise children to respect their elders and reproduce the family. Domesticity is imbued with the values of responsibility, hierarchy, caste and ethnic identification, intense sociality and emotional attachment, and the performance of domestic ritual and life-cycle rites. In direct contrast to secular individualism, most Hindus view material prosperity as not simply the fruit of one's own effort but a blessing that enhances one's ability to meet social and religious obligations and to enjoy life.

True to the stereotype, the Hindu ethos of a good and loving family means that its members should be, and generally want to be, interdependent and intensely involved in each other's lives. If Indian activists and social scientists use the politicized discourse of inequality to critique power dynamics within the home, then Hinduism employs an alternate language of duty and protection. Superiors are responsible for protecting their dependents, so parents are duty-bound to meet the basic needs of their children: Ensuring physical health, providing education, and finding a suitable spouse. In return, children are to be respectful and devoted to their parents; sons and their wives in particular are to look after the son's parents as they age. Of course, as is true everywhere, not all families conform to the ideal, but a loving family is supposed to be characterized by intense attachment and shared goals. There is little evidence that Hindus generally experience this as suffocating or that they crave privacy and solitude. Even if a wife might feel relieved to live separately from her mother-in-law, people separated from their families (by migration, job, or schooling) generally describe intense loneliness. Most Hindus aspire to have a caring family, good health, fertility, material prosperity, and a home filled with the laughter, activity, and the mischief of children.[3]

Sadhus reject this vision of domestic well-being to cultivate detachment (*vairagya*) from worldly life in pursuit of spiritual enlightenment. Precisely because domestic life is built on obligation, desire, and attachment, many sadhus (but not all) find it necessary to abandon domestic life in order to pursue this alternative goal. This abandonment might be quiet and gradual, or it might occur with a dramatic flourish as when the initiation of some highly placed person received media coverage. Householders have varied responses to the sadhu's critique of domestic life. One is that sadhus contribute little to society but make no demands, so they are irrelevant to most householders. Thus, some people generally ignore sadhus, except for the occasional donation, personal encounter, or passing reference.

A second view is that intense spiritual practice gives at least some sadhus wisdom and insight, so they can help householders who feel anxious, confused, or depressed. Indeed, it can be easier to confide in someone outside one's family sphere, both because the home may be the site of one's problems and because loyalty requires one to protect its reputation from gossip. A sadhu who is trusted is presumed to be neutral, disinterested, discreet, and wise. Someone who seeks out a trusted renouncer for advice is likely to see that person as exceptional, as an authentic saint who rises above the mass of posers who are not what they claim to be.

A third response is outright hostility. Householders also critique sadhus as people who have shirked their familial obligations, perhaps abandoning a spouse and children, for their own selfish goals. More ominously, a sadhu is suspect precisely because of his or her unmooring from kinship and other social ties that generally constrain behavior. How can one know if a sadhu is who he or she pretends to be? This is not merely the questioning of modern skeptics, for classical texts suggest that when spies were sent out by Indian rulers to learn about rival kingdoms, they often adopted the disguise of a wandering mendicant (Rocher 2012: 221). Could celibacy and simplicity be a smokescreen for greed and lechery? Might asceticism be a good route for a criminal trying to escape the police? Cultural discourses about sadhus include indifference, reverence, and suspicion.

The Contemplative Life

If images of the good life evoke large, boisterous families, and if the household is a central institution of society, then the world of renunciation exists, literally and figuratively, on its margins. Despite stories of aspirants who simply disappear from home without a word, the more compassionate ones consult their families and then face their disapproval. Almost all the women renouncers I met talked of families who tried to stop them from leaving, using logic, emotional appeal, or force. However, men (young men in particular) also face opposition from families, for sons are vessels into which all parental dreams are poured—dreams of new brides, grandchildren, and long-term security. Daughters generally marry and leave home, but sons are the bedrock that ensures continuity of the family.

Once a person leaves home and undergoes initiation into a contemplative tradition, they are expected to live itinerantly or among other sadhus of their religious order, avoiding attachment to people and place and minimizing their eating, talking, and interactions with lay people. A vow of silence, for example, is a common ascetic discipline that constitutes social withdrawal, and silence might be observed for several hours each day or for years at a time.

Renouncers generally avoid urban areas, preferring instead to wander or reside in uninhabited mountains or forests or on the outskirts of cities, towns, and villages.[4]

The transformation that results from initiation is not just social but legal as well. Hinduism has a variety of ascetic traditions, but the English term 'renunciation' tends to refer to the tradition of *sannyasa*, which tends to be emphasized in elite forms of modern Hinduism. A person who undergoes formal initiation into *sannyasa*, and abandons property and social life by, for example, ceasing to reside with a spouse, is legally recognized as a renouncer. The initiate performs his or her own (symbolic) cremation and thus becomes 'dead' to their previous social and civil identity. After civil death, a son no longer inherits from his relatives; a sadhu may acquire and hold private property, but it will devolve to disciples rather than natural heirs (Narayanan 1993: 288). The state neither tracks nor regulates donations given to sadhus as it does for charitable donations given to secular nonprofit organizations. Renouncing worldly life releases one from the obligation to provide financial support to kin and fulfilling social obligations, such as participating in marriages or funerary rites, but it also means one has no legal claim on kin for assistance. Renunciation is a radical act that results in ritual, social, and legal transformation, and those who choose this path exist on the margins of familial and state authority.

Not all Hindu ascetic traditions require celibacy and abandonment of domesticity. And yet, sadhus are reputed to be asocial. This is true even for those aligned with elite, Brahmanical Hinduism that tends to homogenize the diversity of local belief and practice. Sadhus need not adhere to conventional standards of etiquette, proper dress, social reciprocity, hospitality, or polite small talk; they are granted leeway to be nonconformists. Some ascetics are downright antisocial, and examples abound in Hindu myth, legend, folktales, and hagiography. Among deities, Shiva is the 'bad boy' of Hindu mythology and is known for his extreme asceticism and antisocial behavior (O'Flaherty 1981). Shiva-worshipping sadhus of the Aghori order engage in ritual practices that break taboos regarding pollution; most middle-class Hindus find them distasteful and even frightening (Parry 1994; White 2006). Tantric cosmology understands creation as the result of sexual union, so tantric practitioners seek liberation through embodiment and erotic technique.

In contrast, the devotional bhakti tradition incorporates romantic sexuality as a metaphor for approaching the deity. The fifteenth-century poetess Mirabai, for example, worshipped Krishna as her husband. Her devotion to Krishna not only overshadowed her conjugal obligations to her human, princely husband, but also led her to ignore conventions of modesty and respectability and to leave the palace to mix with other devotees, including male devotees of the lower classes. Even though venerated today as a saint, Mirabai, as a young wife in a conservative royal household, faced sanction by in-laws during her lifetime. Contemporary sadhus of varied sectarian affiliation tend toward the antisocial.

To say that sadhus exist on the fringes of mainstream society does not mean that they are completely separate from it, for they give up paid employment and depend on householders to provide food and clothing. They may do this explicitly by extending their begging bowl or indirectly by living in institutions that depend on donations. They minimize their physical needs and also acknowledge that this dependence puts them at risk for being pulled back into worldly life. A popular folktale posits the boundary between sadhus and householders as dangerously permeable. One version goes something like this: A sadhu lived as a hermit in the woods, with a loincloth and a hut as his only possessions. His only problem was that mice nibbled at his loincloth. Local villagers, always so helpful, advised him to get a cat. The cat would not stay without milk to drink, so he obtained a cow. The cow would not give milk without grass to eat, so he enlisted a servant to graze the cow. The servant missed his family, so the sadhu told him to bring his family from the village to live with him in the woods. One day the sadhu asked the servant why he was so happy, and the latter replied that he was happy because he had a wife and children whom he loved. The sadhu had no happiness and so decided to marry too. Thus, he ceased to be a hermit. This cautionary tale warns sadhus about the risk of too much intimacy with householders. It also suggests that even the tiniest desire, such as attachment to a loincloth (and thus to one's identity as an ascetic), creates more desires, and from this emerges the entire phenomenal world (Narayan 1989: 114–119).

This narrative about the accumulation of possessions may seem familiar to Americans. Graham Hill is an American tech entrepreneur who enjoyed a sudden windfall before age thirty and threw himself into a frenzy of consumption. He soon found himself with one luxury home in Seattle and another in NYC, crammed full of the hottest gadgets. Once he realized that his life of consumption was consuming *him* with worry and complication (such as having to manage a personal shopper), he traded his 3600-square-foot house for a 420-square-foot studio equipped with a fold down bed, six dress shirts, and no compact disks. His epiphany was not only that his life has environmental and social consequences, but also that 'relationships, experiences and meaningful work are the staples of a happy life' (Hill 2013). American experiments in simple living include Shaker and Amish lifeways, utopian communities inspired by American Transcendentalism (which was influenced by Hindu teachings), and today's tiny house movement. Ironically, my own interest in Hindu renunciation was sparked long ago by a fascination with American homesteading, self-sufficiency, and utopian communities. Sadhus also 'opted out' of society.

Eventually, however, sharing the day-to-day lives of Hindu renouncers taught me that *their* simplicity is not in the interest of self-sufficiency or environmental sustainability. The voluntary simplicity of Graham Hill is about 'quality of life': Having less stuff and more time to pursue passions and cultivate human relationships. Hindu renunciation does not have quality of life as its goal. Rather, its goal as inspired by Vedanta is to deconstruct human ego, which alienates one from Divine Reality and keeps one tethered to the cycle of birth, death, and rebirth. Vedanta proposes the possibility of release from this cycle. The non-dual philosophy of Advaita Vedanta, which underlies some of Hinduism's most prominent ascetic traditions, proposes that the Self is ontologically distinct from thoughts and mental processes; meditative techniques can help one observe one's own mental processes in order to recognize one's difference from them. This idea that witnessing the mind enables control of the mind, notes Mani (2009), dovetails nicely with cherished US notions that the individual is one's greatest resource and that individual effort yields results, whether material or spiritual. However, sadhus do not valorize the mind as an instrument of rational thought; rather, they identify it as a cause of much suffering. Even if detachment from material things fits with Puritan austerity and self-reliance, what the Hindu renouncer seeks is detachment from his or her own social identity, expectations, and ego (Mani 2009: 111–115). These sadhus seek an understanding that worldly life, even 'the good life,' is fleeting and illusory. Their submission to ultimate reality may allow for great freedom in daily life, but it is the opposite of self-sufficiency when it involves organizing one's life to ensure future security. Unlike Americans who opt to radically simplify in order to gain control of their lives, sadhus actively seek to give up control and to cultivate detachment not only from material objects but also from their own identities as male or female, rich or poor, high caste or outcaste.

It is not simply that sadhus live apart from society, and according to a different set of rules, for they embody a profound challenge to domestic life that goes something like this: Family life is good, and householders should fulfill their duties according to moral guidelines. However, domestic life revolves around ego, pleasure, and accumulation of wealth. These things are not 'sinful,' and if pursued according to duty, they will result in a good rebirth and happiness. But this happiness is fleeting and worldly life is full of worry, sadness, and suffering. Just as yo-yo dieting is not the path to lasting weight loss, so too the ups and downs of worldly existence signal a life lived in illusion. Sadhus seek true enlightenment defined as release from this cycle, by which, they claim, one achieves 'bliss' (*anand*) or true and lasting happiness.

The interior life of a renouncer is expected to be different from that of the householder, as is their attitude toward the outside world. Depending on the religious tradition into which they are initiated, they might cultivate an inner attitude of detachment from the world and an exterior characterized by emotional poise and equanimity (Khandelwal 2004: 25). Ideally, it is not that they *control* their feelings of anger and anxiety, but rather that they do not experience these negative emotions. Ascetics belonging to devotional traditions may cultivate instead an emotional stance of ecstasy and thus may appear to be 'mad' (McDaniel 1989). Regardless of sectarian affiliation, all Hindu sadhus agree that a life built on desire—for wealth, objects, food, sex, children, fame—will result in pain and suffering and that there is a way out.

A Debate Lasting Two Millennia

The earliest body of Indian literature known as the Vedas describes the ideal person (envisioned as male) as a married householder who studied the scriptures, fathered sons, and, with his wife, fulfilled ritual obligations with the help of highly trained Brahmin priests. These elaborate Vedic rituals had the goals of ensuring longevity, progeny, and material prosperity. By the sixth century BCE, peripatetic seekers were beginning to challenge the authority of the priestly class and the efficacy of ritual sacrifice and to favor a life of renunciation. Out of this context emerged two movements that rejected the authority of the Vedas and eventually came to be recognized as distinct religions: Buddhism and Jainism. A new corpus of texts, the Upanishads, reinterpreted (rather than rejected) fire sacrifice as symbolic rather than literal, as a mystical, interior state of being. Its adherents established the earliest forms of Hindu renunciation that did not break with the Vedas. If the Vedas promoted ritual acts to ensure prosperity in this life and the next, the Upanishads held out the possibility of release from the cycle of rebirth through ascetic practices. If the Vedas emphasize correct ritual practice in order to obtain progeny, prosperity, and long life, these goals depend on an established social order and heterosexual marriage; thus, women were necessary participants. The Upanishads rejected conventional social hierarchies and authority of Brahmin priests. However, their rejection of domestic life marginalized women who had a crucial role to play in Vedic culture; as the influence of renunciation grew, women increasingly came to be seen as temptresses who would lead celibate men astray. The two sets of texts offer alternative visions of the human condition.

Hindu renunciation rejects the institutions, lifestyles, and emotional orientations of domestic life. South Asia is a region permeated by both organized monasticism and the figure of the solitary ascetic, and this ascetic orientation is integral to Buddhism, Jainism, and Hinduism. Are renunciation and domestic life mutually exclusive or can one accommodate the other without taint of compromise? Is renunciation an abstract ideal irrelevant to the demands and desires of quotidian family life? The perspective expressed in ancient ethical codes is that renunciation is the culmination of life stages appropriate for the high-caste male, so life is to proceed sequentially: Student, householder, retiree, renouncer. The tension is acute around the issue of sex. As Jamison observes, sexual abstinence can be affirmed as a goal even in the midst of family life when, for example, temporary chastity is required during rituals, during certain parts of a wife's menstrual cycle, etc. The trope of 'the seduced ascetic' is found even in the Rig Veda, the earliest Sanskrit text. Here we meet an ascetic who practices such extreme austerities that his power wreaks havoc on the cosmos and social order. In response, a god sends a celestial nymph to seduce the sage and thereby restore order (Jamison 1996: 16).

At least since the colonial encounter, western scholars have been fascinated, critics say too much so, with Hindu asceticism. Colonial officials and missionaries criticized ascetics as unproductive parasites who do not earn their living, and this critique persists today. Defenders assert that sadhus are to be distinguished from beggars because their poverty is intentional and purposeful. It is not that they've failed to achieve house and family and stable livelihood, they say. Rather, they have walked away from these goals in pursuit of something higher. Of course, this is also the point on which they are vulnerable to critique, for skeptics suspect that they most likely have renounced familial life because of some tragic loss or failure (bad marriage, fights with kin, job loss, etc.). In the Indian census, sadhus are lumped together with ordinary beggars. This fact is a challenge for researchers, but it also suggests skepticism on the part of the state. Renouncers live on the edges of familial and status authority (Narayanan 1993), and this is one reason for the ambivalence towards them.

Renouncers do not proclaim that others should follow their lead and abandon domestic life, for they recognize the folly of such a stance. First, their path is physically and emotionally difficult and not appropriate for everyone. Second, without householders to raise children and to produce that which is needed for life, society would collapse. Men need wives, and women need husbands. Children need parents, and parents need children. The social order and material world is also part of divine play. To obtain a spouse, children, health, and material prosperity is to be blessed with good fortune. To be a moral person is to fulfill one's obligation to kin. Third, without householders, renouncers themselves would have no support. Renouncers acknowledge that they depend on householders to meet the most basic bodily needs and so express basic respect for household life. They aim to let go of their own expectations, but also understand that parents *must* have expectations of their children to raise them properly, to fulfill their duty. They do not condemn those who pursue domestic life. Nor do they seek to transform society. Instead, they opt out and focus inward to transform the Self. They are rebels but not revolutionaries (Ramaswamy 1992).

The Middle Ground

Social movements, subcultures, and individual people have found ways to reconcile the responsibilities and comforts of domestic life with the sadhu's promise of escape from the suffering it inevitably entails. I offer four examples from the contemporary period to illustrate this point, though one could just as easily find them in history. The first two describe how domestic life and worldly activity have been accommodated within ascetic life. The third and fourth examples describe ways in which in the discourse of detachment imbues activities firmly situated in worldly life.

While all renunciant traditions in India emphasize detachment (*vairyagya*) from worldly desires and expectations, not all have required abstaining from sex. Kasturi (2009) suggests that the emphasis on celibacy in monastic life and its incompatibility with domesticity may be a relatively recent development that emerged under colonial rule. During the 1840s, prior to the consolidation of colonial law, some ascetic orders allowed their monastic head (*mahant*) to marry and succession was structured along the lines of kinship; other orders that emphasized celibacy also (unofficially) accommodated women and children who lived within their institutions. Women attached to male ascetics were wives, companions, or concubines; children were born from these unions or were sometimes runaways. Thus, domestic life was accommodated to varying degrees in ascetic institutions. Court cases from the late nineteenth to early twentieth centuries indicate that sometimes wives inherited property from their ascetic husbands and sons succeeded their fathers to become head of monastic institutions. However, legal regimes had a transformative effect during the late colonial period, for they ignored customary practices that allowed for flexible domestic arrangements and enforced a rigid distinction between legitimate and illegitimate births. According to Anglo-Hindu law, then, a guru could neither marry nor have legitimate children who might claim inheritance. The law thus sharpened what had been a rather fuzzy distinction between asceticism and a life involving marriage, sexuality, and progeny.

It was in this context that a variety of socioreligious reform movements also emerged in the nineteenth century and became highly influential among middle-class Hindus. They diverged in their politics, but all seemed to agree that ascetic masculinity was an important cultural resource for cultivating physical and moral strength and for furthering the cause of anticolonial nationalism (Kasturi 2009). Modern reformist groups defined Hinduism in term of elitist, pan-Indian textual tradition of Vedanta, and emphasized the quest for liberation. Prominent reformers envisioned sadhus who were involved in the world and householders who were ascetic-like in attitude. Rammohan Roy, who founded the Brahmo Samaj in 1828, embraced Vedanta, but rejected the notion that one must go off to the forest in order to control one's desires. As Hatcher notes, Roy and his middle-class contemporaries educated in colonial schools proposed that the desire to increase one's wealth and fame is good to the extent that it motivates people to work hard. The goal for these reformers was not to eradicate all desire, but rather to cultivate self-restraint and to engage in business with right intention and concern with the well-being of others (Hatcher 2007: 315).

The spirit and discourse of detachment is not confined to monastic orders or forest-dwelling sadhus. It finds its way into many contexts situated firmly within social and domestic life. The Hindi word *dan* is often translated as 'charitable gift.' However, it defies classical anthropological theories that posit gifts as constitutive of social relationships, because the giver of *dan* can accept nothing in return. Hindu religious gifts deny the basic reciprocity of social life and are for this reason dangerous for the recipient (Parry 1994). Bornstein argues that *dan* is distinct from liberal philanthropy in that it takes renunciation as its model. Philanthropy, which is the foundation of many modern charitable practices, favors giving to abstract, needy, and deserving others and is interested to the extent that it is concerned with the outcome, hence the need for accountability. Hindu *dan*, in contrast, is expected to be impersonal and disinterested. Money given to kin is obligatory, and *dan* is given not to kin but to strangers. It is more about cultivating *vairagya* or detachment (from one's money) than it is about fixing a problem, so one should not be overly concerned with the outcome of giving or with 'accountability' (Bornstein 2012).

The discourse of renunciation and its critique of desire finds its way into unlikely Indian contexts as well, including the world of nondominant sexualities. *Hijras* are phenotypic males who dress as women and perform an exaggerated femininity in public. Some are born intersexed, with ambiguous genitalia. Others with male bodies aspire to undergo a ritual emasculation (removal of penis and testicles); those who follow through with this rite gain status within their communities. Often called 'eunuchs' in earlier times and 'transgendered persons' today, *hijras* do not define themselves strictly by their sexuality. They seek respect through their traditional occupation of dancing at births and weddings to confer fertility and through their identification with Hindu renouncers. Paradoxically, even those who claim to identify with the figure of the renouncer may be quite open about their sex work activity. The *hijras* who appear in Reddy's study (2005) look down on 'homosexuals' who dress as men and have sex with other men for pleasure and excitement. The point I wish to emphasize here is that the *hijras* whose voices appear in Reddy's book consider themselves to be more respectable because they engage in sex out of necessity, for money, and do not gain pleasure from these encounters. Even though they are not celibate, they nevertheless emphasize *vairagya* in their approach to sexual activity.

Thus, Hindu negotiation between domestic life and renunciation is ongoing. Marriage is important and valued, and many religious practices revolve around aspirations of a happy domestic life. Renouncers walk away from householder life (marriage, family, livelihood) in pursuit of goals that they say cannot be fulfilled while living at home, so they seek solitude and shed material comforts. Although the ideal is to take this radical step only after ensuring that needs of family members are met, in actuality, some abandon their domestic and financial obligations and thus face accusations of being selfish and irresponsible. Hindu family life emphasizes duty and responsibility to others, and the act of renouncing is seen as selfish, even if for a higher goal. Despite efforts to stake out a middle ground, the tension persists.

Renunciation as Argument

Amartya Sen said it best when he observed that Indians like to argue and that these arguments can be quite substantive. He suggests that this tradition is one reason India has produced an exemplary non-western democracy. There is recognition that, when it comes to life's big questions, there are often two reasonable sides, two contrary arguments that seem equally reasonable. Over the centuries, for example, India has produced both arguments in support of caste hierarchies and an array of anti-caste movements, ideologies, practices. It has produced religious traditions of all stripes, but also atheist philosophies that deny the existence of god. So it is with domesticity and renunciation. As A. K. Ramanujan once noted with some amusement, this ambiguity frequently exasperated English observers, who complained of Indian hypocrisy: 'They do not mean what they say, and they say different things at different times' (Ramanujan 1989: 44). This apparent inconsistency presented a challenge to colonial technologies of rule, for governance necessitated mapping out Indian society in a way that was comprehensible to the English. Ramanujan's answer to such colonial frameworks was to suggest that Indians operate within a logic of context-sensitivity rather than universality; both ethics and meaning derive from the situatedness of person, place, and time. What is right and appropriate behavior for a sadhu (because of their stage of life, disposition, etc.) is not so for a householder, and so on. The constitution of democratic India marks a radical shift as it seeks to define the universal Indian citizen, equal and free of context.

The western fascination with sadhus has been criticized as Orientalist, and with good reason, but Hindu renunciation as a frame of reference touches most aspects of the culture, not in the sense that it is the only game in town, but in the sense that all Hindu philosophies, values, and practices must be in dialogue with renunciation. The strong skepticism towards those who opt out of the ordinary social order also suggests the centrality of the sadhu's critique. Because they live on the margins of society, not completely outside of it, and because they interact with householders, they cannot be completely ignored or dismissed. Thus, the tension between leaving the world and living within it presents an ongoing space of argument and cultural innovation.

Summary

Hinduism has kept alive a long-standing debate between two distinct and seemingly incompatible life-orientations that play out in scripture, myth, ritual, popular culture, and the lives of actual people. This debate has no easy resolution. Most Hindus aspire to a vision of 'the good life,' which can only emerge with a strong domestic and familial life. Weddings are iconic events that symbolize key values of this aspiration: Fertility, health, beauty, pleasure, and material prosperity. Sadhus renounce this vision of domestic well-being in favor of the contemplative life in pursuit of spiritual enlightenment. In doing so, they avoid attachment to people, places, things, and to the desire for security. Renunciation exists on the margins of familial and state authority, and is treated with both reverence and suspicion. Even if this tension is widely expressed in ancient and contemporary expressive genres, there are also many ways in which Hindus attempt to stake out a middle ground between goals that seem to face in opposite directions.

Discussion Questions

1. In what ways are domestic life and renunciation different, both in terms of social practice and goals?
2. In what ways do these seemingly opposite ways of being in the world influence each other?

3.   How is Hindu renunciation similar to, and different from, social move-
     ments and ideals of simplicity prevalent in the United States?
4.   In what ways might gender matter in the pursuit of renunciation?

Notes

1   An ashram can refer to a small hermitage housing a handful of ascetics or a sprawl-
    ing monastic institution with managers and other employed staff and the capacity
    to feed hundreds daily.
2   One exception is the elaborate ornamentation found in ashram temples, though
    not all ashrams have temples within their premises.
3   The models of domesticity described here as mainstream are particularly hege-
    monic among middle-class and upper-caste Hindus. However, there are matrilineal
    castes and subcultures within India, and scholars disagree on the degree to which
    this idealized, patrilineal family ideal is shared by poor, low-status groups, whether
    they identify as Hindu or not. It is also clear that gender dynamics within the
    household cannot be universalized in Indian society or even Hindu society. Some
    scholars suggest that poor, low-status families (where women necessarily engage
    in productive or waged labor) tend to have more egalitarian marriages than those
    found in middle and upper-status families (Susan Seymour 1999). In the latter,
    women may have comforts due to their class status and respectability, but they lack
    authority and real control over economic resources within the family. Other schol-
    ars suggest that there is more gender inequality in families that are economically
    marginalized (Jain and Banerjee 2008: 414).
4   Because of the high value placed on domestic and familial life, barrenness is a ter-
    rible fate for women. Folklore suggests that an infertile woman might visit a sadhu
    to be blessed with progeny. Celibacy is thought to result in male virility, including
    the power of semen, but there are legal reasons that a monk might be an appropri-
    ate solution to female infertility, for someone who is 'dead' can have no legal claim
    on a child regarding paternity or property. See O'Flaherty (1981) on the erotic
    power of the yogi.

Selected Readings

Narayan, Kirin (1989). *Storytellers, Saints, and Scoundrels: Folk Narrative in Hindu Reli-
    gious Teaching*. Philadelphia: University of Pennsylvania Press.
Pechilis, K. (2004). *The Graceful Guru: Hindu Female Gurus in India and the United
    States*. New York: Oxford University Press.
Hausner, Sondra L. (2007). *Wandering with Sadhus: Ascetics in the Hindu Himalayas*.
    Bloomington: Indiana University Press.
Knight, Lisa I. (2011). *Contradictory Lives: Baul Women in India and Bangladesh*. New
    York: Oxford University Press.
Madan, T. N. (2010.) *The T. N. Madan Omnibus: The Hindu Householder*. New Delhi:
    Oxford University Press.

Bibliography

Alter, Joseph (1992). 'The Sannyasi and the Indian Wrestler: The Anatomy of a Rela-
    tionship.' *American Ethnologist* 19, No. 2: 317–336.
——— (1994). 'Celibacy, Sexuality, and the Transformation of Gender into National-
    ism in North India.' *Journal of Asian Studies* 53, No. 1: 45–66.

Bornstein, Erica (2012). *Disquieting Gifts: Humanitarianism in New Delhi*. Stanford: Stanford University Press.

DeNapoli, Antoinette (2009). 'Beyond Brahmanical Asceticism: Recent and Emerging Models of Female Hindu Asceticisms in South Asia.' *Religion Compass* 3, No. 5: 857–875.

Dumont, Louis (1980). *Homo Hierarchicus: The Caste System and Its Implications*. Chicago: University of Chicago Press.

Gold, Ann Grodzins (1989). 'The Once and Future Yogi: Sentiments and Signs in the Tale of a Renouncer-King.' *Journal of Asian Studies* 48, No. 4: 770–786.

Hatcher, Brian (2007). 'Bourgeois Vedanta: The Colonial Roots of Middle-class Hinduism.' *Journal of the American Academy of Religion* 75, No. 2: 298–323.

Heesterman, J.C. (1985). *The Inner Conflict of Tradition*. Chicago: University of Chicago Press.

Hausner, Sondra (2007). *Wandering with Sadhus: Ascetics in the Hindu Himalayas*. Bloomington: Indiana University Press.

Hill, Graham (2013). 'Living with Less. A lot Less.' *New York Times*. March 9. http://www.nytimes.com/2013/03/10/opinion/sunday/living-with-less-a-lot-less.html?_r=0

Jain, Devaki and Nirmala Banerjee (2008). 'The Tyranny of the Household'. In *Women's Studies in India: A Reader* (pp. 411–414). Ed. Mary E. John. New Delhi: Penguin.

Jamison, Stephanie W. (1996). *Sacrificed Wife/Sacrificer's Wife*. New York, Oxford: Oxford University Press.

Kasturi, Malavika (2009). '"Asceticising" Monastic Families: Ascetic Genealogies, Property Feuds and Anglo-Hindu Law in Late Colonial India.' *Modern Asian Studies* 43, No. 5: 1039–1083.

Khandelwal, Meena (2004). *Women in Ochre Robes: Gendering Hindu Renunciation*. Albany: SUNY Press.

Khare, Ravindra S. (1976). *The Hindu Hearth and Home*. Durham: Carolina Academic Press.

Madan, T.N. (2010). *The T.N. Madan Omnibus: The Hindu Householder*. New Delhi: Oxford University Press.

Mani, Lata (2009). *SacredSecular: Contemplative Cultural Critique*. New Delhi: Routledge.

McDaniel, June (1989). *Madness of the Saints: Ecstatic Religion in Bengal*. Chicago: University of Chicago Press.

Mody, Perveez (2006). 'Kidnapping, Elopement and Abduction: An Ethnography of Love-Marriage in Delhi.' In *Love in South Asia* (pp. 877–914). Ed. F. Orsini. New York: Cambridge University Press.

Narayan, Kirin (1989). *Storytellers, Saints, and Scoundrels: Folk Narrative in Hindu Religious Teaching*. Philadelphia: University of Pennsylvania Press.

Narayanan, Vasudha (1993). 'Renunciation and Law in India.' In *Religion and Law in Independent India* (pp. 279–291). Ed. Robert D. Baird. New Delhi: Manohar.

O'Flaherty, Wendy Doniger (1981). *Siva: The Erotic Ascetic*. London and New York: Oxford University Press.

Olivelle, Patrick (1984). 'Renouncer and Renunciation in the Dharmasastras.' In *Studies in Dharmasastra* (pp. 81–152). Ed. R.W. Lariviere. Calcutta: Firma KLM Private, Ltd.

Parry, Jonathan P. (1994). *Death in Banaras*. New York: Cambridge University Press.

Pechilis, K. (2004). *The Graceful Guru: Hindu Female Gurus in India and the United States*. New York: Oxford University Press.

Ramanujan, A. K. (1989). 'Is there an Indian Way of Thinking'? *Contributions to Indian Sociology* 23: 41–58.

Ramaswamy, Vijaya (1992). 'Rebels-Conformists? Women Saints in Medieval South India.' *Anthropos* 87: 133–146.

Reddy, Gayatri (2005). *With Respect to Sex: Negotiating Hijra Identity in South India.* Chicago: The University of Chicago Press.

Rocher, Ludo (2012). *Studies in Hindu Law and Dharmasastra.* Ed. Donald R. Davis. London: Anthem.

Roy, Parama (1998). *Indian Traffic.* Berkeley: University of California Press.

Sen, Amartya (2005). *The Argumentative Indian: Writings on Indian Culture, History and Identity.* London: Penguin Books.

Seymour, Susan (1999). *Women, Family, and Child Care in India: A World in Transition.* New York: Cambridge University Press.

Sharangpani, Mukta (2010). 'Browsing for Bridegrooms: Matchmaking and Modernity in Mumbai.' *Indian Journal of Gender Studies* 17: 249–276.

Sinclair-Brull, Wendy (1997). *Female Ascetics: Hierarchy and Purity in an Indian Religious Movement.* New York: Routledge.

Singh, Supriya (2006). 'Towards a Sociology of Money and Family in the Indian Diaspora.' *Contributions to Indian Sociology* 40: 375–398.

Srinivasan, Priya (2011). *Sweating Saris: Indian Dance as Transnational Labor.* Philadelphia: Temple University Press.

Van der Veer, Peter (1987). 'Taming the Ascetic: Devotionalism in a Hindu Monastic Order.' *Man* 2, No. 2: 680–695.

White, David Gordon (2006). 'Digging Wells While Houses Burn? Writing Histories of Hinduism in a Time of Identity Politics.' *History and Theory* 45: 104–131.

13 Vedic Sacrifice in Modern India

Frederick M. Smith

Modern Hindu worship is strongly influenced by (but by no means exclusively grounded in) the texts of the ancient Vedas and Vedic sacrificial ritual. It is therefore important that we examine this body of ancient ritual and its continuity into modern Hinduism. In this way, we can begin to appreciate the ways in which the system of ancient Vedic ritual gave rise to and interacted with religious forms that succeeded it (Renou 1960; Halbfass 1991). It helps to think of the Vedic ritual system as operating like a complex entity made up of hundreds of moving and interlocking parts. Over time, some of these parts were lost or became discontinued, but many were either transformed or have remained largely intact for more than three millennia. The primary reason this preservation has been so successful is because the process is grounded in a textual record (i.e. the Vedas) that has been rigorously and ceaselessly transmitted from generation to generation. The most authoritative canonical sources for these rituals are a series of texts called Shrauta Sutras, 'Aphorisms of Vedic Ritual Performance.' These compendia of ritual instructions, linked to different branches of Vedic literature, date from the fifth to the third centuries BCE (Kashikar 1968; Gonda 1977). These texts provide instructions for ritual officiants whose families have maintained the textual and performative knowledge of the sacrifices as expressed in the Rig, Sama, and Yajur-Vedas (*shruti*). Thus, the name given to the body of rituals prescribed therein is called *shrauta*, derived from *shruti*, the word for Vedic 'revelation.'

Nevertheless, the Shrauta Sutras were not the only sources of authority for the performance of *shrauta* ritual. A large number of much more detailed practical and explanatory manuals subsidiary to each Shrauta Sutra were composed in order to elucidate particular rituals or specialized parts of rituals, thus facilitating performance. These were written at all periods throughout the last two millennia but rarely received little more than local distribution. Although these were invariably based on the Shrauta Sutras, they contained options, recitations (*mantras*), or performative sequences in much greater detail, and several of them achieved the literary and liturgical exactitude of a classically composed play or opera libretto. In addition to this body of ancillary *shrauta* literature, the character of *shrauta* ritual performance has, since the beginning, been guided by unwritten local style and practice that contributed to a traditional choreography that differed, often greatly, from one community to another.

Thus, one must speak with caution of 'the *shrauta* tradition,' a single *shrauta* (or for that matter of a single Vedic) tradition that was invariable from one region to another. The word 'tradition' often implies a standardization and invariability in doctrine and practice. However, variation and change in form and interpretation have been instrumental in the dynamism and survival of the Vedic traditions. Indeed, Indian religious traditions (including Vedic traditions) were almost never apprehended through national or sectarian organizations or hierarchies that guided and enforced a standard set of beliefs and practices. Thus, these rituals were not always identical from community to community, but they were close enough to be recognized by those in other related or nearby communities. Their modifications, variations, and regional differences were due to environmental, linguistic, and religious change. Nevertheless, detractors from within and without often describe these traditions as tableaux of enfeebled constancy, citing as proof the existence of an avalanche of ritual minutiae known only to a few tiny and widely dispersed brahmin communities with a long history of maintaining these rituals.

Three kinds of ritual that were most often performed by brahmins but could be sponsored by anyone, which today increasingly includes people from the lower castes, were noted from the most ancient periods to the modern: (1) obligatory rites, to be performed regularly (*nitya*); (2) those reserved for special occasions such as birth, marriage, or death (*naimittika*); and (3) rites to satisfy specific desires, such as a desire for male offspring or to acquire property (*kamya*). Obligatory rites are what we shall address here. These obligatory *shrauta* rites range from simple to complex in consonance with the calendar. A simple offering of rice or milk, with clarified butter (*ghee*), with a minimum of ancillary offerings and choreography, is offered at the sunrise and sunset (*agnihotra*). This is performed daily. The fire is never allowed to go out; it is preserved by burying balls of smoldering cow dung in the western of the three fireplaces beneath a thick layer of sawdust. The western fireplace (*garhapatya*) is round and accepts only offerings to the household deities. The eastern fireplace (*ahavaniya*) is square and receives offerings to the great Vedic deities, while the southern fireplace, half-moon in shape (*dakshinagni*), receives offerings to the deceased ancestors. These are separated by an altar called *vedi*, strewn with long grass blades on which the gods come and sit when invoked in order to enjoy the sacrifice (see Image 13.1). The smoldering buried sacred fire easily lasts for twelve to fifteen hours. It is then uncovered and reignited by contact with coconut husks or other flammable material. In this way, the fire remains pure; no matches or paper are necessary to keep a Vedic ritual fire burning for very long periods of time. With a single lapse in the sixteenth century, the sacred fires of one of my teachers in South India had been burning constantly for nine hundred years, since the twelfth century.

Figure 13.1 Vedic fire altars

The next in the series of Vedic rituals is the offering to the new and full moons (*darshapurnamasa*), always performed on the morning after the new moon or full moon. This complicated ritual takes about two and a half hours, and requires four priests in addition to the sacrificer and his wife, and considerable choreographing. The gestures and movements, plus the places where the ritual officiants sit, are only partially written into the ancient instructional texts and are therefore dependent for their preservation on the maintenance of local knowledge. The offerings, always to one or more of a large number of Vedic deities, are primarily clarified butter, offered in thin, long-handled wooden spoons. At the center of the performance, rice flour balls (placed in large, wooden spoons) are offered to various deities: Agni, the fire and the god of fire, the priest of the gods and the god of the priests; Prajapati, the creator deity and giver of offspring; Indra, the king of the gods who defeated the powerful and world-threatening demons; Surya, the sun and the sun as a deity; the Maruts, the storm gods and helpers of Indra; Soma, the personification of the soma drink and the regulator of coolness, the one who balances the heat of Agni, the bestower of divine visions; and others.

A series of three seasonal performances offered every four months (*chaturmasya*) is more complex still. Every six months, the sacrificial patron is required to perform an independent animal sacrifice. This requires five priests and encompasses offerings on the model of the sacrifices to the new and full moon, but adds a very complicated animal sacrifice in three separate parts. This is rarely performed, and there is not much evidence that it was ever regularly performed, at least in historical times. Once every year, in the spring or fall, a *soma* sacrifice was required.

Soma is a beverage originally intended to induce visions and help the ritualists sit up all night and recite their Vedic texts. But knowledge of the true identity of *soma* has been lost for millennia, since at least the eighth century BCE. The *soma* sacrifice is a grand affair, still performed regularly, albeit with substitutes for the *soma*, a point that will be discussed below. It employs seventeen priests, and is a minimum of five days in length, including several days of preliminary rites. Some *soma* sacrifices, such as one requiring the construction of a massive bird-shaped altar out of a thousand bricks, two hundred in each of five layers (*agnichayana*, Staal 1983), will take from three to four weeks. The *soma* is not just to be drunk by the ritualists at various points, but is to be offered, by pouring it into the fire, to many Vedic deities. The corpus of *soma* sacrifices in the Vedic texts is vast; dozens of variants are mentioned. But only a few are performed, especially in modern times.

Decline of Vedic Ritual

Textual and inscriptional evidence reveals that *shrauta* rituals were performed throughout the Indian subcontinent. But at present, their provenance is extremely limited. Today, there are about one hundred male patrons who, along with their wives, have established the *shrauta* fires (only married couples are eligible). Most of these couples reside in central Tamilnadu and coastal Andhra Pradesh, and by family tradition follow a single textual and performative tradition (the Apastamba textual lineage of the Yajur-Veda). In the early years of the second decade of the twenty-first century, perhaps forty ritual patrons of this and other ancient schools of performance survive in both Tamilnadu and Andhra Pradesh, a handful in Kerala and Karnataka, about fifteen in Maharashtra (most of them in one unique Vedic memory school near Barsi in Solapur district), and two or three in all of North India (Kashikar and Parpola 1983; Smith 2001).

Several reasons may be cited for the decline in *shrauta* performance. First and foremost is the undisputed fact that religious form constantly changes. What was interesting, meaningful, and necessary in one era may be abandoned entirely in the next one. Modernization and its attractions are not just twentieth- and twenty-first-century phenomena, but have been active forces for thousands of years, drawing people away from old forms of religious practice and towards new ones. These, in turn, create the conditions necessary for backlash and revival, however small. In this case, the *shrauta* rituals ceased to be practicable and meaningful for most people; and in the small enclaves where they did survive in form, they were usually assigned updated and recontextualized meanings that were very different from those explained in the Vedic texts themselves (Staal 1979 on their meaninglessness, Witzel 1992 on their meaningfulness). The eschatological significance of *shrauta* ritual, even in the earliest times performed only by a minuscule and highly educated priestly elite, eventually disappeared for most Hindus, who generally prefer hands-on, participatory domestic, and temple-based religion where meaning is derived very differently (Smith 2011). Not only is such religion and its defining ritual participatory, but it is most often inclusive of nearly everyone in the community. Equally important, it is colorful, fluid, and provides a wide berth for local expression of mood (which can be raucous). As *shrauta* ritual receded into the religious backwaters, religious forms such as deity worship and temple consecrations arose because they are more personally engaging and socially relevant. Vedic sacrifice could not have been all but eradicated as long as popular demand for it lasted. The growth of other forms of religious practice is testimony to the ultimate ineffectiveness of Vedic sacrifice in addressing popular religious and spiritual concerns.

Second, *shrauta* ritual, which, as noted, was never practiced by large numbers of people but carried prestige and long enjoyed the patronage of kings (many of whom are named in inscriptions of the first millennium CE) and institutions (including the great Shankara, Madhva, and Ramanuja temple complexes in South India with dedicated endowments for this esoteric and demanding ritual). Eventually, this institutional patronage tapered off, although it has not completely ceased to this day. Because the sacrifices were no longer deemed religiously meaningful or important, benefactors, especially institutional donors, became difficult to locate. Because the expenses involved in their performance increased, local brahmin performers became more and more dependent on their client and peer communities to bear the expenses of their sacrifices. In addition, public fundraising, never practiced before, became an important aspect of sacrificial performance.

Third, the comparatively public presence of *shrauta* ritual became problematic from about the twelfth century CE onward, especially in North India. One of the great differences between religion in North India and that in South

India is that in the south religion is, as a rule, more public, where the religion of towns, cities, and regions often revolves around great temples. In the north, however, much more of the religious activity is enshrined in small, often private, quarters. The primary reason for this was the greater Muslim power in North India, which forced much Hindu, especially brahminical, religious activity indoors. One of the main casualties of this enforced privacy was Vedic ritual performance. This is why, in North India outside of Varanasi and a few towns in Braj (a district in western Uttar Pradesh), Rajasthan, and Gujarat, hardly any performances of *shrauta* ritual have occurred for hundreds of years. The most visible exception would be the great sacrifices of Mahahaja Jai Singh of Jaipur in the early eighteenth century, who expressed his kingship in this deeply Sanskritic manner after two centuries of Muslim rule in that area.

Fourth, the pressures of survival in a changing society forced many brahmins away from the strenuous educational demands required for the performance of *shrauta* ritual. Brahminical education became increasingly geared towards performance of domestic offertory services called *puja* and other temple and household rites, thus providing little motivation for students in schools specializing in the memorization of Vedic texts to learn the arcane duties or recitative techniques required in the *shrauta* rituals.

Fifth, performance of complicated *shrauta* rituals, especially *soma* sacrifices, required active collaboration of experts in the Rig-Veda, Sama-Veda, and Yajur-Veda. In most of India, the tradition of Sama-Veda recitation disappeared centuries ago. In Andhra Pradesh, and to some extent in Tamilnadu, the surviving practitioners of *shrauta* ritual, who have historically specialized in and memorized only small parts of the ritual libretto because others have been there to recite and perform the remaining parts, have been forced to learn for themselves the parts for which practitioners can no longer be found. This is necessary to the survival of the *shrauta* traditions themselves. However, this did not occur in most of the rest of India, the result being the abandonment of *shrauta* practice due to the loss of the Sama-Veda, which requires the most specialized and subtle singing of the ancient Rig-Vedic mantras. Indeed, the imminent loss of the Sama-Veda in most of South India will soon force more of the remaining *shrauta* tradition into extinction. Fortunately, at present, an effort is underway in Maharashtra to preserve the Sama-Veda by bringing some of the few remaining teachers in Kerala and Karnataka to teach a few young students. This will keep a few of the *shrauta* traditions alive for at least one further generation.

Vedic Ritual Today

We can now turn to the current state of Vedic ritual. A general view suggests two basic motivations for its continued performance: on the one hand, *shrauta* rituals are often performed with an eye to continuing inherited tradition; on the other hand, they can be enacted with more explicitly revivalist intentions. The two objectives are not unrelated: ritualists responsible for revivalist performances are, first and foremost, learned and experienced in their own inherited traditions. But for reasons that vary from one practitioner to another, they have decided to introduce *shrauta* ritual to people outside their local traditions. The hereditary ritualists either have a sense of their own traditions disappearing and see interest elsewhere, or they actively propagate *shrauta* ritual outside their communities as the historically most significant form of 'Vedic dharma,' of ancient socioreligious law that is the source of their present beliefs and practices.

In either case, revivalist performance represents a very small, though increasingly visible, segment of *shrauta* performance. It is these motivations, combined with personal interests in reexamining and recapturing earlier (often imagined) strata of their own ritual traditions, and bringing to the performance a sense of public spectacle, that defines a Vedic sacrifice as revivalist. Such sacrifices have inevitably succeeded in inviting public attention and scrutiny, and in creating major shifts in patronage and ideology. While reinterpreting Vedic sacrifice as offerings to the well-known deities of Hinduism as well as verifiable experiments in modern environmental science, Vedic ritualists have reached towards both the traditional Hindu and the newly dominant, scientifically educated middle classes for patronage (Lubin 2001a, 2001b). For example, it is not unusual now for ritualists in Maharashtra to advertise their sacrifices as an ancient scientific practice that purifies the environment, touting scientific experiments that show how the smoke from the sacred fire eliminates pollution.

Revivalist performances have also engendered new alliances between ancient ritual schools, as well as renewed discussion about what constitutes properly performed Vedic sacrifice. Such revivalism and realignment has met with considerable resistance within the older, local traditions; those responsible for revivalist sacrifices are often distrusted by communities that consider themselves to be the true representatives of orthodoxy. It is important to understand that revivalism here is similar to revivalism in other religious traditions. This is analogous to advocates of Christian fundamentalism in America today who state that Christianity was exactly like this in antiquity, when in fact it never looked like this at any point in history. In the case of revivalist Vedic ritual in India, the forces that shape it are entirely new, and elements appear in it now that have never been there before.

Vedic sacrificial traditions are constituted by both region and textual affiliation. In each region of India, ritualists belonging to particular branches of the Rig-Veda, Yajur-Veda, and Sama-Veda have adapted their procedures and style to fit with each other in arrangements that date back hundreds, if not thousands, of years. Thus, each region or locality has its own distinct flavor of sacrificial performance. However, this is changing now because for the last thirty or forty years, the children of these Vedic ritualists, descending as they do from an old educated elite, have abandoned their traditional educations and professions in favor of new ones in engineering, computer technology, and medicine. For example, one of the great experts in Vedic ritual and traditional knowledge in central India, whom I knew well, had five sons. All had PhDs in scientific fields, four had left India, and none retained their Vedic ritual practice, even if all of them maintained their practice of reciting the Vedas every day. One of the facts of Hinduism is that all religion is local. Forms of recitation, styles of offering, ideologies and interpretations that accompany and even structure the rituals in the minds of the performers, and social interactions that arise from residing in close-knit communities are now undergoing dramatic changes that are forcing subtle but major changes in the rituals, from patronage to organization to performance to social and spiritual meaning.

One example of this may be seen in the state of Kerala on the south-west coast of India. The Kerala *shrauta* traditions have received considerable scholarly attention in recent decades, thanks to the work of Frits Staal (1983) and others. The recipients of this tradition are an extended clan of brahmins called Nambudiri whose Vedic lineages have been healthy and full. Most follow a branch of the Yajur-Veda called Baudhayana or a branch of the Sama-Veda called Jaiminiya (one of the few branches of Sama-Veda to survive into the present day, and at that just barely). Several follow a lineage of the Rig-Veda called Shankhayana. This has enabled them to perform their Vedic rituals for hundreds of years using personnel from within their own community. They have also developed recitational styles that are unique; even if they follow the same texts and phrase accentuation as Vedic scholars and ritualists elsewhere in India, the articulation is very different (Staal 1961). Formerly the Nambudiris performed their sacrifices by utilizing their own resources derived from extensive land holdings. However, due to land redistribution by recent Communist governments of Kerala, the Nambudiris have been largely stripped of their inherited property, the major source of their resources. This, plus the rapid disappearance of experts in the Sama-Veda, has threatened their tradition. The local ritual traditions have now been forced to borrow from other networks of ritualists in order to survive, and this has not been easy. The effects of modernity, including the Internet and the overhaul of local economies and culture by national and multinational corporations on what had been local lineage, ritual, and linguistic networks, have yet to be assessed.

The basic requirements for realizing and maintaining one's status as a patron of the Vedic ritual are the initial establishment of the sacrificial fires and the regular performance of the daily morning and evening fire offerings and the offerings at the time of the new and full moon. These are the basic ritual and family duties and are often viewed as spiritual practice. But they are not often performed with great regularity, in part because the patrons who perform them seek greater prestige and power in their communities through the performance of much grander and visible *soma* sacrifices, the bigger and more complicated the better and more prestigious (the latter because of the former). In order to achieve this, they often dispense with the daily rituals. Indeed, except in the Vedic ritual communities in central Tamilnadu and coastal Andhra Pradesh, the *soma* sacrifices are most often performed within the public domain, with spectacle as one of their objectives even if the priests' focus is strictly on the ritual choreography and recitations.

These performances are considered by the ritualists not just as opportunities to support Vedic traditions for their own sake and for the spiritual advancement of the performers, especially the sacrificer, but as ideal occasions to educate the public about Vedic ritual and other areas of Hindu thought and practice. Because practically no one who attends a *soma* sacrifice as an observer has the slightest idea about what's actually going on (Smith 2011), and because thousands usually attend—they are billed as Vedic and (thus) as merit producing religious spectacles—a good deal of energy is channeled into public discourses on dharma and other popular, often sectarian, religious topics (Smith 2000). These are often timed to coincide with important offerings, which usually occur several times every day. Other supplementary activities occur outside the sacrificial arena, but are close enough to its periphery to provide a conceptual proximity. These include organized singing of popular religious songs and performances of religious dramas, both of which are greatly appreciated by the public as gateways of access to the remote and arcane world of Vedic ritual. These are part of the process of educating the public about the Vedic antecedents to their own religious culture, and are utilized to solicit much needed funds for the sacrifices themselves. Because Vedic sacrifice is an isolated phenomenon on the landscape of Hindu practice—in fact, its very survival can be attributed to its isolation, miraculously enduring the many currents of sectarian practice and orthodoxy in a kind of internal exile—funds collected from the public can be reliably counted on to contribute to the sacrifices. Additionally, both of these phenomena, the religious isolation of Vedic sacrifice and the precarious funding situation for most of them, have discouraged *shrauta* performances from becoming venues for Hindu nationalist political activism. In short, the sponsors, performers, and hosts of these unusual sacrificial rituals are today reenvisioning and resituating themselves in the public discourse of Hinduism because they have to in order to make themselves relevant, whereas in previous periods in which sponsorship and patronage were in the hands of private institutions and small tightly knit communities, it was not important that they were even then out of step with cultural trends. Previously, they did not require or solicit much of an audience, in spite of much ballyhooed sacrifices mentioned in the Sanskrit epics, the Mahābhārata and Rāmāyaṇa.

In different parts of India, different rituals have emerged as the most important bearers of prestige for the ritualists. It is important to note this in order to avoid the notion that the character and culture of Vedic ritual has been more or less the same everywhere. Regional developments within Vedic ritual culture have contributed to differentiation in Hindu ritual and practice. For example, in the Kathmandu valley in Nepal, the ancient *agnihotra* ritual has been appropriated by the local Tantra-accented practice to produce unique religious forms that are deeply etched in the very geography of the cities surrounding Kathmandu (Witzel 1986, 1987). In Tamilnadu and some parts of

Andhra Pradesh, where the ancient traditions are not as seriously endangered as elsewhere, the injunction to perform a yearly *soma* sacrifice is often interpreted to mean that (at least) one *soma* sacrifice should be performed in the community every year, but not one by every qualified ritualist. This is a luxury that these Vedic ritualists can afford, for nowhere else in India are there actually communities of such ritualists. The greatest spectacle among Vedic sacrifices, for both the performers and the public, is a *soma* sacrifice that accompanies the construction of the great bird-shaped altar (*agnichayana*), and the *soma* sacrifice that accompanies a unique chariot race and a ritual ascent to heaven of the sacrificer and his wife, who mount, with great fanfare, a stairway and platform that is built for this occasion (the *vajapeya* rite). These very unusual sacrifices invariably attract large crowds, and offer the sacrificer considerable prestige within Vedic and greater Hindu communities. They are, however, not often performed; perhaps two dozen have occurred in the last twenty-five years in South India and Maharashtra, and even once (a *vajapeya*) in New York City (in June 2000). These and other Vedic rituals have a long history of influencing Hindu practice, even if the sources are in the end diverse (Renou 1960).

The problems associated with performing a Vedic sacrifice outside India are many and often intractable. Although Hinduism has been transplanted to the West through the growing and comparatively well-off diaspora community, replete with temples, sectarian representation, and festivals (although pilgrimage to sacred places, so much a part of Hinduism, is impossible), the attempt to perform old style Vedic ritual in the West has proven to be daunting. A well-known sacrificial patron from Madhya Pradesh, with a very good team of seventeen priests from Maharashtra and South India (which already represented a major shift in ritual community alignments), and a large support staff, tried twice to perform *soma* sacrifices outside India. The first was a normal *soma* sacrifice in a public park in London (which is extremely complicated by any normal standard), where the challenges were too much to truly render it successful (Smith 2000). The second was a *vajapeya* in New York in 2000. Although most of the surface rites were reasonably well done, the grand scale of the *vajapeya* was dwarfed by its alienness in a large foreign city.

It was performed in the Gujarati Samaj Hall in Queens, directly beneath the Brooklyn-Queens Expressway, and the events scheduled for outdoors were inaudible because of the noise from the expressway, and the sight of highly educated and respectable ritualists circling a couple of city blocks in a marginal neighborhood carrying American children's toys as ritual representations of chariots, in place of the grand chariot race, was one of cultures that were at odd angles to each other. Part of the purpose of the performance was to introduce Hindus in America to the religion of their ancient ancestors, but, as in India, this required constant explanatory comments by the sacrificial patron to the approximately two hundred people who showed up (and who sponsored the event). Of course, many substitutions were necessary, including for the animals and the main ingredient, the *soma* itself.

Substitutions

Regardless of the unusual nature and uneven success of these Vedic rituals beyond the borders of India, substitutions (*pratinidhi*) for prescribed material have been regularly employed for thousands of years (Smith 1987). Thus, the idea was not at all novel. Substitutions can occur in nearly any context and for almost any reason. Surrogates are the rule for exotic substances such as *soma*, alcoholic preparations (*sura*), unusual grains, exorbitant fees given to the priests (for example, a token amount in rupees, such as fifty, or seventy-five, although a thousand or more is also attested, for each cow in a *soma* sacrifice in which one hundred and twelve cows are enjoined as the fee), and even for entire sacrifices (*agnihotras* that are not performed for a fortnight are often replaced with a single large offering consisting of the entire amount that would have been offered over that time period). The usual substitution for *soma* is the stalky succulent *Sarcostemma brevistigma*, which fortunately was available in England and New York, called creeping milk-hedge. Rice serves as the substitute for unusual grains and one kind of wood is usually substituted for three or four that are enjoined.

Unquestionably the most contested of substitutions are those for the sacrificial animal. As mentioned above, animal sacrifice may be performed independently or as a part of a *soma* sacrifice, in which the immolation of at least three animals is prescribed. More problematic, though only by degrees, are some of the major *soma* sacrifices, which require the immolation of large numbers of animals (for example, the *vajapeya* prescribes the sacrifice of twenty-three animals). Awareness of this problem has been building for thousands of years. Indeed, by the middle of the first-millennium CE, objection to animal sacrifice began to appear in the sectarian religious histories called Puranas. Eventually animal sacrifice, along with much more in the corpus of ancient Vedic ritual, was prohibited by legal texts for performance in the present Dark Age (*kali-yuga*). Although the Vedic sacrifices have remained ritually unchanged, or at least subject to their own rules of change, they have been reinterpreted as offerings to the great deities of Hinduism such as Shiva and especially Vishnu, and animal sacrifice was increasingly frowned on, even while it was clearly prescribed in the earliest Vedic texts. For example, in the highly influential *Bhagavata Purana* (11.18.7), Krishna states that he should not be the recipient of a Vedic animal sacrifice (Bhaktivedanta 1972). The much earlier *Shatapatha Brahmana* (1.2.3.6–7) states, in a passage often cited by Vedic ritualists, that for one with proper knowledge, an offering of grain can bring about the same effects as the sacrifice of an animal (Eggeling 1882). Animal sacrifice in Sanskritic culture has become more contentious as the alleged sacredness of the cow has become a political issue in modern India (Jha 2002), in which many well-intentioned (and politically involved) Hindus will neither believe nor accept that animal sacrifice and meat eating were acknowledged parts of life among elites in ancient and classical India.

This is indicative of a long tradition of privileged access to mystical knowledge, which in this case allows Vedic ritualists to justify substitutions for the animal sacrifice. The fourteenth book of the great Indian epic, the *Mahab-harata*, which describes the action surrounding a horse sacrifice designed to legitimate the reign of Yudhishthira, the king of the Pandava clan, ends on a decidedly ambivalent note in declaring that the virtue of generosity, the gift of a few handfuls of flour by a hungry family to a mendicant guest, is greater than the performance of a horse sacrifice. Another strategy for deal-ing with the problem is reflected in a series of verses composed by the great sixteenth century philosopher and ritualist, Appayya Diksita. On pondering the agony suffered by animals upon their death, and how the glorious eternal Vedas could have enjoined such a thing, Appayya Dikshita concluded that the word of the Vedas must be followed, that the soul cannot be cut with a knife, and that to die as a sacrificial victim is to conquer death (Ramesan 1972: 79–80). Many modern ritualists add to this that a sacrificed animal obtains a higher rebirth, a religious argument that updates classical philo-sophical argumentation regarding the problem of sacrificial violence (Gune 1993; Houben 1999).

As a result, many of the surviving ritual traditions attenuated the practice of Vedic animal sacrifice. A first step occurred quite likely as early as the third century BCE, under the influence of Buddhists and Jainas, when virtually all of the regional traditions accepted the practice of substituting goats for other prescribed sacrificial animals, including sheep and bulls. Second, independent animal sacrifice decreased in frequency, and, as mentioned, is rarely if ever performed today.

Several methods of offering the animal in the context of *soma* sacrifices are followed today: (1) offering of the actual animal, (2) replacing it with a dough or papier-mâché replica, and (3) offering ghee as a substitute. Only the most rigorous among learned Vedic ritualists in South India and Maharashtra have maintained the practice of slaughtering the prescribed animals, and this is now largely performed in secret, by smothering the animal according to Vedic injunction, but in the middle of the night when nobody will see it. At least one member of each surviving ritual community still retains the surgi-cal skills required to cut the animal open and remove the pericardium and parts of the internal organs and select pieces of flesh to be offered into the fire and consumed by the ritualists. If parts of the animal are in fact consumed, it is usually after storing them overnight in a refrigerator and boiling them for several hours, often with large quantities of salt or sugar. On no other occa-sion will these Vedic brahmins eat meat. Today, based on a passage from the post-Vedic *Laws of Manu* (5.37), the offering of a dough or ghee animal is accepted as a legitimate alternative (see Bühler 1969). The passage from Manu states that if one has a strong desire to eat meat, but has no legitimate reason to kill an animal, then he should make—and presumably consume—a ghee or dough animal. The most visible practitioners of Vedic ritual today employ these substitutes, in no small measure because their visibility renders the use of actual animals risky. As discussed, most of these practitioners are parts of new collegial arrangements with a much more national cast, while the patrons themselves represent either new lineages or revivals of old ones.

Conclusion

In sum, the old Vedic traditions were held together within specific brahmin communities by individuals whose knowledge and ritual skills were specialized even within these communities. If four roles were necessary, then four individuals were entrusted with learning the roles from four distinct specialized lineages of textual and performative knowledge. If even one of these specialized lineages were to disappear for any reason, then the entire tradition would disappear along with it. This has occurred often in the history of Vedic ritualism, in which case the local style of performance would either disappear or be replaced piecemeal by ritualists from elsewhere. This has proven to be awkward, even if compromises have been made to compensate for it. Such reorganization of the ancient traditions is now giving way to new methods of keeping the traditions alive, if barely, by dissemination of knowledge across the Internet and through other means of networking, the effects of which will be known only by the mid-twenty-first century. Thus, the Vedic traditions have remained alive through creative response to change, whether it is in the form of substitutions of offering or other material or because of the necessity of forging new and awkward collegial arrangements.

With respect to Hinduism as a whole, the processes described here are fairly representative. Tradition is highly valued even as elasticity in performance, ideology, patronage, and personnel is more the rule than the exception, at least in the long run. Due to the fidelity with which the Vedas have been maintained across the millennia, the Vedic rituals have remained remarkably stable, even as the numbers of Vedic ritual specialists has thinned out considerably. The idea of the constancy of the Vedas has transferred to the much larger and more mutating corpus of Hindu Tantric and bhakti ritual. But this has conferred an aura of antiquity, and therefore of authority, onto Hindu ritual, and at least internally, to Hinduism itself.

Summary

The Vedic sacrificial rituals were the most visible of the ancient Indian religious forms. One reason for that is because they were the products of 1,500 years of oral literature that survives intact today and because they have a 3,500-year tradition of performance. They still survive today in a few pockets of southern India. This chapter briefly describes some of the most important of these rituals and addresses the issues and challenges surrounding their survival in modern India. These rituals have survived because they have adopted modern Hindu ways of thinking into the interpretive edifice that has carried them through these three and a half millennia. Vedic ritual is often viewed as inflexible and incomprehensible. However, its survival, or the long-term survival of any religious tradition, is in part due to its flexibility and dynamism, its ability to adapt to changing religiocultural, political, and environmental changes.

Discussion Questions

- What is it about the ancient Vedic forms of Indian religion that distinguish them from classical Hinduism?
- What enabled these forms of ancient Indian religion to survive 3,500 years of political and cultural changes, revolutions, and the rise (and fall) of other religions such as classical Hinduism, Buddhism, and Jainism?
- What does the coexistence of Vedic brahmanical religion with more modern forms of religion tell you about the processes of religious syncretism and the ability of distinct cultural groups to survive in isolation?

Suggested Readings

Lubin, Timothy (2001a). 'Science, Patriotism, and Mother Veda: Ritual activism in Maharashtra.' *International Journal of Hindu Studies* 5, No. 3: 81–105.

Lubin, Timothy (2001b). 'Veda on Parade: Revivalist Ritual as Civic Spectacle.' *Journal of the American Academy of Religion* 69, No. 2: 377–408.

Smith, Frederick M. (2000). 'Indra Goes West: Report on a Vedic Soma Sacrifice in London in July 1996.' *History of Religions* 39, No. 3: 247–267.

——— (2011). 'A Brief History of Indian Religious Ritual and Resource Consumption: Was there an Environmental Ethic?' *Asian Ethnology* 70, No. 2: 163–180.

Staal, Frits (1983). *Agni: The Vedic Ritual of the Fire Altar.* Vols. I & II. Berkeley: Asian Humanities Press.

This is a major production and can be found only in libraries. However, it is well worth the effort to see that your library has a copy.

Bibliography

Bhaktivedanta, A.C. (1972). *Srimad-Bhagavatam.* New York: Bhaktivedanta Book Trust.

Bühler, Georg (1969). *The Laws of Manu.* New York: Dover.

Eggeling, Julius (1882). *The Shatapatha-Brahmana, According to the Text of the Madhyandina School.* Oxford: Clarendon Press.

Gonda, Jan (1977). 'The Ritual Sūtras.' In *History of Indian Literature* (vol. I, p. 2). Ed. J. Gonda. Wiesbaden: Otto Harrassowitz.

Gune, Jayashree (1993). 'Paśu Sacrifice and the śāstras.' *Annals of the Bhandarkar Oriental Research Institute* 74: 153–167.

Halbfass, Wilhelm (1991). *Tradition and Reflection: Explorations in Indian Thought.* Albany: State University of New York Press.

Houben, Jan E.M. (1999). 'To Kill or Not to Kill: The Sacrificial Animal (*yajña-paśu*)? Arguments and Perspectives in Brahmanical Ethical Philosophy.' In *Violence Denied: Violence, Non-Violence and the Rationalization of Violence in South Asian Cultural History* (pp. 105–183). Ed. Jan E.M. Houben and Karel R. Van Kooij. Leiden: Brill.

Jha, D.N. (2002). *The Myth of the Holy Cow.* London and New York: Verso.

Kashikar, C.G. (1968). *A Survey of the Śrautasūtras.* Bombay: University of Bombay. [Also found in *Journal of the University of Bombay* 35 (n.s., pt. 2). 41 (September 1966).]

Kashikar, C.G. and Asko Parpola (1983). 'Śrauta Traditions in Recent Times.' *Staal* 2: 199–251.

Lubin, Timothy (2001a). 'Science, Patriotism, and Mother Veda: Ritual activism in Maharashtra.' *International Journal of Hindu Studies* 5, No. 3: 81–105.

—— (2001b). 'Veda on Parade: Revivalist Ritual as Civic Spectacle.' *Journal of the American Academy of Religion* 69, No. 2: 377–408.

Ramesan, N. (1972). *Sri Appayya Diksita.* Hyderabad: Srimad Appayya Dikshitendra Granthavali Prakasana Samithi.

Renou, Louis (1960). *Le destin du Veda dans l'Inde. Etudes védiques et pāṇinéennes.* Vol. 6. Paris: Boccard. [Trans. Dev Raj Chanana as *The Destiny of the Veda in India.* Delhi: Motilal Banarsidass, 1965.]

Smith, Frederick M. (1987). *The Vedic Sacrifice in Transition: A Translation and Study of the Trikāṇḍamaṇḍana of Bhāskara Mishra.* Poona: Bhandarkar Oriental Research Institute.

—— (2000). 'Indra Goes West: Report on a Vedic Soma Sacrifice in London in July 1996.' *History of Religions* 39, No. 3: 247–267.

—— (2001). 'The Recent History of Vedic Ritual in Maharashtra.' *Vidyārṇavavada-nam. Essays in Honour of Asko Parpola.* Eds. Klaus Karttunen and Petteri Koskikallio. *Studia Orientalia* 94: 443–463.

—— (2011). 'A Brief History of Indian Religious Ritual and Resource Consumption: Was there an Environmental Ethic?' *Asian Ethnology* 70, No. 2: 163–180.

Staal, Frits (1979). 'The Meaninglessness of Ritual.' *Numen* 26, No. 1: 2–22.

—— 1983. *Agni: The Vedic Ritual of the Fire Altar.* Vols. I & II. Berkeley: Asian Humanities Press.

Staal, J. F. (1961). *Nambudiri Veda Recitation.* Disputationes Rheno-Trajectinae, 5. The Hague: Mouton.

Witzel, Michael (1986). 'Agnihotra-Rituale in Nepal.' In *Formen kulturellen Wandels und andere Beiträge zur Erforschung des Himalaya: Colloquium des Schwerpunktes Nepal Heidelberg, 1.-4. Februar 1984* (pp. 156–187). Ed. Bernahrd Kölver. Sankt Augustin: VGH Wissenschaftsverlag.

—— (1987). 'The Coronation Rituals of Nepal, with Special Reference to the Coronation of King Birendra in 1975.' In *Heritage of the Kathmandu Valley* (pp. 417–467). Eds. Niels Gutschow and Axel Michaels. St. Augustin: VGH Wissenschaftsverlag.

—— (1992). 'Meaningful Ritual.' In *Ritual, State, and History in South Asia: Essays in Honour of J. C. Heesterman* (pp. 774–827). Eds. A. W. van den Hoek. D. H. A. Kolff, M. S. Oort. Leiden, New York: E. J. Brill.

14 Visual and Media Culture

Karline McLain

While living in the bustling city of Mumbai (formerly Bombay), India many years ago on a research sabbatical, I used to ride the bus daily between my centrally located research site and my rental apartment in a northern suburb. This was an air-conditioned bus, a slower but more comfortable commute than the notoriously packed commuter train cars of Mumbai, and the white-collar passengers who could afford the bus ticket sat in comfort, and peacefully read the newspaper, catnapped, or chatted quietly with their neighboring passengers as we trekked across the congested city. At the Irla stop, the bus stand was located right next to a small street shrine dedicated to Shirdi Sai Baba (see Image 14.1). Seated within the bus, I could gaze through the tinted windows directly into the shrine, taking in its small statue, called a *murti*, and its various posters of the god-man.

The central poster presented an image of the large, marble *murti* that is at the center of the Sai Baba temple at the main pilgrimage complex in Shirdi, Maharashtra, while other posters featured Sai Baba alongside Dattatreya and Hanuman, Hindu deities that are popular in western India. Day after day, I watched as residents of this northern suburb paused to express their devotion at the shrine, walking up to it and folding their hands in prayer while looking upon the images and making a small offering of cash or fruit. I watched as the shrine's caretaker engaged in ritual worship, or *puja*, each morning: ringing the small bell, offering new flowers and a fresh coconut, and lighting incense. And I watched as my fellow commuters also expressed their devotion. As the bus stopped to allow passengers to enter and exit, several of the regular commuters would turn to face the shrine, staring intently at the posters and *murti* of the god-man for the duration of the stop. Usually, these passengers would fold their hands together in a greeting of *namaste* as they gazed upon the images and softly mutter 'Om Sai Ram.' During the morning commute each Thursday—the day most sacred to Shirdi Sai Baba—one passenger would open his window and hold out a cash offering, which the shrine's caretaker would quickly accept and stuff into the metal donation box.

On first observation, my fellow passengers' devotion to this shrine seemed so fleeting and casual as to be almost insignificant. But the compounding effect of

Figure 14.1 Street shrine to Shirdi Sai Baba

witnessing such devotional behavior twice a day, day after day, week after week, and then month after month as the year drew to a close caused me to reevaluate its significance in the everyday lives of these commuters. This reevaluation was further strengthened through conversation with some of these commuters about the significance of the shrine to them. Such conversations began when I finally asked one commuter, with whom I regularly exchanged pleasant conversation, whether she ever got off the bus to visit the shrine in person. Wide-eyed, she asked: 'Why? I can take *darshan* [auspicious sight] from right here, in the A/C.' But, I persisted in asking, does such transitory devotion 'count' the same as a proper visit to a temple? She replied: 'This street *mandir* [shrine], it may not look as important as Mahalaxmi Mandir [one of Mumbai's most famous temples]. But to me it is even more important. It is hard to find time to go to the temple. I work long hours, I have two sons at home, my husband is often out of station for work. Where is the time? And I am not so religious that I keep a *mandir* at home, like my mother did. So, this *mandir* helps me to make time for God in my life every day. Twice a day I take *darshan* at this *mandir* as the bus goes by. Like this, I am able to take *darshan* and find some peace.' Opening her purse, she also showed me what she called her 'wallet *mandir*,' which consisted of a small image of Shirdi Sai Baba nestled into her billfold. 'God is not just in the temple. God is also here,' she said, pointing at the billfold picture, 'and here,' she said, pointing at her heart. 'So why wait in line at the temple, when I can just see him on the bus or watch *Shirdi Ke Sai Baba* at home?'

In thinking about the place of visual and media culture in Hinduism, this seemingly casual example of drive-by devotion stands out as instructive for four primary reasons, each of which will be explored further in the sections that follow. First, it demonstrates the centrality of the visual in interacting with the divine in everyday Hinduism. Second, the common usage of god posters in shrines located beyond the boundaries of formal temples only begins to suggest the wide range of visual and new media that are commonly invested with sacred power in Hindu culture. Third, this shrine to Shirdi Sai Baba calls our attention to the rise of new religious figures under the widespread umbrella of modern Hinduism whose popularity has flourished through visual and new media. And fourth, it alludes to the importance of discussions of and debates about the place of Hinduism and other religions in India today.

The Centrality of the Visual in Everyday Hinduism

While textbooks have often introduced students to Hinduism through its sacred scriptures, especially the *Bhagavad Gita*, and its philosophical concepts and traditions, the above example of drive-by devotion is actually quite typical of the everyday encounter with religion in India and the centrality of the visual to that encounter. Indeed, as Vasudha Narayanan writes: 'At best, it seems that a large part of what is portrayed in textbooks on Hinduism is not rampant in everyday life—Hindus do not usually walk around worrying about their karma or working toward *moksha* (liberation), nor are most folk familiar with anything more than the name Vedanta among the various schools of philosophy.' (Narayanan 2000: 762) Yet it is not an overstatement to state that all Indians are familiar with such street shrines (see Image 14.2), no matter whether they are Hindu or not or whether they actively worship at one or not, for these street shrines are ubiquitous throughout urban and rural India.

Significantly, the visual can frequently be a more primary or common means of interacting with the divine in everyday Hinduism than the textual. In my conversation with the woman cited above, she spoke of taking *darshan* twice a day as she looked in upon the images of Shirdi Sai Baba in the street shrine while the bus stopped. *Darshan* is understood to be a reciprocal exchange of glances between the devotee and the deity. Diana Eck has discussed *darshan* in detail: 'The central act of Hindu worship, from the point of view of the lay person, is to stand in the presence of the deity and to behold the image with one's own eyes, to see and be seen by the deity. . . . Since, in the Hindu understanding, the deity is present in the image, the visual apprehension of the image is charged with religious meaning. Beholding the image is an act of worship, and through the eyes one gains the blessings of the divine.' (Eck 1998: 3)

This *darshanic* exchange of glances can and does take place in large Hindu temples, as it has since premodern times, where the central *murti* has been ritually installed by a priest who performs a formal eye-opening ceremony to bring to life the deity's presence in the image. But the rise of print technology and the reproduction of popular posters of Hindu deities and saints enables this auspicious *darshanic* exchange to take place in other, less formal venues as well. In the late nineteenth century, several major publishers of god posters

Figure 14.2 Tree shrine

established lithographic presses in India: the Calcutta Art Studio, founded
in Bengal in 1878; the Chitrashala Press, founded in Maharashtra in 1878;
and the Ravi Varma Fine Art Lithographic Press, founded outside of Bombay

(Mumbai) in 1894. Initially, Christopher Pinney notes, these publishers printed images of the Hindu gods in a series of portfolio albums, much in the tradition of earlier European artists in India. However, 'finding an enthusiastic market for their images as artefacts in domestic ritual, [they] subsequently produced chromolithographs to be sold individually.' (Pinney 2004: 30) The enthusiastic market for these images has persisted into the twenty-first century.

Today, these god posters (also commonly known as calendar art, bazaar art, and framing pictures) are omnipresent throughout India, where they can be seen not only in small street shrines and large temples, but also in Hindu homes, in all manner of places of business, in taxis, buses, and rickshaws and other means of conveyance, and even in purses and billfolds. These posters are significant for making the *darshanic* exchange available to devotees outside of the temple and the priest's purview. As such, they have helped to make the Hindu gods more accessible to their devotees. However, it is only in the past several decades that scholars of Hinduism have begun to acknowledge the significance of such god posters and to study them. As Richard H. Davis has pointed out in his study of god posters, such scholarship is important for it allows us to 'begin to see these prints of the gods both as an evolving, changing genre of popular art and as an integral part of the history of modern Hinduism and modern India.' (Davis 2012: 3)

Encountering the Divine through New Media

In addition to god posters, a wide range of visual and new media is commonly used for *darshan* in modern Hinduism. The devotee cited above, for example, also includes as valid sources for visual communion with the divine not only the images in temples and shrines and in her wallet, but also the 1977 mythological film *Shirdi Ke Sai Baba* that recaps the life of Shirdi Sai Baba and the miracles associated with him. God posters, films, television, comic books, the Internet—each of these media can become a medium for seeing and being seen by the divine. Thus, a second reason that this example of drive-by devotion is instructive is that it demonstrates not only the common usage of visual and new media in modern Hinduism, but also the need to study what becomes sacred to Hindu viewers and the conditions by which such sacralization occurs. This area of study is what David Morgan has referred to as the 'sacred gaze,' which entails 'the manner in which a way of seeing invests an image, a viewer, or an act of viewing with spiritual significance. The study of religious visual culture is therefore the study of images, but also the practices and habits that rely on images as well as the attitudes and preconceptions that inform vision as a cultural act.' (Morgan 2005: 3).

In studying the sacred gaze within modern Hinduism, scholars have therefore begun considering not only the images that act as the focus of the *darshanic* gaze, but also the creation and reception of such images. The mythological genre of Indian cinema has proven to be especially fertile ground for such study. One of India's first filmmakers, D. G. Phalke, is often credited with the birth not only of the mythological genre, but indeed with Indian feature filmmaking more broadly. Phalke released *Raja Harishchandra*, a fifty-minute feature film based on an episode from the *Mahabharata* epic, in 1913. Following this film, he produced dozens more that were also based upon Hindu epic and Puranic stories. As Rachel Dwyer notes, the mythological genre was thus the founding genre of Indian cinema, and one of the most productive genres of its early cinema. Though the genre's popularity has ebbed and flowed over the years, it remains important to this day (Dwyer 2006: 14–15). In creating mythological films, a variety of techniques have been used to foster the *darshanic* exchange of glances between the viewer in the audience and the divine figure appearing on screen. Foremost among these is the aesthetic of 'frontality,' which arises out of earlier visual media and portrays the divine object of attention directly facing the viewer so that the viewer-devotee can look into the eyes of the divine figure (G. Kapur 1993). Such frontality is enhanced by an array of cinematic editing techniques, including zooming in on the face of the divine figure, pausing for an extended close-up of the divine figure's face and eyes, and interspersing shots of the divine figure with shots of the devotee within the film to model the exchange of glances that is central to *darshan* in the context of ritual worship (Lutgendorf 2006: 231–234).

Viewing such films is frequently not solely a source of passive entertainment, but simultaneously a source of active religious experience. An audience of predominantly Hindu viewers attending a popular mythological film screening may demonstrate a variety of participatory viewing practices: engaging in *darshan* with the deity on screen, singing *bhajans* or devotional hymns, and throwing coins or flowers at the screen. Such interactive devotional viewing also takes place in response to televised mythological serials. Philip Lutgendorf has written about the televised 'Ramayan' serial (directed by Ramanand Sagar) that aired weekly on India's government-run television network, Doordarshan, from January 25, 1987 to July 31, 1988. He reports that this televised epic was greeted with unprecedented acts of mass devotion among its Hindu viewers, as televisions were placed in public areas and then 'sanctified with cow dung and Ganges water [and] worshipped with flowers and incense' before being watched by crowds of neighborhood residents (Lutgendorf 1995: 224). Originally slated to run for fifty-two episodes, the serial was extended three times because of popular demand, and eventually grew into a main story in seventy-eight episodes, followed after an interval of several months by a sequel incorporating the events detailed in the seventh book (the *Uttarakanda*, or epilogue) of the Sanskrit *Ramayana* epic. When all was said and done, it had topped the charts to become the most popular program ever shown on Indian television—and this despite the protests of elite Indian critics that it was a 'technically flawed melodrama' (Lutgendorf 1995: 217).

In my own research on the immensely popular Indian comic book series called *Amar Chitra Katha* (or ACK), I learned that Anant Pai founded the series in 1967 because he wanted the generations of Indian children growing up from the late 1960s onward to become familiar with Hindu mythology. He feared that these children were receiving westernized educations and were becoming increasingly alienated from their Hindu heritage. Recognizing the popularity of imported comics, he turned to the comic book medium to retell classical epic and Puranic stories of the Hindu gods. Yet he did not actually intend for these comics to be used ritually; indeed, he specifically directed his cover artists not to depict the deities frontally, so as to forestall the *darshanic* exchange of glances lest he offend any especially orthodox Hindus who might be upset by any visual innovations taken by the artists. Nonetheless, many Hindu readers still concluded that the comics embodied a powerful, efficacious force within. In the words of one reader, '*Amar Chitra Katha* makes an Indian proud of his or her heritage. . . . My eyes become moist thinking of the good that *ACK* has done to India's children. *Amar Chitra Katha* is not just a comic book. It radiates a spiritual force.' (McLain 2009: 1)

While most readers do not actually pray to the images in these comic books or otherwise engage in ritual activity with them, many did report investing them with spiritual significance in a variety of ways, including making special cardboard binders to store them in so that the cover image of the deity would not be damaged, storing the comics indefinitely rather than disposing of them for fear of angering the deity in the storyline, and rereading an issue when ill out of the belief that it might help to bring about the god's blessing and restore one's health. In this way, these Indian comic books are notably different from their American, European, Japanese, and other global counterparts in that they are invested with a sacred gaze and become part of the spectrum of the sacred for many of their Hindu readers (McLain 2009: 17–18). This was brought home to Anant Pai himself after he 'modernized' the story of the god Krishna in his first comic book issue by removing the miracles, which he had doubts about. Though readers loved the comic series, they repeatedly asked him why he didn't present the miracle of Krishna lifting the Govardhan Mountain, among other miracles commonly associated with the god. In the end, Anant Pai produced a revised version of the *Krishna* comic, this one featuring the miracles. Anant Pai explained to me that he felt compelled to make the revision because he realized that his readers looked upon the comics as a legitimate source of these sacred stories. 'Now I don't tamper with mythology,' he said, 'I present it as it is, because mythology is sacred.' (McLain 2009: 35)

Visual Media and the Changing Hindu Pantheon

A third reason that this example of drive-by devotion is instructive is that it demonstrates the rise of new religious figures under the widespread umbrella of modern Hinduism whose popularity has flourished through visual and new media. The shrine in this example is dedicated to Shirdi Sai Baba, a saint or god-man who died in 1918 in the village of Shirdi, in the western Indian state of Maharashtra. His religious upbringing is disputed, with some devotees claiming he was born to Muslim parents and others claiming he was born to Hindu Brahmin parents. Regardless, during his lifetime he came to be revered among a small circle of devotees from Hindu, Muslim, and other religious backgrounds. By the 1970s, Shirdi Sai Baba devotion had spread throughout western and south-central India. Today, Shirdi Sai Baba's name and face are known throughout India. Much of the spread of his devotion is due to his promotion through new media, including photography, posters, film, and television.

Discussing god posters, Richard H. Davis notes that the mass production and dissemination of this medium educated modern Hindu viewers as a collectivity by engendering a shared visual understanding. Images of some deities like Krishna were standardized, which helped to unify this famously heterogeneous religious tradition, while local or regional deities and saints that were often associated with particular temples or pilgrimage sites gained a broader pan-Indian following through wide distribution of their prints (Davis 2012: 5). This is certainly the case for Shirdi Sai Baba, who had transformed from a regional god-man associated with Shirdi into a pan-Indian presence by the end of the twentieth century.

In addition to posters, Shirdi Sai Baba's popularity throughout India has also been spread through a spate of Hindi language devotional films and televised serials produced from the late 1970s to today. It is worthy to take note of the 1977 mythological film *Shirdi Ke Sai Baba* (directed by Ashok Bhushan), which was mentioned by the devotee on the bus. This film secured a sizeable viewing audience, especially after it began airing nationwide on the Doordarshan television network in 1988. Although hard statistics for the viewership of *Shirdi Ke Sai Baba* are impossible to come by, anecdotal evidence I have gathered while interviewing devotees of Shirdi Sai Baba suggests that the film was instrumental in bringing many new devotees into a relationship with Shirdi Sai Baba.

One example would be C. B. Satpathy, the founder of the Shri Shirdi Sai Heritage Foundation Trust in New Delhi, India, which has established over two hundred Shirdi Sai Baba temples. In the late 1980s, Satpathy was living in New Delhi, where he worked as an officer in the Indian Police Service. He recalls that at this time he was increasingly curious about Shirdi Sai Baba, whose image he was beginning to encounter everywhere—posters of Shirdi Sai Baba hung in neighborhood shops, rings and lockets with photographs of him were worn by friends and acquaintances, stickers with his face and popular sayings adhered to taxis and rickshaws. One day he decided to rent the film *Shirdi Ke Sai Baba* to learn more. He writes in his memoir that, because of this film viewing, 'My life would stand transformed in a matter of a few hours.' (Satpathy 2001: 27) He credits this film with his personal transformation from a curious skeptic to a true believer in Shirdi Sai Baba, and reports that the very next morning after viewing the film he left for Shirdi, where he accepted Shirdi Sai Baba as his divine guru (McLain 2012: 198).

Another example of a new religious figure whose popularity has spread substantially through visual and new media is Santoshi Ma, the 'goddess of satisfaction,' who was the focus of the 1975 mythological film *Jai Santoshi Maa* (directed by Vijay Sharma). Prior to the making of this film, Santoshi Ma was a little-known Hindu goddess. But through word of mouth, the film became a surprise blockbuster success, with audiences packing cinema halls in both urban and rural areas of India. Philip Lutgendorf, who has studied this film and its reception in detail, writes, 'audiences commonly engaged in ritual and devotional behavior during its screenings, and temples and shrines to its titular goddess soon began to appear in many parts of India. As the years passed, the film acquired the status of a "cult classic," and was regularly revived, especially for women's matinees on Friday, the day associated with the *vrat* or ritual fast and worship of Santoshi Ma; by all accounts, hundreds of thousands and perhaps millions of women periodically participated in such worship.' (Lutgendorf 2002: 11) Lutgendorf argues that this film became a super hit among lower-middle-class Hindu women, in particular, because it addressed their aspirations and suggested that a happy ending could be found for their marital and familial woes—just as the film's heroine, Satyavati, achieves her own happy ending—through ritualized devotion to the goddess of satisfaction, Santoshi Ma (Lutgendorf 2002: 35).

But perhaps the best-known example of the role of visual media in the spread of a new religious figure is Bharat Mata or Mother India. Mother India first arose as a new deity in the late nineteenth century in the context of colonial India's struggle for independence from British rule, and is first invoked in the 'Vande Mataram' hymn in Bankim Chandra Chatterji's 1882 novel *Anandamath*—the hymn that would later be transformed into song by Rabindranath Tagore and would eventually become independent India's national song. However, in her study of the pictorial history of Mother India, Sumathi Ramaswamy demonstrates that images arose at the same time as textual descriptions of Mother India, and that these images disclose 'the undercurrent of Hindu sentiments and sensibilities, even Hindu nationalism, that has dogged the mother's hymn almost from the start.' (Ramaswamy 2010: 121) Exploring how the map of India as a national territory became equated with the Indian nation envisioned as a mother goddess, Ramaswamy demonstrates the power of such images—posters, paintings, and other pictures—in convincing Indians to not only identify with India, but to ultimately become martyrs for it.

Many of these images depict patriotic young men dying for Bharat Mata—offering their own decapitated heads to Mother India while their blood flows over the national territory. She points out that for many Indians, Mother India stood as an icon of pluralism and even secularism. If the nation of India was the metaphorical mother of its citizens, then all the children of India—Hindus, Muslims, and others—became siblings. Many politicians and freedom fighters then argued that since their mother was enslaved by the British, these siblings now needed to unite together to free her. Yet more strident Hindu nationalists have also used the same Mother India figure to stand for the essential Hindu identity of the nation of India and all those who should reside within the boundaries of this geo-goddess. Thus, Ramaswamy points out, because Mother India is regularly depicted as a Hindu mother goddess, based on the iconographic practices of Hinduism, she may actually alienate—rather than unite—those Indians who do not share Hindu sensibilities and may even have a tradition of opposing what is deemed idolatrous (Ramaswamy 2010: 70).

Envisioning the Place of Religion in India Today

A fourth and final reason the example of drive-by devotion is instructive is that it suggests the importance of discussions of and debates about the place of Hinduism and other religions in India today. When the devotee on the bus showed me her 'wallet *mandir*,' the small image of Shirdi Sai Baba nestled into her billfold featured him standing, wearing a white robe, with his index finger pointing to the heavens above and his eyes gazing out at the viewer. A different religious symbol occupies each corner of the image: the Hindu Om, Muslim crescent moon, Sikh Ek-Onkar, and Christian cross. Beneath Shirdi Sai Baba, in bold Devanagari print, is the Hindi phrase 'Sabka Malik Ek,' 'Everyone's Lord is One.' As noted above, Shirdi Sai Baba's religious upbringing is uncertain and disputed. But for many of his followers, this ambiguity is a positive thing. These followers claim that Shirdi Sai Baba was both Hindu and Muslim, for he studied with teachers from both traditions, and, as such, his life is a prime example of composite culture, the intermixing or synthesis of Hinduism and Islam in India. They further claim that his teachings, which drew upon both Hindu and Muslim scripture and practices, provide a powerful foil to sectarian visions of India by calling for a united nation that equally values Hindus, Muslims, and members of other religious communities.

A similarly themed image can be seen in Image 14.3, the home shrine of a devotee. In this poster, Shirdi Sai Baba is again presented in a frontal position in the center of the image. His eyes make direct contact with viewers, blessing them with his gaze, while an auspicious ray of yellow light emanates from his hand raised towards viewers. Behind him, four buildings fill the background: in the upper-right corner is a Hindu temple, and beneath that is a Muslim mosque; a Sikh gurdwara is in the upper-left corner, and beneath that is a Christian church. Across the top of the poster reads the Hindi slogan, 'Ek Bano, Nek Bano,' 'Be United, Be Virtuous.' Because this statement is printed in the orange, white, and green colors of the Indian flag, the message of national unity in diversity presented in this poster is unmistakable. Here, Shirdi Sai Baba wants all Indians to look at him—not just Hindus, but also Muslims, Sikhs, and Christians—and in so looking, he wants all Indians to be transformed into unified, virtuous citizens of the nation (McLain 2011: 24).

This image, and others like it that embrace religious pluralism and emphasize national unity in diversity, stand as an alternative to images that depict India as an exclusively Hindu nation or assert that Hinduism should be the national religion and culture of India. Perhaps the most widely distributed such Hindu nationalist images in recent decades are those that feature the Hindu god Rama. Throughout the twentieth century, a handful of powerful Hindu nationalist groups arose that are collectively known as the Sangh Parivar (Family of Associations). Prominent among these are the Vishva Hindu

Figure 14.3 Shirdi Sai Baba, home shrine

Parishad (VHP), founded in 1964, and the Bharatiya Janata Party (BJP), founded in 1980. During the 1980s and 1990s, these and other Hindu nationalist groups employed a range of tactics that drew upon Hindu religious symbolism in the effort to unify and mobilize a large voting bloc.

One such tactic was the chariot procession (*rath yatra*) that was coordinated by the VHP and BJP in 1990. This procession featured at its head a DCM-Toyota van that was decorated as the god Rama's chariot, and wound

throughout northern India for over a month, culminating in the city of Ayodhya in Uttar Pradesh state, said to be the site of the prehistoric kingdom of
Rama, an incarnation of the Hindu god Vishnu. Within Ayodhya, the focus
was the Babri Masjid, a mosque built in the early sixteenth century by the
Mughal Emperor Babar, which the procession's organizers claimed had been
built atop the ruins of a Hindu temple marking the very birthplace of Lord
Rama after Babar ordered his Muslim henchman to tear it down. In his study
of the procession, Richard H. Davis has demonstrated that it utilized widespread devotion to Lord Rama among Hindus in northern India, and drew
upon visual and ritual traditions to mobilize a national Hindu identity in
opposition to both the Muslim minority and the pro-secular Congress Party
government (Davis 1996).

On December 6, 1992, the VHP and BJP organized another rally in Ayodhya, which resulted in the demolition of the Babri Masjid. Throughout the
1990s and even into the twenty-first century, the campaign to (re)build the
Ramjanmabhoomi (Rama's birthplace) temple has remained a central component of Hindu nationalist politics. During the 1980s and 1990s, as the BJP and
VHP focused on Ayodhya, they issued new posters of the Hindu god Rama.
Anuradha Kapur has argued that these posters entail an iconographic shift in
images of Rama from a smooth-limbed, soft-bodied, tranquil deity to one who
is 'exercised, determined, ready to punish' (A. Kapur 1993: 104). She discusses
in detail an image produced by the VHP, and widely copied, in connection
with its Ramjanmabhoomi temple-building campaign. In this image, an angry
Rama stands against a backdrop of dark clouds while the wind whips his hair
and saffron loincloth. With his heavily muscled arms, he holds a bow and
arrow at the ready, prepared to face the coming storm, whatever it may be. He
towers above a temple, beneath which is printed in Hindi: 'The proposed Shri
Ram Temple at Shri Ram's birthplace in Ayodhya.'

Commenting on such Hindu nationalist imagery, Gwilym Beckerlegge
writes that the 'promotion by the Hindu Right of Hindu mythological symbols
as symbols of Indian nationhood may prove alienating to the sizeable number
of Indians who are not Hindus, and offensive to those Hindus for whom the
ideals of an inclusive secular state remain beacons of hope' (Beckerlegge 2001:
109). Clearly, such images present a very different vision of the nation for
those Hindus and non-Hindus alike who are alienated or offended by Hindu
nationalism and other rigidly sectarian movements. In its inclusive vision, the
image of Shirdi Sai Baba provides an alternative to Hindu nationalist images
in two interconnected ways. First, instead of presenting an exclusively Hindu
nation closed to Muslims and other minorities, it depicts multiple-faith communities as equals under the national tricolor flag. Second, this vision of Indi-
anness is not premised on acts of violent martyrdom for a bloodthirsty Mother
India, or on destructive virility for an angry Lord Rama, but instead on acts
of virtue and the union of all Indians under the tranquil blessing of Shirdi Sai
Baba (McLain 2011: 25).

Conclusion: Image Making in Modern Hinduism

Diana Eck describes India as a visual and visionary culture, one in which the eyes have a prominent role in the apprehension of the sacred. Likewise, she describes Hinduism as an image-making religious tradition in which the sacred is seen as present in the visible world (Eck 1998: 10). As was the case with a range of medieval devotional movements, there have been several important Hindu movements in the modern era that have rejected image making and worship as idolatry and called instead for the worship of a formless or *nirguna* god. The two most prominent examples are the Brahmo Samaj, which was founded in 1828 by Rammohun Roy, and the Arya Samaj, which was founded in 1875 by Swami Dayananda Saraswati (Salmond 2004).

Both Roy and Saraswati were attuned to criticisms of Hindu religion and culture then being raised by missionaries and others in the colonial context. Such criticisms included not only the allegation that Hinduism was barbaric for its polytheism and abundant idolatry, but also for its treatment of women and lower castes. Though there were many differences in their ideals and approaches to socioreligious reform, both Roy and Saraswati believed that Hinduism as practiced in their time was a corruption of 'true' or 'pure' Hinduism as found in the Vedas and Upanishads. They stridently argued against idol worship, declaring the practice to be harmful to the effort to realize the true nature of God on the grounds that as a transcendent reality, God could not be limited by human or symbolic form, and that the earliest Hindu scriptures did not advocate image making and worship. They also stridently argued against many of the customs sanctioning gender and caste disparity on the grounds that the earliest Hindu scriptures allowed for widows to remarry, for women to be educated, and for caste to be understood as a professional classification entered into upon adulthood. Nancy Falk points out that despite the limited membership of the samaj organizations—most members were highly-educated, English-speaking men from upper-caste groups—their work for social improvement, especially in women's education and uplift organizations, has had a substantial impact (Falk 2006: 110).

Yet their critique of image making and worship has had far less of a lasting impact. Despite the existence of Arya Samaj temples in which images of the divine are eschewed in favor of fire rituals, from on the ground in India, it is evident that Hinduism remains rich with image worship. When riding the bus in India, walking through cities and villages, conducting business in bazaars or shops, dining in chai stalls or cafes, attending the cinema or watching television, or entering temples and homes, one is surrounded by vibrant, engaging, and accessible images of Hindu gods and saints. Not only has Hinduism remained an image-making religion, but as the discussion above shows, all manner of visual and new media have been embraced and put to image-making purposes in modern Hinduism. Indeed, for a great many Hindus—though by no means all Hindus—worshiping the divine through images is central to 'true' or 'pure' Hinduism as they understand it, and the sacred is arguably ever more present in the visible world than before through the increasing array of new media.

Summary

Images of the Hindu gods are ubiquitous throughout India today. They can be seen in street shrines when walking through cities and villages, hanging on the walls of chai stalls, cafes, and businesses, adhered to the windows and dashboards of taxis and other vehicles, in the movie theater, and framed in home altars. They appear in a wide array of visual and new media: posters, photographs, stickers, comic books, films, television, and online. These vibrant, engaging, and accessible images of Hindu gods and saints teach us about the centrality of the visual to the everyday encounter with the divine in modern Hinduism, wherein the reciprocal exchange of glances between devotee and deity is a central, religious practice. Through a study of these images, as well as the conditions by which they are invested with sacred power, we gain significant insight into many facets of modern Hinduism, including how the divine is ritually worshipped by Hindus today, how the Hindu pantheon is changing in the modern era as the popularity of different divine figures waxes and wanes, and what debates are taking place about the place of Hinduism and other religions in modern India.

Discussion Questions

- In what ways does the study of Hindu visual culture enrich and even complicate our understanding of Hinduism?
- In what ways have visual and new media helped to create new Hindu beliefs and practices or transform older Hindu beliefs and practices?
- In what ways have Hindu beliefs and practices helped to create a unique visual aesthetic in India?
- What does the visual culture of Hinduism have to say about religious diversity and pluralism in modern India?

Suggested Reading

Babb, L. and S. Wadley, eds. (1995). *Media and the Transformation of Religion in South Asia*. Philadelphia: University of Pennsylvania Press.
A collection of essays describing the flourishing of media in modes of religious expression in India with the guiding question of whether such media has homogenized religious practices and beliefs.
Davis, R. H. (2012). *Gods in Print: Masterpieces of India's Mythological Art: A Century of Sacred Art (1870–1970)*. San Rafael: Mandala Publishing.
A collection of Hindu gods and goddesses as they have been represented in lithographs and prints for a century, with scholarly analysis of each era of printing and each individual print.

Dwyer, R. (2006). *Filming the Gods: Religion and Indian Cinema.* New York: Routledge.
Examines how film in India provides a link between modernity and tradition through
   its depiction of religious life.
Pinney, C. (2004). *Photos of the Gods: The Printed Image and Political Struggle in India.*
   London: Reaktion Books.
A history of Hindu nationalism examined through the lens of the printed image,
   including how other forms of media interacted with the printed image.
Ramaswamy, S., ed. (2003). *Beyond Appearances?: Visual Practices and Ideologies in Mod-
   ern India.* New Delhi: Sage Publications.
A collection of essays analyzing the complex visual culture of modern India, focusing
   on how they connect with the ideological and political threads of society.

Bibliography

Babb, L. and S. Wadley, eds. (1995). *Media and the Transformation of Religion in South
   Asia.* Philadelphia: University of Pennsylvania Press.
Beckerlegge, G. (2001). 'Hindu Sacred Images for the Mass Market.' In *From Sacred
   Text to Internet* (pp. 57–116). Ed. G. Beckerlegge. Farnham, U.K.: Ashgate.
Davis, R. H. (1996). 'The Iconography of Rama's Chariot.' In *Contesting the Nation:
   Religion, Community, and the Politics of Democracy in India* (pp. 27–54). Ed. D. Lud-
   den. Philadelphia: University of Pennsylvania Press.
——— (1997). *Lives of Indian Images.* Princeton: Princeton University Press.
———, ed. (2007). *Picturing the Nation: Iconographies of Modern India.* Hyderabad: Ori-
   ent Longman.
——— (2012). *Gods in Print: Masterpieces of India's Mythological Art: A Century of
   Sacred Art (1870–1970).* San Rafael: Mandala Publishing.
Dwyer, R. (2006). *Filming the Gods: Religion and Indian Cinema.* New York: Routledge.
Eck, D. L. (1998). *Darśan: Seeing the Divine Image in India.* 3rd edition. New York:
   Columbia University Press.
Falk, N. A. (2006). *Living Hinduisms: An Explorer's Guide.* Belmont: Thomson
   Wadsworth.
Jain, K. (2007). *Gods in the Bazaar: The Economies of Indian Calendar Art.* Durham:
   Duke University Press.
Kapur, A. (1993). 'Deity to Crusader: The Changing Iconography of Ram.' In *Hindus
   and Others: The Question of Identity in India Today* (pp. 74–109). Ed. G. Pandey. New
   York: Viking.
Kapur, G. (1993). 'Revelation and Doubt: *Sant Tukaram* and *Devi.*' In *Interrogating
   Modernity: Culture and Colonialism in India* (pp. 19–46). Eds. T. Niranjana, P. Sudhir,
   and V. Dhareshwar. Calcutta: Seagull.
Larson, G. J., P. Pal, and H. D. Smith (1997). *Changing Myths and Images:
   Twentieth-Century Popular Art in India.* Bloomington: Indiana University Art
   Museum.
Lutgendorf, P. (1995). 'All in the (Raghu) Family: A Video Epic in Cultural Context.'
   In *Media and the Transformation of Religion in South Asia* (pp. 217–253). Eds. L. Babb
   and S. Wadley. Philadelphia: University of Pennsylvania Press.
——— (2002). 'A Superhit Goddess/A Made to Satisfaction Goddess: *Jai Santoshi Maa*
   Revisited.' *Manushi, a Journal about Women and Society* No. 131: 10–16 and 24–37.
——— (2006). 'Is There an Indian Way of Filmmaking?' *International Journal of Hindu
   Studies* 10, No. 3: 227–256.

Lyden, J. C. (2003). *Film as Religion: Myths, Morals, and Rituals*. New York: New York University Press.

Mankekar, P. (1999). *Screening Culture, Viewing Politics: An Ethnography of Television, Womanhood, and Nation in Postcolonial India*. Durham: Duke University Press.

McLain, K. (2009). *India's Immortal Comic Books: Gods, Kings, and Other Heroes*. Bloomington: Indiana University Press.

—— (2011). 'Be United, Be Virtuous: Composite Culture and the Growth of Shirdi Sai Baba Devotion.' *Nova Religio* 15, No. 2: 20–49.

—— (2012). 'Praying for Peace and Amity: The Shri Shirdi Sai Heritage Foundation Trust.' In *Public Hinduisms* (190–209). Eds. J. Zavos, P. Kanungo, D. S. Reddy, M. Warrier, and R. B. Williams. New Delhi: Sage Publications.

Mitchell, J. P. and S. B. Plate (2007). *The Religion and Film Reader*. New York: Routledge.

Morgan, D. (2005). *The Sacred Gaze: Religious Visual Culture in Theory and Practice*. Berkeley: University of California Press.

Narayanan, V. (2000). 'Diglossic Hinduism: Liberation and Lentils.' *Journal of the American Academy of Religion* 68, No. 4: 761–779.

Neumayer, E. and C. Schelberger (2003). *Popular Indian Art: Ravi Varma and the Printed Gods of India*. New Delhi: Oxford University Press.

—— (2008). *Bharat Mata: India's Freedom Movement in Popular Art*. New Delhi: Oxford University Press.

Pinney, C. (1997). *Camera Indica: The Social Life of Indian Photographs*. Chicago: University of Chicago Press.

—— (2004). *Photos of the Gods: The Printed Image and Political Struggle in India*. London: Reaktion Books.

Rajadhyaksha, A. (1987). 'The Phalke Era: Conflict of Traditional Form and Modern Technology.' *Journal of Arts and Ideas* 14–15: 47–78.

Rajagopal, A. (2001). *Politics after Television: Religious Nationalism and the Reshaping of the Indian Public*. Cambridge, U.K.: Cambridge University Press.

Ramaswamy, S., ed. (2003). *Beyond Appearances?: Visual Practices and Ideologies in Modern India*. New Delhi: Sage Publications.

—— (2010). *The Goddess and the Nation: Mapping Mother India*. Durham: Duke University Press.

Salmond, N. A. (2004). *Hindu Iconoclasts: Rammohun Roy, Dayananda Sarasvati, and Nineteenth-Century Polemics against Idolatry*. Waterloo, Canada: Wilfrid Laurier University Press.

Satpathy, C. B. (2001). *Shirdi Sai Baba and Other Perfect Masters*. New Delhi: Sterling Publishers.

Scheifinger, H. (2009). 'The Jagannath Temple and Online Darshan.' *The Journal of Contemporary Religion* 24, No. 3: 277–290.

—— (2013). 'Hindu Worship Online and Offline.' In *Digital Religion: Understanding Religious Practice in New Media Worlds* (pp. 120–127). Ed. H. A. Campbell. New York: Routledge.

Taylor, W. (2002). 'Penetrating Gazes: The Politics of Sight and Visual Display in Popular Indian Cinema.' *Contributions to Indian Sociology* 36, Nos. 1 & 2: 297–322.

Uberoi, P. (2002). '"Unity in Diversity?" Dilemmas of Nationhood in Indian Calendar Art.' *Contributions to Indian Sociology* 36, Nos. 1 & 2: 191–232.

Vitsaxis, V. (1977). *Hindu Epics, Myths, and Legends in Popular Illustrations*. Delhi: Oxford University Press.

Zitzewitz, K. (2008). 'The Secular Icon: Secularist Practice and Indian Visual Culture.' *Visual Anthropology Review* 24, No. 1: 12–28.

Part V

Critical Social and Political Issues

15 Public Hinduism and Hindutva

Pralay Kanungo

The task of defining Hinduism is famously challenging. One way to address this challenge is to think of Hinduism less as a monolithic or unitary religious tradition and more as a multitude of faiths or perhaps as a plural universe consisting of a plethora of gods, gurus, sects, sampradayas, traditions, communities, and castes. In this respect, the sheer complexity of Hinduism stands in sharp contrast to the modern concept of Hindutva. In a literal sense, the term means 'Hinduness,' which is to say the quality or state of being Hindu. Precisely because Hindutva purports to confidently identify the essential quality of Hinduness, it has become a highly contested concept in the politics of contemporary India. As originally expounded by V. D. Savarkar in his influential tract *Hindutva* (1923) and later popularized by the Sangh Parivar, or 'family of organizations'—the Rashtriya Swayamsevak Sangh (RSS), Vishwa Hindu Parisad (VHP), and Bharatiya Janata Party (BJP)—claims of Hindutva serve to advance an exclusivist political ideology. That is, claims about Hindutva are effectively also claims about India as a Hindu nation, a nation that excludes all those who are non-Hindus, not least Muslims and Christians.

It is important at the outset to clarify that while Hinduism and Hindutva share the same etymological root and manifest semantic proximity, they play very different roles in public discourse; if Hinduism is a faith/religion, Hindutva is a marker of identity employed to make ideological claims about the Indian nation.

As Hindutva seeks a tryst with state power and becomes an ever more serious contender for power in the arena of democratic politics, it has also struggled to shed any association with an exclusivist politics. This it does by offering new meanings and interpretations of Hindutva which would make it appear accommodative and inclusive. However, such attempts to redefine Hindutva have really led to no serious modification of Hindutva ideology, largely because its proponents are unwilling to tamper with the core principles of Hindutva self-assertion. At best, we find gestures aimed at 'softening' the Hindutva message by yoking it to more liberal interpretations of Hinduism, such as that advanced by Sarvapelli Radhakrishnan (1888–1975), a Vedantic philosopher and statesman who famously defined Hinduism as 'a way of life' rather than a religion. Radhakrishnan's goal was to suggest that, unlike dogmatic religions (with their claims to supremacy and histories of internecine conflict), Hinduism represented a kind of experience that was spiritual, undogmatic, and tolerant. Hindutva ideologues adopt similar language, but in a less irenic and ecumenical mode than Radhakrishnan. Their goal is to present Hindutva as the single, all-encompassing 'way of life' that makes India what it is. Ironically, the very Vedanta that allowed Radhakrishnan to celebrate Hindu inclusivity provides Hindu nationalists with a tool for gathering all religious difference under the sole umbrella of Hindutva (see Hatcher 1999).

It is worth noting that in a number of important legal cases involving claims about Hinduism, the Courts in India have tended to follow Radhakrishnan by delivering judgments in which Hinduism is defined as a way of life. Most importantly, in a 1995 decision, the Supreme Court of India announced that '[t]he term "Hindutva" is related more to the way of life of the people in the subcontinent. It is difficult to appreciate how . . . the term "Hindutva" or "Hinduism" per se, in the abstract, can be assumed to mean and be equated with narrow fundamentalist Hindu religious bigotry'(quoted in Kapur 2014: 114). This pronouncement has enormous ramifications, not least for the way in which it conflates Hindutva with Hinduism. In one stroke, it overlooks both issues of historical complexity and immediate political context and absolves Hindu nationalism from the charge of exclusivism or 'bigotry.' One might say that the modern tendency to understand Hinduism as a 'way of life' is so banal that it allows for proponents of Hindutva to easily conflate the two concepts.

Against this terminological and political backdrop, the objectives of this chapter are three-fold: first, to introduce into the discussion the concept of Public Hinduism as way to understand the complex evolution of the tradition from ancient to modern times and to demonstrate how Public Hinduism has been produced, disseminated, and enacted in relation to a range of Hindu symbols; second, to explore the emergence of the discourse of Hindutva out of colonial-era attempts to address questions of community consciousness, anticolonial resistance, and identity politics; and, third, to show how the Hinduism-Hindutva interface in the modern/postcolonial public sphere has tended to blur any meaningful distinction such that we might almost today begin speaking of something called 'Public Hindutva.'

The Evolution of Public Hinduism: Ancient to Modern

When one looks over the long historical development of Hinduism, one notices that the private and the public have always existed in something more like a relationship of interconnection rather than one of opposition. While one could say that the interior life of Hinduism has always remained highly personal and experientially private, its exterior has been famously exuberant and multifarious. Yet even so, these represent in fact two complementary modalities of Hinduism, both integral and indispensable to the development and expression of the tradition. In the great literature of Hinduism beginning already with Vedic hymns to gods like Indra, Varuna, and Rudra, one sees the dynamic fusion of the personal and the public. And from the Vedic era onward, ritual activities associated with the sacrificial fire and the chanting of *mantras* have characterized both the experience and expression of Public Hinduism.

If we look to the vast corpus of Hindu mythology, we notice that the most venerated sages—figures like Valmiki or Vashishtha tended to seek privacy deep in the forests and high in the mountains, where they could pursue knowledge of the divine and personal salvation. Even so, these same sages often hesitated to remain reclusive and anonymous, preferring at times to venture into the public arena in a variety of ways, whether by disseminating knowledge, performing miracles, or destroying demons. In the Hindu tradition, such figures are thus remembered not just as sages (*rishis*) but as 'royal sages' (*rajarshis*). That is to say, their public presence made them fit to counsel the greatest rulers; thus Vashishtha is remembered as the spiritual and political advisor of Ayodhya's king Dasaratha and his son Rama.

Shifting from myth to history, we can note that, over the centuries, the quest of Hindu rulers for legitimacy and supremacy has included explicit gestures aimed at making Hinduism public, whether by holding massive sacrifices, building temples, honoring Brahmins, or by patronizing religious processions and festivals. The great Harsha Vardhana, the seventh-century ruler of Kanauj (modern-day Uttar Pradesh), became an exemplar of charity; the Gajapati kings of Puri (in eastern India) made Lord Jagannath's chariot festival (*rath-yatra*) an annual event of great spectacle. Such public expressions of Hinduism tended to reveal the characteristic diversity of the tradition, since, across time and space, different kings and gurus advanced the interest of different Hindu sects, whether Vasinava, Shaiva, or Shakta. There was a necessary measure of competition within such a religious landscape as the various sects and devotees struggled to promote the interests of their cults while attracting royal patronage. Thus we can think of a vibrant public arena shaped by the construction of shrines and monasteries, the promotion of sectarian religious rituals, and the performance of various public festivals. Meanwhile, alongside the grand displays of what some refer to as the 'great tradition' of Sanskritic Hinduism, we have to also note the existence of innumerable 'little traditions' each displaying their own brand of folk Hinduism—which might include animal sacrifice and the propitiation of local deities for protection from epidemic as well as the performance of minor vows and more elaborate rites of possession or fire walking. This is to speak of a world of vernacular Hindu publics, whose practices continue unabated even today.

While Hindutva ideologues famously associate the arrival of Islam in South Asia with the destruction of their sacred sites and the persecution of their religious leaders, it makes more sense to think of the many ways in which the development of South Asian Islam provided further impetus to the public expression of Hinduism. Religions are not air-tight compartments and it would be only natural for distinctive aspects of Islamic belief and practice to begin shaping some forms of Hindu religious life, whether we think of the Islamic practice of gathering for collective prayer or the construction of monumental mosques. And indeed, Hindu temple building scarcely lagged behind mosque building, and the shaping of new Hindu temple publics continued likewise. At the same time, the private expression of religiosity was surely shaped by the intermittent sense of threat posed to Hinduism by varieties of Muslim iconophobia. This may help explain the increased practice of image worship in the home context. Likewise, the social and moral teachings of Islam must necessarily have posed challenges to Hindu conceptions of social order, as conceptions of human equality jostled with long-standing traditions of *varna* hierarchy and practices of outcasting. But if some view the fear of religious conversion as an impetus behind an increasing rigidity to Public Hinduism in the medieval era (expressed in the articulation of more rigid rules of caste and ritual duty), it is also the case that the same period witnessed a positive open-ing up of Hinduism in terms of new modes of religious devotionalism, often referred to as Bhakti Hinduism.

Here we think of the great Hindu saints like Chaitanya and Kabir, whose teachings and subsequent sectarian movements led to new modes of both pri-vate and public worship. If the devotion of Kabir to a formless (*nirguna*) ulti-mate supported more private kinds of experience, Chaitanya's ecstatic love for Krishna as a god with visible form (*saguna*) provided the impetus for new modes of public devotion associated with the singing and chanting of god's names. In fact, in either case, one can say that while the primary urge of the devotee (*bhakta*) was to find immediate personal connection to the divine, such devotion found expression within a larger public sphere. As a response to Islam, Bhakti Hinduism sought new and more inclusive modes of wor-ship, often challenging even fundamental distinctions of caste and gender. This helped make Hinduism public in new and significant ways. New Hindu festivals were created in which deities were taken out in street processions; religious discourses were conducted before large and diverse audiences, and the practice of singing and chanting enthralled wider and wider portions of the public.

Over centuries of 'living together separately,' Hindus and Muslims in pre-modern South Asia thus developed unique and vibrant cultures with vectors of intellectual, aesthetic, and religious change flowing back and forth. It was this vibrant religious world that European Christians first encountered fol-lowing the arrival of the first explorers at the end of the fifteenth century. This encounter between Europe and South Asia, leading in time to the rise of colonialism and the establishment of British imperial rule, was to be both as disruptive and as creative as had been the earlier encounter with Islam. The complexity of that history is illustrated across the chapters of this book. While the British were officially committed to a policy of noninterference in religious matters, in actual fact, imperial rule brought both the active introduction of Christianity and the vigorous pursuit of 'reform' in matters closely connected to Hindu private and public life. Even so, the story was complex, with the colonial government for a period actively engaged in the management of

Hindu Temples even as Evangelical voices pressed for the vigorous introduction of Christianity. As other chapters in this volume demonstrate, through legal decisions, state-sponsored reform, and administrative fiat, colonialism eventually served to crystallize Hindu identity in ways it had not been before. Indeed, some would say it was only in the colonial era that 'Hinduism' really emerged as the name for an integrated and unitary religious identity.

Colonial India was characterized by new modes of religious creativity, cultural protest, and the rise of anticolonial resistance that led in time to the movement for Indian independence. In time, as mobilization toward national liberation gained momentum, there arose a new discourse of identity and the articulation of what it meant to be Hindu went hand in hand with a process of 'othering' that supported new tensions in the areas of religion and politics.

In the last quarter of the nineteenth century, Bankim Chandra Chatterjee invoked the concept of the nation as 'Mother India' (*Bharat Mata*). The song he composed in her honor, 'Hail to the Mother' (*Vande Mataram*) would in time become a powerful national slogan deployed against British colonialism. However, its decidedly Hindu symbolism made it an implicit (and often explicit) tool for expressing Hindu solidarity over against non-Hindus, Muslims in particular. At roughly the same time, Swami Vivekananda called for a new public role of for the Hindu ascetic (*sannyasi*) and charted a mission of popularizing Public Hinduism both in India and the West. His calls for a new Hindu manliness were powerful tools for mobilizing incipient nationalist fervor, which first came to clear expression in the Swadeshi Movement of 1905, which called for a boycott of foreign goods and the development of India along its own cultural and religious lines. Sri Aurobindo made the rejection of foreign goods a religious sacrifice, while Surendranath Banerjee invoked the Hindu concept of *dharma* as a kind of ethical standard for political behavior. All of this suggests the degree to which Hinduism was fast becoming the primary medium for mobilizing Indians in the national struggle. In Maharashtra, Bal Gangadhar Tilak effectively transformed the annual worship of Ganesha (or Ganapati)—which had hitherto been largely a private, household affair—into a public festival imbued with political import. Seeking to unite Hindus as a collectivity, he chose Ganesha because he was a deity with wide appeal across different castes and subregions. Soon, large images of Ganapati were being installed in decorated pavilions in public places, while the familial mode of the festival was quickly transformed into collective endeavor. Such organizational innovations worked to further create a more unified conception of the Hindu public sphere.

Hinduism and Hindutva

Colonialism changed the very discourse of Hinduism by turning a part of it towards identity politics and Hindu mobilization. We see this in the rise of the discourse of 'unity' (*sangathan*) itself and the rise of explicitly Hindu societies (*sabhas*) around India, culminating in the formation of the All India

Hindu Mahasabha in 1915. In the 1920s, Savarkar became the leader of Hindu Mahasabha. If Tilak's mission of Hindu mobilization signaled identity politics within the arena of Public Hinduism, Savarkar took identity politics beyond Hinduism and converted it into a political ideology. Savarkar defined a 'Hindu' as any person who regards India as his Fatherland (*pitrbhumi*) and Holyland (*punyabhumi*). In Savarkar's Hindutva, two phrases were emphasized: Hindu Rashtra and Hindutva. The former means 'Hindu nation,' and by juxtaposing this with Hindutva, we see clearly that, for him, Hinduness is synonymous with the nation. It is Indian history in its entirety. As such for him, Hinduism is only a fraction of this history; it is subsumed within the larger totality of Hindutva (Savarkar 1949).

On this, Savarkar was clear: Hindus have to profess Hindutva rather than Hinduism as the first defining characteristics of their identity. He listed three criteria for confirming the Hinduness of a person: geographical, racial, and cultural. It was an identity based on a common nation, a common ethnicity (*jati*), and a common culture. The first two essentials of Hindutva, nation and ethnicity, are clearly captured in the concept of the 'fatherland,' while the third is implicit in the 'holyland,' which suggests a shared culture of rituals, ceremonies, and sacraments.

A Hindu is thus someone who follows a religion that had originated in India. This means that Sikhs, Buddishts, and Jains are all rendered 'Hindu.' At the same time, Muslims and Christians are in one stroke excluded—their holylands lie outside India! And since in the case of Muslims and Christians the fatherland is not identical with the holyland, their patriotism is suspect. At the same time, Hindutva gathers under its one umbrella a wide array of theologies, sects, and movements, not just monists, monotheists, polytheists, and atheists, but Sikhs, Arya Samajis, Jains, and Buddhists. All such apparent distinctions are pragmatically erased or perhaps resanctified through invoking Hindutva as a common culture, common civilization, and common history.

Subscribing to Savarkar's formulation of Hindutva, Dr. K.B. Hedgewar founded the RSS in 1925 to serve as a disciplined cadre of volunteers dedicated to the idea of the Hindu nation. His successor, M.S. Golwalkar, amplified RSS ideology in such key writings as *We or our Nationhood Defined* (1939) and *Bunch of Thoughts* (1966). In these works, Golwalkar proposed that the idea of a nation is a compound of five, distinct factors (or 'unities') fused into one whole: geography, race, religion, culture, and language. Of India, he asserted: 'We repeat; in Hindustan, the land of the Hindus, lives and should live the Hindu Nation—satisfying all the five essential requirements of the scientific nation concept of the modern world' (Golwalkar 1939: 18).

While Savarkar had clearly identified Muslims and Christians as the other, he had not gestured toward any solution of this threat to national unity. Golwalkar does so, making it clear that such groups fall outside the five-fold unity of the nation and therefore have no place in national life. The only solution for them would be to abandon their allegiances and adopt the religion, culture, and language of the Hindu nation. The RSS henceforth undertook a mission to unite Hindus, even if they were careful to insist their work was not overtly religious. Its self-styled 'cultural' program focused on imparting physical and ideological training to its members so they would be equipped to deal with the 'others' in their midst.

While Savarkar and the RSS were contemplating India as a nation exclusively for Hindus, Mahatma Gandhi imagined a more pluralist India where every religious community was an equal stakeholder. Even so, Gandhi himself often resorted to Hindu idioms and symbols in his public life. He venerated the Ramacaritmanas of Tulsidas and the figure of the divine Rama and talked openly of his goals in terms of a utopian 'rule of Ram' (*Ram Rajya*). But Gandhi also invoked *Allah* in public prayer and wasn't afraid to reject those passages in Tulsidas that were offensive to women and lower castes. And while he seldom visited Hindu temples, he fought for the right of 'untouchables' to gain entry. And when it came to the final partition of India, many Hindu nationalists faulted Gandhi for being too conciliatory to Muslim feelings. Thus it was a close associate of Savarkar, Nathuram Godse, who killed Gandhi for his purported 'betrayal' of the Hindus.

The RSS was banned after Gandhi's assassination. When the ban was eventually lifted in 1951, it launched its political party, the Bharatiya Jana Sangh (BJS). Since the Party had to work in the democratic arena, it worked to shed the appearance of extremism and began to swear oaths in the name of 'Indian' instead of 'Hindu' law. Still, there was no doubting their conviction that India was a Hindu Rashtra. One BJS leader, Balraj Madhok, even argued that Christians and Muslims living in India could be counted as Hindus if India and Indian culture commanded their first and foremost allegiance. And so the Bharatiya Jana Sangh offered a subtle ideological shift, which took the form of identifying India with Hindutva, rather than Hindutva with India (Sharma 2002: 24). In keeping with this shift, the present-day Bharatiya Janata Party (BJP), successor to the BJS, prefers to represent Hindutva as a nationalist and not a religious concept, effectively treating its mission as one of cultural nationalism.

Public Hinduism-Hindutva Interface in Postcolonial India

Even with its overwhelmingly Hindu majority, the independent Republic of India became a secular state; it embraced its composite culture, granted minority rights and adopted state symbols and emblems aimed at representing India's complex religious heritage. Thus the three colors of the Indian flag—saffron, green, and white—are meant to symbolize Hinduism, Islam, and other religions, respectively. Nonetheless, it can be said that the Indian Constitution demonstrates a 'Hindu bias' as evidenced in the naming of India as 'Bharata' (an ancient Sanskrit name), in on-going official prohibition of cow slaughter, and the adoption Hindi (written in the Devanagari script) as its official language (Singh 2005).

Furthermore, Indian secularism is articulated differently than in countries like the United States. Rather than denoting a strict separation between the state and religion, Indian secularism understands it to be the state's duty to treat all religions equally. As this works out in practice, the state is often called upon to intervene in Hindu religious affairs. It makes laws to run temples, celebrates festivals, regulates processions, allows temple-entry to former untouchables under the pretext of social reform, and even trains some temple priests. In some cases, the level of state patronage to grand, Hindu festivals like the celebration of Dussehra in Mysore, Durga Puja in Kolkata, and the Kumbh Mela in Allahabad has made them virtually state Hindu festivals. And as revealed elsewhere in this volume, by codifying Hindu laws, the state has homogenized and standardized Hinduism.

The expression of Public Hinduism in the modern period is associated with a range of visual imagery. Beginning in the nineteenth century, woodcuts, lithographs, and paintings of Hindu gods and goddesses soon gave way to more vibrant polychrome prints, photography and eventually film and video. Such images have often played an important role in political and ideological contestations in India. For example, during the freedom struggle, these so-called God-photos assumed political connotations, not least offering symbolic representations of the nation (Pinney, 2004). Thus an image of the powerful goddess Durga overcoming the buffalo demon Mahisa might be used to symbolize 'Mother India's' defeat of demonic colonialism—an conceptual linkage originally fostered in Bankim Chandra Chatterjee's novel, *Anandamath* (*The Abbey of Bliss*). Likewise, during the 1980s as the Sangh Parivar combine gained increased political clout, images of the god Rama were deployed in the campaign to reclaim the supposed birthplace of Rama in Ayodhya. So-called chariot processions (*rath yatra*), building on a traditional idiom of Hindu festival culture, were organized across India, focusing the media spotlight on more than one campaign to 'reclaim' mythological sites that had supposedly been usurped by Muslims. The same visual and media strategies originally deployed for anticolonial resistance were thus repurposed by Hindu nationalists for new aims during this era.

When Ramanand Sagar produced a serialized version of the *Ramayana* in seventy-eight episodes for national television in the late 1980s, nearly 100 million people tuned in for some of the most popular episodes. Before viewing, devotees often garlanded their television sets with flowers and performed *arti* and *puja* in honor of the Hindu deities. Many Hindus claimed to take *darshana* during the viewing, considering the televised appearance of the deity as equivalent to a deity seen in other worship contexts. Simultaneous with the Ramayana telecast, the Sangh Parivar worked to mobilize Hindus around the cause of building a Rama Temple on the site of the Babri Mosque in Ayodhya. The Ramayana serial contributed significantly to the transformation of an obscure campaign into an epochal event in Indian politics, especially following the violent destruction of the Muslim mosque in 1992 (Rajagopal, 2001). Throughout this same period, there was a noted shift in the iconography of Rama away from a benign figure with a beatific smile toward a symbol of military prowess. In this way, the TV serial helped cement a more militant understanding of Hindu community and nation.

The agenda of the Sangh Parivar has also profited from the active participation—and visual iconography—of prominent Hindu holy men (*sadhu*), renouncers (*sannyasi*), and gurus (McKean 1996). During the peak of the Ram Janmabhoomi Movement, these *sadhus* (and some prominent female *sadhvis*, such as Uma Bharti and Rithambara) received ample news coverage, becoming celebrated, powerful voices adding legitimacy to the nationalist project. Despite being notionally ascetics, such figures clearly have not remained 'outside the world' in the terms associated with classical treatises on renunciation. While it is by no means unprecedented for renouncers to become engaged in politics and even violent warfare (see Pinch 2006), the combination of overt appeals to Hindu spiritual values and the articulation of a nationalist agenda is more novel. Indeed, holy men and women have been an integral part of the Vishwa Hindu Parishad (VHP) from its inception. In 1966, they organized a large protest before Parliament demanding a ban on cow slaughter. Put simply, the conjuncture between Public Hinduism and the ideology of Hindutva took a critical turn with the increased involvement and abundant media representations of these important figures.

The rise of more aggressive forms of Hindutva politics must also be situated within an increasingly dynamic transnational environment of diasporic Hinduism and international Hindu movements. From the early appearance of holy men like Swami Vivekananda and Paramahamsa Yogananda in the United States around the turn of the twentieth century, Hinduism has been an early pioneer in what we might think of as the New Age Movement. During the counterculture period of the 1960s and '70s in the United States, Hindu religious leaders were once again prominent, not least figures like Prabhupada (A. C. Bhaktivedanta Swami) and Maharshi Mahesh Yogi, who respectively launched the global 'brands' of ISKCON and Transcendental Meditation. Coupled with changes in South Asian migration in the wake of European decolonization and the relaxing of US immigration rules after 1965, Hinduism has become increasingly globalized. In places like the United States, U.K., and Canada, especially, the successful integration of Hindus into the social and economic landscape has occasioned the development of Hindu *satsangs*, new temple communities, and other forms of religious activity. And the spiritual concerns and self-understanding of diasporic Hindus in such contexts is integrally related to developments in India, facilitated in part by any number of transnational religious movements and charismatic gurus.

Today, many important Hindu teachers such as Sri Sri Ravi Shankar and Baba Ramdev have expanded their overseas visibility, building upon their strong presence within India. Such teachers, like their New Age counterparts, have effectively combined spirituality with market considerations, becoming spiritual entrepreneurs who can appeal to the spiritual demands of both the Indian and diasporic middle classes. Ravi Shankar's Art of Living Foundation has a presence in more than 150 countries and is one of the world's largest, contemporary, new religious movements (Tollefsen 2011). Not surprisingly, boasting huge mass following and significant resources, such teachers have become social and political activists. Their support for the anticorruption movement led by Anna Hazare in 2011 helped bolster the anti-Congress propaganda of the Bharatiya Janata Party. When the BJP later contested the 2014 Parliament elections, the same Hindu teachers not only endorsed its BJP candidate Narendra Modi, but also mobilized their spiritual resources by organizing yoga camps and using their charisma to bolster support for Modi. With his skillful use of modern social media and his invocation of business success, Modi has not only established himself within the Indian context but has formed significant connections to a base of support in places like the United States.

As a result, the public representation of Hinduism can at times become a matter of real controversy in the United States. Today, American scholars who tackle controversial issues within Hindu culture or venture new readings of the tradition are often confronted by the ire of local Hindus. And true to our globalized world, these controversies are often batted back and forth between India and the West, as was tellingly illustrated in 2014 when Hindutva advocates in India won a legal battle against the publication of Wendy Doniger's book, *The Hindus* (2009). Indeed, the question of who has the right to represent Hinduism has become a major point of contestation both inside the academy and in the general public (Reddy 2013). In the United States, this was forcefully illustrated in the California textbook controversy of 2005–2006, when Hindu nationalist voices complained about the representation of Hinduism in sixth-grade textbooks. Both the Hindu Educational Foundation (HEF) and the Vedic Foundation (VF) were vocal in protests to the California State Board of Education (SBE) and mobilized American Hindus to lobby against the original textbooks. In the United States, as in India, we see the gradual attempt to conflate Public Hinduism with Hindutva.

Conclusion

Public Hinduism has existed by some accounts since time immemorial; it is a heterogeneous tradition made up of countless sects, communities, and worship traditions that have come into varying relationships with ruling powers and political states over the past two millennia at least. But the forces of colonialism led to a consolidation of the idea of Hinduism and simultaneously occasioned attempts to redefine its mission and form. In the postcolonial era, the Hindu public sphere has expanded dramatically, moving Hinduism from the local and regional to the global and transnational; today, Public Hinduism engages a range of agencies and actors in India and the diaspora, and draws upon a plethora of traditional as well as innovative symbols, medias and technologies to advance its various spiritual and worldly goals.

Hindutva, which first emerged in colonial India and has subsequently consolidated its political power in postcolonial India, has made use of the vibrant Hindu public sphere to expand and strengthen its ideology, even successfully capturing state power in a democratic India. While some actors in the Hindu public sphere actively support Hindutva politics as patrons and collaborators, others unwittingly contribute to the overall agenda of Hindu nationalism (Berti, Nicolas, and Kanungo 2011). As Hindutva proponents have expanded their ambitions, they have also at times attempted to cloak their religious agenda behind a more benign banner of cultural nationalism. But such new vocabulary does not indicate a revision of the core principles of Hindutva. Reluctant to dilute what it takes to be the fundamental idea of a Hindu nation, it oscillates for now between militancy and moderation, depending on the political climate. But its successes suggest that what we may be witnessing is the emergence of a new religion of the public sphere, which we might choose to call 'Public Hindutva.'

Summary

Despite having an intense private domain, Hinduism, whether elite or popular, has always had a passionate engagement with the public sphere. Over the centuries, Public Hinduism has been plural, diverse, and multilayered. Colonial interventions helped construct new understandings of Hinduism. In the period of anticolonial struggle, new discourses and new modes of representation molded the disparate forms and agencies of Hinduism into a common sense of identity; in the process, Hinduism and the Indian nation became intertwined in discourses and political practice. Out of the dynamics of Hindu nationalism emerged the discourse of Hindutva, or Hinduness, which deploys an array of symbols from the rich repository of Hinduism in order to mobilize Hindus around the vision of a unitary Hindu nation. In the process, the complexity of Public Hinduism becomes blurred and the particular meanings produced by Hindutva spokespeople are internalized as the truth of the religion called Hinduism. Lord Rama's transformation during the Ram Janmabhoomi Movement from an object of religious devotion to an icon of a longed-for Hindu nation suggests the tensions at the heart of the Public Hinduism-Hindutva conundrum. Are we witnessing the resolution of those tensions in the emergence of something we could call Public Hindutva?

Discussion Questions

1) How would you define Hindutva? How does the author contrast it with Public Hinduism?
2) What is the Sangh Parivar and what sorts of activities have its supporters engaged in since the early twentieth century?
3) Can you think of ways to connect concerns raised in this chapter with those addressed elsewhere in this volume?
4) What does the author mean by suggesting we may be witnessing the rise of something called Public Hindutva?

Suggested Readings

Berti, Daniela (2011). 'Introduction.' In *Cultural Entrenchment of Hindutva: Local Mediations and Forms of Convergence* (1–25). Eds. Daniela Berti, Nicolas Jaoul, and Pralay Kanungo. London, New York, and New Delhi: Routledge.

Copely, Antony (2003). 'Introduction. Debating Indian Nationalism and Hindu Religious Belief.' In *Hinduism in Public and Private: Reform, Hindutva, Gender, and Sampraday* pp. 1–27). Ed. Antony Copely. Oxford and New York: Oxford University Press.

Zavos, John, Pralay Kanungo, Deepa S. Reddy, Maya Warrier, Raymond Brady Williams, eds. (2013). *Public Hinduisms*. New Delhi: Sage.

Bibliography

Berti, Daniela, Nicolas Jaoul and Pralay Kanungo (2011). *Cultural Enrichment of Hindutva: Local Mediations and Forms of Convergence*. New York: Routledge.

Copely, Antony, ed. (2003). *Hinduism in Public and Private: Reform, Hindutva, Gender, Sampradaya*. New Delhi: Oxford University Press.

Dalmia, Vasudha and H. Von Stietencron, eds. (1995). *Representing Hinduism: The Construction of Religious Traditions and National Identity*. New Delhi: Sage.

Golwalkar, M. S. (1939). *We or Our Nationhood Defined*. Nagpur: Bharat Prakashan.

Hatcher, Brian A. (1999). *Eclecticism and Modern Hindu Discourse*. New York: Oxford University Press.

James, Jonathan D. (2010). *McDonaldisation, Masala McGospel and Om Economics*. New Delhi: Sage Publications.

Kanungo, Pralay (2002). *RSS's Tryst with Politics: From Hedgewar to Sudarshan*. Delhi: Manohar.

Kapur, Ratna (2014). 'A Leap of Faith: The Construction of Hindu Majoritarianism through Secular Law.' *The South Atlantic Quarterly* 113, No. 1: 109–128.

McKean, Lise (1996). *Divine Enterprise: Gurus and the Hindu Nationalist Movement*. Chicago: University of Chicago Press.

Pinch, William (2006). *Warrior Ascetics and Indian Empire*. Cambridge: Cambridge University Press.

Pinney, Christopher (2004). '*Photos of the Gods*'. *The Printed Image and Political Struggle in India*. Chicago: The University of Chicago Press.

Rajagopal, Arvind (2001). *Politics after Television: Hindu Nationalism and the Reshaping of the Public in India*. Cambridge: Cambridge University Press.

Reddy, Deepa S. (2012). 'Hindu Transnationalisms: Organisations, Ideologies, Networks.' In *Public Hinduisms* (pp. 309–323). Eds. John Zavos, P. Kanungo, D. Reddy, M. Warrier, and R. B. Williams. Thousand Oaks: Sage Publications.

Savarkar, V. D. (1949). *Hindutva: Who is a Hindu?* Poona: S.P. Gokhale.

Sharma, Arvind (2002). 'On Hindu, Hindustan, Hinduism and Hindutva.' *Numen* 49, No. 1: 1–36.

Singh, Pritam (2005). 'Hindu Bias in India's "Secular" Constitution: probing flaws in the instruments of governance.' *Third World Quarterly* 26, No. 6: 909–926.

Tollefsen, Inga Bardsen (2011). 'Art of Living: Religious Entrepreneurship and Legitimation Strategies.' *International Journal for the Study of New Religions* 2, No. 2: 255–279.

Zavos, John et al., eds. (2013). *Public Hinduisms*. New Delhi: Sage.

16 Caste and Untouchability

Rupa Viswanath

In the first decades of the twentieth century, when Indian anticolonial nationalists were loudly proclaiming the glories of an Indian cultural heritage that drew on Hinduism, B. R. Ambedkar, a civil rights activist, principal author of postcolonial India's constitution—and also a member of a so-called untouchable caste—made the bold and counterintuitive claim that Hindu society simply 'does not exist' (Ambedkar 2014 [1936]). This chapter will allow us to understand why Ambedkar made this remark, as well as what makes it so important to Indian society today. Put simply, Ambedkar considered the constitution he helped draft to be only the first step in promoting a just and egalitarian society. As he saw it, whatever the constitution might say about equality, it could not in fact ensure that all of India's citizens received the same treatment at the hands of the law, government officials, and society more generally. The root of the problem lay in the differences *between* groups of Indians, which in Ambedkar's opinion did more to inform the way Indian society operated than values, customs, or traditions those groups might share. In Ambedkar's diagnosis, the principal problem was caste. It was caste that stood in the way of India's progress toward becoming a democratic society characterized by genuine fellow feeling. Hence, he argued that there was no Hindu society if by that one meant a group of people who shared common values and interests; such commonalities were shared only within castes.

In order to understand Ambedkar's concerns, we need to take up the topic of caste, one of the most remarked-upon features of the Indian subcontinent. For several hundred years, caste has befuddled observers, generating a slew of heated academic debates and public controversies. It has managed to remain a central feature of Indian life down to the present day, as indicated by the profusion of caste-based political parties in contemporary India. This is despite the many transformations brought about by the intensified spread of global markets and transnational migration in the last century. The persistence of caste has thus defied widespread expectations that the onset of global modernity would witness the disappearance of this apparently outdated social arrangement.

What is caste? In the simplest of terms, it is a pattern of social organization defined by what anthropologists call endogamy, the practice of marrying within the group. Today in India, there are tens of thousands of such groups for whom endogamy is still very much the norm. The tight social control over marriage within such groups suggests in turn that the control of women and women's sexuality is central to the preservation of caste boundaries. Thus, in cases where men and women from different castes attempt to marry one another against the wishes of their families, kinsmen often react with outrage and even violence, invoking a concern to 'protect' the honor of 'their' women. One could well say that patriarchy and caste are two sides of the same coin (Rege et al. 2013; Rao 2003).

In Indian languages, the most common term for caste is *jati*, whose root meaning emphasizes the fact that birth (*janma*) determines one's caste. Another defining feature of caste in India is its relationship with the Hindu religion. Thus, when Ambedkar refers to the society that practices caste, he often simply speaks (as in the above quotation) of 'Hindu society.' Those we identify as Hindus in India today hold a wide range of views on what caste means to them and in their lives, but most would agree that the practice of caste and caste-related values are linked in some way to norms of ritual purity, and most accept that a hierarchically organized division of labor was divinely mandated. While the practice of caste can be found among non-Hindu groups (including Jains and Muslims), for critics like Ambedkar, it is essential to recognize the tight correlation between the values of Hinduism and the justification of caste.

'Varna': An Ideology of Social Hierarchy

In ancient India's classical texts, the earliest of which date back to the pre-Christian era, castes were arranged in a fourfold hierarchy. This hierarchical organization is called *varna*, and is another term used in Indian languages to refer to caste, but is much less common than jati. Varna describes not the actually existing endogamous groups in Indian society, but an idealized vision of a fourfold Indian society represented in texts composed exclusively by elites over several millennia. These elite litterateurs were members of the jatis that aligned themselves with the highest varna, the Brahmin or priestly caste; it is hardly surprising that every one of these texts lists Brahmins as the highest. But what values inform the desire to rank among the highest varnas?

According to traditionally held Hindu ideas of ritual purity, some castes are inherently more 'pure' than others, which are correspondingly understood to be more 'polluted.' Being 'pure' in this specific ritual sense means being entitled to engage in many forms of social interaction, including entering into and worshipping at Hindu temples; this is stereotypically true of Brahmins, the so-called priestly varna. On the other end of the hierarchy are those who are considered the most 'polluted,' the Sudras and Untouchables. Such groups have not only historically been prohibited from entering Hindu temples, but they have also been ostracized and confined to occupations considered degrading or unfit for the higher varnas. As the French sociologist Louis Dumont (1980) famously observed, the logic underlying the hierarchical ranking of varnas is one based on the dichotomy of purity and pollution: the higher the caste, the more pure their ritual status. After the Brahmin, in order of decreasing purity, come the other three varnas as described in classical sources: *Kshatriya*, warriors and kings, *Vaishya*, merchants, and *Sudras*, workers and servants. One of the most famous of the ancient sources on varna is a metaphoric description of a cosmic man found in a hymn from the Rig Veda, a text dating to approximately 1500–1000 BCE. In this hymn, the different parts of the man's body are likened to the different varnas, clearly establishing both their hierarchical relationship and the social division of labor.

> The Brahman was his mouth,
> of both his arms was the Rājanya [Kshatriya] made.
>
> His thighs became the Vaiśya,
> from his feet the Śūdra was produced.[1]

In a later period, elaborate codifications of rules for governing castes and their interrelations began to be composed in India. The most well-known of these is the *Laws of Manu*, or *Manusmriti*. This highly influential text appeared in its current form around the first century CE. It lays down in very concrete terms different moral codes and forms of punishment for each caste. In the process, it enshrines in law the superior privileges of the Brahmin and the other two higher *varnas*, the Kshatriyas and the Vaisyas. Collectively, these three upper varnas are called 'twice-born,' because the men of these castes are eligible to undergo an initiation ceremony that represents a kind of second, spiritual birth. The text also recommends the violent enforcement of the practice of deference among the lower castes. For instance, we read that 'A once-born man (a Sudra) who insults a twice born man with gross invective shall have his tongue cut out, for he is of low origin,' and 'If he (the Sudra) arrogantly teaches Brahmins their duty, the king shall cause hot oil to be poured into his mouth and ears.'[2] It is no surprise that Ambedkar publicly burned this text in a defiant political act in 1927.

It is essential to understand that this four-varna scheme never corresponded to social reality. What we observe empirically instead is the operation of the jatis, endogamous caste groups of more or less local reach. At various times and for a variety of mostly political reasons, different jatis have made claims about their ranking in the varna hierarchy. The influential scholar Louis Dumont, mentioned above, has thus been thoroughly criticized for taking the ideology of varna at face value. In doing so, he painted a picture of Indian society as essentially bound in an unchanging varna system, and insisted ritual ideas of purity were the sole key to understanding Indian society. But scholars like M. N. Srinivas, through a careful study of rural caste relations, showed that other factors were influential in determining caste ranking, not least wealth and power. Srinivas showed that in the absence of high varna status, a particular caste could still become the most important—what he called 'the dominant caste'—in a given region (Srinivas 1956, 1959). In such cases, a ritually 'low' group might then use the varna scheme to provide legitimation for their claims to power (see also Singer and Cohn 1968; Fox 1969). For instance, when a subset of Nadars, a hitherto low-ranking Sudra caste in southern India, became more powerful and wealthy through the establishment of trading networks, they successfully claimed Kshatriya status (Hardgrave 1969). In a pattern found throughout Indian history, they then effectively formed a new caste; henceforth they would not agree to marry other Nadars who had not also been successful in claiming status as Kshatriyas. It is processes like these, involving local contests for political and economic power, that have given rise to the very large number of jatis in India, revealing that the relative position of jatis in the caste hierarchy is not fixed for all time. And it is these bids for improved local status, successful or otherwise, that are the means by which the ideology of social difference (varna), represented in Indian textual traditions, is linked to the pragmatic actions of different endogamous social groups (jatis).

The appearance of a nation-wide census in British India in 1872 added a further dimension to how people could imagine the relationship between varna and jati (Cohn 1990; Barrier 1981). Since the British did not just record jati names, but also varna positions for each jati across the Indian subcontinent, it became possible for the first time for Indians to imagine a shared caste identity with persons from unrelated jatis beyond the locality. This made a new kind of supralocal caste mobilization and caste politics possible for the first time (Dirks 2001). The new public prominence that the theory of varna acquired through the process of its becoming a census category meant that classical accounts of varna, based on ideals of ritual purity, achieved even greater social recognition than before. And in the process, more and more people came to see caste as primarily a matter of purity and pollution.

Caste Differences and the Caste Difference

As we noted above, the varna scheme should not be taken at face value as a description of social reality. In fact, if one were to go by classical accounts of caste difference, one would entirely overlook the very question that the remainder of this chapter takes as its focus. Put most simply, there is a single marker of difference that is arguably more socially salient than any of the aforementioned differences among the four varnas—and, ironically, it is not even represented in the classical fourfold varna scheme. This is the difference between all castes that fit into the varna scheme and another broad group of persons who are sometimes called 'untouchables' and who are today widely known as Dalits. The postulate of a fundamental difference between Dalits and all other varna groups is premised on a single *qualitative* distinction: Dalits are set apart from all other so-called caste Hindus (that is, those whose jatis are supposed to correspond to one of the four varnas). While Dalits also have jatis, these jatis are not thought to fall within any of the four classical varnas. For this reason Dalits are sometimes called 'outcastes.' But it is analytically important to recognize that Dalit difference is of a unique kind; it is not a question of being further down the scale, but of not existing on the same scale that accounts for other caste differences.

One might ask why, if all castes enjoy differing levels of social prestige in relation to how they conduct specific rituals and to which gods they pray, we couldn't say that Dalits simply occupy the extreme end of a spectrum of caste difference? In order to appreciate why this is not the case, it will help to consider three features of Indian society that determine Dalit lives. First, Dalits were and often still are distinguished in terms of the political economy of agrarian life. Throughout history, they have been almost universally associated with slavery or bonded labor; these have typically been among their only means of survival. There were certainly caste Hindus who lived as poor farmers tilling the fields of their landlords, but only Dalits were actively prevented from owning land. Second, Dalits have been set apart spatially. All other castes in a village, even if segregated residentially from one another along different streets or in contiguous neighborhoods, nevertheless shared the village proper. By contrast, Dalit settlements had to be kept apart from the living areas occupied by caste Hindus; this is still overwhelmingly the case. Such spatial segregation is not merely a question of maintaining separate quarters for workers. It also entails differential access to all the resources any village might hold, such as access to pasturage and water sources, both of which can quite literally be a matter of life and death in an agrarian setting. Third and finally, the basic differences between Dalits and caste Hindus are compounded by widespread practices of exclusion and humiliation—for instance, the prevention of temple entry or even entry into shared secular spaces like village teashops, on the grounds that Dalits are ritually 'polluted,' the demand that Dalits publicly display humility and respect to other castes, and the widespread negative stereotyping about Dalits as dirty and immoral.

One important consequence of such stigmatizing of Dalits and the devaluation of their shared humanity is that Dalit women are placed at great risk of sexual violence perpetrated by caste men (Rao 2009: 217–240; Teltumbde 2010). The sexual exploitation of Dalit women—who, unlike their better-off counterparts of higher castes, must leave the safety of their homes and neighborhoods to work in fields and factories in order to survive—is rampant (e.g., Amnesty International 2001). Sadly, such exploitation rarely garners the kind of media attention that more high-profile cases of sexual assault do, once again pointing to the systemic marginalization of Dalits. Viewed in terms of the foregoing three ways of conceptualizing Dalit difference, we can see that the ritual discrimination associated with 'untouchability' is but one component of a much more extensive structure of domination (cf. Mendelsohn and Vicziany 1998). When understanding the situation of Dalits in India, it becomes even more clear that when theorists of caste, such as Louis Dumont, focus on ritual purity and pollution to the exclusion of violence, domination, and economic inequality, they risk painting a highly inaccurate and apologetic picture of caste.

Dalit Difference: In Their Own Eyes and in the Eyes of Others

How Dalits themselves understand the nature of their own discrimination is often in sharp contrast to how most other Indians do so. Here is how one Tamil Dalit activist named P. Samuel described things in 1918 in a magazine directed at other Dalits:

> In considering [the social position of] any [upper] castes in the world, we can see that wealth alone is the principal reason for . . . their superiority. It is money that makes things possible . . . [and] indeed, as everyone knows, there is no respect in this world for those without it.[3]

In the view of Samuel and of many other Dalit activists over the course of the last century, caste is a matter of wealth and power. In this view, economic control over Dalit livelihoods gives caste Hindus the power to enforce practices of segregation and exclusion. And as Dalits know well, failure to conform can be routinely met with violence. The brutal acts of anti-Dalit violence that take place from time to time throughout India are almost always the result of perceptions that Dalits are not 'minding their place' (Narula 1999). Adopting a Dalit perspective, especially as articulated through the voice of activists, allows us to identify unjust political-economic relations as the cause of their subordination. Dalit activists do not see these relations as natural, but as the result of oppression, a condition that can only exist and be perpetuated through the sustained efforts of oppressors.

It is striking to observe how sharply non-Dalit, and especially high-caste, views of caste relations diverge from such an explanation. Ursula Sharma has documented a range of ways in which elite Indians speak about caste (Sharma 1999), including by invoking purity and pollution, and by drawing upon the doctrine of *karma*. Karma refers to the Hindu theory of rebirth, according to which one's deeds in a past life determine one's position and fortunes in the present. If Dalits accepted this doctrine, as many believe all Hindus do, Dalits might be expected to understand their own low social position as the result of previous misdeeds. This is what elite commentators and scholars have sometimes authoritatively asserted (Weber 1964: 63). The problem is that it is very hard to find any evidence that Dalits actually hold this view! On the contrary, as Gerald Berreman has pointed out on the basis of his fieldwork among Dalits in North India:

> No one said, in effect, 'I am of low status and so are my family members and my caste-fellows, and justly so, because of our misdeeds in previous lives.' . . . Rationalizations of caste status which are . . . convincing to those . . . who benefit from them seem much less so to those whose deprivation they are expected to justify or explain. (Berreman 1971: 12)

This difference between how Dalits and others think about caste has meant that while Dalits have often sought to gain political and economic power, even while they criticized Hinduism for providing an ideological justification for caste subordination, the vast majority of well-meaning elite reformers have continually restricted their efforts at improving the condition of Dalits to the reform of Hinduism, since Hinduism's acceptance of the doctrine of purity and pollution would seem to be the source of the problem. Most famously, Mohandas K. Gandhi adamantly refused to allow Dalits their own independent political voice, and instead asked his fellow caste Hindus to treat Dalits better; needless to say, this entailed that they remain in the same menial occupations that Dalits contend are the very source of their oppression in the first place (Zelliot 1992; Jaffrelot 2005: 31–51). Gandhi insisted that the 'removal of untouchability' was a crucial responsibility for caste Hindus, but nevertheless maintained that Dalits must provide 'service through physical labour.'[4] His argument was based on the assumption that 'every person,' according to his or her caste, 'is born with certain definite limitations he cannot overcome.'[5] His incomplete embrace of social change is signaled by the name he chose for speaking of Dalits: Harijans, 'children of God.' For Gandhi, the redemption of the Harijan had to come through religious means—they were children of *God* above all else—and the agents of change had to be caste Hindus like himself. In contrast to their caste benefactors, then, Dalits were pictured as a being in need of nurturing and protection—in other words they were *children* of God.

Dalits and Hinduism

Are Dalits Hindus?

Let us take stock by considering three ways in which we have seen that Hindu caste in general and Dalit subordination in particular have been seen as linked within a unified social system. First, Hindu sacred texts have described the fourfold scheme of varna, a divinely mandated social hierarchy; this scheme has been used by jatis across India to legitimize their caste status and to support movements for upward mobility. Second, because varnas are arranged on a scale of increasing ritual purity, those considered so low as to not even be included in the schema, namely Dalits, are viewed as exceptionally impure or polluted. In most accounts, it is this alleged impurity that is supposed to explain their degraded position; some have even argued that it is natural they should be despised in view of their supposedly polluted nature. Third, it has been argued that since the Hindu sacred texts deploy the concept of varna, the ideas of caste, hierarchy, and purity are themselves religious values; they are in some sense part and parcel of what it means to be Hindu.

If Hindus have themselves justified caste subordination on the basis of religion, it should come as no surprise that some of the most powerful critiques of Indian society voiced by Dalits have been themselves indictments of Hinduism (see Ambedkar n.d.). But this raises an interesting and, as we will see, politically very sensitive, question: are Dalits best understood as Hindus in the first place?

As scholars of religion, we are not required to provide a definitive answer to this question. If someone claims to be a Hindu, and is considered by others in his or her social world to be a Hindu, it is not the scholar's place to disagree. Determining who really does and does not count as a member of a religious community is a matter best left to religious authorities. So our task here is to examine instead who asks this question, why they ask it, and what consequences follow from answering it in one way as opposed to another.

A turning point in the history of this question came in 1932. Religious identity and political power became intimately linked with the introduction by the British colonial government of the so-called Communal Award. The Award meant that political representation would be apportioned according to the numerical strength of respective religious 'communities': the actual numbers of a religious group became significant in an entirely new way. In regions like Punjab, Hindus came to believe that their majority status was threatened by the presence of other communities like Muslims. It thus became important that Dalits be counted as Hindus. Questions of identity were subsumed under the census logic of a communal 'politics of numbers' (Webster 1992).

A long tradition of Dalit activists and scholars has argued that it is by no means evident that Dalits are Hindus. Dalit religious life, they argue, is different from that of high-caste people, even if it shares much with other low-caste groups (Ilaiah 1996; Juergensmeyer 1982: 93–108; Lamb 2002; Viswanath 2012b). Furthermore, there is evidence both from the colonial period as well as today that Dalits themselves use the term Hindu to refer only to caste people (Searle-Chatterjee 2008). At the same time, it does not appear that caste Hindus saw Dalits as sharing in their religious community prior to the twentieth century (Frykenberg 1997). Indeed, it was only in the precise political context discussed above that Gandhi suggested that the problem of Dalits was a Hindu problem that only Hindus could solve. What was, when Gandhi formulated it, a very idiosyncratic idea, soon became a matter of national common sense—and one that benefitted the interests of caste Hindus by incorporating Dalits into their majority community, thereby increasing Hindus' measure of political power.

Some twentieth-century political leaders, like B.R. Ambedkar (see Image 16.1), did understand Dalits to be Hindus but admittedly Hindus of a very peculiar kind, thoroughly marginalized and prevented from sharing in the communal life of Hindus of other castes. Ambedkar therefore believed that in addition to struggling to ensure political-economic and political equality, Dalits should, as a mark of self-respect, convert out of Hinduism, the religion that justified caste discrimination. Deeply disappointed by the hypocrisy and casteism of his fellow politicians, Ambedkar famously converted to Buddhism with some 500,000 of his followers in 1956, a strategy Dalit leaders have adopted both before and since (Aloysius 1998; Ayyathurai 2011; Beltz 2005).

Dalits have also predominated among those converting to Christianity in India in the modern period (Webster 1992; Grafe 1990); still others have chosen to convert to Islam (Khan 1983). Given its direct connections with political power in the colonial period, and its explicit critique of dominant

Figure 16.1 Ambedkar

society, Dalit conversion, for over a hundred years now, has been a powerful political tool and occasion for debate and scandal. Every call for Dalits to convert to another religion is taken as a sign of anti-Hindu (even antinational) agitation and attracts attention far and wide. In short, we can say that Dalits have long maintained an ambiguous relationship to mainstream Hinduism. It is therefore necessary to recognize that any claims about their 'true' religious status—Hindu or otherwise—are always political claims.

Do Dalits 'Accept' Caste?

One way scholars have tried to make sense of the question of whether Dalits are Hindus is to consider whether Dalits themselves accept the idea that people can be ranked according to levels of purity and pollution. The backdrop of this debate was the extraordinarily influential theory of Louis Dumont mentioned earlier. According to Dumont, caste is a unified system, and everyone in India ultimately accepts the theory of purity and pollution. The problem with this view is that it seems to rely heavily on a theory of varna, which, as we have seen, does not conform to the Indian reality of a multiplicity of jatis (cf. Roberts 2008).

One Dumontian anthropologist, Michael Moffatt, argued that Dalits accept pan-Indian ideas of purity and pollution because the Dalit castes in the village in South India where he worked seemed to be hierarchically arranged, with higher ranked subcastes claiming greater purity than their lower caste fellows (1979). As Moffatt contended, this demonstrated their 'consensus' with the system of caste according to which the broader Indian society discriminates against them. Moffatt's argument implies that Dalits accept the position they are in; but it also flies in the face of the overwhelming evidence of Dalit discontent. Furthermore, a large range of arguments and data directed against the Dumontian theory of caste undermine the theory of consensus that Moffatt advances (e.g., Berreman 1971; Deliège 1992; Lynch 1977; Mencher 1974; Mosse 1994). These accounts stress that purity and pollution are merely upper-caste justifications for a complex system of entrenched inequality that includes political-economic domination. Nor can this justification be taken to reflect the views of Dalits themselves, who, however much they might conform in the presence of their social 'superiors,' view society in class-like terms; in their eyes, the economic power differentials at play reveal caste practices to be associated most strongly with selfishness and oppression. We should bear in mind that conformity and consensus are two very different things. Since Dalits who fail to conform to caste-based practices often face the threat of violence, outward behavior that comports with socially enforced norms can hardly be taken to imply consensus with or approval of those norms.

In a more promising vein of scholarship, Lynn Vincentnathan (1993) offers a sophisticated analysis of Dalit oral narratives of caste origins, drawing on examples taken from across the Indian subcontinent. These tales decry the injustice of Dalits' current position, describing it as a trick perpetrated by others who act selfishly to make themselves 'high.' Here is one example of a Dalit narrative provided by Vincentnathan:

> [There were once] four original Brahman brothers, one of whom was their founding ancestor. In a spirit of cooperation and brotherly love, their ancestor removed a dead cow from the brothers' common kitchen. The other three gave priority over kinship to their concept of pollution and thus banished the 'scavenger' brother, who was for all time defiled. (Vincentnathan 1993: 65, citing Kolenda 1964: 75)

The fact that all the castes were originally brothers expresses the widespread Dalit view that castes are in fact equal; they share the same blood, even if self-interest has caused some to differentiate themselves from others. For many Dalits, then, ritual purity is not seen as the permanent inherited status that caste Hindus believe it to be (Vincentnathan 1993: 63–66). And nor is ritual status justified; such a view accords nicely with the widespread rejection, noted above, of the theory of karma amongst Dalits.

Despite all this evidence, in the last two hundred years, a wide range of public commentary has spread the erroneous view that Dalits have been content with their lot and have accepted their caste position. Given that purveyors of this view are invariably high-caste elites, it is also a remarkably self-exculpatory position, and its roots go deep. Such a view must have multiple origins, but one of its earliest proponents was the British colonial state, for whom it was convenient not to place too much emphasis on the severity of Dalit subordination. The British were more interested in ensuring the stability, productivity, and profitability of the agrarian economy, which was fueled by cheap Dalit slave labor. Indian political elites quickly came to echo the view that Dalits were really not so badly off and were, if not happy, at least resigned to their lot (Viswanath 2014).

Dalits, Hinduism, and the Postcolonial Indian State

India is a secular state. The postcolonial government has, to a great extent, managed to put in place the laws and institutional means to ensure that the state does not treat people differently on the basis of religion and to refrain from interfering in religious freedom. This official position is undermined, however, by the fact that the state has sought to decisively settle the question of the relationship of Dalits to Hinduism (Galanter 1971). Most ordinary Indians today do not realize that Dalits have been made to belong to the community of Hindus by administrative fiat.

To understand how this is so, we need to consider the issue of reservations. In India, 'reservations' are the affirmative-action-style policies that guarantee a certain percentage of seats in government-run educational institutions and in government offices for people from a number of historically disadvantaged groups, including Dalits (Galanter 1984).[6] But in the case of so-called untouchables the state does not employ the designation 'Dalit.' Instead, the official rubric is 'Scheduled Castes' (or SCs), a nomenclature based on the fact that all their jati names are found on an official 'schedule,' or list. But the matter is not as simple as this, since there is a very specific stipulation as to who will be considered SC for legal-administrative purposes: 'No person who professes a religion different from the Hindu [or the Sikh or the Buddhist] religion shall be deemed to be a member of a Scheduled Caste.'[7] The government's definition of Scheduled Caste therefore entirely omits vast numbers of Christian and Muslim Dalit who are converts to those faiths (Viswanath 2012a). As such, converts cannot benefit from state-sponsored welfare schemes. In effect, this is a state-sponsored direct disincentive to conversion to those religions; and this represents something of an anomaly for a secular state whose professed mandate is to protect freedom of religion. Even less often publicly acknowledged is the fact that Dalits who fall outside the official definition of SC thereby also lose protection under the Prevention of Atrocities Act, which affords special penalties against perpetrators of caste-based violence against Dalits. Since such violence has shown no signs of abating in the last half century, this too represents a significant disincentive to prospective converts (Narula 1999).

The implied premise of the currently existing basis for the definition of a Scheduled Caste person is that being a Dalit and being a Hindu are so intimately linked that, without the one, the other disappears. By now, the limitations of such a premise should be clear. Yes, we have seen that Hinduism does provide legitimation to caste inequality and has used the logic of purity and exclusion to ostracize and suppress Dalits. And we have seen that important

Dalit leaders like Ambedkar understood the connection between Hinduism, caste, and Dalit experience to be critical. Hence, Ambedkar famously advocated conversion to Buddhism as a means for securing dignity and freedom from caste oppression. At the same time, we have seen that due to the census logic of twentieth-century politics, Hindu groups have sought to enhance their power by including Dalits among those counted as Hindu. It should also be clear that this is not how many Dalits see themselves.

Thus it is no surprise that even leaders like Ambedkar who advocated conversion did not think the problem of Dalit discrimination could be entirely solved by a change of religion. There had to be legal and political means for securing equality, and not just reservations for voting but also access to economic resources: hence Ambedkar's repeated insistence on the importance of the redistribution of land. And yet, despite the awareness of the need for legal and economic reform, we see that the peculiar definition of Scheduled Caste persists. The error of assuming that Dalits experience an immediate end to discrimination and disadvantage upon conversion should be readily apparent. Discrimination against Dalits is something that is practiced by caste people of all religions. Numerous studies have shown that Dalit Muslims and Dalit Christians are in a comparable situation to their caste fellows of any other religion when judged by external indicators like educational attainment, literacy, poverty, and employment (Report of the National Commission on Religious and Linguistic Minorities 2007). One of the most striking illustrations of the persistence of caste outside of Hinduism can be found in the walls built to segregate corpses according to caste in Catholic cemeteries in South India, in order to prevent Dalits from 'polluting' their fellow Christians even after death.

It is no surprise, then, that Dalit Christians and Muslims have actively been trying to get themselves included in the list of Scheduled Castes (Mosse 2012). What is surprising is that the currently existing definition of SC passed muster with the whole phalanx of elite lawmakers who put it into the Constitution, even as it flies in the face of overwhelming sociological evidence.

Conclusion: Dalits, Race, and International Solidarity

As we have seen, focusing on religion, the discrimination justified by Hindu theories of purity and pollution can very easily obscure fundamental issues of political and economic inequality. For this reason, it is a matter of great importance how one defines Dalit subordination. For most of modern India's history, makers of public opinion have overwhelmingly come from the same elite groups who drafted the constitution. At the moment, there are only a handful of Dalit journalists writing in the English language anywhere in India, and Dalits are alarmingly underrepresented in academia, politics, and other elite spheres—despite representing some 16% of the population. Seeking to define for themselves what it means to suffer discrimination, and being able to propose their own solutions to the problem, is thus a major political struggle for Dalit groups. In this they have sought inspiration from African-American civil rights leaders and activists. Dalit parties throughout India call themselves Dalit Panthers, after Malcolm X's Black Panther Party.

With this in mind, let us conclude by considering how scholarship and politics, the state and Dalit activism, recently came together on the occasion of the UN-sponsored Conference Against Racism and Xenophobia held in Durban, South Africa in 2001. Dalit activist groups lobbied to have the discrimination they faced recognized as a form of racialized discrimination, a move they hoped would publicize their plight and perhaps persuade the Indian government to be more accountable for the enforcement of laws like the Prevention of Atrocities Act. But among many Indians, this was felt as a betrayal, an antinational airing of dirty laundry.

In response, Indian academics (all of elite background) and political figures penned editorials and gave speeches in order to insist that caste and race are entirely different matters and that there were no real racial differences in India (Béteille 2001; Gupta 2001). But debates about whether these categories, as defined in academic sociology, are or are not the same, misses the much greater political point. Both caste and race are systems of inherited discrimination and therefore activists engaged with either can learn from one another. We need not assume caste and race are identical to acknowledge this. Even the forms of what are widely agreed upon as being racial discrimination are hardly identical all over the world—South African apartheid, segregation in the southern United States, and the treatment of the Roma in Europe are all both alike and different. So, as in the case of defining who is a Hindu, deciding what counts as racism is also a political matter, and in this case, elite Indians of widely diverging political stripes nevertheless decided that it was not up to Dalits to highlight the similarities between what they faced and what racialized groups face all over the world in an attempt to build international solidarity and demand that more be done to end their plight.

Dalits went ahead with their delegation despite the disapproval of the central government. In Durban, they made common cause with a variety of other groups discriminated on the basis of descent. Their courage and forthrightness would no doubt have pleased the Maharashtrian Dalit poet Daya Pawar (1935–1996). In one of his poems, 'You Wrote from Los Angeles,' he describes how a high-caste friend who had traveled to the United States during the 1950s experienced racial discrimination. First Pawar takes on the voice of his friend, who was outraged that 'Indians and curs' are 'measured by the same yard-stick' in the United States, where words like 'Niggers' and 'Blacks' are thrown in their faces. The high-caste friend tells Pawar that he felt this abuse like the sting of a 'thousand scorpions.' But Pawar then shifts to his own voice in the poem, using his friend's bitter experience to force him (and millions of Indians like him) to reckon with his own complicity in perpetuating similar practices in India. He tells his friend that when he learned what he had experienced in America, he 'felt *so damn good!*' Now, he says, finally, 'you've had a taste of what we've suffered' for generations in India.[8]

Through poetry like this, Pawar reminds us that moments of confrontation can sometimes be transformative. The relentless humiliations experienced by Pawar are here transformed into poetry and activism. He graphically suggests how one high-caste man's unexpected encounter with discrimination leads him to recognize a problem so often ignored or misunderstood by those in his high-caste milieu. Only the startling juxtaposition of caste and race is able to unsettle this high-caste perspective. As Dalit intellectuals and activists have long understood, such recognition of discrimination is a necessary first step towards a more just social order.

Summary

Castes are social groups that practice endogamy, that is, marriage within the group. The control of marriage entails control over women's sexuality: patriarchy and caste therefore go hand in hand. Caste status is fixed by birth, and castes are understood to be arranged hierarchically. While all castes maintain some separation from one another, the difference between Dalits (members of the 'lowest' castes) and all others is of a distinct kind. Most Dalits were once unfree laborers, and today continue to be discriminated against socially, ritually, and economically. The Hindu religion justifies this treatment by viewing Dalits as 'impure.' Dalits have retaliated by struggling for civil rights, and sometimes by converting to Buddhism, Christianity, or Islam. It is not clear that this should be labeled conversion 'out of Hinduism' since it is unlikely they were understood as Hindus prior to the rise of modern politics. It was only with modern electoral politics that it became important to retain Dalits 'within the fold' in order to secure Hindu electoral majorities. These politics shape even the policies of the secular state, which does not grant affirmative action benefits to Dalits who have converted. The latest attempt by Dalits to reframe discussion of their plight—their efforts to have casteism recognized by the UN as on a par with racism—was opposed, not only by nationalistic state officials, but even by some 'objective' Indian academics, illustrating the challenges still facing Dalit communities.

Questions for Discussion

- Can you describe caste in terms of the categories of varna, jati, purity, and hierarchy?
- What factors contribute to the identification of certain groups as Dalits?
- Both activists like Ambedkar, and more recent Indian sociologists like M.N. Srinivas, insist that Hinduism is impossible to imagine without caste. What is at stake in such claims? Do you agree?
- What factors might shape Dalit decisions to convert to a religion other than Hinduism? What consequences does such a decision have for the lived experience of Dalits?

Notes

1 Rig Veda, 10:90.12 (Griffith 1896).
2 *The Laws of Manu*, ch. 8, vv. 270 and 272 (Buehler 1886: 302)
3 'South Indian Oppressed Castes, their Income and their Expenses,' (*Teṇintiya Oṭukkappaṭukiṟa Jātikaḷum, Avarkaḷuṭaiya varavu-celavukaḷum*), *Vaḷikāṭṭuvōṉ*, February 1918, p. 48, translation mine.
4 *Young India*, 4 June 1931, p. 129.
5 *Modern Review*, October 1935, p. 413.
6 Reservations are also given to those known (in administrative parlance) as Other Backward Classes or OBCs. OBCs make up a wide variety of castes, most of whom are commonly understood to be Sudras in varna terms. Since reservations are meant to bring representation closer in line with proportions in the general population, the largest percentage of reserved seats in politics and education are in fact granted to OBCs.
7 Constitution of India Scheduled Castes Act of 1950.
8 Quoting from Daya Pawar's 1974 collection *Kondwada* (translated by Graham Smith) as cited in Zelliot 1992: 301.

Suggested Readings and Films

Ambedkar, B. R. (2014). *Annihilation of Caste*. Foreword by Arundhati Roy, Annotated by S. Anand. Delhi: Navayana.
A searing critique of caste society, both a political document and an insightful sociological analysis.
Berreman, Gerald (2009). 'Caste and Race: Reservations and Affirmations.' In *Against Stigma: Studies in Caste, Race, and Justice Since Durban* (pp. 47–77). Eds. Balmurli Natrajan and Paul R. Greenough. New Delhi: Orient BlackSwan.
An anthropologist draws on extensive fieldwork in India and his experiences living in Alabama to reflect on similarities between caste and race.
Hamermesh, Mira, Director, Writer, and Producer (1990). *Caste at Birth*.
A documentary film that powerfully reveals the reality of caste, even in urban settings.
Rege, Sharmila (2013). *Against the Madness of Manu: B.R. Ambedkar's Writings on Brahmanical Patriarchy*. New Delhi: Navayana.
A wonderful collection of writings by Ambedkar linking caste and gender discrimination.
Sharma, U. (1999). *Caste*. Buckingham, UK; Open University Press.
An excellent introduction to caste.

Bibliography

Aloysius, G. (1998). *Religion as Emancipatory Identity: A Buddhist Movement among the Tamils under Colonialism*. Bangalore: Institute for the Study of Religion and Society.
Ambedkar, B. R. (1945). *What Congress and Gandhi Have Done to the Untouchables*. http://www.ambedkar.org/ambcd/41A.What Congress and Gandhi Preface.htm
——— (2014). *Annihilation of Caste*. Foreword by Arundhati Roy, Annotated by S. Anand. Delhi: Navayana.
——— (n.d.). *Riddles in Hinduism*. http://www.ambedkar.org/riddleinhinduism/21A1.Riddles%20in%20Hinduism%20PART%20I.htm
Amnesty International (2001). *India: The Battle against Fear and Discrimination: The Impact of Violence against Women in Uttar Pradesh and Rajasthan* http://www.amnesty.

org/en/library/asset/ASA20/016/2001/en/c23e3527-db7b-11dd-af3c-1fd4bb8cf58e/asa200162001en.html

Ayyathurai, G. (2011). 'Foundations of Anti-Caste Consciousness: Pandit Iyothee Thass, Tamil Buddhism, and the Marginalized in South India.' PhD Dissertation. Columbia University.

Barrier, N. Gerald, ed. (1981). *The Census in British India*. New Delhi: Manohar.

Beltz, Johannes (2005). *Mahar, Buddhist, and Dalit: Religious Conversion and Socio-political Emancipation*. Delhi: Manohar.

Berreman, Gerald D. (1971). 'The Brahmanical View of Caste.' *Contributions to Indian Sociology* 5: 16–23.

Béteille, Andre (2001). 'Race and Caste.' *The Hindu*. March 10. http://www.thehindu.com/2001/03/10/stories/05102523.htm

Buehler, G. (1886). *The Laws of Manu*. Oxford: Clarendon Press.

Clark-Dèces, I. (2005). *No One Cries for the Dead: Tamil Dirges, Rowdy Songs, and Graveyard Petitions*. Berkeley: University of California Press.

Cohn, B. S. (1990). 'The Census, Social Structure and Objectification in South Asia.' In *An Anthropologist among the Historians and Other Essays* (224–254). Ed. B. S. Cohn. Delhi: Oxford University Press.

Deliège, R. (1992). 'Replication and Consensus: Untouchability, Caste and Ideology in India.' *Man* 27, No. 1: 155–173.

Dirks, Nicholas (2001). *Castes of Mind: Colonialism and the Making of Modern India*. Princeton: Princeton University Press.

Dumont, Louis (1980) [1966]. *Homo Hierarchicus: The Caste System and its Implications*. Chicago: University of Chicago Press.

Fox, Richard G. (1969). 'Varna Schemes and Ideological Integration in Indian Society.' *Comparative Studies in History and Society* 11, No. 1: 27–45.

Frykenberg R. E. (1997). 'The Emergence of Modern "Hinduism" As a Concept and As an Institution: A Reappraisal with Special Reference to South India.' In *Hinduism Reconsidered* (pp. 82–107). Eds. G. Sontheimer & H. Kulke. New Delhi: Manohar.

Galanter, M. (1971). 'Hinduism, Secularism, and the Indian Judiciary.' *Philosophy East and West* 21, No. 4: 467–487.

——— (1984). *Competing Equalities: Law and the Backward Classes in India*. Delhi: Oxford University Press, 1984.

Grafe, Hugald (1990). *History of Christianity in India, Vol 4, pt. 2: Tamilnadu in the Nineteenth and Twentieth Centuries*. Bangalore: Church History Association of India.

Griffith, R.T.H. (1896). *Hymns of the Rgveda*. Benares: Lazarus.

Gupta, Dipankar (2001). 'Caste, Race, Politics.' *Seminar* 508. December. http://www.india-seminar.com/2001/508/508%20dipankar%20gupta.htm

Hardgrave, R. (1969). *The Nadars of Tamilnadu*. Berkeley: University of California Press.

Ilaiah, K. (1996). *Why I Am Not a Hindu: A Sudra Critique of Hindutva Philosophy, Culture and Political Economy*. Calcutta: Samya.

Jaffrelot, C. (2005). *Dr. Ambedkar and Untouchability: Analysing and Fighting Caste*. London: Hurst.

Juergensmeyer, M. (1982). *Religion as Social Vision: The Movement against Untouchability in 20th-Century Punjab*. Berkeley: University of California Press.

Khan, Mumtaz Ali (1983). *Mass-Conversions of Meenakshipuram: A Sociological Enquiry*. Madras: Christian Literature Society.

Kolenda, Pauline (1964). 'Religious Anxiety and Hindu Fate.' *Journal of Asian Studies* 23: 71–82.

Lamb, R. (2002). *Rapt in the Name: Ramnamis, Ramnam and Untouchable Religion in Central India.* Albany: State University of New York.

Lynch, O. (1969). *The Politics of Untouchability: Social Mobility and Social Change in a City of India.* New York: Columbia University Press.

————— (1977). 'Method and Theory in the Sociology of Louis Dumont.' In *The New Wind: Changing Identities in South Asia* (pp. 239–262). Ed. Kenneth David. The Hague: De Gruyter.

Mencher, J. (1974). 'The Caste System Upside down, or the Not So Mysterious East.' *Cultural Anthropology* 15, No. 4: 469–493.

Mendelsohn, Oliver and Marika Vicziany (1998). *The Untouchables: Subordination, Poverty and the State in Modern India.* Cambridge: Cambridge University Press.

Mines, D. (2005). *Fierce Gods: Inequality, Ritual, and the Politics of Dignity in a South Indian Village.* Bloomington: University of Indiana Press.

Moffatt, M. (1979). *An Untouchable Community in South India: Structure and Consensus.* Princeton: Princeton University Press.

Mosse, D. (1994). 'Replication and Consensus among Indian Untouchable (Harijan) Castes.' *Man* 9, No. 2: 457–461.

————— (2012). *The Saint in the Banyan Tree: Christianity and Caste Society in India.* Berkeley: University of California Press.

Narula, S. (1999). *Broken People: Caste Violence against India's 'Untouchables.'* New York: Human Rights Watch.

Rao, A., ed. (2003). *Gender and Caste.* New Delhi: Kali for Women.

————— (2009). *The Caste Question: Dalits and the Politics of Modern India.* Berkeley: University of California Press.

Rege, S., J. Devika, K. Kannabiran, M. John, P. Swaminathan, and S. Sen (2013). 'Intersections of Gender and Caste.' *Review of Women's Studies. Economic and Political Weekly* 48, No. 18 (May 04): 35–97.

Report of the National Commission for Religious and Linguistic Minorities (2007). New Delhi: Ministry of Minority Affairs. http://www.minorityaffairs.gov.in/sites/upload_files/moma/files/pdfs/volume-1.pdf

Roberts, N. (2008). 'Caste, Anthropology of.' In *International Encyclopedia of the Social Sciences* (pp. 461–463). Ed. W. Darity. New York: Gage Cengale.

Searle-Chatterjee, M. (2008). 'Attributing and Rejecting the Label 'Hindu' in North India.' In *Religion, Language and Power* (pp. 186–201). Eds. N. Green and M. Searle-Chatterjee. New York: Routledge.

Sharma, U. (1999). *Caste.* Buckingham, U.K.: Open University Press.

Singer, M. and B. S. Cohn, eds. (1968). *Structure and Change in Indian Society.* Chicago: Aldine.

Srinivas, M. N. (1956). 'A Note on Sanskritization and Westernization.' *The Far Eastern Quarterly* 15, No. 4: 481–496.

————— (1959). 'The Dominant Caste in Rampura.' *American Anthropologist* 61, No. 1: 1–16.

Teltumbde, Anand (2010). *The Persistance of Caste: The Khairlanji Murders and India's Hidden Apartheid.* Delhi: Navayana.

Vincentnathan, L. (1993). 'Untouchable Concepts of Person and Society.' *Contributions to Indian Sociology* n.s. 3, No. 1: 53–82.

Viswanath, R. (2012a). 'A Textbook Case of Exclusion.' *Indian Express*. 13 July. http://archive.indianexpress.com/news/a-textbook-case-of-exclusion/973711/

—— (2012b). 'Dalits/ Ex-Untouchables.' In *Brill Encyclopedia of Hinduism* (Vol. 4, pp. 779–787). Ed. Knut Jakobsen. Leiden: Brill.

—— (2014). *The Pariah Problem: Caste, Religion and the Social in Modern India*. New York: Columbia University Press.

Weber, Max (1964) [1922]. *The Sociology of Religion*. Trans. Ephraim Fischoff. Boston: Beacon Press.

Webster, J.C.B. (1992). *The Dalit Christians: A History*. Delhi: ISPCK.

Zaehner, R.C., trans. (1966). *Hindu Scriptures*. London: J.M. Dent, 1966.

Zelliot, E. (1992). *From Untouchable to Dalit: Essays on the Ambedkar Movement*. New Delhi: Manohar.

17 Gender and Sexuality

Ruth Vanita

It is often remarked that whatever one says about India, the opposite is also true. Indicating the accretive and mobile quality of the traditions that have come to be called Hindu and that form the substratum of Indic cultures, this maxim is even more valid in India today, when an average Hindu's hand is as inseparable from a mobile phone as from a puja thread round the wrist, and when he or she eats white bread and toffees from the corner store as habitually as roti or rice cooked at home.

Continuing Debates

Contradictory attitudes to gender and sexuality coexist in every religious text and tradition; they are particularly common, however, in Hinduism since adherents acknowledge the sanctity of not just one but hundreds of texts, teachers, and deities, while new ones are constantly coming into being. On the one hand, women's subservience is often justified by referring to devoted wives in scriptural narrative; on the other, vigorous debates around these same heroines have continued over centuries, for example, the question of epic hero Rama's injustice to his wife has been reworked through numerous written and oral retellings in many languages (Kishwar 2001; Gokhale & Lal 2010), for example, the fourteenth-century *Adbhut Ramayana* where she outdoes him in martial exploits (Vanita 2005b).

The question of whether gender should restrict women to certain spheres has also been debated among Hindus for centuries. The more recent phases of this debate occurred, first, during nineteenth-century Hindu social reform movements and the Gandhi-led nationalist movement, which focused on women's education, the status of widows and girl children, and freedom of choice in marriage and employment. The second phase was in women's movements from the 1970s onwards, which added emphases on violence against women and, somewhat later, sexual freedom (Chaudhuri 2005). Most political parties today claim to espouse equality and all have active women's wings. Hindu right-wing parties' rhetoric contradictorily endorses separate spheres based on gender while also espousing women's empowerment in the public sphere (see Hancock 1995).

With some exceptions (such as the controversy around the 1998 film *Fire*), Hindu and Muslim right-wing parties, secular left parties, and many women's organizations have tended to favor the censorship of sexual expression considered Westernized or obscene, such as beauty contests or explicit films and songs (Ghosh 1999). The nonparty left, especially women's and LGBT groups, have made changes in the last decade, arguing for the right to self-expression and choice, for example, in the case of the bar dancers of Mumbai whose rights have lately been upheld by the Supreme Court.

In the same period, extremist right-wing Hindu organizations in north India have taken to campaigning against Valentine's Day, violently attacking stores and restaurants that offer special deals, and beating up dating couples. Despite this, however, the celebrations continue. The celebrants are arguably more in tune with Hindu traditions than are the denunciants, because fourth-century texts represent the public celebration of Madanotsava, the spring festival of the God of Love. The festival of Holi, when people drench one another in colored water, imbibe intoxicants, and engage in erotic play, is a remnant of that tradition: Krishna and his milkmaids are supposed to have engaged in Holi revelries, several Hindu and Muslim kings played Holi with their queens and subjects, and some Sufi mystics met their male beloveds during Holi festivities (Vanita and Kidwai 2000: 137, 147).

An early example of the gender debate occurs in the epic Mahabharata, composed circa 200 BC. Sulabha, a woman ascetic, challenged by famous philosopher-king Janaka on the propriety of her appearing unescorted at his court and engaging in a philosophical debate with him, argues on the basis of Hindu doctrine that the body is constantly in flux and takes many forms while the spirit is not gendered so there is no difference between a man's and a woman's spirit and no reason why two spirits should not meet or fuse in debate (Vanita 2003). Modern media, from print to television, has allowed such debates to reach much wider populations than before.

Because of the nationalist movement's emphasis on gender equality, Indian mass media has tended to be very supportive of feminism and LGBT issues. From the 1990s onward, the movement's own publications, like *Bombay Dost*, the first LGBT magazine, founded in 1990, and pioneering books like *Same-Sex Love in India* have been supplemented by mainstream media's efforts. Television talk shows frequently focus on LGBT issues, and soap operas are coming up with remarkable story lines, featuring disapproved sexual relations, including adultery and homosexuality. For example, a 2010 Hindi serial set in Haryana, *Maryada Lekin Kab Tak?* (*How Long to Preserve Honor?*), had a sympathetic portrayal of a nonstereotypical gay male couple who gradually come out to their families. Lesbian couples' marriages and suicides were sympathetically reported in the press since 1980, a while before the movement came to the aid of these couples.

In the last decade, the internet, now available on ubiquitous cell phones, has made it possible for LGBT people from rural areas and small towns to contact one another. Fewer and fewer young people grow up feeling that they are the only ones with unusual desires. The LGBT movement has great visibility in the media, and increasingly in the academy as well. In the last decade, I have spoken on my research not just at elite colleges like Miranda House where I studied and taught for years (homosexuality was never mentioned in class when I was a student) but at Hindi-medium colleges in remote areas, and have been impressed by students' volubility. Several feminist NGOs now conduct sexuality studies workshops both for rural women and for activists and academics.

Paradoxically, the legacy of Nehruvian secularism has ensured that it is hard to come out as a Hindu in left-wing, LGBT, and feminist circles. Any positive take on Hindu practice tends to be simplistically equated with right-wing Hinduism. Beyond these circles, though, a quieter and older, Gandhi-type secularism continues to thrive in the lives of religious practitioners along with unobtrusive steps towards sexual freedoms. A few thinkers are beginning to discuss the positive connections between religion, gender, and sexuality (Mani 2009, 2011, 2013).

Violence and Religion?

When I worked at the prominent journal *Manushi*, visitors from the West frequently asked whether violence against women was caused by Hinduism or Islam. They did not, however, in the same fashion ascribe wife-beating, wife-murder, or rape in the West to Christianity. My response to such questions has been framed by my conviction that violence against women is caused not by religion but by women's powerlessness, which is compounded of many elements, such as economic dependence, virilocality (shifting to the husband's home), lack of family support, lack of access to housing and physical mobility, unsafe conditions, and fear internalized over time as a result of these factors.

Gender discrimination is prevalent worldwide and may or may not be religiously grounded. In India, the laws are relatively egalitarian but are hard to implement because of cumbersome procedures and corrupt enforcers. Outsiders often mistake local cultural practices as religiously mandated; for example, in some Hindu communities, women are denied higher education and are expected to do all the housework, obey elders, and veil themselves in the presence of men. However, these are cultural rather than religious practices, and practitioners are aware that other Hindus do things differently and that any attempt to claim religious sanction for such rules would be futile. Thus, when justifying their own practices, they appeal not to Hinduism but to local custom, saying something like, '*Hamare mein aise hota hai*' ('This is how it is done among us'—that is, in their village or region).[1]

In India, the family is the most important support system on which people fall back in times of crisis. Family support is the crucial factor that enables women (and men) to achieve success and power. Thus wives who resist abuse usually do so with the backing of natal families; victims who came to *Manushi* for help almost always were accompanied by parents or brothers.

Goddesses and Kinship

Goddesses render Hindu religious culture distinctly different from others (Hawley and Wulff 1996). Goddesses are alive, healthy, and proliferating—from the Vedic river-goddess Saraswati reformulated in late antiquity into the presiding deity of education and the arts, to the twentieth-century Santoshi Ma (Mother of Contentment), a creation largely of Hindi cinema, whom millions of worshipers propitiate with fasts (Pintchman and Sherma 2011). Modern media has had the effect of turning local, religious practices into national and even international ones, for example, over the last fifty years, the pilgrimage to goddess Vaishno Devi's mountain shrine in Jammu has grown exponentially, necessitating the widening of the roads and the entrance to her cave temple (Singh 2010).

Whether goddess worship positively influences ordinary Hindus' attitudes to women is a matter of debate among feminists. I would argue that in what may be termed 'the goddess effect,' even those Indian men who oppress women in their families are usually respectful to a woman boss, employer, or political leader and are relatively more accepting of women in positions of power than men in many other societies. Witness the large number of Indian women politicians from widely varying caste, class, and familial backgrounds, married, single, and widowed, all often addressed as mother or sister, and iconized as goddess figures. India has a long tradition of Hindu queens (and even the occasional Muslim queen, disallowed in Muslim-majority countries), and in modern times, has had a female prime minister, a female president, and many women chief ministers of major states. The current head of the ruling Congress party is an Italian woman who is a naturalized Indian citizen.

Nor has the sexuality of these women stood in their way. At least two women chief ministers are known to have had long affairs with now-deceased male leaders of their parties, and the connection is important to their popularity. India has had a never-married man as well as a widow as prime minister. The unmarried woman chief minister of Tamil Nadu has an inseparable 'life-friend,' a married woman who lived with her and performed with her many Hindu rituals and ceremonies normally performed only by married couples (Vanita 2005a: 115–118). This tradition of women in power is comparable to the European acceptance of women rulers, which is not unrelated to centuries of worship of Mary and the female saints.

The goddess effect is also related to the Hindu tendency to respect older women more than younger ones. In south India, the term '*amma*,' meaning 'mother,' is attached as an honorific or affectionate suffix to the names of all females, including little girls. As a woman grows older, she gains status, especially if she has children or if she acts in a motherly way to those around her. The same is true of men too, but symbolic fatherhood does not carry the same charge as symbolic motherhood. One of the most famous speeches in Hindi cinema occurs when a rich but corrupt man tauntingly asks his virtuous, poor brother what he has that can match the rich brother's car, house, and money.

The poor brother, with whom their mother lives, replies, '*Mere paas maa hai*' ('I have mother'). This oft-quoted line never fails to bring the house down, indicating as it does Hindu ideas of the ultimate wealth—a close relationship with one's mother, representing virtue, love, and dharma or the normative life.

Indians traditionally address everyone, even strangers, in kinship terms—older people as grandparents, uncles, or aunts, and younger people as brothers or sisters. Hindus institutionalize several kinship relations through ritual. For example, on the north Indian festival of *rakhi*, women tie sacred threads on the wrists of their brothers and feed them sweets; the brothers in turn give them gifts. This symbolizes the brother's duty to protect the sister; if her husband turns violent, the brother must provide her with a home. This symbolism changes with the times. A famous legend tells of a Hindu queen who averted war by sending a *rakhi* thread to a Muslim king who thenceforth considered her his sister and consequently could not fight her husband. Today, when many women are employed and may be earning more than their brothers, the gift-giving is often mutual. Also, the category of brother includes cousins as well as friends whom a woman chooses to consider her brothers (Vanita 2013).

Some of these ritualized relationships are based on assumptions of inequity, for example, fasts kept by women for their husbands' or sons' longevity (Pintchman 2007). One such fast, *karva chauth*, which used to be regional, has rapidly spread, partly through cinematic exposure, to wider swathes of the country. On this day, wives eat before dawn and then fast until they see the moon, after which they feast. They do no work all day; instead, they dress in their best finery and celebrate in groups. Both in life and in cinema, people have recently been redefining this fast, some men keeping it along with their wives. Recently, a lesbian activist couple living in Kolkata kept the fast and posted pictures of their celebration on Facebook. They faced a storm of criticism from other lesbians for supposedly aping heterosexual norms, while a few lauded them for appropriating the festival.

Divinity, Gender, and Sex

The visual presence of gods and goddesses is important for the ways it influences ideas of gender and sexuality. Hindu gods are sexual beings, and their gender and sexuality are colorful and flexible. Consider, as one example among many, Kartikeya or Murugan, a popular south Indian god, son of Shiva. He has no biological mother since he sprang from Shiva's semen, which, in various versions of the story, was swallowed by the god of fire Agni and then cast into the river Ganga or into river reeds (Vanita and Kidwai 2000: 77–80). Icons of this god are a study in diversity. He may be a beautiful bachelor, armed, enthroned on a peacock, and leader of an all-male army, or a lover of many females (see Image 17.1). He is also a cute son, in cozy domestic scenes with Shiva, his wife Parvati, and her biological son Ganesh. In modern pictures, stickers, and magnets, he appears as a meditating, smiling child, with shoulder-length hair, holy beads round his neck, and a *tilak* on his forehead. In this last representation, he appears girl-like to uninitiated viewers.

This androgynous appearance is not unique to him. The gods are almost always young and smooth-skinned, without facial hair (while demons sport large moustaches), bedecked in colorful clothing and jewelry, smiling,

Figure 17.1 Murugan

large-eyed, and curly-haired. To the uninitiated eye, they are hard to distinguish from goddesses. Radha and Krishna, and Shiva and Parvati often look very much like one another. Nor is this likeness accidental. It has theological foundations since all things and all categories are, in Hindu ontology, manifestations of spirit.

Each deity is both male and female and ultimately neither male nor female; likewise, gods are not always represented as human-like but may take the forms of animals, plants, rivers, and mountains. In the Gita, Krishna is praised as the best in each category of being, from mountains to snakes to planets to trees to sages. This is true of every deity. A typical eulogy in the Mahabharata identifies Shiva with a series of apparently exclusive attributes: 'Thou art male, thou art female, thou art neuter.' (Ganguly 1998: I. IX: 326). This foundational premise is expressed in Shiva's *ardhanarishwara* (half-female) form, the right side of which is male and the left female.

While acknowledging all the gods and goddesses, individual Hindus generally choose one for special worship. In this *ishta devata* (chosen deity), the worshiper sees all possibilities; thus, for example, goddess hymns identify her as creator, preserver and destroyer, father and mother, beginning, middle, and end of the universe.

Hindus also tend to see the divine as immanent in everything in the universe, and most Indian languages gender all things. From the Vedas onwards, rivers and the earth tend to be gendered female, while mountains may be either male or female. The earth is a mother goddess, hence many nationalists envisioned India as a motherland and a goddess (Bharat Mata) rather than, say, the fatherland celebrated in the Soviet Union. Some Muslim and Communist leaders objected to this characterization as it conflicted with their beliefs.

Alternatives to Marriage

If goddesses are ubiquitous, so are female gurus (Pechilis 2004). There are great women gurus who have millions of followers worldwide, like the late Anandamayi Ma and the Mother of Sri Aurobindo's ashram or Gurumayi and Mata Amritanandamayi. Equally important are numerous unknown *sannyasinis* or female ascetics who are locally venerated. For example, in Landour, Mussoorie, where I spent a month in 2013, a cheerful and sprightly eighty-five year old named Swamini Gurupriya, clad in an orange synthetic sari, fluent in English, Hindi, Gujarati, and Sanskrit, lives alone in a little room filled with books and pictures of Sri Ramakrishna and Swami Vivekananda, to whose lineage she belongs. She is seen climbing mountains at all hours; locals address her as Mataji (mother) and consider her highly knowledgeable. Our widowed landlady introduced her to us, and she gave free daily yoga lessons to my partner and son. Such women act as alternative role models for young women. They are living embodiments of renunciation, the age-old Hindu safety valve for men and women from all castes and classes who do not wish to marry, reproduce, or pursue a profession.

Following the nineteenth-century Hindu reform movements and Mahatma Gandhi's celebration of singleness and childlessness, which itself drew on the lives of medieval women mystics who refused marriage, a secular version of the ancient guru ideal emerged in modern India in the form of women teachers and social workers. This new type of woman significantly modified the conventional Hindu idea that all respectable women apart from ascetics must be married. Up to the 1970s, most educational institutions had numerous single women teachers. Many of my teachers in school and college were single women. At colleges like Miranda House, singleness was by no means a dour or empty existence. As early as the 1950s, women professors drove their own cars, pursued research, traveled in the country and abroad, went on hikes, and attended concerts in groups. Some single women lived in pairs and were treated as couples. Others maintained long-term relationships with men; this last would have been more difficult in a smaller town.

Although young Indians, especially women, who refuse marriage often face great opposition, even persecution, by their families, wider society often views singleness as impelled by devotion to the greater good. Thus, when Madhu Kishwar and I lived and worked together for over a decade on *Manushi*, the women's magazine and organization we founded in 1978, neighbors in Lajpat Nagar, our lower-middle-class area of Delhi, respectfully referred to us as having eschewed marriage for community welfare. On *Kanya Puja*, the festival when the goddess is worshiped in the form of young girls, they sent us the special food they prepared, because as unmarried women, we were perceived as virgins despite our openly interacting with large numbers of men and women.

Another type of alternative role for women, that of the courtesan, which was built into urban life for at least two millennia, has been erased over the last century (Soneji 2012). The courtesan or *nagarvadhu* (bride of the city), connected to both court and temple, appears as a powerful and auspicious figure in ancient Hindu narrative and drama. Up to the nineteenth century, both Hindu and Muslim courtesans living in women-dominated households wielded considerable economic, political, and cultural power in cities. These women developed and transmitted traditions of classical music, dance, and poetry; they customarily entered into long-term liaisons with one man at a time, and their closest relationships were often with other women (Vanita 2012).

Beginning in the colonial era and especially after 1857, social reformers and nationalists, influenced by Western mores, grew ashamed of sexual arrangements that did not conform to the modern Western ideal of heterosexual monogamy. Courtesans were equated with prostitutes, condemned as immoral and outlawed. Dance and song were gradually taken over by middle-class women living in patrilineal households. A woman-centered way of life disappeared with courtesans.

Sexual Expression

Modern Hindus have a somewhat fraught relationship to ideas of sexual pleasure. On the one hand, a long-standing understanding of sex as play—the play (*leela*) of the gods—reflected as aesthetic and pleasurable enjoyment (*rasa*) among humans, persists, as expressed, for example, in film songs and dances. On the other hand, there is considerable embarrassment regarding talking about sex, though this of late has been eroded in the media. Many Indian couples, including married couples, do not touch in front of others. But many Hindus habitually engage in sexual activities they will not speak about; at the risk of generalization, Hindu cultures tend to be shame rather than guilt-oriented. Today shame or embarrassment can be seen as a fall-out from the late colonial, nationalist era, when the open expression of varied sexualities was labeled licentious and oppressive to women. Indian masculinities that did not conform to the Victorian norm were derided, a process first explored by Ashis Nandy (1989).[2]

Another example of change in attitudes spawned by colonial rule can be seen in attitudes to nudity. British missionaries were shocked when they found Hindu and tribal women in parts of India, especially the south, going topless like men, a practice suitable for the extreme heat. British missionaries and educationists made the blouse a universal garment in India. Today, ironically, Indians are often scandalized when Western tourists wear shorts, skirts, or bikinis.

Kama or desire is one of the four aims of human life recognized in Hindu scriptures. Kama is also the name of the ancient Hindu god of desire, a handsome youth who makes people fall in love by shooting flowery arrows at them. But Kama is no longer widely worshiped today. Other gods, such as Krishna, have absorbed his characteristics. Krishna, known as Madanmohan (enchanter of Kama), is the mischievous lover of numerous milkmaids, many of whom are married, and is generally worshiped not with a wife but with Radha, his beloved who was married to another man. The mystical explanation is that such extramarital love symbolizes selflessness since it involves social disrepute and separation rather than the domestic comforts. Nevertheless, the polyamorous Krishna both complements and counterbalances the monogamous Rama.

Groups that today might be classified as gender or sexual minorities develop patterns of worship that legitimize their existence, for example, *hijras* (transgendered men) who identify as female and live in highly organized communities, worship their own goddess Bahuchara, and celebrate annual festivals around the story of Krishna's marriage to Aravan, a hero destined to die in an epic battle. To enable Aravan to experience sex, Krishna took the female form of Mohini and married him for one day. Identifying both with Krishna and with Aravan, the *hijras*, who term themselves *aravanis*, celebrate the wedding by adorning themselves as brides and then mourn Aravan's death the next day like traditional widows.[3]

Weddings are traditionally occasions when sex is freely spoken about in ribald songs, jokes, and mimes, often separately among women and among men. On the other hand, weddings are also occasions of mourning, when a girl is separated from her family and friends, and is carried away to a strange family. This is particularly true in north India, where marriages tend not to be arranged within the same village. Among some south Indian Hindu communities, conversely, marriages between cross-cousins or between maternal uncle and niece are allowed. Hindu marriage law recognizes the diversity of custom with regard to permissible marriages.[4]

Hindu laws of marriage and inheritance vary widely, based on local custom. Hindu law books decree that custom always takes precedence over written statutes; the British rulers also recognized this principle. After independence in 1947, the central government in the 1950s attempted to reform Hindu law by passing uniform statutes for the whole country. Intended to institutionalize gender justice, these laws often eradicated more egalitarian practices in favor of uniformity, for example, matrilineal inheritance systems prevalent among some Hindu communities were replaced by a nationwide patrilineal system. While Indian Muslim men can legally marry up to four wives, monogamy was imposed on Hindu men. This was intended to remove sexual double standards; in practice, however, the small number of Hindu men who married more than one wife continued to do so, with the difference that the second wife and her children now have no legal rights or status. Polygamy was outlawed, but so was polyandry, practiced in a few regions.

Today, the law incorporates the diversity of Hindu marriage practices by recognizing as legal any form of marriage that is customary in either partner's community. No obtaining of license or registration with the government is necessary. Many women's organizations want to make marriage registration compulsory, which will impose more uniformity and outlaw certain types of marriages, including same-sex marriages, which now take place with community consent but without government recognition.

Most Hindus ignore state laws and live by community custom. This has both positive and negative effects for gendered practices. For example, dowry was outlawed in 1961 but continues to be almost universally practiced. Dowry has often been incorrectly identified as the cause of wife-murder, whereas in fact the root cause is women's powerlessness in virilocal family structures (Oldenburg 2002); it also, however, functions as women's only inheritance in families where sons alone inherit their parents' assets and are responsible for the care of aged parents.

Likewise, the modern emphasis on uniformity, whether institutionalized in law and state-sponsored education, or spread by mass media, has mixed effects. On the one hand, it has resulted in wider acceptability of women's education and remarriage of divorcees and widows. On the other hand, the son-preference that was much stronger in parts of north India than in southern and western India has been spreading all over the country for the last century, as evidenced by the steadily declining sex ratio. (In certain pockets, the scarcity of women has given rise to innovations, such as Hindu men in Haryana villages importing brides from Kerala. This leads to hybridity not only in food and language but also in gender roles, as Kerala women are used to greater freedom than is normally available to young women in Haryana; for example, it is considered inauspicious in south India for women to cover their heads while many north Indian Hindu women are required to veil themselves before elders and unrelated men.)

Love, Marriage, and Rebirth

Marriage practices among Hindus constantly change with changing conditions. Hindu scriptures recognize eight types of marriage, including *gandharva vivaha*, wherein partners choose each other and marry without witnesses, officiant, or parental permission. This type of marriage, termed 'love-marriage' in Indian English, is celebrated in cinema, and has led to the evolution of what may be called 'arranged love.' It is now common for Hindu parents to introduce young people and have them converse in the presence of chaperons. After they consent, an engagement takes place and some may go out on supervised dates. Such couples often fall in love in conformity with patterns absorbed from literature and cinema, talking and messaging every day on cell phones and exchanging Valentine's Day and birthday cards even if they have never met.

Conversely, when young people find their own partners, parents who may initially disapprove often come around and go through all the procedures of arranging the marriage, thus turning the 'love-marriage' into the simulacrum of an arranged one. This has happened for some same-sex couples too (Vanita 2005a: 64–65, 130). The opposite, however, also happens, when families persecute young couples, forcing them to separate and to marry others judged more suitable, or even kill them or drive them to suicide. Joint suicides by young lovers, both cross-sex and same-sex, occur in all communities, but among Hindus, it is often accompanied by the dying wish to be reunited in the next birth (Vanita 2005a).

The doctrine of rebirth, specific to Hinduism and the three religions that arose from it, Buddhism, Jainism, and Sikhism, is perhaps the single most important feature distinguishing Indic religious ideas of gender and sexuality from those prevalent in the Abrahamic religions. The spirit (*atman*), whether conceived of by Hindu dualists as an eternal individual in relation to God or by non-dualists as a temporary manifestation of universal spirit (*paramatman*), has no inherent characteristics. Caste, class, gender, abilities, and temperament are all transient features that change from birth to birth. Thus gender in the ultimate analysis is unreal. If the body, as Krishna says in the *BhagavadGita*, is like clothing that the spirit assumes at birth and discards at death, then gender, since it pertains to the body, is inessential to the self.

On the other hand, what does persist from one lifetime to the next is attachment. Unfulfilled desires and attachments impel the spirit to be reborn. Therefore those who seek liberation try either to fulfill their desires and move beyond them or to empty themselves of desire. At the everyday level, Hindus tend to explain inexplicable attachments of all kinds (from preferences for certain foods or activities to falling in love at first sight to irrational likes or dislikes) as traces of attachment from a former birth. So universal is this idea that Indians who are not Hindu also semiplayfully refer to former births as the reason for mysterious privileges or predilections.

These two dimensions of rebirth—the nonpersistence of categories like gender, and the persistence of attachment—are often invoked together to legitimize socially disapproved behaviors and relationships. Stories in ancient Hindu texts explain and justify cross-caste and cross-class love as well as sex-change as stemming from attachment in a former birth. Several modern Hindu priests and teachers explain same-sex love in this way, and also justify on this basis their officiating at same-sex weddings (Vanita 2005a).

Struggling against strong attachments is perceived as futile. The dharma of the individual, that is, the law of his or her being, requires the working through of attachments from former births, not their repression. When this individual dharma comes into conflict with social dharma, for example, when an individual desires to marry someone perceived by the family and community as unsuitable, the resulting impasse is hard to resolve. But many preceptors would advise against forcing the individual to abandon his or her deepest predilections; for example, pioneering gay activist Ashok Rowkavi, who joined the Ramakrishna Mission, was advised by senior monks not to choose celibacy as a way of escaping his sexual inclinations but rather to embrace the latter and work through them.

Hindu marriage is a sacrament, not a contract, so if the spirit is genderless, there is no reason why the body's gender should override the spirit's inclinations. Numerous medieval male mystics, whose songs are widely sung today, figured themselves as the brides of a male god. Some devotees known as Radhapyaris even live their entire lives as women, identifying with the girlfriends of Krishna's beloved, Radha.

The well-known epic story of Sikhandin is another fruitful narrative for transgendered people and same-sex relations. In this story, princess Amba wishes to revenge herself on an invincible hero named Bhishma who she thinks prevented her from marrying. She dies possessed by the desire for revenge, which impels her birth as the daughter of a king who is an enemy of Bhishma. The king raises princess Sikhandini as a boy named Sikhandin and marries her to another girl. When the bride discovers that the groom is a woman, she complains to her father and a war seems imminent. A forest-spirit takes pity on Sikhandini and agrees to temporarily exchange his gender with hers. However, when the god in charge of the forest-spirit discovers the exchange, he makes it permanent. Although Sikhandin is now a biological male, Bhishma refuses to fight him, saying he will never fight one who was once a woman. Therefore, Sikhandin is able to kill him. The word *sikhandin*, literally, a crested peacock, is now used to refer to a *hijra*, a transgendered man or a womanly man. There are many such stories of sex-change, both temporary and permanent, in the Hindu scriptures, which suggest that gender is fluid rather than fixed (Vanita and Kidwai 2000).

Hindu approaches to gender and sexuality continue to evolve, assimilating outside influences, especially in today's context of Hindu migration to all parts of the world and the phenomenon of non-Indians becoming Hindus. Hinduism's diversity has always been its great strength, and it is to be hoped that this can be retained in the face of greater pressures towards uniformity.

Summary

Hindus have diverse and constantly changing approaches to gender and sexuality. Some distinctive features that provide continuity are the range of gods and goddesses who are complexly gendered beings, the presence of many female gurus, the notion that all things are manifestations of spirit, which is itself ultimately beyond gender, and the doctrine of rebirth whereby beings may change their gender from one lifetime to the next but do not change their attachments until these are worked through. While the colonial and nationalist eras fostered puritanical uniformity in sexual attitudes and a mistrust of pleasure, modernity also introduced new types of discourse, such as the mass media, which allow centuries-old debates about gender and sexuality to reach more people.

Discussion Questions

- Do you think the female visual presence in the form of goddesses, saints, or angels is likely to make a difference to popular perceptions of real-life women's capabilities?
- In what kinds of ways might the idea of rebirth influence our feelings about our own gender and sexuality and that of others?
- Do you think religious practices and rituals that are inequitable with regard to gender should be abandoned, appropriated, and refashioned, or dealt with in some other way?

Notes

1   Hindu sanction has been claimed for a few types of violence, most notably Sati or the burning of widows on their husbands' pyres. As Lata Mani demonstrates, this practice, long outlawed, was always restricted to certain regions and practiced selectively when families wished to rid themselves of widows, generally for economic, not religious, reasons (Mani 1998).

2   Urban men's abandonment of traditional colorful clothing, cosmetics, and jewelry is a consequence of this, as is the antisodomy law imported by British rulers in 1861. Although the British have long since overturned this law in their own country, in India, it was overturned only a few years ago by the Delhi High Court ruling on a petition filed by LGBT activists, and now awaits a decision by the Supreme Court (Narrain 2011).

3   *Hijras* have been much studied lately (see Reddy 2005). They are almost all from economically poorer backgrounds, and they engage in a mix of Hindu and Muslim practices. Homosexually inclined men also gravitate towards these communities (Revathi 2010). Some *hijras* undergo ritual castration or, these days, take hormones and have sex-change surgery; others do not. All, however, identify as female, taking women's names, wearing women's clothing, and sometimes having

sex with men. Yet they generally do not seek to pass as women. Living in distinct communities, they are easily identifiable as *hijras*, not women. Many Hindus think *hijras* have special powers. *Hijras* sing and dance on ceremonial occasions, and their blessings are considered auspicious for newlyweds and newborns, while their curses are feared.

4   Hindu weddings vary widely from elaborate ceremonies that stretch over five days to simple mutual garlanding before witnesses. Most Hindu weddings involve walking around the fire as witness, exchanging garlands and vows, feeding one another, playing games, singing songs, and a feast. Same-sex weddings vary similarly. A number of female runaway couples have been married by priests in temples. Some weddings have been hosted by parents at home in the traditional fashion. Some couples devise their own hybrid ceremonies and ask friends to officiate.

Suggested Readings

Falk, Nancy Auer (2006). *Living Hinduisms: An Explorer's Guide*. Belmont: Thomson Wadsworth.

Manushi: A Journal about Women and Society, especially issues 42–43 and 50–51–52. Back issues available on website: www.manushi-india.org/back-issues.htm

Pintchman, Tracy and Rita D. Sherma, eds. (2011). *Woman and Goddess in Hinduism*. New York: Palgrave Macmillan.

Vanita, Ruth (2005). *Love's Rite: Same-Sex Marriage in India and the West*. New York: Palgrave-Macmillan.

Bibliography

Chaudhuri, Maitrayee, ed. (2005). *'Feminism' in India*. New Delhi: Kali for Women.

Eck, Diana (2012). *India: A Sacred Geography*. New York: Harmony.

Falk, Nancy Auer (2006). *Living Hinduisms: An Explorer's Guide*. Belmont: Thomson Wadsworth.

Ganguly, K.M. (1998). *The Mahabharata of Krishna-Dwaipayana Vyasa*. Vol. III. New Delhi: Munshiram Manoharlal.

Ghosh, Shohini (1999). 'The Troubled Existence of Sex and Sexuality: Feminists Engage with Censorship.' In *Image Journeys: Audio-Visual Media and Cultural Change in India* (pp. 482–518). Eds. Christiane Brosius and Melissa Butcher. New Delhi: Sage.

Gokhale, Namita and Malashri Lal, eds. (2010). *In Search of Sita: Revisiting Mythology*. New Delhi: Penguin.

Hancock, Mary (1995). 'Hindu Culture for an Indian Nation: Gender, Politics, and Elite Identity in Urban South India.' *American Ethnologist* 22, No. 4 (November): 907–926.

Hawley, J.S. and D.M. Wulff, eds. (1996). *Devi: Goddesses of India*. Berkeley: University of California.

Kishwar, Madhu (2001). 'Yes to Sita, No to Ram: The Continuing Hold of Sita on Popular Imagination in India.' In *Questioning Ramayanas: A South Asian Tradition* (pp. 285–308). Ed. Paula Richman. Berkeley: University of California.

Mani, Lata (1998). *Contentious Traditions: The Debate on Sati in Colonial India*. Berkeley: University of California.

―――― (2009). *SacredSecular: Contemplative Cultural Critique*. New Delhi: Routledge.

―――― (2011). *Interleaves: Ruminations on Illness and Spiritual Life*. New Delhi: Yoda.

———— (2013). *The Integral Nature of Things: Critical Reflections on the Present*. New Delhi: Routledge.

Nandy, Ashis (1989). *The Intimate Enemy: Loss and Recovery of Self under Colonialism*. New Delhi: Oxford University.

Narrain, Arvind, ed. (2011). *Law like Love: Queer Perspectives on Law*. New Delhi: Yoda.

Oldenburg, Veena Talwar (2002). *Dowry Murder: The Imperial Origins of a Cultural Crime*. New York: Oxford University.

Pechilis, Karen, ed. (2004). *The Graceful Guru: Hindu Female Gurus in India and the United States*. New York: Oxford University.

Pintchman, Tracy, ed. (2007). *Women's Lives, Women's Rituals in the Hindu Tradition*. New York: Oxford University.

Pintchman, Tracy and Sherma, Rita D., eds. (2011). *Woman and Goddess in Hinduism*. New York: Palgrave Macmillan.

Reddy, Gayatri (2005). *With Respect to Sex: Negotiating Hijra Identity in South India*. Chicago: University of Chicago.

Revathi, A. (2010). *The Truth about Me: A Hijra Life Story*. New Delhi: Penguin.

Singh, Rana P.B., ed. (2010). *Sacred Geography of Goddesses in South Asia: Essays in Memory of David Kinsley*. Newcastle upon Tyne: Cambridge Scholars Publishing.

Soneji, Davesh (2012). *Unfinished Gestures: Devadasis, Memory and Modernity in South India*. Chicago: University of Chicago.

Vanita, Ruth (2003). 'The Self is Not Gendered: Sulabha's Debate with King Janaka.' *NWSA Journal* 15, No. 2: 76–93.

———— (2005a). *Love's Rite: Same-Sex Marriage in India and the West*. New York: Palgrave-Macmillan.

———— (2005b). 'Sita Smiles: Wife as Goddess in the *Adbhut Ramayana*.' In *Gandhi's Tiger and Sita's Smile: Essays on Gender, Sexuality and Culture* (219–235). Ed. Ruth Vanita. New Delhi: Yoda.

———— (2012). *Gender, Sex and the City: Urdu Rekhti Poetry in India 1780–1870*. New York: Palgrave-Macmillan.

———— (2013). 'The Romance of Siblinghood in Bombay Cinema.' *South Asia: Journal of South Asian Studies* (Special Issue: 'Unfamiliar Ground: Security, Socialisation and Affect in Indian Families') 36, No. 1: 25–36.

Vanita, Ruth and Saleem Kidwai, eds. (2000) [2008]. *Same-Sex Love in India: A Literary History*. New Delhi: Penguin.

18 Hinduism and Environmentalism in Modern India

Eliza Kent

How do religious worldviews affect perceptions and experiences of the natural world and shape actions within it? This question defines the academic subfield of religion and ecology, which was launched in 1967 by Lynn White, Jr.'s groundbreaking article in the journal *Science*, "The Historical Roots of Our Ecologic Crisis" (1967). Drawing on his expertise in medieval history, White argued that the Western Christian view of nature as a resource created by God solely for the benefit of human beings has been instrumental in fostering attitudes towards the natural world that legitimate unchecked exploitation. White decried the philosophical dualism of the dominant theologies of the West, which attributed spirit to human beings alone, consigning animals, plants, forests, mountains, stars, and rivers to the status of inert matter. In his search for new theologies that would support a more sustainable ecological ethos, White saw room for hope in the religions of Asia, inspiring generations of scholars to seek theological, mythological, and symbolic resources for an ecological ethos in Asian religions, including Hinduism.

But does Hinduism necessarily foster more sustainable ways of relating to the natural world? As is arguably true for all the world's religions, Hinduism has long supported both environmental destruction and environmental care. The ecological history of India stretches back millennia and has seen considerable androcentric transformation of the landscape, much of which gained meaning through religious discourse. For example, the destruction of the Khandava forest and its terrified inhabitants by the fire god, Agni—depicted in the great Hindu epic, the Mahabharata—gives an idea of the pressing need and desire already in ancient India to 'tame' sparsely populated regions to make them suitable for a new kind of civilization centered on settled agriculture (Thapar 2001). Similar surges in deforestation accompanied the settling of frontier territory during the medieval and early modern period. At this time, sovereigns eager to support a growing population and enhance revenue bestowed land grants on those willing to undertake the difficult work of clearing forests for cultivation. On the other hand, India also harbors one of the world's richest traditions of sacred grove conservation, where small forests or groves of trees have been protected by religious taboos for decades, perhaps centuries, even in the face of mounting demand for timber, fuel-wood, fodder, and land for agriculture (Kent 2013). Like all the great religions of the world, Hindu theological and normative traditions were consolidated long before the emergence of complex problems like rampant species loss and climate change. But now, the challenges of climate change, species loss, and industrial pollution press down upon us all. Just as in other moments of tremendous change, people of faith today are adapting their inherited traditions to meet the demands of the time. How have modern-day Hindus drawn on the mythological and symbolic traditions of their faith to address our current ecological crisis? What political and social significance does religious environmental rhetoric acquire in India's pluralistic religious context, in which religion has become increasingly politicized?

As many authors in this volume have noted, Hinduism is a complex and internally variegated religion. Within it, one can cautiously identify three main strands of thought and practice. First, there is Brahmanical Hinduism, which represents the 'great tradition' transmitted largely through Sanskrit scriptures by Brahman priests, scholars, itinerant and monastic ascetics, and gurus. This tradition represents itself historically as orthodoxy, and was taken as such by Western observers during the British colonial period (Oddie 2006). Second, we might speak of the popular 'little tradition' that varies greatly according to region, but in which worship frequently entails shamanistic traditions of ecstatic trance, spirit possession, and animal sacrifice. Third, we may refer to what is sometimes called Renaissance Hinduism, neo-Hinduism, or reform Hinduism; all three terms point to varieties of Hinduism that emerged out of a series of reform movements that sought to purify the tradition of 'backward' practices such as widow immolation and animal sacrifice and to make its Brahmanical core more widely available through vernacular translations and lay leadership. It is important to recognize that this threefold schema identifies broad similarities and difference. In practice, these strands are deeply intertwined, in addition to borrowing from and also identifying themselves in opposition to other influential religions in the subcontinent such as Islam, Christianity, Jainism, Buddhism, and so on.

In this chapter, I analyze several environmental movements that have drawn inspiration from the various strands of Hinduism, including efforts to restore two of India's most sacred—and polluted—rivers, the Ganga and Yamuna; projects that seek to preserve and restore sacred groves; and Chipko, a grassroots movement that directly challenged policies allocating forests to distant corporations at the expense of local populations, which is regarded as the first Indian environmental movement. In my analysis, I seek to discern what strands of Hinduism leaders have drawn upon in order to address the unique challenges of modern industry and agriculture and their resultant ill effects on the environment. I highlight how individuals and groups have drawn on religious discourse to promote action (and sometimes foster inaction) in the face of well-resourced, multinational corporations, intransigent government agencies, and popular inertia and ignorance.

A (Very) Brief Environmental History of India

While androcentric transformation of the environment has been taking place for millennia, it accelerated dramatically in the modern era under British colonial rule. The British introduced railroads and coal-based energy production, technologies that facilitated the large-scale use of natural resources for industrial production. Under the British, the forests of India were depleted as the British took for themselves what they assumed were rights of Indian sovereigns to absolute control over forests. In fact, early modern Indian kings did not possess unrestrained title to forests, but rather shared access to timber and nontimber forest products (honey, fodder for animals, leaf mulch, roofing material, wild game animals, etc.) with a wide range of users, including the indigenous inhabitants of mountain forests, local political leaders, merchants, and regional kings, each of whom customarily had access to different kinds of forest produce. These rights were all swept away when the British took possession of India's 'public' forests. They proceeded to extract as much timber as they could to help support the British navy and provide raw materials for British industry (Gadgil and Guha 1992). The British also assumed the traditional role of Indian sovereigns as controllers of another precious and commonly held resource, water, initiating water management practices such as dams and canals to divert river flow for agricultural purposes.

After India gained political independence in 1947, the Indian government continued to prioritize economic development through industrialization, but according to a socialist model of centralized control of the economy, with attendant environmental consequences. Big, state-sponsored development projects like the creation of enormous dams—famously hailed by India's first prime minister, Jawaharlal Nehru, as the temples of modern India—bore great promise as ways to bring both electrical power and irrigation water to growing populations, especially in cities of the plains. However, as we will see, such dams became the focus of intense opposition by environmentalists, some of whom employed religious rhetoric to support their campaigns.

With the liberalization of its economy in the 1990s, India launched a social transformation nearly equal in significance to the liberation of India from colonial rule in the 1947. New federal policies eliminated restrictions on imports and abolished quotas for industrial production, lifting economic growth rates into the double digits. The expansion of the economy brought opportunities to millions and helped create India's burgeoning middle class. It also made consumer goods from electric fans to televisions to cars available on a mass basis, while the explosion of television channels through satellite technology gave advertisers innumerable new outlets for fostering desires for these goods. Whether celebrated or lamented, the twenty-first-century transformation of India's economy from a centralized, socialist-style economy to a consumer capitalist powerhouse has had one indisputable effect: the intensification of environmental destruction. Indians today face mounting pollution of rivers, soils, and air, habitat and species loss to development, groundwater depletion, deforestation, and extraordinary challenges in managing solid waste production. In coming decades, climate change promises to bring even more disruption. Already, populations are reeling from cataclysmic floods in the Himalayas in the north and years-long stretches of drought in the south.

Anti- and Pro-Environmental Ethics in Brahmanical Hinduism

The scriptural canon of Brahmanical Hinduism is dually anchored in the Vedas, a vast collection of songs, chants, and incantations revealed to enlightened sages at the beginning of the world, and the Upanishads, philosophical commentaries on the often cryptic poetic images of the Vedas. From this foundation, Hindu orthodoxy has developed in a variety of different directions. Among the most prominent schools of thought, Advaita Vedanta, affirms the unity, or non-duality, of all existence, asserting that our innermost spiritual essence, the *atman*, is identical with the divine foundation of the entire cosmos, *Brahman*. Self-realization, in this view, consists in overcoming the false sense of individual distinctiveness to recognize our identity with Brahman—'thou art that,' as the Upanshadic formulation concisely expresses. At first glance, this worldview seems to have positive implications for environmental thought insofar as it underscores a fundamental axiom of ecology: that we are inseparable from the larger unity of Nature. But as Lance Nelson has argued in an influential essay, 'The Dualism of Non-dualism,' this school of thought actually supports a stark metaphysical dualism in that it sees the *atman* or spirit as enmeshed in the matrix of the material world—*maya* or *prakriti*—which is illusory, both in the sense of being ultimately unreal and a seductive snare. In asserting that the only true and ultimately real dimension of reality is pure spirit, Advaita Vedanta valorizes extreme asceticism, urging seekers to see the natural, material world as of 'no more worth than the excrement of a crow' (Nelson 1998: 81). Nelson argues that Advaita Vedanta thus fosters an attitude of indifference to environmental decay and destruction by viewing the natural world as ultimately valueless relative to the absolute spirit.

Is this dualistic religious worldview responsible for one of the most puzzling contradictions in the study of religion and ecology in India, namely, the fact that India's sacred rivers are among its most polluted? The contradiction between the physical condition of the Ganges River awash in sewage, garbage, and industrial effluents and its religious status as an embodied goddess whose holy waters can purify devotees of all sins has astonished Western observers for years. Mark Twain wrote of seeing pilgrims sip Ganges water just yards away from a floating corpse and a pipe discharging sewage into the river: 'The sewer water was not an offence to them, the corpse did not revolt them; the sacred water had touched both, and both were now snow-pure, and could defile no one. The memory of that sight will always stay by me; but not by request' (Twain 1897: 499). In her influential anthropological study,

On the Banks of the Ganges: When Wastewater Meets a Sacred River (2002), Kelly Alley provides a more culturally sensitive investigation of the attitudes towards the river's purity and pollution. Alley discovered that a starkly dualistic worldview, not unlike the metaphysical dualism of Advaita, shapes people's perception of the holy river. Accordingly, people accept that mother Ganga—the powerful goddess who takes embodied form in the river itself—may become dirty (*gandaji*) while nonetheless holding that such material dirt does not affect her spiritual purity (*pavitrata*) or her capacity to wash away both the sins and the filth of humanity. In particular, she found that Brahman priests (*pandas*) and boatman whose livelihood depends on the steady flow of pilgrims to the Ganges were adamant in seeing Her as infinitely capable of absorbing and neutralizing whatever pollution, spiritual or material, that humanity could throw at her (Alley 2002: 80). Alley writes: 'When asked whether Ganga can purify all this dirty material without becoming impure, one *panda* replied, "Why not, she is Ma Ganga! How much sin have we taken to her already!"' (Alley 2002: 102). This idea gets translated popularly into quasi-scientific terms when devotees marvel at the supposedly self-purifying qualities of the Ganges—whether because the unusually high presence of bacteriophages or some other more mysterious reason, Ma Ganga is seen above all as a patient, loving, nurturing, and forgiving mother, who tirelessly cleans up her filthy children, not worrying if her own garments get soiled temporarily in the process (Alley 2002: 99). It is not difficult to see how this position supports inaction, or in any case, does not spur a sense of urgency in efforts to clean up the river.

These beliefs are supported by myths known throughout the subcontinent, which depict the goddess Ganga as a daughter of the Himalayan mountain range. Ganga descended to earth in response to the intense asceticism of a devout young man, Bhagirathi, who wanted to save the souls of his deceased ancestors suffering in a state of limbo. Having stumbled across their pitiful condition, Bhagirathi stood on one foot for years, until Lord Brahma granted his wish that the purifying waters of the Ganga would descend to earth. However, were the Ganga to directly unleash her waters, the earth would be destroyed, so Lord Shiva caught the waters in his tangled dreadlocks, cushioning her fall. A Vaishnava myth foregrounds the actions of Lord Vishnu in Ganga's history, recounting how Vishnu once took form as a dwarf, Vamana, to outwit a tyrannical demon who had taken over the world. Vamana pleaded with the demon for the boon of land equivalent to three strides. Thinking that would not amount to much, the demon agreed. Vamana encompassed the earth with his first step, the heavenly realms with his second, and kicked the shell of the cosmic egg with the third, causing the Ganga to come gushing down over Vishnu's foot and into the locks of Lord Shiva, who broke Ganga's fall. Today, millions of pilgrims come to Varanasi (Benares) or other holy sites along the Ganga to immerse the ashes of their deceased relatives in hopes that their sins will be washed away, adding both to its reputation as a site for the outpouring of divine grace and its pollution load.[1]

Scientists and environmental activists involved in campaigns to clean up the Ganga generally have a different, more naturalistic view of the rivers' pollution, and yet whether out of deference to the devotional attachment of the 'masses' or their own piety, they too frequently advance a dualistic view of the Ganges that distinguishes her 'dirty' material form from her divine essence, which ever retains its capacity to purify. In 1985 when Prime Minister Rajiv Gandhi launched the Ganga Action Plan, an ambitious program to address the river's pollution backed by scientific data gathering and parliamentary authority, he immediately reassured his audience that 'the purity (*pavitatra*) of the Ganga has never been in doubt.' But action was needed because 'we have allowed the river to become polluted' (qtd in Alley 2002: 161). Similarly, without questioning the purifying powers of the Ganga, there are religiously devout and scientifically educated leaders of the Sankat Mochan Foundation, an environmental NGO, who claim that Mother Ganga has become unclean (*aswaccha*) as a result of popular practices like bathing with soap or excreting on the river bank or due to the practice of municipalities to dump untreated or semitreated sewage into the river (Alley 2002: 182–187). Drawing on people's love for Mother Ganga, members of the Sankat Mochan Foundation urge residents to refrain from such acts, and likewise pressure city officials to keep the Ganga clean. However, it is possible to detect a paradox in the environmental rhetoric surrounding Ma Ganga: the more her divine powers are extolled as infinite and unalterable—and the more those powers are seen as distinct from her material embodiment—the less urgency there is to clean her physical river form. It becomes in effect unthinkable to imagine that the great Ma Ganga needs our help. This is the sort of problem highlighted by Nelson, whereby the dualism of Advaita theology blunts the urgency of calls for ecological restoration.

That said, not all Brahmanical Hindu thought is so dualistic. In fact, some would argue that the dualistic philosophical worldview worked out so systematically in Advaita Vedanta (and echoed in the perspectives of religious specialists in Varanasi) represents only a minority point of view within Hinduism. It is possible to go further and claim that the traditions of Advaita Vedanta were seized upon and foregrounded by colonialist scholars of Hinduism and European Christian missionaries in order to depict Indians as too 'otherworldly' to manage their own country (Oddie 2006; Haberman 2006). The fact that many neo-Hindu thinkers affirmed some version of Advaita Vedanta means that one legacy of colonialism has been to reduce the meaning of Hinduism to just one dominant feature of the Brahmanical worldview. In order to correct for the bias of both colonial and neo-Hindu discourse, it can be pointed out that Advaita Vedanta has in fact had very little influence on popular Hindu religious thought and practice, in which a more world-affirming interpretation of the ancient Vedic texts prevails. In such Hindu attitudes, the divine is thought to be immanent rather than completely other than worldly realities.

David Haberman's research on the religious environmental activism surrounding another sacred river afflicted by pollution, the Yamuna, shows how an immanental philosophical position supports an attitude of engaged concern for the river that translates, for some, into active service in cleaning up the river's pollution. Haberman's informants draw on the Bhagavata tradition, which employs a very different interpretation of the Brahmanical scriptural canon. Like Advaita Vedantins, Bhagavata theologians follow the Vedas and Upanishads in affirming the fundamental unity of the cosmos, but they regard Brahman as immanent in the material world, rather than being ontologically distinct from it. Where Advaita Vedanta regards the ever-changing material world as inert matter, which is ultimately unreal, theologians in the Bhagavata tradition regard it as the manifest (*vyakta*) form of the divine Brahman, which complements Brahman's unchanging, formless, unmanifest (*avyakta*) modality. At a level of reality higher than either manifest and unmanifest Brahman, suffusing and supporting them, this theistic tradition affirms the existence of a third level of reality—Bhagavan, the Supreme Person or Lord. Bhagavata scriptures like the Bhagavad Gita, for example, identify Krishna (regarded as the Supreme Lord) with the Purusha of the Vedic canon, the immense person out of whose body emerged the entire universe—moving and unmoving, animal, plant, and human, formed and formless (Haberman 2006: 34–36). Within varieties of Hinduism that participate in this theological tradition—for example, Gaudiya Vaishnavism and the Pushti Marg of Vallabhacharya—the seeker of truth is urged to see this world as the divine body of God, and to approach it with an attitude of love, seeking to deepen his or her relationship with the divine present in all beings through *bhakti*—devotional loving worship.

Taking up the case of the Yamuna River, Haberman notes that like the Ganges, it is both heavily polluted and yet widely revered as a Mother Goddess. Whereas the Ganges river is associated with death and dying because of the centuries-old tradition of immersing the ashes of the deceased, the Yamuna is envisioned as the vibrant goddess of love, closely associated with Krishna, as his lover and partner in creation (Haberman 2006: 60–61). In Haberman's interviews with ordinary devotees and religiously motivated environmental activists alike, he found that a theology of immanence informed by Bhagavata traditions can be a powerful motivator of environmental action. Those working to save the Yamuna lament the fact that those who pollute her do not recognize her true form; that is, they don't recognize that her waters are themselves the embodied form of the goddess. If they were to do so, they would not throw their garbage in her. As some devotees articulate it, this point of view contains a trace of the metaphysical dualism we saw among the Brahman pandas in Varanasi. They assert that Yamuna's waters, though surrounded by garbage and filth, are never themselves really polluted. But, importantly, while the presence of such filth cannot harm the goddess herself, it is harmful to devotees because its presence compromises our ability to see the true form of the Goddess and thus impairs our ability to act lovingly and respectfully towards her, in the way that leads to salvation (Haberman 2006: 184).

All that is required within the Bhagavata context is a change in perspective. Through active worship (*seva*), one can come to see the Goddess's true form. As Haberman writes: 'Once that true nature is revealed and one has an experience of its marvelousness, one enters spontaneously into an appreciative and worshipful attitude and engages naturally in acts of loving service aimed to care for it' (Haberman 2006: 186). This reinforcing cycle whereby loving acts of service allow one to see the Goddesses' true form more clearly, inspiring more love and joyful service, has inspired some leaders of the environmental movement in Vrindavan to dedicate their lives to the uphill battle of restoring the Yamuna River to health.

Popular Tamil Hinduism and the Preservation of Sacred Groves

Other dimensions of popular Hinduism lend support to a range of beliefs and practices that have tended to support environmental conservation. For instance, Tamil Nadu boasts one of the richest and most studied forms of the 'sacred groves' phenomenon found throughout India and around the world, where religious taboos protect small forests or stands of trees from human over-use, creating islands of biodiversity in landscapes otherwise denuded of forest. Besides playing important roles in popular Tamil Hinduism, sacred groves also provide precious habitat for endangered and endemic taxa in landscapes otherwise denuded of forest. Madhav Gadgil, a senior Indian environmental historian, established one of the key ideas that brought attention to this phenomenon, namely, that the groves provide an ecologically significant *refugia* for plant and animal species. Gadgil drew on the work of evolutionary biologist G. F. Gause, whose experiments with protozoa demonstrated that, in an environment where no limits were placed on the population of either prey or predator, one could prevent the extinction of prey species only by providing them with an area inaccessible to predators, from whence they could repopulate and colonize other areas (Gadgil and Guha 1992: 24). Sacred groves, Gadgil argued, essentially provide that kind of shelter from human use to both plants and animals. By restricting or regulating the use of forest products, the taboos surrounding sacred groves limit the overutilization of species by human beings, allowing sacred groves to serve as a kind of 'Noah's Ark' for endangered and endemic species.

But with this instance of religiously inspired Hindu environmentalism, the behaviors that lead to conservation do not flow from people's reverence directly for the butterflies or termite mounds found in sacred groves. My own fieldwork suggests that the religious complex that sustains them has four components that are each integral aspects of what we might call popular Hinduism, as it is instantiated in Tamil Nadu: 1) respect and reverence for the fierce deities who preside over the groves; 2) taboos protecting the forest, construed as the deity's temple and property, from inappropriate usage; 3) tales of the supernatural punishments meted out against those who defy these taboos; and 4) rituals of possession and sacrifice meant to restore harmony between forest-dwelling deities and the communities they shelter and protect.

The deities who reign over forested shrines in Tamil Nadu are typically lineage deities traditionally associated with the protection of boundaries such as the horse-riding village protector god, Ayyanar, and fierce versions of village mother goddesses, or *ammans*, who reside at the outskirts of the village. As befits their use of violence to protect the social order, these deities are, with the exception of Ayyanar, all nonvegetarian deities, whose worship involves animal sacrifice, mostly of fowls and goats. Even the vegetarian deity Ayyanar frequently has a guardian deity in close proximity to his own shrine, such as Veerabhadran or Muniyandi, who receives animal offerings from devotees. While these forest-dwelling deities normally direct their violence against ghosts, demons, or disease, and shielding their devotees from harm, these quixotic gods can also inflict harm when offended or neglected.

When people suspect a supernatural cause for trouble in their lives, they often resort to a medium (a *kotanki* or *camiyati*) who enters a trance-state enabling a god to speak and act through his or her body. The possessing deity can then tell whether he or she, another deity, or a disturbed ghost sent the affliction, and what needs to be done. Often, the remedy for having offended or neglected the deity is to offer a sacrifice. The offering of a chicken or goat is meant to make up for the moral lapse that led to the god's displeasure, whether a forgotten vow, a taboo unknowingly violated, or regular worship that has gone undone. Similarly, gratitude for boons or services obtained (such as the driving out of ghosts or becoming pregnant after a period of infertility) is often expressed through sacrifice. Forested shrines occupy an important place in this religious system because they represent the homes and temples of these deities. Forests are their special domain. Residing in forests suits these gods' irritable nature by putting them out of earshot of the cacophony of domestic life. Mostly neglected during the year, sacred groves are the sites of heightened ritual activity during the annual festival (*tiruvila*), when lineages deities speak through their human *camiyati*. Typically, this involves providing a narrative of how they arrived in the village, which serves to connect communities to their mythologized pasts and to anchor and integrate community identity.

Overall, then, we find a variety of beliefs and practices that frame the reverence associated with sacred groves, including taboos on the use of forest produce, tales of divine punishment for transgression, possession rituals to ascertain the will of the divine, and sacrifices to restore harmony between humans and deities, whose connectedness to a mythologized past cements a community's group identity. All of these constitute a kind of ideological system that helps place constraints on the human use of the natural resources found in sacred groves (Kent 2013: 182–183). However, my research suggests that there is perhaps not much in the beliefs and practices surrounding sacred groves that resembles an ecological ethos, if by that we mean a recognition of the ecological value of species diversity or the spiritual value of nature as such. If anything, the village residents I spoke with are practical people; they tend to draw on all the resources around them—material, social, and spiritual—for strength in materially difficult circumstances. Some might recognize that there is a kind of ecological wisdom in their practices, even if it is not present at a conscious level. Yet, the attribution of unconscious wisdom seems to me to stretch the meaning of 'consciousness' and 'wisdom' beyond credibility, and moreover participates in a kind of romanticization of the 'ecological primitive.' Even in the absence of conscious ecological motivation for practice, however, the practices surrounding sacred groves can be shown to have beneficial and measurable ecological side effects. It has been noted, for instance, that in some regions, such practices have led to higher levels of species diversity in sacred groves than in state-run reserve forests (Visalakshi 1995; Ramanujan and Kadamban 2001).

Should we regard the maintenance of sacred groves as a kind of grassroots religious environmentalism, or not? This is more than a rhetorical question. Today, sacred groves in India are the object of a great deal of interest on the part of environmentalists, foresters, and botanists alike. The environmentalist Gadgil, among others, has argued that because village residents do not value these groves for the same reasons that environmentalists do, the groves are in danger of being cleared for other purposes. Gadgil argues they should be monitored, if not taken over and managed by the state (Gadgil and Vartak 1975: 320). We may relate his position to that enunciated in the most recent formulation of Indian national forest policy, known as the Intensification of Forest Management Scheme (IFMS) of 2009. This includes a provision for the protection and conservation of sacred groves, beginning with a state-led inventory of all sacred groves, and plans for their 'improvement' through the creation of signage, paths, labeling of significant species, etc.[2] Such a vision capitalizes on the environmental education potential of sacred groves, but it threatens to turn them into secularized parks, with meanings quite different from those which have supported their survival over what may be centuries (Kent 2013: 5).

The Influence of Reform Hinduism in the Chipko Movement

Such plans to protect sacred groves by transforming them into state-run nature reserves or parks shed light on the problem of importing strategies for the conservation of natural resources from the industrially and economically developed West for use in developing countries like India. In a densely populated country where a large proportion of the population lives in direct dependence on natural resources, is the creation of human-free zones for the protection of nature viable or advisable? In addressing this question, it is useful to consider some of the features that broadly distinguish Western environmentalism from Indian environmentalism. With intellectual roots in the writings of John Muir and Henry David Thoreau, Western environmental movements typically find inspiration in romantic ideas about nature that have emerged out of the modern West's experience of the industrial revolution, such that undisturbed nature (i.e. wilderness) is highly valued as a zone of redemption, a crucial antidote to the moral and material pollution of industrialization. Certainly, environmental movements in North America, Australia, and Western Europe take diverse forms, and varieties that are not based on the notion of 'wilderness,' such as the environmental justice movement, are gaining in significance. But, arguably, the most popular forms of Western environmentalism, such as the slogan 'reduce, reuse, and recycle,' take on meaning only in postindustrial contexts in which people live at a remove from the resource extraction necessary for all human life.

Distinguishing between the 'full-belly' environmentalism of the global North and the 'empty-belly' environmentalism of the global South, Ramachandra Guha and Juan Martinez-Alier argue that Indian environmental movements have a very different genesis, arising more out of conflict over access to natural resources. India in particular has a long history of social movements driven by people whose direct use of forests and rivers for housing, food, building materials, and medicine has been threatened by commercial or industrial firms seeking to utilize those resources for the benefit of people in cities. Recently, one has also seen resistance around the creation of nature reserves where indigenous inhabitants have been displaced so that foreign and indigenous elites can enjoy ecotourism experiences, such as contact with charismatic species such as the Indian Tiger (Guha 2006: 125–151). As Guha and Martinez-Alier argue, one's perspective on 'nature' is very different when one's livelihood directly depends on it.

This kind of conflict over natural resources is seen clearly in the social movement widely recognized as the first environmental movement in India, Chipko. In 1973, the Indian government granted the right to fell trees in the Alakananda valley in the Himalayas to a sports equipment manufacturer from faraway Allahabad. Previously, a local, Gandhian, nongovernmental organization (NGO) that focused on promoting livelihood development had bid on the right to use the same forest for smaller-scale production of agricultural implements and had been refused by the government. In response to this blatant favoritism, the local people—led by women since the men of the community were away on government business—ran to the forest before the contractors arrived and clung to the trees vowing not to move. The phrase Chipko means 'to hug' or 'embrace' in Hindi. Their bravery sparked a series of similar actions in the Himalayan region of Uttar Pradesh as peasants employed classic Gandhian tactics (*satyagraha*, or nonviolent nonresistance) to stop felling by loggers. When activists brought their complaints to Delhi through public demonstrations, word of the movement spread throughout India and the world (Guha 2000).

As Ramachandra Guha has argued, the two leaders of the Chipko movement who received the most public attention, Chandi Prasad Bhatt and Sunderlal Bahuguna, differ greatly from each other in terms of personal philosophy and practice. They also illustrate two different components of the Gandhian style of Reform Hinduism, which has had profound influence on Indian environmentalists. Before discussing the ways these two leaders developed Gandhi's techniques and religious philosophy in the service of environmentalism, let me briefly sketch Gandhi's sociomoral vision and its foundation in Reform Hindu thought with a focus on its potential for supporting an environmental ethos.

It is ironic that Gandhi is hailed by many as India's first environmentalist given that Gandhi himself was decidedly not a nature lover. As Vinay Lal writes: 'His writings are entirely devoid of any celebration of untamed nature or rejoicing at the chance sighting of a wondrous waterfall or an imposing Himalayan peak' (2000: 184). Nonetheless, Gandhi had a profound sense of the unity of all beings, which underlay many of his personal moral and political choices—from his vegetarianism to his tireless work for the poor and marginalized in Indian society. Born to a well-to-do family in the western region of Gujarat and trained as a lawyer in England, Gandhi was raised a Vaishnava with considerable influence from Jainism. Along with many other educated, elite Indians, Gandhi chafed under the inequity of colonial rule, but his distinctive contribution to the Independence movement was a framing of resistance through a wholesale critique of modern, industrial, consumer-oriented society. In his masterpiece, *Hind Swaraj* [*Indian Home Rule*] (1909), Gandhi sharply critiqued that variety of civilization that made 'bodily welfare the object of life' (2009 [1909]: 34). 'This civilization,' he wrote, 'is irreligion [*adharma*], and it has taken such a hold on the people in Europe that those who are in it appear to be half mad.' By seizing on all the modern conveniences that the British had brought to India (from mechanized production and transportation to modern medicine and law), Indians had weakened themselves and lost touch with the foundational strengths of true civility (*dharma*). Deftly melding the ideas of nineteenth-century critics of industrial civilization like Tolstoy, Ruskin, and Thoreau with his own readings of the Bhagavad Gita, Gandhi argues that true civilization entails not the speedy satisfaction of individual desires, but the restraining of desire through a sense of duty and humility.

Like many modern Hindu reformers, Gandhi absorbed ideas from innumerable sources, but his religious social vision was primarily grounded in his religious faith. Gandhi's reading of the Bhagavad Gita emphasized the text's Vedantic vision of the oneness or non-duality of the cosmos, where 'all embodied life is in reality an incarnation of God' (Gandhi 2000 [1926]: 17). Following the Gita, Gandhi regarded the means to self-realization as the ability to 'see divinity' in all creatures, and to love them as oneself.[3] This perspective deeply informed his political activism on behalf of the most marginalized members of society. It also informed his ethos of restraint, where unbridled consumption was seen as inflaming egoistic, selfish desire, in an unhealthy, self-reinforcing cycle.

Famously, Gandhi predicted that if the people of India were to catch the 'disease' of industrialized civilization, and embark on economic exploitation the way the British did, the whole world would be consumed as if by a swarm of locusts (cited in Guha 2006: 231). The restoration of Dharmic civilization, he pronounced, would begin by rejecting the false convenience of machine-made goods, and simplifying one's life: 'The tinsel splendour of glassware we will have nothing to do with, and we will make wicks, as of old, with home-grown cotton, and use hand-made earthen saucers for lamps' (Gandhi 2009 [1909]: 108). It is well known how such views led to the political strategies of economic boycotts and nonviolent noncooperation for which Gandhi is justly celebrated. Less well-known is how influential they have been in inspiring generations of environmentalists in India.

Chandi Prasad Bhatt embodied the values of Gandhian grass roots organizing for economic development. He espoused the view that the forests of the Himalayas should be used, but in a sustainable fashion that would benefit local people rather than distant corporations. Inspired by the example of selfless service he found in post-Independence era Gandhians such as Vinoba Bhave (1895–1982), Bhatt became involved in the Sarvodaya (literally 'uplift for all') movement. Through such work, he became acquainted with the hardships of hill country peasants in the upper Himalayas where the Chipko movement began. His experience in social organizing helped him to channel local people's long-simmering resentments into effective challenges to the state's extractive economic policies. After the Chipko movement subsided, Bhatt continued his grassroots organizing in the Himalayas through an NGO, called the Dashauli Village Self-Help Association (Daushali Swarajya Seva Mandal), which advocates for women's rights, economic self-reliance, and the development of appropriate technology meant to improve the lives of people of the region (Guha 2006: 184).

Though the son of a temple priest, Bhatt's own religiosity reflects a particularly intense commitment to public service (as signaled by the word 'seva' in the name of his NGO). His commitment draws not only on the example of Gandhi, but also on the life and work of Sri Aurobindo and Swami Vivekananda. All three neo-Hindu leaders advocated for a new kind of religious practice that linked spiritual knowledge to disciplined action, or *karma yoga*. Wisdom such as Gandhi found in the Gita would be coupled with the Gita's own teachings about the value of work. Thus it was possible to think that, by engaging in work for the public good, or *seva*, one could strip away the selfish desires associated with the personal ego. Here it is worth noting that while in traditional contexts *seva* is most closely associated with the kinds of service provided temple worship, modern Hindu reformers like Gandhi and Vivekananda broadened the sphere of religious service to encompass society at large. In connection with this new conception of *seva*, we may think of the monks of the Ramakrishna mission established by Swami Vivekananda; of Gandhi's satyagrahis engaged in nonviolent direct action against unjust British policies; or of those devotees who even today plant trees in the name of the internationally famous guru, Mata Amritanandamayi. This reformed conception of service has inspired Hindus of all walks of life to contribute to environmental campaigns.

Sunderlal Bahuguna, in contrast to Bhatt, draws on the prophetic-ascetic side of Gandhian activism and employs explicitly religious rhetoric to argue for the inherent, even sacred, value of nature (Guha 2000: 200). His work reminds us that the forests and rivers of the Himalayas have long been celebrated as *tirthas*, or holy sites, where the divine can be immediately accessed. With his long beard, white garments, and values of simple living, Bahuguna invokes a familiar Brahmanical Hindu paradigm of the renouncer–guru whose distance from the hurly-burly of profane life endows him with the authority to critique society in a disinterested and thus more truthful way. While chroniclers of the Chipko movement disagree over who first consolidated the movement, Bahuguna had already been established as an activist in the region. He gained national attention as a leader of the Chipko movement because of his nearly 4,000-kilometer march through the forests of the Himalayas in 1983 (Guha 1989: 180). This represented a kind of political pilgrimage, or *yatra*, designed to call attention to the ecological and social damage caused by the government's support for industrial forestry. Like many other Indian social leaders, Bahuguna draws from the repertoire of nonviolent strategies employed by Gandhi. During the many mass demonstrations associated with the Chipko movement, Bahuguna undertook fasts and conducted ritualized readings of the Bhagavad Gita to instill in the participants and convey to outside observers the righteousness and moral superiority of their cause. Bahuguna's willingness to undergo physical suffering rather than back down from his position, an example being a fast he underwent in the freezing winter of 1978 in a shepherd's hut in the forest, is recounted with awe even today by peasants in the region, for whom it signifies a variety of moral courage only possible when one's purposes are aligned with the Truth (Guha 1989: 166, 171).

Conclusion

The Chipko movement demonstrated rather early on the effectiveness of Gandhian grassroots mobilization when yoked to peasant unrest over unjust resource distribution; it revealed what could be done when a charismatic leader used long-standing paradigms of religious authority to address broader environmental issues regarding consumption, equity, and sustainability. In something of a coda to the original Chipko movement, Bahuguna emerged once again in the 1980s as a key leader in another movement, this time aimed at blocking construction of a large dam in the Uttarakhand region of the Himalayas. For many years, Bahugana lived alongside the dam site in a small hut, and undertook several long fasts to protest construction of the dam, succeeding at one point in pressuring the Prime Minister to order a halt to the project. His recourse to religious idioms and values at this time had a somewhat different resonance, however, since the same time period witnessed a resurgence of conservative Hindu political activism (discussed elsewhere in this volume). Against a backdrop of politicized Hinduism, Bahuguna's increasingly explicit religious language attracted some criticism. His urgent calls to followers to preserve a threatened Hindu way of life were seen by some as echoing and even supporting the rhetoric of conservative Hindu chauvinists who were prone to use similar rhetoric in order to bully religious minorities and suppress freedom of speech.

By way of conclusion, it would do well to examine this second stage of Bahuguna's career as a religiously-inspired environmentalist to illustrate how the different strands of Hindu religiosity—the Brahmanical, the popular, and the reform—are interwoven in contemporary Hindu environmental discourse. This will also serve to suggest how religious language and symbolism can inspire acts of courageous self-sacrifice, even in the service of very different social and political goals.

Bahuguna's activism for the forests of the Himalayas in the Chipko movement and his work to save its rivers in the Tehri dam opposition movement should be seen as connected. In his voluminous writings, Bahuguna promotes a compelling vision of the Himalayas as an ecologically integrated and deeply sacred region. In this respect, his work exemplifies some of the most creative ecotheological thinking in contemporary India. In this way of thinking, the Himalayan glaciers slowly release water creating the headwaters of the great sacred rivers of North India, the Yamuna, and the Ganges; the roots of the trees that make up the Himalayan forests trap this moisture and slowly release it; and this in turn enables the human inhabitants of the region to benefit from the healing and life-giving properties of the sacred rivers, just as in the myth of Shiva and the Ganges. The Himalayas are also the home of religious ascetics, living in caves, meditating, and performing austerities that generate blessings or good karma for the benefit of humanity. To live in this land, to drink the holy waters of the pure Himalayan mountains is thus to live in a heavenly paradise; here, one needs no more than is necessary to meet one's subsistence needs.

Among the central themes in Bahuguna's activism has been the need to preserve India's distinctive, 'forest culture,' or *aranya sanskriti*, which is his way of affirming the holiness of all life and calling for minimizing human desires in order to respect that life. In his acceptance speech upon receipt of the Right Livelihood Award in 1987, Bahuguna wrote:

> This culture was born and nurtured in the forests where sages and seers— the teachers of society—led a life of austerity and penance with their disciples. They pondered over the problems of humankind and, with their knowledge and wisdom, provided thoughtful guidance to society. The surrounding forests filled them with high ideals and, ultimately, with a new vision of life which held that: There was life in all nature's creation—human beings, birds, beasts and insects, trees and plants, rivers and mountains; and All life should be respected and human beings should particularly have a worshipful attitude towards life. Lord Krishna identified himself with the Himalaya, River Ganges and the fichus tree, when he said: Austerity, should be practiced.[1]

---

1 Acceptance Speech by Sunderlal Bahuguna, 1987 [http://www.rightlivelihood.org/chipko_ speech.html]

One sees here the intertwined strands of Hindu thought and practice that, as I've sought to show in this chapter, have been utilized by environmentalists to inspire action for decades: the celebration of forests as holy sites, reverence for the in-dwelling spirit in all material creation, and the exhortation to restrain one's desires in order to advance spiritually. And yet, not everyone sees the stakes of environmental conflicts in the same way.

The Tehri dam opposition movement was like any significant political movement made up of numerous factions, many of whom argued their case by using meticulously detailed scientific analyses of the dam and its potential ill-effects in the region, including concern with seismic instability in such a mountainous region, displacement of human populations, and the diversion of a huge volume of water from existing river ecosystems (Sharma 2012: 119). In his criticisms of the project, Bahuguna was not above employing scientific reasoning of his own, even if his rhetoric was consistently framed by religious concerns.

Invoking the rich mythology surrounding the Himalayas, whose snowy peaks shelter the headwaters of the Ganges and the Yamuna and innumerable holy shrines, ashrams, and other pilgrimage destinations, Bahuguna sought to harness the religious devotion of Hindus to evoke a sense of urgency about the project. 'If we leave aside the Ganga and the Himalaya,' he wrote, nothing will remain of the high values we cherish. All the preachers of India from Vyas Dev [legendary author of the Mahabharata] to Mahatma Gandhi took inspiration from the Ganga and the Himalaya' (cited in Sharma 2012: 128). While Bahuguna has been widely celebrated for providing a language for environmental activism with broad popular appeal, others criticize his framing of environmental issues in religious terms. Mukul Sharma argues that such framing oversimplified the issues at stake, and overshadowed the equally compelling scientific reasons to oppose the Tehri dam, which would have been more effective and less divisive. Yet, in an effort to activate a sense of urgency, the anti-Tehri dam movement used highly emotional rhetoric drawing on the identification of the Ganga as a threatened mother whose sons needed to rally to her side. By emphasizing that nothing less than the spiritual soul of the nation was at stake in these conflicts over natural resources, Bahuguna's rhetoric can be seen to come very close to the kinds of rhetoric employed by right wing Hindu extremists in groups like the Vishwa Hindu Parishad (VHP) and Rashtriya Swayamsevak Sangh (RSS) (see Sharma 2012).

Indeed, in the 1980s and 1990s, the VHP and the RSS actively joined the campaign against the Tehri dam. In 1998, in one of the first public statements by the VHP against the dam, Askhok Singhal, then president of the VHP, wrote: 'The human monsters that conceived the "damming" of the holy Ganga have displayed a monumental insensitivity to the very soul of Bharat. . . . The enemies of Hindu heritage and Hindu *sanskriti* [culture] seem determined to destroy the Ganga in the name of progress, disguised in the garb of the Tehri dam' (cited in Sharma 2011: 136). In 2000, the VHP organized rallies in Delhi, strikes in Tehri Garwal, and political pilgrimages (the Sri Ganga Raksha Yatra) in Haridwar with the message that Mother Ganga was profoundly threatened by the creation of the dam. Bahuguna joined some of these VHP sponsored meetings and openly endorsed Ashok Singhal's campaign (Sharma 2011: 134, 138). While the campaign against the Tehri dam did not succeed in halting the project, it did attract international attention to the ecological and social costs of massive hydroelectric projects. Along the way, it provided yet another example of the capacity of Hindu religious language and symbolism to shape perceptions about and responses to the natural world. As we have seen in this chapter, not only have several strands of Hinduism contributed to framing contemporary attitudes, but the yoking of Hinduism to the work of ecological preservation can also yield unexpected side effects.

Summary

This chapter analyzes environmental movements that have drawn inspiration from various strands of Hinduism, including efforts to restore two of India's most sacred—and polluted—rivers, the Ganga and Yamuna; projects that seek to preserve and restore sacred groves; and Chipko, a grassroots movement that directly challenged policies allocating forests to distant corporations at the expense of local populations, which is regarded as the first Indian environmental movement. The chapter identifies the major strands of Hinduism that have inspired efforts to address the challenges of modern industry and agriculture and their detrimental effects on the environment. It also highlights how specific individuals and groups have drawn on religious discourse to promote action (and occasionally foster inaction) in the face of well-resourced, multinational corporations, intransigent government agencies, and the changing articulations of Hindu politics.

Discussion Questions

- What different strands within the Hindu tradition can help us understand the kinds of religious, moral or theological resources environmentalists have turned to in their work?
- If the conservation of sacred groves is more of a by-product of village Hinduism than the outcome of explicitly ecological or environmental motives, is it appropriate to think of sacred groves as a kind of grassroots religious environmentalism?
- With its affirmation of the unity, or non-duality, of all existence, is Advaita Vedanta good for the environment? How has it shaped the thinking of religious leaders and activists in relation to the environment?
- Should progressive environmental activists who cherish India's religious pluralism avoid using Hindu rhetoric to rally support for their cause just because some chauvinistic Hindutva activists employ similar rhetoric to advance their aims?

Notes

1   See Brian Pennington's essay on Hinduism in North India, in this volume, for further exploration of the mythology surrounding the Ganges and the surge in pilgrimage activity to the headwaters of the Ganges at Gangotri.
2   The IFMS was implemented in connection with India's eleventh Five-Year Plan
3   Gandhi found special meaning in such verses as 5:16 and 6:32, which praise a kind of Vedantic awareness of oneness.

Suggested Readings

Two well-wrought, edited volumes provide readers with a broad introduction to scholarship on Hinduism and ecology and/or environmentalism:

Nelson, Lance (1998). *Purifying the Earthly Body of God: Religion and Ecology in Hindu India.* Albany: State University of New York Press.

Chapple, Christopher Key and Mary Evelyn Tucker (2000). *Hinduism and Ecology: The Intersection of Earth, Sky, and Water.* Boston: Harvard University.

Hindu environmentalism can be divided into two types: activism surrounding sacred rivers and activism surrounding sacred forests. Two excellent and complementary monographs of how Hindu ideas and practices have informed environmental activism surrounding India's sacred rivers are:

Alley, Kelly (2002). *On the Banks of the Ganga: When Wastewater Meets a Sacred River.* Ann Arbor: University of Michigan Press.

Haberman, David (2006). *River of Love in an Age of Pollution: The Yamuna River of Northern India.* Berkeley: University of California Press.

The following two titles offer an equally stimulating and contrasting pair of studies of Hindu environmentalism in connection with sacred trees and forests:

Haberman, David (2013). *People Trees: Worship of Trees in Northern India.* New York: Oxford University Press.

Kent, Eliza (2013). *Sacred Groves and Local Gods: Religion and Environmentalism in South India.* New York: Oxford University Press.

Bibliography

Alley, Kelly D (2002). *On the Banks of the Ganga: When Wastewater Meets a Sacred River.* Ann Arbor: University of Michigan Press.

Gadgil, Madhav and Ramachandra Guha (1992). *This Fissured Land: An Ecological History of India.* New Delhi: Oxford University Press.

Gadgil, Madhav and V. D. Vartak (1975). "Sacred Groves of India: A Plea for Continued Conservation." *Journal of Bombay Natural History Society* 72: 314–320.

Gandhi, Mohandas (2000) [1926]. *The Bhagavad Gita According to Gandhi.* Ed. John Strohmeier. Berkeley: Berkeley Hills Books.

——— (2009) [1909]. *Hind Swaraj and Other Writings.* Ed. Anthony Parel. Cambridge: Cambridge University Press.

Guha, Ramachandra (2006). *How Much Should a Person Consume: Environmentalism in India and the United States.* Berkeley: University of California Press.

——— (2000). *The Unquiet Woods: Ecological Change and Peasant Resistance in the Himalaya.* Berkeley: University of California Press.

Guha, Ramachandra and Juan Martinez-Alier (1997). *Varieties of Environmentalism: Essays North and South.* London: Earthscan Publications.

Haberman, David (2006). *River of Love in an Age of Pollution: The Yamuna River of Northern India*. Berkeley: University of California Press.

Kent, Eliza F. (2013). *Sacred Groves and Local Gods: Religion and Environmentalism in South India*. New York: Oxford University Press.

Lal, Vinay (2000). 'Too Deep for Deep-Ecology: Gandhi and the Ecological Vision of Life.' In *Hinduism and Ecology: The Intersection of Earth, Sky, and Water* (pp. 183–212). Eds. Christopher Key Chapple and Mary Evelyn Tucker. Boston: Harvard University.

Martinez-Alier, Juan and Ramachandra Guha (1997). *Varieties of Environmentalism: Essays North and South*. London: Earthscan Publications.

Nelson, Lance E. (1998). 'The Dualism of Nondualism: Advaita Vedanta and the Irrelevance of Nature.' In *Purifying the Earthly Body of God: Religion and Ecology in Hindu India* (pp. 61–88). Ed. Lance E. Nelson. Albany: State University of New York Press.

Oddie, Geoffrey A. (2006). *Imagined Hinduism: British Protestant Missionary Constructions of Hinduism, 1793–1900*. New Delhi: Sage Publications.

Ramanujam, M. P. and D. Kadamban (2001). 'Plant Biodiversity of Two Tropical Dry Evergreen Forests in the Pondicherry Region of South India and the Role of Belief Systems in their Conservation.' *Biodiversity and Conservation* 10: 1203–1217.

Sharma, Mukul (2011). *Green and Saffron: Hindu Nationalism and Indian Environmental Politics*. Delhi: Orient Blackman.

Thapar, Romila (2001). 'Perceiving the Forest: Early India.' *Studies in History* 17/1: 1–16.

Twain, Mark (1897). *Following the Equator: A Journey around the World*. Hartford: American Publishing Co.

Visalakshi, N. (1995). 'Vegetation Analysis of Two Tropical Dry Evergreen Forests in Southern India.' *Tropical Ecology* 36, No. 1: 117–127.

White, Lynn, Jr. (1967). 'The Historical Roots of Our Ecologic Crisis.' *Science* 155, No. 3767: 1205.

Conclusion

Brian A. Hatcher

The goal of this volume has been to open up and complicate the rich world of modern Hinduism. The authors gathered here have invited readers to engage intensively with the rich, aesthetic, emotional, historical, theological, and social traditions we associate with Hinduism as these were reshaped and remobilized for a range of concerns during the colonial and postcolonial eras. It is our hope that through an encounter with the richness and diversity of Hinduism in the modern world, readers might be inspired to go still further. This might entail visiting a Hindu temple in their community, reading the writings of Rammohan Roy or the lectures of Swami Vivekananda, exploring the rich world of Hindu iconography, or taking up the practice of yoga or meditation. On the other hand, we also hope readers will continue to ask hard questions about the forces that have shaped and continue to shape the expression of Hinduism in the modern world. Whether we think in terms of contemporary South Asia, home to the majority of the world's Hindu population, or in terms of those communities of Hindus who are today actively reshaping religious, social and political life in disparate locales around the world, our goal should be to ask how Hindu values, customs, and practices both impinge upon and respond to the dynamics of today's world. One goal of *Hinduism in the Modern World* is to provide a starting place for carrying forward such exploration. Using the bibliographies and other study guides in this book, readers are equipped to reflect upon a range of issues that have both historical and contemporary salience, not least concerns over the global economy and environmental degradation, the articulation of Hindu majoritarian politics, or on-going attempts to press for issues of gender equality or social justice.

Above all, it is hoped that readers will be encouraged to develop a nuanced and historically sensitive understanding not just of what it means to be Hindu today, but also of all the factors that have shaped—and continue to shape—the way Hinduism is understood both inside the academy and 'out there' in the so-called real world. To develop such an understanding means being open to the wide range of experiences, beliefs, practices, and institutions that make up contemporary Hinduism while attempting to work skillfully with nearly two centuries of writing about Hinduism, writing that for all its value must also be critically unpacked in order to deal honestly with issues like colonial domination, European supremacy, high-caste privilege, and identitarian (or 'communal') politics. Becoming aware of the ways in which modern Hinduism has been judged, categorized, and mobilized for disparate social and political purposes makes us better students of history, more sophisticated students of South Asian culture, and hopefully more sensitive and sympathetic interpreters of what it means to be Hindu in the modern world.

Glossary

Advaita Vedanta   the 'non-dual' (*advaita*) philosophical school based in the Upanishads (*vedanta*); one of the six orthodox schools of Indian philosophy (*darshana*); emphasizes the oneness of Brahman and the individual soul; reconfigured in the modern era by figures like Swami Vivekananda and Sarvepalli Radhakrishnan; an important dimension of neo-Vedanta

Agnichayana   'piling of the fire [altar],' one of the most lengthy and elaborate of Vedic sacrifices involving the construction of a bird-shaped altar from bricks

Agnihotra   the daily offering into the sacrificial fire (*agni*) of rice or milk along with clarified butter; one of the twice-daily obligatory offerings prescribed for Brahmins

Anusara Yoga   a popular form of Modern Postural Yoga that incorporates aspects of tantric philosophy

Arti/arati   display of lights before the deity during worship, typically involving the waving of oil lamps or lighted camphor

Atman   'eternal self'; distinguished from the empirical or psychophysical self (*jiva*)

Bala vihars   educational groups for children popular among North American Hindus

Bhajan   devotional hymn

Brahman   'ultimate reality'; impersonal absolute taught by the Upanishads and classical Vedanta (q.v.)

Chakra   'centers' of spiritual energy situated along channels (*nadi*) in the subtle body as taught in various forms of yoga and tantra

Darshana   'seeing' or 'point of view'; refers to the auspicious exchange of glances between devotee and deity; to the act of visiting a sacred place, statue, or person; a philosophical school or system of thought

Garbha-griha   'womb-house,' the *sanctum* of a Hindu temple in which the deity is installed

Hatha-Yoga   'postural discipline'; a system of Yoga that aims to calm the mind by purifying the physical and subtle bodies through bodily postures (*asana*) and breath control (*pranayama*)

Karma Yoga   'discipline of action'; as taught by Krishna in the Bhagavad Gita, a philosophy of selfless action performed out of dedication to God; in the modern teachings of Swami Vivekananda this concept is repurposed for invigorating new notions of energy and activity among colonial Indians

Kashmir Shaivism   A school of Tantra (q.v.) that reached its height during the ninth to twelfth centuries, the goal of which is to merge individual consciousness with Shiva, understood as universal consciousness

Kaula Tantra   A type of Tantra that places emphasis on manipulation of the physical body and the use of secret sexual rites

Kundalini   'energy' envisioned as a serpent coiled and resting at the base of the spine; in Kundalini Yoga the goal is to awaken the serpent so that it travels up the central spiritual channel (*nadi*) resulting in Self-realization

Mandir   a temple or shrine

Mantra   a sacred word or phrase that is believed to have spiritual power; may be as simple as *Om* or as elaborate as devotional mantras to particular deities, such as *Om Namo Bhagavate Vasudevaya*

Moksha   'liberation' from the wheel of birth and death (*samsara*); the ultimate goal in many philosophical and devotional traditions

Mudra   'gestures' used in the context of yogic practice and in the iconography of particular sacred beings; for instance, an open hand with the palm facing the viewer symbolizes 'freedom from fear' (*abhaya mudra*)

Murti   lit., the 'form' of a deity; the 'image' that is typically installed within a temple or shrine

Nadi   'channel' through which flows the 'breath' or life force (*prana*) animating the physical body; yogic and tantric texts state there are 72,000 *nadis* in the subtle body

Nirguna   lit., 'without qualities'; applied to the divine when understood to be without any manifest name or form; contrasted with *saguna* (q.v.)

Pativrata   lit., 'she whose vow is her husband'; the ideal Hindu wife

Prakriti   'primordial nature' conceptualized as the feminine material source of the universe; one of two fundamental principles in *Samkhya* philosophy alongside *purusha* (q.v.)

Prana   'breath' conceptualized from ancient times as a kind of life force animating reality; control of the various *pranas* associated with human physiology is an important feature of both yoga and Indian medicine

Pranayama   'restraint of breath'; yogic techniques for controlling the breath and calming the mind

Puja   'worship'; may be as simple as making an offering to a deity to more elaborate ritual processes involving up to sixteen major components, including bathing, feeding, and entertaining the deity

Purusha   'spirit' or 'eternal consciousness' conceived as the masculine principle within creation; one of the two fundamental categories in *Samkhya* philosophy; see *prakriti*

Raja Yoga   'royal yoga,' typically refers to the classic eight-limbed (*ashtanga*) teaching of the *Yoga Sutra*, which includes moral training, physical postures, breath control, and stages of meditation

Rath yatra   chariot procession; an annual ritual especially central in Vaish-nava traditions

Sadhana   'spiritual discipline'; means of gaining an 'attainment'; see *Siddhi*

Sadhu   'holy man' (fem., *sadhvi*); typically a renouncer whose authority is predicated on spiritual practices aimed at distancing him/her from the quotidian world

Saguna   'with qualities'; applied to the divine when thinking of the particu-lar appearance or virtues of a deity that can become the focus for worship and devotion; contrasted with *nirguna* (q.v.)

Samkhya   lit. 'enumeration'; one of the six orthodox schools (*darshana*) of Indian philosophy; teaches the distinction between masculine spirit (*purusha*) and feminine matter (*prakriti*)

Samsara   round of rebirth

Sangh Parivar   lit., 'family of organizations'; applied to the combine of Hindu nationalist groups made up of the Rashtriya Swayamsevak Sangh (RSS), Vishwa Hindu Parishad (VHP), and Bharatiya Janata Party (BJP)

Sannyasi(n)   a renouncer; someone who has abandoned all connection to the world in quest of spiritual release; can be engaged in solitary practices or organized into larger monastic fraternities; given new political salience in the modern era by such figures as Swami Vivekananda

Satsangs   Local worship groups common in devotional Hinduism

Seva   'service'; can be applied to service of a deity through *puja* or of other human beings through selfless work

Shaivite   devotee of Lord Shiva

Shakta   devotee of the Divine Mother (conceptualized as feminine power, or *Shakti*) in her various forms

Shakti   feminine 'power'; often considered to be the dynamic aspect of Shiva; in Yoga associated with *kundalini* (q.v.)

Siddhi   lit., 'attainment'; supernatural powers attained through spiritual practice and Yoga, such as flying, knowing the past and future, and enter-ing another person's body

Shrauta   the 'solemn' rituals of Vedic sacrifice; distinguished from the Gri-hya, or 'domestic' rituals

Shruti   'revelation'; the general term applied to Vedic scripture; often pared with 'tradition'; see *smriti*

Smriti   'tradition'; general term denoting a range of authoritative but non-revealed texts central to the classical Hindu worldview, such as the Mahabharata, Ramayana, Dharmashastras and Puranas

Soma   the divine personification of the drink made by pressing the *soma* plant used in Vedic sacrifice; also the name for a major class of solemn rituals

Tantra   lit. 'loom'; the generic name for a range of esoteric teachings and scriptures dedicated to the immediate realization of the ultimate, often through the practice of secret yogic techniques and occasionally practices forbidden in an orthodox context

Theosophy 'divine wisdom'; a modern coinage associated with Madame Blavatsky and Colonel Henry Olcott; devised in the nineteenth century as the name for a synthetic approach to eastern and western esoteric philosophies

Upanishads otherwise known as Vedanta (q.v.) these are a collection of esoteric texts from ca. 800–200 BCE that reflect on the hidden meaning of Vedic sacrifice and first articulate new modes of mystical spirituality, yogic practice, and the quest for liberation (*moksha*) that would come to shape the expression of classical Hinduism

Vairagya 'dispassion' an attitude of indifference to the sensual world and desires

Vaishnava/Vaishnavite Devotee of Lord Vishnu and his various manifestations (*avatara*)

Vajapeya a major Vedic solemn (*srauta*) Soma ritual involving a chariot race and the ritual ascent to heaven of the sacrificer and his wife

Varna-ashrama-dharma an ancient Hindu way of emphasizing the duty (*dharma*) associated with social class (*varna*) and stage in life (*ashrama*)

Veda the revealed scriptures of Hinduism, composed ca. 1200–200 BCE; see *shruti*

Vedanta lit, 'end of the Veda,' originally indicating the Upanishads as the last layer of Vedic revelation; by extension those philosophical schools (*darshana*) based on the Upanishads; in the modern era often a shorthand way of speaking of the particular *darshana* of 'non-dual' Advaita Vedanta (q.v.)

Vrat ritual vow, often entailing a fast; a common form of religious practice among Hindu women

Vyakulata 'agitation' ardent pining for God

Index